The Marriage between Literature and Music

The Marriage between Literature and Music

Edited by

Nick Ceramella

Cambridge
Scholars
Publishing

The Marriage between Literature and Music

Edited by Nick Ceramella

This book first published 2022

Cambridge Scholars Publishing

Lady Stephenson Library, Newcastle upon Tyne, NE6 2PA, UK

British Library Cataloguing in Publication Data
A catalogue record for this book is available from the British Library

Copyright © 2022 by Nick Ceramella and contributors

All rights for this book reserved. No part of this book may be reproduced, stored in a retrieval system, or transmitted, in any form or by any means, electronic, mechanical, photocopying, recording or otherwise, without the prior permission of the copyright owner.

ISBN (10): 1-5275-8142-X
ISBN (13): 978-1-5275-8142-5

This book is for all the literature and music lovers I know,
but also for those I have never met.
Nick Ceramella

"The high arts of literature and music stand in a curious relationship to one another, at once securely comfortable and deeply uneasy – rather like a long-term marriage."
Will Self

TABLE OF CONTENTS

List of Figures x

Acknowledgements xii

Foreword xiii
Doc Rossi

Introductory Essay xv
Overall View on Origins and Contemporary Development
of the Interweaving Between Music and Literature
Nick Ceramella

Part I: English and Irish Literature

From the *Beggars' Opera* to *The Threepenny Opera*: A Long-standing
Relationship of Text and Music 2
Yuri Chung

George Eliot and her Musical Affinity in *The Mill on the Floss* 18
Sanaz Alizadeh Tabrizi

"The Voice of Nethermere" (A Cantata) 34
Malcolm Gray & Alan Wilson

'Piano': Swinging Between Past and Present 51
Nick Ceramella

Jazz Sounds and Styles in the Fiction of Jean Rhys, Toni Morrison
and Zadie Smith 79
Bethan Jones

Yeats and Crazy Jane: *Words for Music Perhaps* 99
Adrian Paterson

Part II: American Literature

'Smudging the Air with My Song': Bob Dylan's *Murder Most Foul* 128
Sandro Portelli

A Primal Source of Music 137
William Neil

Elusive Tunes: Jazz and Popular Songs in *The Great Gatsby* 146
Gianfranca Balestra

Pynchon, Weaver of Music and Words 159
Christian Hänggi

Part III: German Literature

George Anton Benda: A Global Composer and His Singspiel "Romeo und Julie" (1776) 172
Christa Jansohn

Schubert's *Winter Journey* in "Space-Time": The Power of Solitude 200
Charlotte Stoppelenburg

Part IV: Italian & Latin Literature

The Light Between the Liminal Space: Italo Calvino's *Invisible Cities* and the Music of Indigenous Australians - Archie Roach, Kutcha Edwards, and Christine Anu 220
Jema Stellato Pledger

Ovid - Heroides vs Metamorphosis – A Musical Journey from J. S. Bach to A. Piazzolla 236
Cinzia Merlin & Manuela Kustermann

Part V: World Literature

Vinicius de Moraes: A Multifaceted Brazilian Artist and the Dialogue Between Literature and Music 248
Rita Namé, Izabel Brandão & Nick Ceramella

'Sing of the famous Portuguese / To whom both Mars and Neptune bowed': Camões Recurrence in Portuguese Music 281
Leonor Santa Barbara & Luís A.V. Manuel Bernardo

Two Lodgers in Their Time: Dmitry Shostakovich and Sasha Cherny 301
Elena Lutsenko

Poetry and War: Miguel Hernández Set to Music 315
Patricia Pérez Borrero

Contributors 328

Index 342

List of Figures

Fig. 1: Score of *Belle, bonne, sage* (XV C.) by Baude Cordier.
Fig. 2: Queen Elizabeth I dancing "La Volta" with Robert Dudley, Earl of Leicester. The painter is anonymous, but belonged to French Valois School, c. 1580.
Fig. 3: *The concert* (1623), Gerard van Hornthorst (1592-1656).
Fig. 4: "Introduction to Songs of Experience."
Fig. 5: William Hogarth (1697-1764), Engraved print of *The Beggar's Opera* (1728), Victoria and Albert Museum.
Fig. 6: Image on a Greek vase.
Fig. 7: Nethermere', the area around Moorgreen Reservoir (courtesy of Malcolm Gray)
Fig. 8: Piano at the Lawrences' in Garden Road 57, the Breach, Eastwood (1887-91) (courtesy of Nick Ceramella, henceforth NC)
Figs. 9- 10: Lucas is enjoying being "in the boom of the tingling strings" while his mum is playing for him (courtesy of Charlotte Stoppelnburg)
Fig. 11: Living room at the Lawrences' in Garden Road 57, the Breach, Eastwood (1887-1891) (courtesy of NC)
Fig.12: The Lawrences' in Garden Road 57, the Breach, Eastwood (1887-1891) (courtesy of NC)
Fig. 13: "And her arms, and her bosom and the whole of her soul is bare / And the great black piano is clamouring …" (ll 18-19, 'The Piano'). Tanja Knežević at her piano recital in Radke Fine Arts Theatre at the University of Central Oklahoma, April 25 2021 (courtesy of Tanja Knežević)
Fig. 14. Richard Dadd "Sketch of an Idea for Crazy Jane". London: Bethlehem Hospital, 1855.
Fig. 15: 'Wolf Keys,' photo image created for W. Neil by Elliot Madow.
Fig. 16: Jazz Age Rage (anonymous).
Fig. 17: Jiří Antonín Benda (1722-1795), Czech composer, violinist and Kapellmeister.
Fig. 18: Portrait of Franz Schubert (source: unknown).
Fig. 19: *Wilhelm Müller* by Johann Friedrich Schröter (1770-1836). Engraving ca. 1830.

Fig. 20: *A Schubertiade at Ritter von Spaun's* (Schubert and the singer Johann Michael Vogl at the piano). Oil sketch, 1868 by Moritz von Schwindt.

Fig. 21: 'Guerriero donne', Stradbroke Island, Queensland, Australia (Art piece, courtesy of Jema Stellato Pledger).

Fig. 22: Poster for Ovid – 'Heroides and Metamorphosis' –

Fig. 23: Front cover of 1st edition, Rio de Janeiro 1956.

Fig. 24: *Orfeo playing the lyre.* Roman mosaic floor II c. a. D. Palermo Archeological Museum (Sicily, Italy).

Fig. 25: Landmark 'Garota de Ipanema' bar, Rio de Janeiro (courtesy of NC)

Fig. 26: Original score *Garota de Ipanema* at the bar in Rio (courtesy of NC)

Fig. 27: Film poster *Orfeo Negro*, 1959.

Fig. 28: In the background: Girl on Ipanema Beach, Rio, 2017, Now as Ever. "Look at this wonderful creature / so graceful / It's she, the girl / who comes and just passes / swinging softly towards the sea." (Courtesy Vince Cannatelli).

Fig. 29: Engraved portrait Luis de Camões.

Fig. 30: Galina Vishnevskaya, Dmitry Shostakovich and Mstislav Rostropovich after a concert (courtesy of E. Lutsenko)

Fig. 31: *Satires*, Sasha Chorny. 1st ed.1910 (idem.)

Fig. 32: The article about Galina Vishnevskaya in *Pravda* in January 1961 (idem)

Fig. 33: Galina Vishnevskaya and Mstislav Rostropovich (idem.)

Fig. 34: Miguel Hérnandez haranguing his fellow soldiers.

Acknowledgements

I have to start by thanking my wonderful wife, Marianna. From going through the drafts to bearing with my ups and downs, she was as important to this book getting done as I was.

I would like to thank all the colleagues, artists, and friends who have so generously contributed to making this lifelong dream of mine come true.

In particular, I wish to thank Doc Rossi for his advice and for writing the Foreword to this Volume. I am also indebted to William Neil for his factual help and inspiration through the production of this book. A particular acknowledgment goes to Giovanni Azzinnari for especially arranging the Aria 'Through all the employments of life' from John Gay's *The Beggar's Opera*. Thanks so much to Charlotte Stoppelenburg for kindly offering me two photographs of her son Lucas, and to Tanja Knezević for her photograph on piano. I am so grateful to my friend Daniele Marzeddu, film maker and photographer, for 'rescuing' me with photography artwork. I have to thank Eleonora Semeraro for her help on editorial matters and double checking the translations.

Finally, I am grateful to all the staff involved at CSP and am especially indebted to Rebecca Gladders and Adam Rummens (Commissioning Editors), Clementine Joly (Author liaison), Sophie Edminson (Designer), and Amanda Millar (Typesetting Manager) for their patience and advice.

Rome 14 February 2022

Nick Ceramella

Foreword

I first met Nick Ceramella when I was living in Rome, during my first years as a young academic. Although it was literature that had brought us together, we soon learned that we were both musicians as well. There was an instant bond through our love of literature, the Slow Food movement, and above all, music. I still like to remember our trips to Santa Sofia d'Epiro, Nick's home village in Calabria, and to nearby Bisignano to hang out with and interview luthier Vincenzo de Bonis, whose family has been making musical instruments since the 18th century. This wonderful family tradition continues to this day thanks to the fine work of his niece, Rosalba, who still builds fine instruments in the old family workshop in Bisignano.

At this point, Nick and I have been friends for over 30 years, and if we were in the same room now, we would certainly be celebrating that, and this book, with a toast or two, perhaps even in our favourite Roman *enoteca* (wine shop), L'Angolo Divino.

I elected to do my graduate work at University College London in Literature rather than Music. Since I had done so much work in the theatre, my topic – Shakespeare and Brecht – seemed to bring some unity to my work up to that point. Although I enjoyed doing my doctorate, I eventually learned that academia was not for me – researching, writing, and teaching Literature and Writing not only did not suit my temperament, it took far too much time away from researching, writing, and especially from playing music. I had given academia a decade before I realised that I was decidedly *not* following my bliss, and so I went back to being a musician. I also moved – a lot – going wherever my muse and the gigs took me. There have been many ups and downs, but I don't regret it for a moment; neither do I regret my academic training and work – learning to do rigorous research and write it up in a convincing, readable manner have been invaluable.

I have watched Nick grow and advance in his career: from editing for Loffredo, one of the oldest Italian publishing houses, based in Naples, to his work with Cambridge Scholars Publishing; from his teaching appointments at *La Sapienza*, *Roma Tre*, and *LUMSA* in Rome, as well as other Italian universities, to visiting professorships in Moscow (Russia) and Alagoas (Brazil), and lecturing at Stony Brook and Ottawa; from the many conferences he has organised, to the many works he has published concerning Shakespeare and the literature of the English Renaissance, D.H. Lawrence,

Translation Studies, and the History of English. Nick has been Vice President of the D. H. Lawrence Society of Great Britain since 2017, a position he enjoys as much as he deserves.

This present volume is not the culmination of Nick's academic career - it's not *that* big! - but it certainly is an expansive work, as full of passion as it is of knowledge, and for this he has brought together an impressive team from Europe, Turkey, Russia, Australia, and the Americas.

As Nick points out in his Introductory Essay, Music and Literature have enjoyed a long and fruitful marriage, and much has been written about it. What sets this collection apart are not only the many scholars Nick has invited to contribute, but also the unique perspectives offered by the musicians, singers, actors, and directors who present the results of their work here, many of whom, like Nick and myself, are scholars as well. Taken as a whole, it is a fascinating read across a broad spectrum of topics ranging from Ovid, Bach and Piazzolla to *The Beggar's Opera*, Bob Dylan, and Shostakovich; from George Eliot and D. H. Lawrence to Yeats and Joyce; from Scott Fitzgerald, Jack London and Thomas Pynchon to Jean Rhys, Toni Morrison, and Zadie Smith; from Spain and Portugal to Brazil, extend to Indigenous Australians, who share an enchanting spiritual connection with Italo Calvino's fantastic stories; from Wilson's and Gray's use of music to emphasise nature's voice and Neil's ecomusicological approach, which explores the relationship between music or sound and the natural environment before composing and making these sounds part of the musical fabric, to the close interweaving of libretto and music in opera.

The Marriage of Music between Literature offers an "innovative exploration of how music and words can merge, blur and lose themselves in each other" – a polyphony of words and music bound in a charming book of essays.

31 January 2022 Porto (Portugal)

Doc Rossi

Introductory Essay: Overall View on Origins and Development of the Interweaving Between Music and Literature

> 'Understanding a sentence is much more akin to understanding a theme in music than one may think. What I mean is that understanding a sentence lies nearer than one thinks to what is ordinarily called understanding a musical theme.'
> —L. Wittgenstein, 1986, 527.

This introductory essay is meant to present a paramount picture of the title topic of this volume, covering the mythical origins of the relationship between music and literature to our days. Needless to say, it is not meant at all to offer a thorough analysis of such a varied and extremely long period yet is just an attempt to fill in the 'gaps,' as it were, concerning general aspects and single authors and musicians who, despite their importance, are not dealt with individually in the essays forming this book. Indeed, to pay justice to that, it would certainly take more than one volume. Let me also say that as an anglicist I have concentrated on English authors and society, but without overlooking some of the main European and American musicians, literary authors, musicologists, and philosophers who have played a remarkable role in the relationship of literature and music over the centuries.

To start with, here is the key question at the root of this book: what happens when we add text to music? An immediate reply could be that music, which is abstract by nature, is contextualised thanks to the meaning of the words related to it. In effect, Music and Poetry in particular, have been regarded as sister arts since the days of ancient Greece. However, in recent years, a major impulse coming from the growth of a varied interdisciplinary research, involving new literary and linguistic critical theories and musicology, has helped to open up new ways of analysing this relationship. What has emerged is that, even if each can stand on its own, it is also true that if combined, they can be complimentary and, as is the case when literature lends words to the abstract feelings that music arouses, the latter offers a different viewpoint from literature by illustrating the words and giving an emotional response. To put it bluntly, we may say that poetry has traditionally been a powerful source of inspiration for musicians and conversely, which together have managed to create an ancestral, unique magic circle. This is self-evident when notes and words closely interact not only in operas and songs, but also in narrative, and even in silence, whose aim is to create a dramatic atmosphere through the varying length of pauses.[1] This fascinating approach has led to significant progress in the development of joint studies in Literature and Music over the last three decades. Studying the present relationship in this research area has become a continuously evolving task as it moves through different disciplinary fields. A major contribution to this has been given by the International Association for the Study of Words and Music (WMA) which, coordinated from the University of Graz in Austria, holds an international conference every second year and publishes its own book series, *Word and Music Studies*.

Now we are ready to venture into a very fascinating socio-cultural landscape to see how the relationship between music and literature has grown and evolved through the centuries, starting ...

From Ancient Greece to the Middle Ages

Throughout the Middle Ages, people at large agreed that man was the centre of the universe, and that the earth was at the centre of a rotating planetary system consisting of seven planets which, by rubbing against each other's atmospheres created musical pitches that combined to create heavenly harmony, or the "music of the spheres." Indeed, Greek philosophers such as Pythagoras (580 B.C.– 495 B.C.), who founded one of the most important schools of human thought in Kroton (Calabria, Magna Graecia), together with his followers imagined that this particular music and the relationship between music and words represented the future basis of what was going to develop as literary work. Among the earliest examples of this kind, which lead us back to the dawn of civilization, there is the myth of Orpheus and Eurydice; he was 'the father of songs' and the supreme musician in Greek mythology. (See pp. lxix, 224, 250, 253-4, 262). Equally significant is Homer's *The Iliad* (762 c. B. C.), opening with the famous line, "Sing, o goddess, the anger of Achilles, son of Peleus" (Book 1) where the poet

---

[1] Note that in Sanskrit poetics on music and drama, presented in *Sangita Raknakara* ("Ocean of Music and Dance") by Sarngadeva, a leading Indian musicologist, he declares that music, or rather some sort of drone called 'nada," developed itself in an audible but also an inaudible form.

invokes the muse of epic poetry to help him in telling the story of Achilles' anger and the war over Helen and Troy. It then followed that intellectuals began referring to music and poetry as sharing certain basic principles like timbre and metre. Quite notably, in ancient Greece, they used the term *mousikè* to refer to the three arts inspired by the muses – music, poetry, and dance. The distinction between these different modes of expression was rather vague, and sometimes made it impossible for us to distinguish the *liaison* between lyrical texts and the music accompanying them because they often faded into each other.

In medieval thinking, however, poetry and music took two different directions. The former verged towards rhetoric and grammar and the latter towards mathematics and science, though music has always been linked with the word, especially in its poetical mode. In the following centuries, music and song rose in social importance, as had been theorised by Aristotle (384–322 B.C.) in *Book 8* of *Politics*, and much later by Augustine (354-430) in *Confessions* Book 10, XXXIII, and Boethius (475-524) in *De institutione musicae*; most importantly, they all agreed on the role of music in society as a metaphor for harmony and accordance. Unfortunately, well before that had become normal practice, every form of entertainment was banned from the social scene. That occurred on the fall of the Roman Empire (476 A.D.) as a consequence of the clash between Christianity and Paganism which had a devastating effect not only on the theatre, but also on visual arts and music. It is not until Guido d' Arezzo (991 c.–1033 c.), a Benedictine monk, developed modern musical notation in the eleventh century, that music was gradually allowed to take back its salient role in society at all levels. From then onwards, conditions changed favourably so that musical activity almost everywhere around Europe improved quite rapidly. Alongside music composed in connection with religious services, there was also that originating from popular life of which one of the earliest examples, dating back to about 1220, can be found in England: the anonymous 'Summer is icumen in' (also known as the 'Cuckoo Song'). This piece, celebrating the arrival of spring, is the earliest extant song whose lyrics are written to the same music score. The singers can choose between the Middle English lyrics for the secular version, or the Latin for the religious one. It consists of six phrases distributed across twelve bars through which the voices enter one by one rather than in unison, and after reaching a prefixed point marked with a red cross in the score, they sing together in unison, or at the octave.

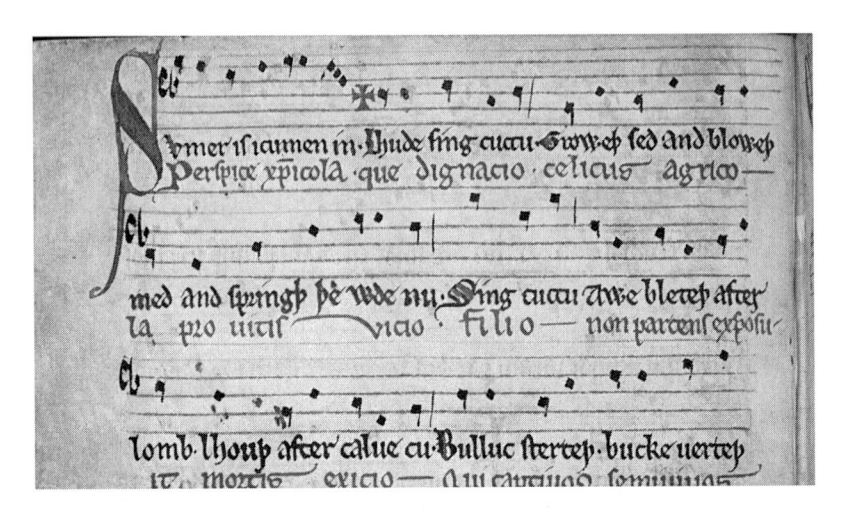

'Summer is icumen in' (anonymous original score).

Worthy of attention, among the most popular literary genres in the Middle Ages, is the poetry and prose inspired by the Arthurian Cycle, starting from the Welsh, Geoffrey of Monmouth (c. 1100-1155) up to Sir Thomas Malory (1415-1471) who used it as his primary source. The Arthurian Cycle includes the most famous part of the Matter of Britain, representing the earliest examples in the Western World which refer to music, namely the Tristan and Isolde legend. Tristan is a master in the arts of the *trivium* – grammar, logic and rhetoric – which are the foundation for the *quadrivium*, the upper division of the medieval education in the liberal arts, comprising music, geometry, arithmetic, and astronomy. He almost always composed poems which he himself put to music on his harp, pretending to be a professional itinerate minstrel, like when he arrived at King Marcus's court in Cornwall. His beloved Isolde learned the *trobar* art from him, just like the minstrels of *chansons de geste* (French, literally, 'song of deeds'), who used to accompany themselves on a string instrument in the courts and on the streets. And that is where we can draw a line between ballads, narrative poems put to music, coming directly from popular tradition, and chivalric romances testifying to the power of noble families and institutions. (See subsection below). This type of literary production had by and large the great merit of guiding and promoting the European sentimental education, represented by the brave and generous fighting knight, who still loved art and convivial life, thus anticipating the writings of Machiavelli and, even more so Castiglione, about the perfect prince and "courtesan."

Troubadour Poetry and Dante's *Divine Comedy*

Music had an even more important function in the allegoric poem than in the chivalric romance. This is a genre, including the 14th century anonymous *Roman de la Rose ou de Guillaume de Dole*, as well as two works by Guillaume de Machaut (1300-77), the autobiographical *Le voir dit* (1360-1363) and the love poem *Remède de Fortune* (1343?), in which emphasis is placed on the importance of sounds. The latter is extant with the score composed by the poet himself, but what makes it particularly interesting for us here is that, as words may remain ambiguous, the characters reveal their inner thoughts through their singing and even the outcome of the story. Arnaut Daniel (1180-1200), an Occitan troubadour, is widely acknowledged to have opened the way to this kind of poetry, which has been put to music ever since his days. As it happens, Ezra Pound (1885-1972), an amazing expert in Medieval poetry, praised him in *The Spirit of Romance* (1910) as one of the best poets ever while Petrarch, the poet who described love as a sensual and overwhelming passion, called him "gran maestro dell'amore" ("great master of love"). (See Pound's version, pp. lxvi).

Dante Alighieri (1265-1321) himself lauded Arnaut as the "miglior fabbro del parlar materno" ("the best craftsman in the mother tongue"), Canto xxvi, 1. 117, *Purgatorio, The Divine Comedy* - 1304–1321). At the end of this Canto, when Dante asks Arnaut who he is, he answers "Ieu sui Arnaut, que plor e vau cantan" ("Io sono Aranaut che piango e vado cantando," ("I am Arnaut that weeps and goes a-singing," 1. 142.) This demonstrates that in Dante's time, singing was naturally connected to poetry, to which he often refers as song. Quite interestingly, he treats music in a different way in each 'cantica.' To start with, the only musical instrument that can be heard in the dark Hell is Nimrod's horn (Canto xxxi, ll. 70-78). which does not produce any music at all. The 'instruments' that can be heard in *Inferno* just make blasts and thumps and not music as such; the rest is shrieks, moans, and lamentation: "Ora comincian le dolenti note / a farmisi sentire; or son venuto là dove molto pianto mi percuote.") ("Now begin the doleful notes to reach me; / am I come where much lamenting strikes me" (Canto v, l. 25-26). The only music reference is to Dante himself saying, "E mentre io gli cantai cotai note" - "And while I sang these notes to him" (Canto xix, l. 119) which he uttered to accuse Constantine of avarice, without actually singing. In *Purgatorio*, Dante often resorts to popular liturgical texts under various circumstances that can be easily referred to certain relevant melodies. Music takes a central role in the Canto II, l. 112 of *Purgatorio*, where the poet meets his friend Casella and begs him to sing for him *Amor che nella mente mi ragiona*. (See opening of

Convivio, III). Just before climbing the "sacro monte" ("sacred mountain"), Dante stops to listen to the song which moves them to feel the nostalgia for the joys of earthly life. Finally, whereas music in *Purgatorio* is discontinuous, in *Paradiso* it is an inherent, uninterrupted, harmonious sonority, suffusing the whole of it. By creating amazing metaphors, while sound and visual effects enhance the narrative development, Dante suggests vivid images like that of the lutist who accompanies a singer describing the joined little flames of Trojan and Ripheus: "E come a buon cantor buon citarista / fa seguitar lo guizzo della corda, / in che più di piacer lo canto acquista" / ("And as on a good singer a good harpist maketh / the quivering of the chord attend, wherein the / song gaineth more pleasantness") (*Paradiso*, Canto xx, ll. 142-144). In the glowing Paradise, there are such sweet sounds, so different from anything heard on earth, making them impossible to memorise: "così vid'io la gloriosa rota / moversi, e render voce a voce tempra / ed in dolcezza ch'esser non può nota, / se non colà dove gioir s'insempra." ("so did I see the glorious wheel revolve and / render voice in harmony and sweetness that may not be known except where joy / maketh itself eternal.") (*Paradiso*, Canto X, ll. 150-154).

Petrarch and *The Canzoniere*

Francesco Petrarca (1304-1374), **commonly** anglicised as **Petrarch**, represents a world apart from Dante. Although, his many references to the effect of music on the human spirit are particularly telling, it is unlikely that he meant all of his *Rerum vulgariun fragmenta* ("Fragments of Vernacular Matters"), a collection of 366 lyric poems in many different genres, known as *Il Canzoniere* ("Songbook"), to be set to music. However, during the period 1520-1630, polyphonic madrigalists often used Petrarch's sonnets to illustrate how poems could be put into music. One example is "Zefiro torna" ("Canzoniere," 310) by Claudio Montevertdi; the work of Luca Marenzio provides another. Petrarch's influence on composers continued for centuries to come. Franz Liszt (1811-86) put to music a poem by Victor Hugo, "O quand je dors" ("Oh when I sleep") in which Petrarch and Laura are invoked as the epitome of erotic love. Listz adapted to music for voice, what he called *Tre Sonnetti del Petrarca* (47, 104, and 123), which he would transcribe for solo piano and include in the suite *Années de pèlerinage* (1842, "Years of Pilgrimage"). (This title refers to Wolfang Goethe's *Wilhelm Meister's Journeyman Years* ("Wilhelm Meisters Wanderjahre"). Given the purpose of our volume, it is worth highlighting that Listz, following the Romantic trend of the time, prefaced most of these compositions with literary passages from authors like Byron, Senancour, and Schiller. This trend has continued to our days, as shown, among others, by the American composer Elliot Carter (1908-2012), who on stressing the close link between music and words said: "How serious music would have developed without its accompaniment of verbage is hard to imagine!" (Carter, n. p., 1972). As a modernist composer, he gives an example of this kind himself with his solo flute "Scrivo in Vento" (Writing in the wind) (1991) which is inspired by Petrarch's Sonnet 212, *Beato in sogno*, a truly modernist piece in the 20th centre sense. The sonnet itself appears with Carter's comment before his score, reading: "*Scrivo in vento*, [...] takes its title from a poem by Petrarch who lived in and around Avignon from 1326 to 1352. It uses the flute to present the contrasting musical ideas and registers to suggest the paradoxical nature of the poem" (Whitall, 2010, 91). Carter's musical adaptation follows Petrarch's pattern of a dream state, imagining a dreamer swimming oceans and going after breezes while writing in the wind (Cf. Dylan's famous song *Blowing in the wind*). The Italian poet as usual creates amazing contrasting images by applying some of his typical literary devices: oxymorons, conceits and paradoxes, which often draw on sensory imagery. "Beato in sogno et di languir contento" / [...] / solco onde, e 'n rena fondo, et scrivo in vento." ("Bless with sleep and content with languor / [...] / Plough waves, build on sand, write in air").

Ballad

On writing about the liaison between music and literature, the ballad certainly deserves a reference of its own, however short it may be, for two good reasons: the important social and cultural role it played in the Medieval society and, obviously, the relevance that this poetical form still has in modern times. Medieval ballads were narrative poems deriving from popular tradition, which were often improvised and sung on a simple musical accompaniment that could include dance from which derives its name. Indeed, ballads originate from the French 'chanson' / 'ballade' and people enjoyed them in countries speaking romance languages before spreading to Ireland and around the British Isles. Unlike songs, which were specially written to be sung, ballads were lyrical poems put to music, and were performed in the streets, market squares, taverns, and fairs. The typical ballad is often anonymous, or has more than one author, and portrays a dramatic, exciting event often using a simple, dialogical narrative. In addition, while were more often than not an emotional expression of the singer, ballads are rather impersonal, a simple retelling of events varying from love and death, adventures, outlaws ('Robin Hood Cycle'), battles ('Chevy Chase'), dangerous trips. Since they were rarely written, there are various versions of the same text, as for example "Lord Randal," a 13th-century Scottish ballad of which there are variations, including one from Bob Dylan as well as others from countries like Germany and Italy. 'Barbara Allen' is another good example, undergoing changes according to circumstances and conditions. In fact, this ballad exists in numerous versions. Like very many medieval ballads, it originates in the border country between England and Scotland, belonging to the 'Scottish Border Ballads,' and in this case probably in the village of Allendale, hence, its title. It continued to be a very popular story for many generations to come. In the 17th century, the diarist Samuel Pepys makes this entry in his *Diary*, on January 2nd 1666: "In perfect pleasure I was to hear her (Mrs Knipp, an actress) sing, and especially her little Scotch song of Barbara Allen." In the 18th century, Oliver Goldsmith says, in one of his essays, that the song made him weep and that its various versions are divided in their presentation of Barbara or Barbry, sometimes representing her as truly penitent for causing the death of her lover, sometimes showing her as unrepentantly cold-hearted. One of the modern interpretations of "Barbara Allen" is sung by the America folk singer Joan Baez. This shows that, although somewhat removed from its roots, the ballad has remained a valid and popular literary form thanks to the continued popularity of artists like Woody Guthrie, Joan Baez, Bob Dylan, and Bruce Springsteen.

Barbara Allen

Anon. 17C
arr. Doc Rossi

© Doc Rossi 2022

'Barbara Allen' by anonymous (1622).

Boccaccio and Chaucer

The close relationship between music and poetical narrative in the 14th century is strongly marked by two of the greatest authors of their time, the Italian Giovanni Boccaccio (1313-1375) and the English Geoffrey Chaucer (1343-1400). Music in *The Decameron* (1348-1353) offers us a precious source of information about the musical instruments of the time, dances, secular songs and religious hymns. In the Preface to *The Decameron*, Boccaccio stresses the important role that music plays in his era, saying: "And I shall also include some songs, which these seven ladies sang for their mutual agreements." The words of the songs they sang set the appropriate atmosphere for the stories day by day, varying from cheerful to sad. Music in Boccaccio's view is a symbol of harmonious friendship in the *brigata*, the ten people who, having self-confined themselves in a villa outside Florence to escape from a devastating plague that was spreading all over Europe, to pass the time pleasantly sing, play, and dance to popular tunes, which Boccaccio mentions through his narration. Music is part and parcel of *The Decameron* since it represents a most important aspect of daily life, though perhaps is not so present as in Dante or Petrarca. Indeed, only Fiammetta and Dioneo can play a musical instrument, the vielle (fiddle) and lute respectively on which they accompany the singing and dancing of the whole group in addition to various other pieces they practice on their own. Both of them have a sensual association to music, with Fiammetta singing more romantic songs and Dioneo those that we could define even as "sexy." In brief, they represent sex and love of the group.

In the following centuries, various madrigalists were inspired by Boccaccio. The Flemish Jacques Arcadelt (1507-1568) wrote many books of songs and madrigals combined with the texts of various poets, such as Petrarch, and also Boccaccio on whose prose romance *Elegy of Madonna Fiammetta* he based a famous madrigal. The French composer Philip Verdelot (1480c.–1552?), who spent many years in Italy, and is even considered the father of the Italian madrigal, deserves particular attention for his "O singular dolcezza del sangue bolognese" drawn from a passage in prose in *The Decameron*.

Boccaccio and music have continued to represent a winning combination through the centuries to these days. The Italian author and film maker Pier Paolo Pasolini (1922-1975), on shooting the film *Il Decameron*, acknowledged how indebted he was to the inherent function that music has in Boccaccio's text, which naturally supports the narrative framework of his Neapolitan reinterpretation of the tales.

Concerning Chaucer, the interest he had in the music of his time is evident in most of his writings which have become an important source of information, besides showing the influence that music had on his own poetry. From the beginning of his career, he resorted to music to create the appropriate narrative environment, but the musical references are still stylised and conventional, as for example in *The House of Fame* and *The Book of the Duchesse*, or in "The Knight's Tale," as well as elsewhere in *The Canterbury Tales*. From the earliest steps in his career, Chaucer used musical instruments as an integral part of the narrative environment, but not as a distinguishing aspect of the characters. Indeed, as Chaucer got to know the changing real world, be it court or the streets, he began to emphasize the inter-relationship between these environments and the many instruments that served symbolic social functions, as can be seen in "The Squire's Tale" in *The Canterbury Tales*, with characters like the Squire himself with his flute. Equally interesting is this passage from the "Miller's Tale" whose protagonist, Nicholas, an Oxford university student, shows not only particular lover's skills with his landlady, the miller's wife, but that he is a good musician, too:

> And Nicholas had stroked her loins a bit
> And kissed her sweetly, he took down his harp
> And played away, a merry tune and sharp.

Everything is fine until another young man, Absalom, a parish clerk, who likes the same woman, enters the scene and seduces her with his outstanding ability as a dancer and fiddle player:

> He used to dance in twenty different styles
> (After the current school at Oxford though,
> Casting his legs about him to and fro).
> He played a two-stringed fiddle, did it proud,
> And sang a high falsetto rather loud;
> And he was just as good on the guitar
> [...].
>
> (Chaucer, 1968, 108)

As we can see, unlike in his earlier period, in these passages Chaucer uses musical instruments to highlight their relationship to the characters in order to stress their social function. Incidentally, this demonstrates that even if musical notation was not widely used in England in the 14th century, there was folk dance, war and love ballads as well church music in the form of hymns. In short, there was a widespread and popular musical culture where music was no longer conventional, but a mirror of the times of which Chaucer was a great interpreter.

Renaissance: XIV-XVI Centuries

When the Medieval period came to its end around 1400, the Renaissance period began and lasted until about 1600, with the beginning of the Baroque age. Music historians agree to divide this long span of time into three periods. Early (1400-1470), Middle 1470-1530), and Late (1530-1600).

In the *Early Period*, musicians were obviously influenced by the late Medieval style, as is the case with John Dunstaple (c.1390-1453), one of the most famous English composers of the time. Owing to the fact that many copies of his works have been found in Italian and German manuscripts, historians have thought that his influence spread from England into Europe, especially in creating the very original new style of the Burgundian School (a group of composers particularly active in France). Dunstaple developed a most influential art known as "la contenance angloise" ("the English countenance"), a term used by the French poet Martine le Franc (1410-1461) in his *Le Champion de Dames*, characterised by the use of "triadic harmony" (three-note chords). Only fifty compositions that are attributed to him are extant, including some masses in which he uses a single melody (*cantus firmus*) instead of Medieval polyphony. There are hardly any songs in English that are considered his. On the contrary, although European musicians continued to write religious music, non-religious works were composed by the German musician Oswald von Wolkenstein (c. 1376-1445), the Dutch Gilles Binchois (c.1400-1460), who composed secular songs, mainly 'rondeaux' like the Franco-Flemish Guillaume Du Fay (c.1397-1474) with his many ballads and 'virelais', and other 'chansons.' On closing this early period, there are certain scores, anticipating today's art interaction, which are true visual artworks worthy of particular notice. Among them there are two by the French composer Baude Cordier (1380-1440): 'Tout par compass,' an eternal canon, where he uses a circular staff shape, and 'Belle, bonne, sage,' a love song shaped like a heart and with some red notes (unfortunately will not be visible here in b/w) indicating a change of rhythm.

Fig. 1: Score of *Belle, bonne, sage* (XV C.) by Baude Cordier.

In the *Middle Period*, Frenchman Josquin des Prez (c.1450-1521) took a leading role as the best composer of the time. His fame is anchored to his highly virtuosic technique and his universally acknowledged mastery of expression, which was imitated up to the baroque era. Even Martin Luther and Baldassare Castiglione praised him both as a composer of religious polyphonic music, masses on popular songs, and completely secular music such as motets and "chansons."

Concerning the place of music generally, one of the leading political figures of the Renaissance humanist movement, Thomas More (1473-1535), who served under Henry VIII as Lord High Chancellor of England, envisaged in his famous *Utopia* (1515) a fantastic state on an imaginary island where he describes three different sorts of bodily 'pleasures' related to senses and health, and stresses that in between

> Real pleasures they [the Utopians] divide into two categories, mental and physical. [...] However, there are also pleasures which satisfy no organic need, and relieve no previous discomfort. They merely act, in a mysterious but quite an unmistakable way, directly on our senses, and monopolize their reactions. Such is the pleasure of music." (More, 1978, Book II, 96)

It may be surprising, but Niccoló Machiavelli (1469-1527), whose claim to fame are his political theories, had an interest in music filtered through poetry. Amongst his verses, all composed between 1524-25, of particular notice are the "intermedi" – which he himself called "canzoni" or "canzonette" – and, as we will see below, are widely considered the precursors of melodrama. He wrote nine of them for his two comedies *Clizia* and *Mandragola*, (e. g. 'Quanto sia lieto il giorno' and 'Amore'). Machiavelli was aware that he had entered an area that was new to him, yet he managed to innovate the role played by the *intermedi* by using them as an integral part of the dramatic action. Among his best poems are 'S'alla mia immensa voglia' and 'Amor, io sento l'alma,' written for Barbara Salvati, the Florentine lady described by Giorgio Vasari in his life of Domenico Puligo. His intention was that, once they were set to music, they were to be sung by Salvati herself with other singers.

In the *Late Period* of the Renaissance (1530-1600), des Prez represents a link to Italian musicians, while choirs became very popular thanks to the School of Venice which developed at the local Basilique of Saint Mark and spread all over Europe. France continued to play a leading role thanks to the foundation of the *Académie de poésie et de musique* in 1574, in the very year when King Charles IX of France died. His mother Catherine de' Medici had certainly influenced him to give his full support, though the mastermind behind the initiative was the poet Jean-Antoine de Baïf, together with the musician Joachim Thibault de Courville. We need to underline that those two artists followed the Neo-Platonic ideals aiming at the revival of Greek and Roman poetry and music, which linked morality and order as the principles to be applied to the construction of a harmonius society. At the same time, the school of Rome, very close to the Vatican, gave an impressive contribution too, thanks to Giovanni Pierluigi da Palestrina (1525-1594), who was the best and most prolific composer of church music and motets of the time. He was also known for combining the needs of the Catholic Church with the most popular music styles during the Catholic

Reformation as a response to the Protestant Reformation. His ideas were welcome all over Europe, where his counterparts were the Flemish Orland de Lassus (1532-1594), and the Englishman William Byrd (1540-1623), who were particularly popular in the second half of the 16th century. There was a lot of competition to hire them in churches and courts. Italy became the most attractive pole for their services as composers, teachers, and performers. There was a free exchange of techniques between sacred and secular music that allowed musicians to get deeply into the texts they were to put to music, which became a way to express personal feelings more freely. Worth mentioning is the English Madrigal School, which flourished between 1588 and 1627 and used direct translations of the leading Italian models. A case in point are the extremely expressive madrigals of Gesualdo da Venosa (1566-1613) which, besides setting an unsurpassable example on the Continent, represent an impeccable combination of poetry and music, expressed at its utmost level of interweaving thanks to the polyphonic structure of the madrigal. Thus, secular music like the German "Lied," the French "chanson," and the Italian "frottola" became independent of churches. Then, towards the end of the 16th century, an early form of opera as the "madrigal comedy," the "monody" and the "intermedi" began to be heard.

In the meantime, the love for music and poetry of Henry VIII and his daughter, Queen Elizabeth, favoured the rise of some outstanding poets like Thomas Wyatt, Edward Spenser, Christopher Marlowe, and Sir Philip Sidney. Their lyrics appeared in various publications set to music, and although none of them composed music, we can say that they intended their poems for singing. In *The Defense of Poesy* (1595), Sidney (1554-86) writes: 'our Poet…cometh to you with words set in delightful proportion, either accompanied with, or prepared for, the well enchanting skill of Music' (Sidney, 2002, 7). When he was only nineteen, he spent two years studying in Venice and Padua where he came into direct contact with the new Italian movements in music and poetry. He wrote from Venice that he was studying 'certain musical subjects.' On 22 May 1580, in one of the rare references to his own work, he wrote to his friend, Edward Denny, stressing the importance of musical settings for his poetry: "remember with your good voyce, to singe my songes for they will one well become another" (Osborne, 1972, 540). Sidney followed a trend of the time, consisting of using poems to be adapted to existing melodies, or using the tunes to give the meter of the poem to be read. His claim to fame is a love sonnet sequence *Astrophel and Stella* dedicated to his illicit love for Penelope Devereux, who married Lord Rich in 1581, thus recalling Petrarch's unrequited love for Laura. The first line of '*In a grove most rich of shade*' puns upon her new name, Penelope Rich. This is set to the melody of a French aria by Guillaume Tessier, which appeared in a book dedicated to Queen Elizabeth in 1582. This is one of three *Astrophel and Stella* sonnet settings that Robert Dowland, the son of the famous lutenist John, included in his *A Musical Banquet* of 1610, which was dedicated to his godfather, Sir Robert Sidney, Philip's brother.

Another outstanding poet is **John Donne** (1572-1631) who composed mainly for the 'happy few.' Among his major poems that were put to music there is, 'Come live with me, and be my love,' which is a parody of Christopher Marlowe's pastoral ballad *The Passionate Shepherd to his Love* and Sir Walter Raleigh's *The Nymph Reply*. This is one of the few poems from Donne's *Songs and Sonnets* to be published during his lifetime, and specifically as a song. Another important theme of his poetry is religion. When he was Dean of St. Paul's Cathedral in London, he wrote *A hymne to God the Father* whose setting to music was most likely commissioned by John Hilton. His biographer Izaak Walton (1593-1683) reported that Donne wanted it "to be set to a most grave and solemn Tune, and to be often sung to the Organ by the Choristers of St. Paul's Church, in his own hearing; [...]" He occasionally said to a friend, "The words of this Hymn have restored to me the same thoughts of joy that possest my soul in my sickness when I composed it. And, O the power of Church-musick!'"

William Shakespeare

In the Elizabethan and Jacobean theatres, between the second half of the 16th century and the beginning of the 17th, music played a much more important role than the bare literary texts can show. This explains why the majority of people tend to overlook the songs and music references on reading a play. Yet playwrights considered them as vital and integral parts of their works. Indeed, to attract larger audiences they often used lyrical poems of already existing famous ballads that were sometimes especially set to music. A good example of this is the Welsh song, "I framed to the *harp* / many an English *ditty* lovely well." (*Henry IV,* Part I, Act 3, sc. 1), or the four songs present in *Volpone* (1605-06) by Ben Jonson (1532-1637), including the popular 'Come, my Celia', an adaptation from the Roman poet Catullus. It is thanks to that practice that many original songs have reached us. However, people in general were not so familiar with the equally good and abundant productions of contemporary music by such eminent composers as Shakespeare's friend Thomas Morley (1557-1602), an expert in making poems into madrigals who also composed the music for the Great Bard's *As You Like It* (1600).

Indeed, **William Shakespeare** (1564-1616), the most popular playwright of the Elizabethan theatre, loved music so deeply that in his works alone, he manages to take us through the whole range of the musical world and its history, going from the philosophical "music of the spheres" to love songs or impertinent ballads. There are three hundred stage directions related to music in his thirty-seven plays, out of which at least thirty-two contain interesting musical references, be it to specific songs, which were to be sung as part of the action, to instructions on how to dance a galliard, or casual allusions to popular pieces as the pastoral song "Come live with me and be my love" by Christopher Marlowe (1564-1593), which Shakespeare borrowed from his friend and quoted it in his play *The Merry Wives of Windsor*. In addition to this, there are witty references and puns, with obvious sexual connotations, where Shakespeare associates music to people, as in *Pericles* (Act I, sc. 5) where the King, in disagreement with his daughter's choice of a husband, says to her: "You are a fair viol and you sense the strings." Music is also used to relieve mental tension, as in *Antony and Cleopatra* (Act II sc. 5) when the latter orders, "Give me some music; music, moody food/ Of us that trade in love. / All say: "The music, ho!" Sensitivity and morality are closely associated in *Richard II* (Act I, sc. 3) when Mowbray, who has been sent into exile by the King, says: "The language I have learn'd these forty years, / My native English, now I must forgo;/ And now my tongue's use is to me no more/ Than an unstringed viol, or a harp;/ Or like a cunning instrument cas'd up, / Or, being open, put into his hands/ That knows *no touch to tune the harmony.*" And here follow some of the most representative songs which, according to the critic and musicologist F.W. Sternfield, are introduced to throw light on the character of the singer, or to create an appropriate atmosphere, or also to examine closely the essence of a dramatic situation: "Tomorrow is St. Valentine's Day" (*Hamlet*), is a common tune sung by Ophelia, which was traditionally known and continued to be used in many 18th century ballad operas. "The willow song" (*Othello*: Act IV, sc. 5) is sung by Desdemona just before being smothered by Othello. She recalls that she first heard it from her mother's maid, Barbary, who had had a similar sad experience and sang it before dying. In fact, the song was as old as it was popular.

Shakespeare's last work *The Tempest* was first written and performed between 1610 and 1611 and published posthumously in the First Folio of 1623. Several instruments and four songs make of it the most musical of the Great Bard's plays. Ariel, a fundamental character in the play, is always accompanied by music when entering and exiting the stage. He is a player of pipe and tabor. Music is an intrinsic part of his nature. He sings 'Come unto These Yellow Sands' (Act I sc. 2), 'Full Fathom Five' (Act I sc. 2),

'Whil you Here Do snoring Lie' (Act II sc. 1), 'Where the Bees Sucks' (Act V sc. 1). Note that these songs support the plot itself and determine the characters' doings.

It is evident that Shakespeare borrowed a lot from musicians of his time, but he became himself a source of inspiration for musicians through the centuries. They go from modern singers and groups like Bob Dylan, Elvis Costello, The Beatles, and Dire Straits, who used the very names of the protagonists of Shakespeare's tragedy *Romeo and Juliet* (1597) to develop a different story of an unrequited love, seeing a disillusioned Romeo singing his disappointment to a careless Juliet. Many of the greatest classical music composers, such as Berlioz, Gounod, Schubert, Schumann, Mendelsohn, Chopin, Bellini, Rossini, Tchaikovsky, Wagner, Britten, and Vaughan-Williams, set Shakespeare to music, or were inspired by Shakespeare's works. See *Grove's Dictionary of Music* for a list of compositions inspired by Shakespeare. Not widely known is the partnership of the Chekoslovakian adopted-German musician Georg Anton Benda and the German poet F. W. Gotter, who translated Shakespeare's *Romeo and Juliet* and adapted it for Benda's eponymous musical setting. (See Essay in this volume, pp. 173-199). For more recent adaptations, there is an operatic version of *The Tempest*, composed by Thomas Adès and performed at the Royal Opera House in London in 2004, and Brett Dean's *Hamlet* (2017) whose world premier was staged at the Glyndenbourne Festival in England in 2017.

At any rate, if there is a musician who undoubtedly deserves our utmost attention for the extraordinary influence that Shakespeare had on his career, he is the greatest Italian opera composer **Giuseppe Verdi** (1813-1901). As indicated by the following titles, Verdi was convinced he could transform great literature into music. Therefore, he was particularly keen on approaching the works of eminent authors such as Lord Byron (*The Corsair – Il corsaro* 1843), Victor Hugo (*Hernani – Ernani* 1843; *Le Roy s'amuse – Rigoletto* 1854); Alexandre Dumas-fils (*La Dame aux camélias – La Traviata* 1852); Eugène Scribe – Charles Duveyrier (*Les vêpres siciliennes - I vespri siciliani* 1855) Joseph Méry (*Don Carlos* 1867). Most importantly, we know that in his later days, he acknowledged he had first read *Macbeth* when he was very young, and that he had been immediately struck by it. He seems to have been virtually haunted by the Great Bard throughout his life. In 1847, he sent his mentor and benefactor, Antonio Barezzi, his first opera based on one of Shakespeare's plays, saying: "Ora, io mando a voi *Macbeth*, che io apprezzo sopra tutte le mie altre opere, e quindi la ritengo degna di dedicarla a voi." [Now, I am sending you *Macbeth*, which I consider above all my other works, and therefore I think it is worth dedicating it to you"] (Weffel, 1973, 122). In 1865, he went back to this opera to extend it and restructure it because he thought he was too young to be up to the task he had set himself. Meanwhile, Verdi enjoyed the great success of one of his best operas, *Trovatore* (1853), when he began to take into consideration adapting *King Lear* into an opera. Antonio Somma offered a libretto twice, but the Maestro rejected it both times. He found the story too complex to be written as a libretto. Later, his friend the librettist Arrigo Boito, knowing how much Verdi cared about Shakespeare, offered him a libretto ready to put to music, but Verdi said, "I am too old for that now!" We should know that, as a rule, before starting to compose, he demanded to go through the libretto first, and, generally speaking, through the period of composing he was tormented. This was certainly the case with *Othello* (1887), an opera based on the eponymous play accomplished in 1887. In the following years, Verdi dedicated most of his time and efforts to his last opera, *Falstaff*, which, except for the failure of his juvenile comedy *Un giorno di regno* (1840), represents his second work of the kind. *Falstaff,* according to most critics, is some sort of "divertissement." Nonetheless, its composition resulted from the merging of *The Merry Wives of Windsor* and *Henry IV* to create coherent characters and a consistent story as conceived by Verdi. We need to emphasise though that it took the collaboration of Boito, a brilliant young poet and critic, whom the aging Maestro trusted most as a collaborator and a friend. There is a particular letter to Boito which I think is most telling about that. An old and depressed Verdi wrote it in 1889:

> As long as we roam in the world of ideas, everything smiles on us; but once we come to earth, and face practical questions, doubts and discouragement arise. In outlining *Falstaff*, have you ever thought of the enormous number of my years? I know well how you will reply, exaggerating the state of my health, good, excellent, sturdy… And let's assume that is so; nevertheless, you must agree with me that I could be accused of great temerity in taking on such task! And what if the effort were too much for me?! And what if I did not manage to finish the music? […]
> (Conati, 994, 139)

Incidentally, this is an unmissable book for whomever is interested in this wonderful friendship built on a twenty-year-collaboration between composer and librettist, which made Verdi's Shakespearean dream come true through their brilliant the composition of *Otello* and *Falstaff*, two of Verdi's greatest operas.

By way of conclusion of this subsection, it will be most interesting to read Jerry Lutz quoting two articles written by George Bernard Shaw (1856-1950), a sophisticated music critic and a playwright himself who emphasises that Shakespeare's plays are so musical in themselves that they could be quite legitimately analysed by music reviewers instead of literary critics. At the provocation of Arthur B. Walkley, *The Times* theatre reviewer, Shaw wrote a review on *Richard III* in 1889, arguing that a music reviewer should actually attend performances:

> As a matter of fact, I did go to the Globe, not because Walkely wished me to hear Mr Edward's fine music with its *leitmotivs* after Wagner's plan" (ah!ah!ah!) but because a musician only has the right to criticize works like Shakespear's earlier histories and tragedies. The two Richards, King John, and the last act of Romeo and Juliet, depend wholly on the beauty of their music. There is no deep significance, no great subtlety, nor variety in their numbers; but for splendor of sound, magic of romantic illusion, majesty of emphasis, ardor, elation, reverberation of haunting echoes, and every poetic quality that can waken the heart-stir and the imaginative fire of early manhood, they stand above all recorded music. These things cannot be spectated (Walkley signs himself *Spectator*: they must be heard. It is not enough to see *Richard III*, you should be able to *whistle* it. (Lutz,1972, 65)

Apparently, Shaw did not drop the idea of Shakespearian music once he became a theatre reviewer. On the contrary, it is repeated constantly throughout his work for the *Saturday Review*–Shakespeare is the supreme dramatic music maker, although the music is composed at the expense of characterization and a philosophical point of view.

Shaw's first Shakespearean review in *The Saturday Review* sets the tone for the rest. He talks about the performance of *All's Well That Ends Well*, one of his favourite plays by Shakespeare:

> What a pity it is that people who love the sound of Shakespear so seldom go on the stage! The ear is the sure clue to him. Only a musician can understand the play of feeling which is the real rarity in his early plays. In a deaf nation these plays would have died long ago. […] In short, it is the score and not the libretto that keeps the work alive and fresh; and this is why only musical [sic] critics should be allowed to meddle with Shakespear [sic].

(ibid., 66)

Music and social life at the turn of the 16th century into the 17th

Between the 16th century and the beginning of the 17th, although the Church was extremely influential and ecclesiastical music for service developed especially thanks to William Byrd (1542-1623), popular songs and ballads increased rapidly in number as the most natural way English people preferred to express themselves. This contributed – also thanks to the widespread use of music – to make England known in Europe as "Merry England." Music was also regularly appreciated and practiced at court: Anne Boleyn, Catherine of Aragon, and Edward VI played the lute and the virginals. It is reasonable to say, then, that there was a music craze, especially during the Elizabethan Age (1558-1603), involving the lowest as well as the highest layers of English society. As for Queen Elizabeth I, she was an enthusiastic virginal player and also loved dancing. The painting that shows her below dancing 'La Volta' with Robert Dudley, Earl of Leicester, now is thought that its title is ironic and mocking.

Fig. 2: Queen Elizabeth I, dancing "La Volta" with Robert Dudley, Earl of Leicester. The painter is anonymous, but belonged to French Valois School, c. 1580.

Fig. 3: *The concert* (1623), Gerard van Hornthorst (1592-1656).

This period was called the "Golden Age" of English music, though great musicians like William Byrd, John Dowland (1583-1626), Orlando Gibbons (1583-1626), John Bull (1562-1628), were still unknown to the general public.

This flourishing musical activity was marked by secular music, carols (mostly anonymous), numerous folk songs like "The Cuckoo", and dance music used at Maypole festivals such as Morris dancing, a ritual folk dance typically performed in the countryside, which reached its apex in the reigns of James I (1603-25), and Charles I (1625-49), who was himself a player of viola da gamba. In the same period, masques became an ever-present form of court entertainment, representing primitive examples of the rising Italian opera. Perhaps the greatest achievement is *Comus*, whose words, written by **John Milton** (1608-1674), were adapted to music by his close friend Henry Lawes; it was performed at Ludlow Castle in 1634. Milton, too, was a fine amateur composer and cello player, and his father had been a chorister at Christ Church Cathedral in Oxford. An anonymous biographer declared that "Hee [Milton] had an excellent Ear and could bear a part both in Vocal and Instrumental Music." His scores appeared in collections with some of the greatest musicians of the time, and he even wrote both words and music of 'Fair Orian' to contribute to Thomas Morley's madrigal collection (*The Triumph of Oriana*, 1601) to pay homage to Queen Elizabeth.

The amazingly wealthy production of those days lasted until Cromwell became Lord Protector and imposed Puritanism on the people in 1642; thus, striking a tremendous blow to everything that had to do with entertainment. A pamphlet called *The Actor's Remonstrance or Complaint for the Silencing of their Profession* (1643) talks about the terrible state that music was in just one year after the theatres were closed down:

> Our music, that was held so delectable and precious, that they [players] scorned to come to a tavern under twenty shillings salary for two hour*s*, now wander with the instruments under their cloaks —I mean, such as we have any—into all houses of good fellowship, saluting every room where there is company with *Will you have any music, Gentlemen?* (Anonymous, 1643, 7)

Then the Restoration of the monarchy, marked by the return of King Charles II (1660-1685), which followed the period of Cromwell's Commonwealth, allowed artists like Milton to concentrate on writing his masterpiece, *Paradise Lost* (1667, 1674). He, like Dante, describes in it how music changes accordingly in Hell and Heaven (the almost completely absent singing of the fallen Angels vs the jubilant heavenly singing). His interest in music was so deep that he also focused his attention on the theory originally developed by Pythagoras, resulting in the connection between music and abstract mathematics, which offered a key to explaining the origin of the universe. This theory, known as the "music of the spheres" (See Intro., xvi, xxx, xlviii), became particularly popular in the Renaissance when it was the basis of the "harmonia mundi" ("harmony of the world"), a metaphor for thinking of God, a concept enhancing a Christian view of the world. Thus, Milton, in *Paradise Lost,* explained in ethical terms why human beings cannot hear "the heavenly tune, which none can hear / Of human mould with gross unpurged ear." (Milton, 1969, 103). With respect to Milton's influence, it will be interesting to compare this use of synaesthesia with John Keats's "Ode on a Grecian Urn". (See Balestra's Essay, xlviii). Even more telling is how *Paradise Lost* proved to be an evergreen and most inspiring literary work for many generations, even up to these days. Among the best examples is its use by Joseph Haydn (1732-1809) as the basis for the libretto for his oratorio *Die Schöpfung* ("The Creation", 1796-98) written, among others, by Baron van Swieten (1733-1803). Then, in our days, let's just consider the title of "Long Hard Road Out of Hell" (1997) by Marilin Manson, which is from a line of the poem. Worthy of particular notice is the musical adaptation of *Paradise Lost* written by Ben Birney and Rob Seitelman, staged in New York City in March 2006. **John Dryden** (1631-1700), another great poet of the 18th century was, like Milton, intrigued by the "music of the spheres." He composed *A song for Saint Cecilia's day* (1687) in homage to the patroness of musicians and based it on two principal themes: *harmonia mundi,* the Pythagorean and Platonic tradition that the world was designed in harmonic intervals; and *musica humana,* or the moral power of music, meant to arouse distinct emotions in the hearer, depending on the instrument that was being played. This ode is the first of two written by Dryden for such an occasion. It was originally set to music by the Italian composer G. B. Draghi (alias Pergolesi, 1710-36) and later by Georg Friederich Händel (1685-1759) in 1739.

On closing this subsection, it must be underlined that, if music and culture in general flourished in England, France was its equal during the long-lasting reign of Louis XIV (The Sun King – Le Roi Soleil, 1643-1715). Madame de Sévigné puts us straight in the picture by saying that "Everything is grand, magnificent at Versaille... and the music and dance are at the very height of perfection." Following the tradition of his father, Louis XIII (1610-1643), who loved the ballet in particular and even composed his own musical scores, the Sun King favoured culture and entertainment by encouraging musicians to compose excellent music to be played, sung, and danced. Again, the example that was set to support the practice of these arts came from ancient Greece where Plato maintained that music not only helps to sow harmony in society but is also good for fostering in individuals "the habit of good order." Hence, with the growing interest for more varied entertainment, playrights, poets, and authors in general realized the need for music in their writings. This leads us straight into the 18th century where the court continued to be the hub of social life.

Enlightenment: 18th century

King Louis XV (1710-74), like his predecessor, besides favouring musicians, gave full support to philosophers, novelists, dramatists, and writers who often showed their appreciation of music in their writings. It will suffice to mention Montesquieu, Voltaire, Rousseau, Diderot, Beaumarchais, and Chénier. I only regret that this essay is not appropriate, especially space-wise, to duly deal with each of them. Anyhow, Rousseau (1712-1778) and Montesquieu (1689-1755) were particularly interested in music. The latter abounds in musical references in *The Persian Letters* and *The Spirit of Laws*, two books in which he discusses laws in relation to the climate and recounts attending the same operas in England and Italy but noticed how music was perceived differently by the audiences in each of those two countries. As the English were cold and phlegmatic while the Italians got emotionally very involved, Montesquieu found that inconceivable in either case. He likened French literature of the time to music as a unifying and harmonious element comparable to the harmony of the Reign of Louis XIV. As for Rousseau, he is worth recalling for the abundance of music in *The Social Contract*, *Rousseau and Education According to Nature*, and *The Confessions of Jean-Jacques Rousseau*. Besides that, there is an interesting article on music written for the *Encyclopédie*, and his opera *Le devin du village* which was performed with great success before the King at Versailles. Instrumental and vocal music did not arise his interest, though, I would like to stress they are particularly predominant in Voltaire, even if he claimed little expertise in music. By contrast, he was keener on opera than on anything else because it was connected to the stage, hence his great passion for the theatre. Beaumarchais (1732-99) too shared the same passion. He is the author of *Barbier de Séville* (1773), which inspired the Italian composers Rossini and Paisiello their respective famous operas *Barber of Seville* (1782, 1816) and *Mariage de Figaro* (1778) from which Mozart himself drew the eponym opera in 1790.

One thing that is peculiar about the century, that we are dealing with in this subsection, are the various names used to refer to it. The "long 18th century" (1685-1815) is a phrase used by British historians to refer to a movement whose participants called the Age of Reason, or simply the

Enlightenment, notably *Illuminism* in France, *Illuminismo* in Italy, and *Aufklärung* in Germany. Whatever the term used, the 18th century corresponded everywhere to a long period of profound changes based on the primacy of reason not only in the scientific field, where the experimental and evidential approach increased its importance, but also in every area of social and cultural life that inevitably included music. Little wonder, then, that the mathematical conception of music, which was quite popular at the time, was particularly developed by many German philosophers, such as Gottfried Wilhelm Leibniz (1646-1716). He, in his *Monadology* (1714), a short text originally written in French, conceived beauty mathematically and arising from harmony, which he defines as "unity in plurality." In his words:

> Music charms us, although its beauty consists only in the agreement of numbers and in the counting which we do not perceive, but which the soul nevertheless continues to carry out, of the beats or vibrations of sounding bodies which coincide at certain intervals. The pleasures that the eye finds in proportions are of the same nature, and those caused by other senses amount to something similar, although we may not be able to explain them so distinctly. (Leibniz, 2014, 300)

Leibniz put that in brief also in a letter to Goldbach (27 April 1712, quoted in O Sacks, *The Man who Mistook his Wife for a Hat*), "Musica est exercitium arithmeticae occultum nescientis se numerare animi", meaning that "The pleasure we get from music derives from counting, though unconsciously. Hence music is nothing but unconscious arithmetic." The German influence was felt all over Europe, as is the case with the English playwright **John Gay** (1685-1732), who enjoyed the collaboration of the German-born composer Johann Cristoph Pepusch (1667-1752), who composed the score for his ballad opera *The Beggar's Opera* (See Chung's Essay, 2-14).

On turning back to England and the English novels of the Georgian period (1714-1837), if we consider the many novelists of that period, the relationship between music and literature did not draw enough attention as perhaps it should have. Despite that, it reached its apex with one of the greatest novelists of that time, **Laurence Sterne** (1713-68), who combined his artistry as a writer with his ability as a fine instrumentalist who played the violin, cello and bass viol. He confirmed in a letter to his daughter that "fiddling was one of (his) [my favourite] amusements" (Sterne 1935, *Letters* 4), which he accompanied with a very good grasp of theory as well as composition. In effect, he took an active role in the current debate of seventeenth century music theory. In his *Compendium Musicae*, he launched an open attack against the French philosopher René Descartes

(1596-1650) by satirising his mathematical discourse on Baroque style in general. Sterne disliked the current trend of Baroque music which relied on mathematics and logic, especially in operatic music. His passion for music is confirmed by the many musical references in *Tristram Shandy* and in *A Sentimental Journey*. In the latter, there is a letter from Amiens, stating that music has a social function, meant to create a joyful gathering of any living creature, people and animals alike:

> La Fleur, in less than five minutes, had pulled out his fife, and leading off the dance himself with the first note, set the *fille de chambre*, the *maître d'hotel*, the cook, the scullion, and all the household, dogs and cats, besides an old monkey, a-dancing. I suppose there never was a merrier kitchen since the flood. (Sterne, 1952, 58)

Similarly, William Freedman declared that, especially in *Tristram Shandy*, there is a "pervasive musicalization" (Freedman, 1978, 188) that Sterne creates by borrowing not only musical terms but also other appropriate features like forms and metaphors. Moreover, in the words of the Austrian musicologist Werner Wolf, *Tristram Shandy* "could be shown to foreshadow some musicalizing devices which have become important in the subsequent history of musicalized fiction." (Wolf 1999, 233) This musicalization of the novel was meant to reflect an illusionary harmony in society, though there where strong tensions between people, which Sterne tries to interpret metaphorically in terms of the opposition between harmony and dissonance (cf. other European countries). In other words, Sterne's view of the universe discord / dissonance is the prevailing element in its chaos, whereas harmony appears only as a transitional element. This recalls the many references to music since the Renaissance, among which the most characteristic is the opposition between discord and harmony that was used metaphorically to stress the passage from conflict and chaos to order and resolution. Hence, Sterne sees the Neo-Platonic resolution of discord into harmony as a possible way out, and argues that in such an unstable, chaotic world, conventional communication through conventional language proves to be inappropriate and limited in itself as, for example, are the musical annotations in Yorick's sermons, such as this one upon *Le Fever*:

> What Yorick could mean by the words *lentamente*, —*tenutè*,—*grave*, and sometimes *adagio*,—as applied to theological compositions, and with which he has characterized some of these sermons, I dare not venture to guess.— .—I am more puzzled still upon finding a *l'octava alta*! Upon one; *Con strepito* upon the back of another;—*Siciliana* upon a third; —*Alla capella* upon a fourth;—*Con l'arco* upon this;—*Senza l'arco* upon that.—All I know is, that they are musical terms, and have a meaning; —and as he was

a musical man, I will make no doubt, but that by some quaint application of such metaphors to the compositions in hand, they impressed very distinct ideas of their several characters upon his fancy,—whatever they may do upon that of others. [...] I something doubt; —because at the end of the sermon (and not at the beginning of it)—very different from his way of treating the rest, he had wrote—Bravo!
(Sterne, 1950, Book VI, ch. 11, 445-7)

It will not be surprising to hear that *Tristram Shandy* had some intrinsic elements, as disrupted chronology, association of ideas, flashbacks, blank pages, and the use of a variety of languages. Such a challenging attitude reveals Sterne's deliberate intention to break away from the traditional system on which he bases his starting point, even at the risk of seeming aligned, but in actual fact he aims to overturn the whole discourse and restore a consequent order. This allowed Sterne to project his novel into the modern literary sphere, thus making him a forerunner of James Joyce. See below the use of musical scores and even blank pages as parts of the main texts. Much more recently, the English musician Michael Nyman (1944-) used *Tristram Shandy* as an inspirational basis to compose an opera as yet unfinished, *Nose-List Song* (for soprano and orchestra), whose fourth part was recorded in 1985. (The song in question is based on "Slawkenbergius's Tale" from Volume IV, Chapter 1.). (Sterne, 1952, 648-649)

In the Georgian era, we can detect not only the social importance of music, but also the metaphorical roles that music played in the writers' literary strategies. At first, it seems that music was not a favourite with the leading novelists as Henry Fielding, who just occasionally mentions music, or **Samuel Richardson** (1689-1761), who shows no interest in music in his debut novel *Pamela* (1740). Conversely, in *Clarissa* in 1748, Richardson resorts to music to identify the protagonist's musical skills as an evident sign of her conventional femininity and as a virtue which could help to create harmony in society.

> My friends were pleased with my choice. They wanted me to be shackled: for early did they doubt my morals, as to the sex. They saw, that the dancing, the singing, the musical ladies were all fond of my company: For who [I am in a humour to be vain, I think!]—for who danced, who sung, who touched the string, whatever the instrument, with a better grace than thy friend?
> (Richardson, 2018, 176)

It will be ironic to see that the English composer and writer Robin Holloway (1943-) spent many years to adapt *Clarissa*, the longest novel ever written in English, into a 'libretto', while he managed to compose the orchestral score in only two weeks in 1976. Some critics saw it as a symphony whose overture is represented by the story of Clarissa's seduction by Lovelace. It was premiered at the English National Opera in 1990. Ironically, Pierre Dubois, in his *Music in the Georgian Novel*, identifies it within the 'musical scenes' such as the excessively melodramatic Italian opera, which was parodied by John Gay in his *Beggar's Opera*. (See Chung's Essay, 2-14).

Jane Austen (1775-1817) a typical representative of the transition from the Age of Reason to the Romantic period closes the 18th century. She was an independent sort of woman, who, like many of her peers loved dancing, played the piano and compiled her albums of sheet music, which was a way to save money to buy them. Indeed, musical references often characterise her female characters. In *Pride and Prejudice* (1813), playing the piano and being knowledgeable about music is an important accomplishment for young women. This emerges in a conversation between Lady Catherine and Miss Bennet:

> '[…] What are you telling me Bennet? Let me hear what it is.'
> We are speaking of music, Madam,' said he, when no longer to avoid a reply.
> 'Of music! Then pray speak aloud. It is of all subjects my delight. I must have my share in the conversation, if you are speaking of music. There are few people in England, I suppose, who have more true enjoyment of music

than myself, or a better natural taste. If I had ever learnt, I should have been a great proficient. (Austen, 2000, 207)

Emma (1815), a novel marking Austen's maturity, is another case in point. There are various scenes, marking the importance that music had for the English middle class. The first scene is the dinner party at the Coles' where a mysterious gift of a Broadwood pianoforte is delivered anonymously from London. This makes Mrs Cole say: "It always has quite hurt me that Jane Fairfax, who plays so delightfully, should not have an instrument" (Austen 1994, 171). Conjectures on who might have sent it become the main topic of conversation for the entire dinner party. In truth, Frank Churchill and Jane Fairfax are secretly in love, so they communicate through her special talent for music. They are warmly invited to have a duet, which serves a double function: entertaining the guests and providing an opportunity for Jane to receive Frank's attention publicly. Everybody is charmed by "the sweet sounds of the united voices" (Austen, 2000, 180). In another scene, Jane Fairfax mentions a living composer, Johann Baptist Cramer (1771-1858), which is something that hardly ever happens in Austen's novels. Fairfax, like Austen, was particularly fond of folk music, which she played to entertain her family, especially a traditional Celtic song, 'Robin Adair' of which the novelist had several versions in her collection. We can deduce that the piano is not just a musical instrument but is used as an integral plot device, just as it was an important element in Austen's life. Frank Churchill "begs" Jane Fairfax to remain seated at the piano.

'If you are very kind,' said he, 'it will be one of the waltzes we danced last night; let me live them over again. […]'
She played.
'What felicity is to hear a tune again which *has* made one happy! […]'
She looked up at him for a moment, coloured deeply, and played something else. He took some music from a chair near the pianoforte, and turning to Emma, said:
Here is something quite new to me. Do you know it? Cramer. And here are a new set of Irish melodies. That, from such a quarter, one might expect. This was all sent with the instrument. Very thoughtful of Colonel Campbell, was not it? He knew Miss Fairfax could have no music here. […] 'She is playing "Robin Adair" at this moment – *his* favourite.' (Ibid. 194)

Also very telling is the scene where Mrs Elton, an amateur pianist, says to Miss Woodhouse, a proficient pianist:

I am dotingly fond of music – passionately fond; and my friends say I am not entirely devoid of taste; but as to anything else, upon my honour my

performance is *mediocre* to the last degree. You, Miss Woodhouse, I well know, play delightfully. […]
"to be quite honest, I do not think I can live without something of a musical society. I condition for nothing else; but without music, life would be a blank to me."   (ivi, 220)

Moving to poetry, and for the purposes of this book, **Robert Burns** (1759-1796), the Scottish national bard, certainly deserves to be mentioned here. He wrote 360 songs in English and Scottish, and wanted to be remembered among the greatest Scottish songwriters. He elaborated a painstaking theory to combine words with music and showed an incredible sense of rhythm in catching the inherent tonal and rhythmic irregularity of the Scottish language, which he said not many poets managed to catch. His claim to world fame is 'Auld lang syne' ('Old long since' in standard English 'Times long past'), a song people sing on Hogmanay (Scottish for New Year's Eve). The song was sung by many artists, reaching its utmost success thanks to the duet performed by Frank Sinatra and Dean Martin. Poems with similar words to Burn's "Auld lang syne" existed before he wrote his own version in 1788. It seems that the melody also existed before Burns wrote down the words. The combination with which we are familiar today did not appear until 1799.

Finally, here is the most representative poet of the 18th century, **William Blake** (1757-1827), who embodied both music and words in his poetry. He cut all links with neoclassical and didactic poetry of the 18th century and rediscovered the lyrical intensive voice of the Elizabethan song, while conceptualizing his art in musical terms. Blake brings to mind the word 'song,' which played an important role in English everyday life, from opera and oratorio for the high layers of society to broad street ballads for the poor. It is known that Blake used to attend the gatherings of wealthy Londoners to whom he offered the musicality and freshness of his verses, which are features of the beautiful poems in the *Songs of Innocence* (1789), a collection that was reprinted together with *Songs of Experience* in 1794. He found again through them his most genuine musical vein, inspiring in him a musical accompaniment for his beautiful singing to entertain his friends at the social events. There are various references to music and singing in the *Songs*, dealing with universal and timeless themes, such as childhood and nature to which he clearly refers to in the *Introduction* to *Songs of Experience*. Note that Blake uses the words 'pipe' and 'sing,' in their different forms, ten and seven times respectively, as if he wanted to say that his poems naturally lent themselves to being sung and set to music.

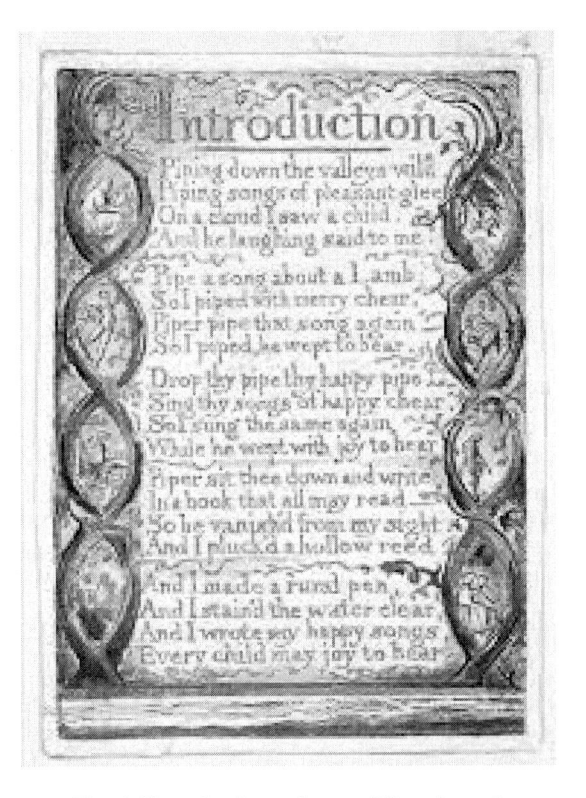

Fig. 4: "Introduction to Songs of Experience."

Piping down the valleys wild,
Piping songs of the pleasant glee,
 On a cloud I saw as a child.
And he laughing said to me: —
"Pipe a song about a lamb:"
So I piped with merry cheer.
"Piper, pipe that song again:"
So I piped: he wept to hear.
"Drop thy pipe, thy happy pipe,
Sing thy songs of happy cheer!"
So I sang the same again,
While he wept with joy to hear.
"Piper, sit thee down and write
In a book, that all may read—"
So he vanished from my sight;
And I plucked a hollow reed,

> And I made a rural pen,
> And I stained the water clear,
> And I wrote my happy songs
> Every child may joy to hear.
> 		(Blake, 1971, 34)

Blake gained the admiration of teachers of music, who would try to transcribe his performances from his time up to these days, as is the case with the English composer and writer, Joseph Andrew Thomson who acknowledges his fascination with William Blake's *Songs of Innocence* and *Songs of Experience*.

> In the title of the book, Blake refers to the poems as 'Songs,' and it has been said he would at times sing them in social gatherings to the delight of those in attendance. […] That these are works of a musical nature is evident, and as a composer, I have always found it hard to read this collection without imagining the kinds of melodies Blake might have paired with his words. In keeping with his storybook design, I hear them as simple, memorable songs, at times sweet, and at others, sinister. They might be sung in a playful voice, and when accompanied, illustrated by a vivid musical texture.
> (Thomson, 2019)

In agreement with the above, Thomson decided to put Blake's poem, *A Poison Tree*, to music, which is included in his band *Astralingua*'s album *Safe Passage*, released in March 2019. Blake's 'Songs' have been adapted by many other popular musicians including Bob Dylan, Bruce Dickinson, and Tangerine Dream, let alone the influence that he had on the American poet Allen Ginsberg (1926-1997). Several musicologists, such as Anthony Newcomb (1941-2018), have agreed that eighteenth-century music, which became a form of independent expression detached from words, could succeed in expressing the ambiguity and heterogeneity of a text and, consequently, lend itself to being explored like a literary narrative text in the structure of fiction. In fact, readers and listeners alike can follow the action through a thematic thread which is expressed with words and music accordingly. Similarly, as overtures are composed to exemplify the idea of the musical piece that follows, prefaces and introductions to novels have a similar function. In both cases, they prepare audiences and readers for the action from the beginning. It goes without saying that composers needed to have a deep grasp of the feelings expressed in the story by the novelist in order to convey the literary idea. Of course, this is not easy at all as Hector Berlioz (1803-1869) stated saying that, while a literary text by its own nature communicates a narrative story, music can only evoke musical images.

19th Century: Romanticism and Victorian Age

In the nineteenth century, despite all the efforts to see how poetry and music could be complimentary, they emerged as separate cultural areas even if they continued to wink at each other. In practice, music went along its own autonomous path thanks to the rise of symphony orchestras and some outstanding virtuosi like Niccolò Paganini and Franz Liszt. Music thus superseded poetry and literature in general, yet the rich middle class became more and more educated in every field, as testified to by about 60,000 novels that were published during the 19th century. It is true though that, with the advent of Romanticism, music became a primary source of inspiration in the literary European world. It varied in importance from country to country, perhaps seeing Germany as the leading nation, followed by England, France, Russia, and Italy.

The way to Romanticism in England was mainly paved by Burns and Blake who brought along their lively interest in music, which contributed to take a fresh, lyrical approach to poetry which their great successors happily shared with them.

William Wordsworth (1770-1850), the 'father' of English romanticism, certainly set an example to emulate with his very intimate, musical lyricism. He was so keen on Nature and its sounds that developed a strong conceptual responsiveness under various circumstances. Just by way of example, take "To the cuckoo," or sonorous Nature in "There was a boy," and "The Solitary Reaper": 'solitary Highland Lass! / Reaping and singing by herself / […] / And sings a melancholy strain' (Wordsworth [1805] 1980, 158) whose voice continues to resound in the valley and in the poet's heart. Wordsworth is such a creative and sensitive poet capable of coming out with an unexpectedly realistic approach to poetry. In "The Power of Music" (1806), he compares a busker, playing in busy Oxford Street, London, with Orpheus. (See Intro., xvi, lxix / Also Brandão' Ceramella's Essay, 251-5, 261-3, 265-6). He plays the violin so beautifully that people stop to listen to him as 'He fills with his power all the hearts to the brim,' making them happy regardless of their everyday problems.

Samuel Coleridge (1772-1834), a great admirer and friend of Wordsworth, was in contact with the romanticists of Germany who showed him the importance of musical inspiration for lyricism and helped him to revitalise the musical themes of romanticism in England. In particular, like Novalis (1772-1801) and Hoffmann (1776-1822), he is aware that in the huge 'concert' of Nature, uniting hills, mountains, weather conditions, rivers, sea, flora and fauna, everything contributes to pay homage to God and to the rising sun ('Hymn to the Earth', 'Hymn before Sunrise,' 'An

Ode to the Rain', etc.). Coleridge however, unlike Wordsworth, was a visionary poet like Blake. When he was under the effects of opium, he composed most of the long poem *The Rhyme of the Ancient Mariner* (1798), recalling how "The dead men gave a groan.' while the larks [...] Around, around flew each sweet sound, / I heard the skylark sing.' Music blends with hallucinations, dreams and nightmares. In *Kubla Khan* (1797), an Abyssinian girl appears and sings songs on a dulcimer; he finds her so charming that he commands his servants to build a new palace for pleasure and recreation. Music merges with dreams and love: "She loves me best whene'er I sing / The songs that make her grieve" (Coleridge, 'Love,' 1950, 101). We know that Coleridge loved the old Scottish folksongs that his nurse sang, and disliked fashionable concerts and singers, where the main reason for the venue was the show itself "Lines Composed in a Concert Room."

Coleridge shared, with two other leading poets of the time, **Percy B. Shelley** (1792-1822) and **Lord Byron** (1788-1824), a peculiar style recalling musical devices such as assonances, onomatopoeias, internal rhymes, alliteration, and repetitions, which have a musical sound of their own, aimed at creating unreal and mysterious atmospheres. In other words, these poets conceived their poems as music in a way that had rarely happened before. In a sense, we can say that they composed music by using words as notes, resulting in an intertwining of music and the sound effects of the words in their poems.

Regarding the link between **Byron** and music, it will be interesting to cite what he wrote to introduce *Hebrew Melodies*, a collection of thirty poems based on melodies from the synagogue service: "The subsequent poems were written at the request of my friend, the Hon. Douglas Kinnaird, for a selection of Hebrew Melodies, and have been published, with the music, arranged by Mr. Braham and Mr. Nathan." (Byron, [Jan 1815], 1994, 76). These tunes are not only still sung in the Jewish religious ceremonies, but have continued to kindle the creativity of musicians such as the English composer Brian Blyth Daubney (1929-1980). In his blog, Daubney describes the inspiration he finds in Byron's poetry and the circumstances which led him to compose three musical adaptations for Byron's love poems, 'She Walks in Beauty,' 'When We Two Parted,' and 'So We'll No More Go A-Roving,' in memory of his friend Marie, an alto. Also, the heavy metal band Iron Maiden had the great merit of getting young people to know Coleridge's *The Rhyme of the Ancient Mariner*. They composed a long song, lasting 13 minutes and 45 seconds, a time sufficient to summarise the story told in that long poem in detail. Quite remarkably, Iron Maiden felt the fascination of other authors, ranging from Edgar Allan Poe to Aldous

Huxley, from Joseph Conrad to William Golding. Nonetheless, as we have already seen, it is not so exceptional that young pop musicians have based some of their works on high literature. Just to mention another example, see *The Sign of Cross* from the *X Factor* (1995) album which was based on *Il nome della rosa* ("The Name of the Rose", 1980), a novel by the Italian semiotician and literary critic Umberto Eco (1932-2016). Eco's novel inspired also the Romanian classical musician Serban Nichifor, who composed the poem *Il nome della rosa for cello* (1989) (and piano 4 hands).

John Keats (1795-1821), in "Ode on a Grecian Urn" (1819), went even a step beyond Coleridge because – without taking any drugs – his amazing power of imagination led him to contemplate and address an inexistent urn. Keats's ability to imagine and create is so limitless that the urn even more paradoxically answers all the questions. He draws his conclusion by saying that

> Heard melodies are sweet, but those unheard
> are sweeter; therefore, ye soft pipes, play on.
> Not to the sensual ear, but more endeared,
> Pipe to the spirit ditties of no tone.   (Keats 1973, 209)

It seems to me that the poet is somehow alluding to the ancient Pythagorean theory of the "music of the spheres" (see Intro., xvi, xxx, xxxvi), and is perhaps also contrasting through synesthesia "unheard melodies" with certain "dull and flat" music unable to see how tormented nature really is, as is the case with Wordsworth's poetry evoking stability and still harmony versus the flying alteration of the "unheard melodies." Among other leading figures of the day, Arthur Schopenhauer (1788-1860) and Honoré de Balzac (1799-1850) refer to the same theory which, ultimately, leads back to Plotinus' *The Enneads*, "… harmonies unheard in sound create the harmonies that we hear and wake the Soul to the consciousness of beauty…" (Plotinus 1969, 59). Since this thought is coherent with the rest of Keats's "Ode," stressing the idea that Art is as eternal as Beauty, we can say that Keats, too, was familiar with Plotinus's metaphysical theory.

Given that Romantic music focuses on provoking emotion and passion, we will now see how important sounds were to Keats for communicating personal feelings. Indeed, following the tradition initiated by Shakespeare, Spencer and Milton, his poetry is characterised by the attention he paid to the exactitude of the sound of the words used. He stated that vowels should be distinguished between the open and closed and should be used like notes that help to produce a particular freshness of sound. In this way, and also by the masterly use of internal alliteration, vowel repetitions, assonant rhyme, and speaking stresses, he manages to create the various moods he felt. Similarly, most European composers in the Romantic Era considered music as having a special role, distinguishing it from any other artistic expression, a particular means suitable to describing the inner varied world of an individual. It is interesting to see that Schopenhauer embraced this metaphorical approach to music by observing that

> Music ... stands quite apart from all the [other arts]. In it we do not recognize the copy, the repetition, of any Idea of the inner nature of the world. Yet it is such a great and exceedingly fine art, its effect on man's innermost nature is so powerful, and it is so completely and profoundly understood by him in his innermost being as an entirely universal language, whose distinctness surpasses even that of the world of perception itself, that in it we certainly have to look for more than that *exercitium arithmeticae occultum nescientis se numerare animi* ["an unconscious exercise in arithmetic in which the mind does not know it is counting"] which Leibniz took it to be. ...We must attribute to music a far more serious and profound significance that refers to the innermost being of the world and of our own self." (Schopenhauer, 1966, n. p.)

In conformity with Schopenhauer's conception of music, Romantic composers around Europe began to pursue the flourishing trends of Romantic literature, visual arts in general and philosophy by creating works that reflected the typically emotional and dramatic approach to life, and often used nature (the landscape in particular) as an open inspirational source. In the meantime, it is thanks to the Romantic cultural revolution that a new sensibility, stressing the inner tumult caused by music, was introduced. In consequence, poets who had used music as just one of the various forms of expression and talked about it as something existing on its own in the external world up to then, began to appreciate it as an amazing but natural source of inspiration. Music, then, declared its autonomy and perhaps even its superiority over literature, becoming itself a narrative style with its own poetics. Even so, some of the greatest composers, such as Berlioz (1803-1869) and Wagner, realised that to enhance and heighten its power of expression music still needed to interact with other forms of art, above all poetry. In that respect, the contribution coming from France is really remarkable thanks to a generation of great romantic authors like Balzac, Stendhal, Gérard de Nerval and George Sand, genuinely eager music lovers whose works have many musical elements in their structures, and, equally important, their articles supporting the proliferation of the popular *revues musicales*. George Sand (1804-1876), once the lover of the Polish musician Fryderyk Chopin (1810-49), thought that music is the most thorough form of communication that can best express the innermost feelings of human beings.

> La musique dit tout ce que l'âme rêve et pressent de plus mystérieux et de plus élevé. C'est la manifestation d'un ordre d'idée et de sentiments supérieurs à ce que la parole humaine pourriat exprimer. C'est la révélation de l'infini. [...] La music est un langage plus complet et plus persuasif que la parole.
>
> (Music describes all the dreams of the soul and expresses everything that is more mysterious and more elevated. It is the manifestation of a certain kind of idea and of superior sentiments which human words could never express. It's a revelation of the infinity. [...] Music is a language more complete and persuasive than words. (*My translation.*).   (Sand, Paris, 2004)

In other words, Sand thought that word and music do not use the same language "ils ne s'expliquent mutuellement que par de mystérieuses analogies." ("they do not make each other understood other than by mysterious analogies" my translation). A few years later, Charles Baudelaire (1821-1867) would develop his poetics based on the "théorie des correspondances" in which *symbolism* played a key role, aiming to represent reality through abstract concepts, symbols and synesthesia when music prevails. A similar idea is expressed by Claude Debussy in 1921, who, in commenting on his decision to put Pélleas et Mélisande of Maeterlinck (1902) to music, declared: "*Je voulai donner à la musique une liberté qu'elle contient peut-être plus que n'importe quel art, n'étant pas borné à une reproduction plus ou moins exacte de la nature, mais aux correspondences mystérieuses entre la Nature et l'Imagination"* (Debussy, 1987, 49). ('I wanted to give music the freedom which it may hold in itself more than any other art, since it is not limited to a somewhat exact reproduction of nature, but to the mysterious affinity between Nature and imagination.' my translation). Perhaps as a reaction to this metaphysical approach, music was adapted to tell stories in a narrative form which prevailed over the musical form itself. With respect to that, Beethoven (1770-1827), without breaking the link with classical 18th century rules, paved the way to auto-biographical music. A particular example is represented by the new programme music (presented through an extensive programme text) of which Berlioz's *Symphonie Fantastique* (1830) splits critics and musicians into two factions: Robert Schumann (1810-1856) and Franz Listz were in favour of an extra-musical inspiration, as the rhapsodic expression of poetry, representing the form through the idea of poetic "substance," that shaped harmony and melody in the composition, whereas François-Joseph Fétis (1784-1871), the head of the newly founded Brussels Conservatory, was against it, and had Johannes Brahms (1833-1897) as the major representative of 'absolute music', also known as "abstract music," which, being non-representational, is not explicitly about anything. Above all, works of these early Romantic composers include the symphonies of

Franz Schubert (1797-1828), who used material from his song cycles (i. e. Lieder) in some of his longer works. (See Stoppelenburg's Essay, 200-215). Setting popular songs and poetry to music became an important source of income for musicians who responded to the growing demand in middle-class households as part of their daily entertainment. Songs were particularly favoured by Schopenhauer's major follower, Friedrich Nietzsche (1844-1900), who, only two months before he was fourteen, wrote:

> God has given us music so that above all it can lead us upwards. Music unites all qualities: it can exalt us, divert us, cheer us up, or break the hardest of hearts with the softest of its melancholy tones. But its principal task is to lead our thoughts to higher things, to elevate, even to make us tremble... The musical art often speaks in sounds more penetrating than the words of poetry and takes hold of the most hidden crevices of the heart... Song elevates our being and leads us to the good and the true. If, however, music serves only as a diversion or as a kind of vain ostentation it is sinful and harmful. (Young, 2010, 37)

It is not surprising that music continued to haunt Nietzsche for the rest of his life. In *Twilight of the Idols, or, How to Philosophize with a Hammer* (1899), he wrote: "What trifles constitute happiness! The sound of a bagpipe. Without music life would be a mistake. The German imagines even God as a songster" (Nietzsche, 1990, 7).

In any case, while German culture, from the romantic period onwards, considers the primacy of music over all arts in general, the French view seems to see literature at the top of this cultural hierarchy. Indeed, one of the major supporters of this approach, especially in France, is Mallarmé (1842-1898) who considered Wagner's compositions highly poetic, which he achieved through his flexible musical prose leading to a thorough reinvention of the poetical language while stressing the musicality of literature even if was not based on sounds but words. A younger generation of great composers from different European countries, including Berlioz, Mendelssohn, and Chopin, who came to be known a little later, were inspired by literary texts. Liszt with his symphonic poems, *Dante Symphony* and *Faust Symphony*, Tchaikovsky's *Manfred Symphony* (1885), and Gustav Malher, who composed his *First Symphony* between 1888-1894 and based it on *Titan*, a novella by Morgan Robertson.

Having dealt with the main cultural movements on the Continent, let's now turn back to the English situation. Queen Victoria (1819-1901) ascended to the throne and marked the whole century as the Victorian Age, lasting from 1836 till her death. During this time, prose superseded poetry by far, though during the early Victorian period, the working class, under the influence of the French Revolution, founded the Chartist Movement, which was very active between 1838-49. This also had an effect on literature since Chartist poets had their poems put to music and sang in their street demonstrations to get people involved. (The best-known example is Ernest Jones' "The song of the Lower Classes.") Conversely, with the passing of time and the wealth of musical inspiration in lyricism, not only in poetry but also in prose, many authors exaggerated with poetical dissertations in their stories. Indeed, it became a fashion. So, even a novelist like **Charlotte Brontë** (1816-55), who was not particularly musical, could not refrain from writing on the sweetness of singing voices. It was 1847 when she had her second novel published, *Jane Eyre*, under the pseudonym Currer Bell. A significant passage shows the protagonist of the eponymous novel, begging her lover, Rochester, to sing for her:

> He duly summoned me to his presence in the evening. [...] I remembered his fine voice; I knew he liked to sing—good singers generally do. I was no vocalist myself, and, in his fastidious judgment, no musician, either; but I delighted in listening when the performance was good. No sooner had twilight, that hour of romance, began to lower her blue and starry banner over the lattice, than I rose, opened the piano, and entreated him, for the love of heaven, to give me a song.He said I was a capricious witch, and that he would rather sing another time; but I averred that no time was like the present.
> "Did I like his voice?" he asked.
> "Very much." I was not fond of pampering that susceptible vanity of his; but for once, and from motives of expediency, I would e'en soothe and stimulate it.
> "Then, Jane, you must play the accompaniment."
> "Very well, sir, I will try."
> I did try, but was presently swept off the stool and denominated "a little bungler." Being pushed unceremoniously to one side—which was precisely what I wished—he usurped my place, and proceeded to accompany himself: for he could play as well as sing. I hied me to the window-recess. And while I sat there and looked out on the still trees and dim lawn, to a sweet air was sung in mellow tones the following strain:—   (C. Brontë, 1983, 299)

In relation to the Brontë sisters, and just to stress how the literature of past centuries still has an influence on the pop music of our time, here is the example of Kate Bush's song *Wuthering Heights* (named after the famous novel of 1847), which appeared on her debut album *The Kick Inside* in 1978. The piece was welcomed by critics and listeners alike. "Heathcliff, it's me, I'm Cathy, I've come home!" sings Kate Bush, showing a great ability to empathize with Catherine, the protagonist of the story.

William Thackeray (1811-63) condemns, though with a great sense of irony, the trend towards excessive imitation in the music of the time (see his satirical, panoramic portrait of *Vanity Fair*, 1848). If we consider the novels written in the early years of the Victorian Age, it appears that there was no well-developed music culture in Britain. However hard they tried, professional musicians, critics, and the audience at large were lacking both the taste and sensitivity one could find on the Continent. Nietzsche wrote, "what [...] offends us about the most human Englishman is his lack of music." (O'Gorman 2014; 101- quoted in). Yet O'Gorman adds that London was, "the metropolitan epicentre of musical activity for most of the [19th] century" (Ibid., 102), as shown by the fact that, among other foreign musicians, Germany's Mendelssohn was good friends with Queen Victoria and Prince Albert.

In those years, one of the most anti-Victorian novelists was arising in the London literary milieu, **Charles Dickens** (1812-1870). But here we will consider him for his great musical sensibility marked by an irregular and surprisingly comical, musical humour. Though conventional romanticism was still popular, Dickens was creating a touching "musical poetry," as is the case with *David Copperfield* (1849-50) in which the Doctor is "music mad," Dora plays the guitar wonderfully, and Agnes sings sweetly. Another example is *A Christmas Carol* (1843), where all the bells sound together in Scrooge's house until the long-dead fiddler appears and makes "old couples seen as in a dream" dance. Yet such intimate poetry of music belonged to the romantic musical heritage. Towards the closing years of the century, **Thomas Hardy** (1840-1928), who was very sensitive to music, as a child he could tune a violin and his father used to play almost every evening for family and friends, moving him to tears thanks to the beauty of the music. Like the Dickens of *Sketches by Boz* (1839) and *American Notes* (1842), on departing further from romanticism, Hardy made benevolent fun of the folk who played, sang ballads and danced at the popular fairs. A typical figure representing all that is Mop, an old fiddler, a dreamer and a drinker, a figure modelled on his father, as it were. We find him in "The Fiddler of the Reels":

> While playing he closed his eyes—invariably; using no notes, and, as it were, allowing the violin to wander on at will into the most plaintive passages ever heard by rustic man. There was a certain lingual character in the supplicatory expressions he produced, which would well-nigh have drawn an ache from the heart of a gate-post. He could make any child in the parish, who was at all sensitive to music, burst into tears in a few minutes by simply fiddling one of the old dance-tunes he almost entirely affected—country jigs, reels, and "Favourite Quick Steps" of the last century—some

mutilated remains of which even now reappear as nameless phantoms in new quadrilles and gallops, where they are recognized only by the curious, or by such old-fashioned and far-between people as have been thrown with men like Wat Ollamoor in their early life. (Hardy, 2002, 114)

In *Tess of the D'Urbervilles* (1891), Hardy tells a funny story that he had known since he was a child. When Tess arrives at Talbothays, looking for a job as a milkmaid, she hears the story of a bull attacking William Dewy on his way back from a wedding after midnight. As he realises that he could not avoid being gored, Dewy stops and plays the bull a jig on his fiddle. "The bull softened down, and stood still, looking hard at William Dewy, who fiddled on and on; till a sort of a smile stole over the bull's face" (Hardy, 1978, 165). When he stopped playing, the bull threatened to attack him again. Having finished all the tunes he knew, he had a brilliant idea, and began to play

> 'Tivity Hymn, just as at Christmas carol-singing; when, lo and behold, down went the bull on his bended knees, in his ignorance, just as if 'twere the true 'Tivity night and hour. As soon as his horned friend were down, William turned, clinked off like a long-dog, and jumped safe over hedge, before the praying bull had got on his feet again to take after him. William used to say that he'd seen a man look a fool a good many times, but never such a fool as that bull looked when he found his pious feelings had been played upon.
> (ivi. 165)

Soon after, William jumped over a hedge and managed to save himself. After all, he had a narrow escape only thanks to music. It is the magic produced by music that pervades the whole village. So, like William, Tess's mother "who likes passionately tunes and songs," enjoys singing lullabies for her little children. Hardy in this way creates a sort of musical heroine in the village. But Tess too, the protagonist of the story, likes going to church because she loves singing, while the curate's son, whom she is in love with, imagines her as a flute player joining "an orchestra" when she is chatting with the other women.

At the same time that humour was competing against lyricism, a psychological current emerged from music thanks to the English essayist **Thomas de Quincey** (1785-1859) who drew it from the German romanticists. To him, musical sounds were often a source of pure pleasure, and in his *Confessions of an English Opium Eater* (1821) he seizes on every opportunity to note them. He sometimes mentions the changes in tone and rhythm in the air played by the clock between 9:30 and 10:00. At other times, he "hears" the silence of the evening over mute Nature, while in a completely different key, one can hear the noise coming from the nearby roaring city. Concerning conventional music, he rejects programme music because, in his philosophical view, music can express ideas, and he prefers silence full of visions. Hardy himself is not indifferent to musical psychology of a realistic sort. In *Jude the Obscure* (1895) a mason, who is abandoned by his wife, learns to play a harmonium and sings along to it. One day he hears a sacred song, "The foot of the cross," which makes him draw the character of the composer. He wants to pay him homage, so goes and visits him, but he has hardly said a word when the musician loses control and expresses his rage over music because he suddenly realises that music does not allow a man to earn his bare living and decides to give it up.

In the second half of the 19th century the overall situation improved when everybody and everything involving music became respectable and was taken more seriously than ever. As we have already seen above, a sign of the changing times was the growth of the middle class, when more and more women were allowed to play the piano and even the violin at home, where music began to be practiced regularly. Hence, classical music took on an important role in English literature in portraying respectability, socio-economic distinctions, and even political identity, which, as we will see later, will become a distinctive element to aspire to in the early decades of the 20th century. This is proved also by the comments about instrumental music and opera made by John Ruskin (1819-1900), who traced the role of music in contemplating a piece of architectural work (*The seven Lamps of Architecture*, 1880). Whereas **Walter Pater** (1839-94), the father of English Aestheticism, identified music as the most perfect kind of art because it expresses itself on its own, as he provocatively summarised in the following dictum in 1893, "All art constantly aspires towards the condition of music" (Pater, 1967, 80).

We know that some painters have pursued this goal as, for example, the Dutchman Piet Mondrian (1872-1944), who tried to convey rhythm and achieve harmony in creating a balance between surfaces and colours. Similarly, the French painter Henri Matisse (1869-1954) focused his efforts on the attempt to create impressions like those deriving from jazz improvisations. These visual artists reinforced a trend of interpreting music as the self-contained art *par excellence*, thus beginning and leading right into Modernist discussions of the musicality of language as opposed or in combination with music itself. By contrast to the prevailing importance of high culture in literature and music, it is particularly interesting to note that, unlike in Blake's time in the second half of the eighteenth century, according to the novels of Arnold Bennett (1867-1931), a true music expert, common people had operas and oratorios to mark their respectability, whereas classical instrumental music was the prerogative of the upper classes. Meanwhile, by the end of the 19th century, alongside painters like Matisse there were composers who were becoming more abstract, as shown by the forthcoming musical and painting forms of Impressionism. Gustav Mahler (1860-1911) is a good example of a composer bridging the Romantic and Post-Romantic Periods, of which an original follower is John Cage (1912-1992), with his entire rejection of aesthetic rules. He was a revolutionary composer, a pioneer of electroacoustic music and non-conventional use of musical instruments. Cage's work as a musicologist contributed to popularising the influential work of the French composer and pianist Éric Satie (1886-1925). And this leads us straight into the twentieth century.

XX - XXI Century: Modernism and Postmodernism

Britain: Modernism

Musicologists have played an important role in today's interdisciplinary world of academic research where increasing attention has been paid to the cultural interaction between literature and music. Among the many literary critics and theorists in the field of word and music studies who contributed to the concept of musicality in literature, I would like to mention, among others, the Frenchman Roland Gérard Barthes (1915-1980) with his theory of literary counterpoint. He maintains that even if readers perceive a linear succession of terms, the terms of various sequences may overlap, thus implying that a sequence is not terminated when the initial term of a new sequence intervenes. This means then that the sequences are arranged in counterpoint. Another major contribution comes from the Russian philosopher and literary critic Michail Michailovič Bakhtin (1885-1975) who saw the novel *The Brothers Karamazov* by Fyodor Dostoevsky (1821-1881) as the first polyphonic novel. Both Barthes and Bakhtin agree that to achieve polyphony an author gradually gives up control over his characters, who should develop autonomously, according to the different tones the author uses in creating them, as do their individual stories. On the American front, the comparatist, Calvin S. Brown, (1909-1989) manifested a great interest in the relationship between music and literature ever since he finished his PhD in 1934, with a dissertation on *The Musical Opus in Poetry*. He became an internationally influential pioneer in the interdisciplinary study of literature and music. On exploring the poetry of Walt Whitman (1819-1892) and Conrad Aiken (1889-1973) in his seminal *Music and*

Literature, he stresses the close link between the two arts in such terms that we would today call intermediality that aims to create a single piece of artistic work. Brown showed how these two poets shared some typically musical analogies such as rhythm, rhyme, meter, alliteration, disharmony, and assonance. He also maintained that, even if many of Whitman's 400 poems refer to instruments, musical terminology, and composers' names, it is quite likely that he could hardly read music. So, we can only conjure up that he was naturally gifted enough to create such musical poetry as that in his magnum opus *Leaves of Grass* (1892 'deathbed edition'). Brown thought that Aiken's love for music proved him unsurpassable in conveying the musicality of his themes as in the case with the collection *Nocturne of Remembered Spring: And Other Poems* (1917) which shows how most of his poems are based on musical principles rather than on poetic ones. Of the many followers of Brown's teaching, worth mentioning is Steven Paul Scher (1936-2004). In one of his earliest contributions to the field of word and music studies, it is *Notes Toward a Theory of Verbal Music* which remains literature centred. He is one of the leading experts in music literary studies whose claim to fame is his theory built on a very simple, clear and efficient three-modality scheme: music and literature, literature in music, music in literature. The *liaison* between music and literature has been growing as one of the most vibrant and involving artistic expressions in the 21st century, to which writers have more and more resorted to dedicate their time.

This brief reference to the main theorists of the music and literature link leads us straight to the writings of the world-renowned modernist authors: D. H. Lawrence, T. S. Eliot, Virginia Woolf, and James Joyce, who used music to mark the difference between social classes. Given that there are two essays entirely dedicated to Lawrence in this volume, we will begin with **T. S. Eliot** (1888-1965). This Anglo-American author had a great interest in music, marked by the central role it has in the poems: *Preludes*, *Rhapsody on a Windy Night*, *A Song for Simeon*, and the most famous *The Waste Land*. This is a 400-line-long poem which is particularly interesting because critics often refer to it as musical rather than discursive in form, implying that it does not follow the conventional plot and time pattern, typical of a temporally constructed narrative, but consists of words and paragraphs related to other words and paragraphs like sections of music are related to one another. Equally important is *Four Quartets*, a set of four poems ('Burnt Norton', 'East Coker', 'The Dry Salvages', and 'Little Gidding'), written over a seven-year period, 1935-1942. They are intertwined reflections on religious and philosophical questions, whose purpose is to have different themes interconnected with each other, continuously recalling each other just as happens with the sections of musical images. The English critic Helen Gardner, in *The Art of T. S. Eliot*, states that readers should try to listen to the cadences and rhythms in the poem as a whole instead of analysing the meaning of any particular point in it. She seems to believe that Eliot's main aim is to make the readers see each of the five sections of the poems as 'movements – usually containing a counter-movement' – which continue the main musical theme of time while exploring the movement that precedes. Therefore, they complete a pattern based on an evident sense of circularity which confirms that the poet had a musical analogy in mind, especially regarding structure. The analogies to music that emerge are theme and variation, statement and counterstatement, tempo variation vs mood variation. Although the wide use of such devices allowed Eliot to avoid monotony, which was a typical feature of philosophical poems like *Four Quartets*, in his *The Music of Poetry* (1942), written with Beethoven in mind as a model, he acknowledges that one should not exaggerate with that to clarify the non-discursive nature of poetry. To end this brief presentation of Eliot's affinity with music, here is a must, *Old Possum's Book of Practical Cats* (1939), which outsold *The Waste Land*. It is a collection of extravagant and playful poems about the socio-psychological behaviour of cats and describes how human beings give names to their pets. In 1981 *Old Possum* was a London West End smash, adapted into a musical by Andrew Lloyd Webber, under the title *Cats*, a still-running worldwide musical. *Cats* develops through music and songs with no dialogue, though every now and then music accompanies verse. Webber resorts to a variety of styles, reflecting the song cycle on which the show itself is based, in order to amplify the contrasting personalities of the characters. Besides Webber, Eliot had quite an influence on other modern composers and writers like Iani Christou (1926-1970), a Greek composer, who, in 1957, adapted six poems by Eliot for mezzo-soprano and piano.

Virginia Woolf (1882-1941) is another leading modernist author. Early in her career, Woolf humorously played with the idea of funding a community 'where there shall be no marrying – unless you fall in love with a symphony of Beethoven – no human element at all except what comes through Art – nothing but ideal peace and endless meditation' (Woolf 1975-80, *L*1 41-42). Music continued to be a constant presence in her life and writings. She had many friends who were musicians and was closely related to one of them, the composer Ralph Vaughan Williams, who in 1897 married Adeline Fisher, her friend and cousin. We know from her diaries and letters that she also befriended other popular musicians like Saxon Sidney-Turner and Ethel Smyth who led her to becoming a regular concertgoer. Woolf was so passionate about music that as soon as the gramophone was available, she bought an expensive one on which she habitually listened to records while writing. Woolf even said that she conceived her stories as music before she wrote them down. We can assume, then, that it is more than likely that the short story, 'The String Quartet' (1921) was inspired by such an original and involving experience. On 9 March 1920, she wrote in her *Diary*: "I went up to Campden Hill to hear the Shubert quintet" in order to "take notes for my story (Woolf 1977-84, *Diary* II, 24). This short story consists of three separate moments, echoing the four parts of the string quartet form (Allegro, Moderato, Minuet, Sonata-Rondo) [actually, it echoes sonata form rather than the four movements of this piece]. The story is practically an impressionistic account of the narrator's consciousness and a setting of the scene in the concert hall. The first moment is before the concert begins when the conversations of the spectators are intermingled with the chords and the tuning up of the musical instruments. The second moment covers the time when the musicians appear on the stage and describes the impressions that the music produces on the protagonist. Woolf's dramatization of the first few notes of the musical performance clearly recalls that:

> Here they come; four black figures, carrying instruments, and seat themselves facing the white squares under the downpour of light; rest the tips of their bows on the music stand; with a simultaneous movement lift them; lightly poise them, and, looking across at the player opposite, the first violin counts one, two, three – (Woolf, 1997, 86)

In the third part of the story, with the return of the audience to the hall during the interval, there are their comments: "That's an early Mozart, of course –' 'But the tune, I like all his tunes, makes one despair – I mean hope. What do I mean? That's the worst of music! I want to dance, laugh, eat pink cakes, yellow cakes, drink thin, sharp wine. […] The second violin was late you say?" (Ibid., 86). When in the final part, all the instruments play together in a crescendo reaching the apotheosis, alongside the images deriving from the impressions, there follows a second and much longer piece of music. It is true that, while reading 'The String Quartet,' one has the sensation of listening to a string quartet unfolding through the exposure of words, colour, and even texture linked by a series of associations. In the midst of the heap of impressions and images that cross the protagonist's mind while she is listening to the music, there are two themes: the first is the contrast between appearance and reality, and the second is that of old age focused on Mrs. Munro, a blind old lady who is the first to leave the concert hall which is in clear contrast to the 'flourish, spring, burgeon, burst!' (Ibid., 86) of music. In a review of the short story, "*Monday or*

Tuesday" in 'The Dial' of August 1921, T. S. Eliot acknowledged that he was so fascinated by 'The String Quartet' to note Woolf's indirect reference to the musical performance she was dramatising. Virginia Woolf dedicated her whole life to catching this essence of reality which, according to her experimentation, could be achieved by applying the techniques of music and painting to fiction, and also by pulling down the traditional barriers that divided the different writing genres. Her feelings, her stream of consciousness, and her masterful use of language reflect her passion for music, a passion that she manifested through her continuous attempt to translate musical impressions into images.

In addition, before closing this subsection dedicated to Virginia Woolf, here are some references to two novels and a short story on which music has a strong impact. The first instance is the novel *To the Lighthouse* (1927), recalling the three usual parts of a symphony which share the concern with texture and form. Woolf's style in this novel is characterised by a lasting rhythmical movement where punctuation is used in a very original way to regulate the flux of words. This can be exemplified in the following passage, in which interestingly it seems that she is afraid of stopping, almost as an omen of death related to the terrible sound of the breaking waves that announces an imminent

> destruction of the island and its engulfment in the sea and warned her whose day had slipped in one quick doing after another that it was all ephemeral as a rainbow – this sound which had been obscured and concealed under the other sounds suddenly thundered hollow in her ears and made her look up with an impulse of terror. (Woolf, 1991, 21)

The second instance is another short story "Blue & Green" in which Woolf uses some typical features of poetry (e.g., rhythm, and rhyme), to create a rhythmic and poetical prose that sounds like a poem. This experimental little masterpiece resulted in free style prose writing that she would develop further in her future works. Our final example is the novel *The Waves* (1931) where the relationship between words and music evolves and widens in an attempt to exploit the musical qualities of language, breaks the restricting barriers between prose and poetry, and creates a novel that has been justly defined 'a long poem.' *The Waves* was written 'to the rhythm' of Beethoven's sonatas and quartets as she states in her *Diaries* on 22 December 1930:

> It occurred to me last night while listening to a late Beethoven quartet that I would merge all the interjected passages into Bernard's final speech, & end with the words O Solitude: thus making him absorb all those scenes, & having

no further break. This is also to show that the effort, effort, dominates: not the waves: & personality: & defiance: but I am not sure of the effect artistically; because the proportions may need the intervention of the waves finally so as to make a conclusion. (Woolf 1977-84, 336; see also 139, 339)

Indeed, Bernard's final soliloquy has a counterpart in Beethoven's quartet, notably the structure of op. 133 'Grosse Fugue,' whose characteristic are the movements that are linked to each other just as the six friends' monologues are on their lives. Interestingly enough, they are eventually woven by one of them, Bernard, who, as Woolf herself reports in her Diary, tries to imitate the counterpointed texture and circular movement of sonata and fugue.

James Joyce (1882-1941), with his *Ulysses*, wrote a novel comparable to *The Waves*. He too had a genuine interest in music and was quite a fine musician, too, who could play both the guitar and the piano. He loved Verdi and Puccini and, having a tenor voice like his father even thought of becoming a professional singer. He did not do that, but became a close friend of John McCormack and John Sullivan, two highly reputed Irish tenors. Joyce equally enjoyed the friendship of his Italian friend and writer Italo Svevo (1861-1928), who was an amateur violin player. (His passion for the violin is evident in *La coscienza di Zeno*, where the untalented violinist Zeno Cosini loses his beloved to Guido Speier, an extremely gifted musician.) No wonder Joyce entitled his first work, *Chamber Music*, which is a collection of poems based on his research on Iranian popular music, known as 'Siki Siki baba.' Following the example of Pater, Flaubert, Dujardin, and the symbolist poets, he saw the possibilities of combining music and literature. The majority of critics agree that the analogy with music surely helps to analyse the complex structure of *Ulysses* in which Joyce once again went beyond the work of his precursors by exploiting the intrinsic musicality of language. He uses syncopated syntax, linguistic refrains, and onomatopoeia, the most obvious feature of a language, to create some sort of 'tonalities;' he also uses musical devices such as 'overture' phrases and counterpoint, allowing a contrapuntal arrangement of themes, and *leitmotif* which are employed over and over again to create a sense of 'musical' development. A most interesting musical example in *Ulysses* is Ithaca (episode 17) which parallels Book 17 of *The Odissey*. While Odysseus and Telemachus plan to recapture the former's palace and attack the suitors, in Joyce's book, Stephen Dedalus and Leopold Bloom, while chatting about music and politics, go to the latter's house. After drinking a cup of cocoa in the kitchen, Bloom coaxes Stephen to sing a song. What is of particular interest to us here, is the inclusion of the sheet music for the ballad 'Little Harry Hughes' – an anti-semitic song – sung by

Stephen. Right below is the score that Joyce reproduced with the lyrics in his handwriting and inserted in the text as "the first (major) part" and "the second part (minor) of the legend."

[…]

Little Harry Hughes and his school fellows all went out for to play ball. Went out for to play ball. And the very first ball little Harry Hughes played He drove it o'er the Jews garden wall. He drove it o'er the Jews garden wall. And the very second ball little Harry Hughes played He broke the Jews windows all. He broke the Jews windows all.

[…]

Then out there came the Jews daughter And she all dressed in green. Come back Come back you pretty little boy And play your ball again And play your ball again

(Joyce, 1973, 611-612)

Just as interesting from the musical point of view is Episode 11, "Syrens," characterised by a predominance of musical style. For example, the first 62 lines of the episode sound like some sort of "overture" introducing key aspects of both plot and language. Incidentally, this recalls Virginia Woolf's short story "The String Quartet." In particular, the first moment, before the concert begins, the conversations of the spectators are intermingled with chords, scales, and the tuning up by the musicians, while practicing the difficult phrases. As Patrick Hastings says: "It is cacophony here, but it will all make sense when properly arranged and elaborated upon in the performance/chapter ahead." (Hastings 2020, n. p.) Worth remembering is also the situation when, at the Ormond Hotel bar, they ask Simon to sing 'M'appari':

> – Go on, blast you, Ben Dollard growled. Get it out in bits.
> – *M'appari*, Simon, Father Cowley said.
> [...]
> –   Cowley sang:
> *M'appari tutt amor:*
> *Il mio sguardo l'incontro ...*
> [...]
> – Go on, Simon.
> – Ah, sure, my dancing days are done, Ben , , , Well . . . Mr Dedalus laid his pipe to rest beside the tuningfork and, sitting, touched the obedient keys.
> – No, Simon, Father Cowley turned. Play it in the original. One flat. The keys, obedient, rose higher, told, faltered, confessed, confused. Up stage strode Father Cowley.
> – Here, Simon, I'll accompany you, he said. Get up.
>   (Joyce 1973, 270-1).

In *Ulysses*, the atmosphere in the city of Dublin seems to be imbued with music and myth, which accompany the protagonists' thoughts. A very good example of that is the famous episode of the Sirens where Joyce highlights "the ability of the mind to process multiple streams of information simultaneously" (Prieto, 2002, 59). This shows that the structure of the fugue, typical of music, focuses on the possibility to juggle concurrently with different tasks as is the case with the stream-of-consciousness technique which governs this episode and most of the novel itself. The Homeric episode 17 represents the arena where all that is put in practice, resulting in what Joyce called "fuga per canonem," complete with counterpoint and polyphony. Indeed, *Ulysses* is structured in such a way that we can detect the typical features of a symphony: its prose takes place in a continuous present like music, which has no present or past and materialises as the musicians are playing and we are listening to them; the rhythm created by its punctuation is functional to the continuous flow of words and sentences and never gives the impression of being added as an external element; the nuance (i.e. colouring) of the sentences is as consistent as the musical nuances (i.e. sound colours) which convey emotions, mood and feelings perceivable through practice, especially thanks to one's absolute pitch. To say it with Will Self, "and perhaps most significantly of all, the entire work is conceived of as a grand exercise in the contrapuntal, as the psyches of Leopold Bloom and Stephen Dedalus call and respond to one another." (Self, *Guardian* 5 Oct. 2011). Another key feature of Joyce's method is in his last novel, *Finnegans Wake* (1939). It consists in his attempt to transform each word into a miniature 'image' allowing him to express various themes simultaneously and create a new vision of the world. He was helped in doing that by his love for and understanding of music which enhanced the auditory nature of his imagination, thus making him create some wonderful visual images resulting from a combination of rhythm and sound. *Finnegans Wake* is often described as a novel full of musical references; even its title was borrowed from a popular Irish ballad. On concluding we cannot overlook the influence Joyce had on modern musicians: it is most likely that The Beatles were inspired by *Finnegans Wake* when they composed 'I Am a Walrus.' The American band "Jefferson Airplane," based the song 'Rejoyce' (1966) and the album *After Bathing at Baxters* on a stream of themes and characters taken from *Ulysses*. Syd Barrett, one of the founding members of Pink Floyd, on his first solo album, *The Madcap Laughs*, sings "Poem V" from Joyce's *Chamber Music*. Kate Bush took the inspiration to write the lyrics for 'The Sensual World,' appearing on her album of the same title, where she adapts Molly's famous monologue from *Ulysses*. Moreover, great classical composers like Luciano Berio, John Cage, Pierre Boulez, David Del Tredici, Gilberto Mendes, Victor Gerard, Tod Machover, Elizabeth Lauer, used Joyce's texts for inspiration.

Aldous Huxley (1894-1963) is another great English novelist of the first half of the 20th century, who had a particular interest in music. Among his works he can boast *Point Counter Point* (1928) certainly comparable to Woolf's *The Waves*. As suggested by the title, the writer meant to use this form as if he were a musician writing a complex composition, based on the weaving of various themes at times running in parallel, at other times converging. The whole meaning is not evident until their convergence towards the end of the book. In chapter twenty-two, Philip Quarles, the character who is widely considered Huxley's spokesman throughout the novel, draws this comment about the musical make up of a novel in his notebook: "The musicalization of fiction. […] Get this into a novel. How?

The abrupt transitions are easy enough. All you need is a sufficiency of characters and parallel, contrapuntal plots." (Huxley, 1928, 349-350) Though *Point Counter Poi*nt offers a clear idea of what music meant to Huxley, it may be even more interesting to learn about the author's essay 'Music at Night' (1931), dealing with his thoughts about love, death, and pain; in brief, the things that human beings can experience but not often express. All the rest, in Huxley's view, is silence. He believed that after silence what comes nearest to expressing what is impossible to express is music. He adds that

> Silence is an integral part of all good music. Compared with Beethoven's or Mozart's, the ceaseless torrent of Wagner's music is very poor in silence. Perhaps that is one of the reasons why it seems so much less significant than theirs. It "says" less because it is always speaking. (Huxley, 1970, 257).

This is what Victor Hugo made explicit in his own words: "Ce qu'on ne peut pas dire et ce qu'on ne peut taire, la music l'exprime." (Hugo 1880, 76) ("What cannot be said and what cannot be put into words, music can express." *My translation*). Therefore, we can conclude that the most complete experience of all, the only one superior to music, is silence. According to Huxley, "When the inexpressible had to be expressed, Shakespeare laid down his pen and called for music. And if the music should also fail? Well, there was always silence to fall back on. For always, always and everywhere, the rest is silence." (Huxley, 1957, 22).

Ezra Pound (1885-1972), alongside his literary work as an avantgarde poet, critic, and translator, wrote music and poems quite different from the modern free verse for which he is famous. Pound taught himself musical composition to master rhythm. One of his early works is *Parody of a Medieval Rota* (1915), which is based on *Sumer is icumen in* (1220), written in the Wessex dialect of Southwest England. He used both the original language and the music structure. (See Intro., xvii-xviii). In February 1924, Pound began to compose a work based on Sestina Altaforte, a poem inferred from a Provencal text originating from Bertrand De Born, a Medieval warlord, placed by Dante in Hell, and in whose castle, Altoforte, the poem is set. On writing it, Pound followed the traditional sestina form—invented by the Provençal poets of the Middle Ages—consisting of six sestets and a concluding tercet. (Incidentally, over a decade later, in 1931, he wrote a letter to the famous pianist and singer Agnes Bedford, that composing in the 'sestina' pattern was a particularly difficult task: "I do think musical notation is the damndest thing to get simple facts from ever invented. Perfectly simple AFTER the fact, but impenetrable before it.') Following the chronological order of events, in 1923, Pound composed his first opera in collaboration with an avant-garde composer George Antheil *Le Testament* ("The Will", 1489), inspired by the eponym poem by François Villion (1431-1463), which Richard Taruskin acclaimed as a "modernist triumph." This opera was staged only a few times because of its great rhythmic difficulty, recalling Stravinsky's rhythmic unconventionality. Another great achievement in Pound's production is represented by 'The Sappho aria *Poikilothron,*' *which is a key piece* in his incomplete third opera Collis O Heliconii. He had hardly ever imitated the Greek music accompanied by lyre before and had even less so attempted to imitate the melodies but wrote fresh ones. Through the melodies in it, Pound shows an enormous ability in recreating a variety of emotions, such as invocation, pleading, and persuading, that he imagined Sappho expressed, by using literary devices as stress, timbre, assonance, and the like. Pound's musical production includes also some pieces for solo violin, *Sestina: Altoforte* and *Sestina in Homage* (1924), both based on the 'sestina' structure. His last and third work for solo violin follows the rhythms, the tonal leadings of words as they are uttered and used in Dante's 'sestina' of *Al poco giorno e al gran cerchio d'ombra* [To the short day and its great arc of shadow. *My translation*] belonging to a group of poems called *Rime Petrose* from the name of a lady addressed with the epithet Petra (stone). Arnaut Daniel invented the 'sestina' form with his poem 'Lo ferm voler qu'el cor m'intra ("The firm will that my heart enters" *My translation*), which is Dante's way to pay homage for doing that. (See Intro., xix, lxvi). It is quite legitimate at this point to wonder why Pound was so interested in the 'sestina' form, it seems that it is because it allowed him to show how the role of the image in poetry was changing and that Imagism was no longer found interesting. In 1914, Vorticism followed from Imagism as an idea of movement in music, having a strong energy which developed from a central theme characterised by the close relation between words with clear musical traits, which in turn create some sort of vortex in both melody and asymmetric rhythm. This is demonstrated in the unfinished virtuosic composition *Sestina: Altaforte*, representing Pound's most vorticist musical violin piece. Finally, and most importantly, here is Pound's second opera *Cavalcanti* (1931-33). This work dramatises the life of Guido Cavalcanti (c. 1250-1300), a good friend of Dante, in which the American poet uses eleven of his philosophical 'canzoni' and ballads. Through this opera, Pound meant to show that music may take the role of literary criticism and can also help to save the ancient poetry by renewing both its original rhythm and overall structure. Noteworthy is the fact that these were the basic guidelines he applied for setting words to music as intended through the analysing and rearranging of his endeared medieval repertoire.

Post Modernism

From the second half of the 20th century right into the 21st century, we can count many examples of fiction relying on music as the narrative drive. A case in point is the novelist and critic **Anthony Burgess** (1917-93), who was also an accomplished composer who wrote classical, popular and jazz. His repertoire includes symphonies, concertos, musicals and operas, chamber music especially for piano solo, ballets, music for films, etc. Burgess combined quotations from songs of the 1910s and War World One, as well as from Stravinsky and Wagner, recited by a narrator whose reading is woven together with a soprano, accompanied by four instruments: piano, cello, flute, and an oboe. Ludwig van Beethoven's *Symphony nr. Nine* has a very important function in the structure of his best-known novel *A Clockwork Orange* (1962). This is the story of the conflict between the individual and society (i. e. state), exemplified in the novel by fifteen-year-old Alex who, due to his criminal acts, is imprisoned and subjected to 'Ludovico's Technique' (note that Ludovico is a clear variant of Ludwig van Beethoven). This is a frightening experiment, consisting of therapy that forces a 'patient' to experience nausea when thinking of violence, thus developing a rejection to violent behaviour. As one can see through the novel, Burgess loved classical music and Beethoven's in particular, just like Alex. The following passage from the novel shows how much this teenager was a lover of the beauty of classical music.

> Oh, bliss, bliss and heaven. I lay all nagoy to the ceiling, my gulliver on my rookers on the pillow, glazzies closed, rot open in bliss, slooshying the sluice of lovely sounds. Oh, it was gorgeousness and gorgeosity made flesh. The trombones crunched redgold under my bed, and behind my gulliver the trumpets three–wise silverflamed, and there by the door the timps rolling through my guts and out again crunched like candy thunder. Oh, it was wonder of wonders. And then, a bird of like rarest spun heavenmetal, or like silvery wine flowing in a spaceship, gravity all nonsense now, came the violin solo above all the other strings, and those strings were like a cage of silk around my bed. Then flute and oboe bored, like worms of like platinum, into the thick thick toffee gold and silver. I was in such bliss, my brothers.
> (Burgess, 1962, 29).

But both Burgess and Alex equally detested pop music. The former called it 'twanging nonsense,' and the latter, on entering a record shop, shows all his belittled 'popdiscs' and 'teeny pop vesches.' (In Burgess's especially made-up language, 'teenager's pop things'). He says, 'I accepted the Beethoven symphony as a kind of musical ultimate, something that the composers of our own age could not aspire to [...]' (From *The Music of a Clockwork Orange*). Among the writer's other works where music appears, there are the following novels: *Napoleon Symphony: A Novel in Four Movements* (1974), dealing with Napoleon's life, and in turn based on Beethoven's *Eroica* Symphony; *Earthly Powers* (1980) is about the hard life of a film composer; *The Pianoplayers* (1986) is inspired by Burgess's father's experiences as a piano player in pre-War Manchester; *Mozart and the Wolfgang* (1991) features among its characters Beethoven himself; and *Byrne* (1993), a verse novel which tells the story of the hardships of an Irish composer. Finally, Burgess was an admirer of D. H. Lawrence for the intrinsic musicality of his language, which in his view was something he shared with James Joyce, another one of his favourite writers. He paid homage to Lawrence by setting four of his poems as a song cycle, entitled *Man Who Has Come Through* (1985). (See Ceramella's Essay, 51-68).

Kazuo Ishiguro (1954-) was born in Nagasaki, Japan, and took British nationality in 1983. In an interview, with the Italian journalist, Leonetta Bentivolglio, he said: "Ever since I was a child, I have been playing the piano, and since my adolescence the guitar, and when I was young, I used to dream of becoming a songwriter like Bob Dylan or Leonard Cohen or your Fabrizio De André. Between fifteen and twenty-three I composed about a hundred songs by going through many styles, from the self-contemplative to the experimental and the poetic-visionary." (from "Biografia Kazuo Ishiguro," 9/11/2018; *My translation*) In 1985, Ishiguro came out with a novel, *The Unconsoled*, whose plot develops over a period of three days and is about Ryder, a world-famous pianist who, during a tour in a central European city, realises he cannot even remember honouring all the commitments he has before giving his concert there. From 2002 onwards, Ishiguro has been writing the lyrics for several songs for the jazz singer Stacey Kent and her husband, sax player Jim Tomlison. In 2007, he wrote the lyrics for Stacey Kent's album *Breakfast on The Morning Tram*, which inspired his *Nocturnes: Five Stories of Music and Nightfall* (2009). This collection of short stories came after six novels which had already gained him fame and prestige. As the subtitle suggests, each story focuses on music and musicians, and the end of the day. Most peculiarly, the book was conceived as a record with five songs. His latest collaboration with Stacey Kent was his contribution to the album *I Know I Dream*. In an interview with Kate Kellaway, he says how important writing songs has been throughout his career: "One of the key things I learnt writing lyrics – and this had an enormous influence on my fiction – was that with an intimate, confiding, first-person song, the meaning must not be self-sufficient on the page. It has to be oblique; sometimes you have to read between the lines." (*The Guardian*, 15 March 2015).

Many other authors have resorted to the collective imaginary of music. **Salman Rushdie** (1947-) is an Indian writer and essayist who naturalised as a British citizen. *The Ground Beneath Her Feet* is an adaptation of the Orpheus and Eurydice myth adapted to today's world, with allusions to pop stars like John Lennon and Madonna. (See Intro. xvi, lxix and Brandão' Ceramella's Essay, 251-5, 261-3, 265-6). 'The Ground Beneath Her Feet' is also a song from the novel. It appears in Wim Bender's *The Million Dollar Hotel* in which the first track is sung by Bono. In a telephone interview with David Fricke for the magazine *Rolling Stone*, Rushdie declared: "That something that was designed to exist only on the page should burst into the real world – I like that enormously." He said that Bono, to whom he had sent a copy of the MS, asked him if he could extract the sections where there were lyrics. "A few weeks afterwards, he said he'd written this melody." (*Rolling Stone* 13-05-1999)

USA

On turning to the USA, we find **Tony Morrison** (1931-2019), a most relevant author to the topic of this book. She grew up in a musical world at home. In the following article, Daphne A. Brooks says that Morrison told her during her *Opera America Keynote* in 2005:

> I was surrounded by all kinds of music as a girl [...] All the adults in my family, it seemed, could play instruments when they picked them up. None of them could read music, but all of them could hear music and then repeat it." And while it was her mother who possessed all of the talent in this realm—"My mother sang opera, she sang sentimental Victorian songs, she sang arias from *Carmen*, she sang jazz, she sang blues, she sang what Ella Fitzgerald sang, and she sang 'Ave Maria.'" (Brooks, 2019).

The passion for music was accompanied by her love for literature. Throughout her first three novels, *The Bluest Eye* (1970), *Sula* (1973), and *Song of Solomon* (1977), Morrison employs the language of music, or rather the metaphor of music in the varying forms of the structure of song. In each song Morrison's use of the language of music takes a different shape according to contrasting values such as friendship, respect, and the ideas of good and bad. However, music invariably seems to allow a sense of belonging to a cultural and ethnic community. Indeed, *Song of Salomon* even more evidently than the other two novels, shows that songs are a powerful means to dig out and proudly preserve one's African roots and identity. There followed the trilogy, including *Tar Bay* (1981), *Beloved* (1987), and *Jazz,* which appeared in 1992. Focusing attention on *Jazz*, we are immediately struck by the style she applied there that recalls the rhythms of jazz. In that novel, she presents some challenging theories about jazz as being invented by black people, thus revealing their philosophical approach to life, which in her view represented one of the living elements of a new era to come. At the end of *Beloved* some 'singing women' emerge to comfort the protagonist Sethe, exorcising the ghosts of slavery by using their voices. This is the true story of an escaped slave, Margaret Garner, which gained her the Pulitzer Prize for Literature in 1988. Morrison is an incredibly eclectic artist, who surfed different genres and even enjoyed writing the lyrics for original classical music scores. She collaborated with the German American composer and pianist on *Honey and Rue*, a song cycle in 1992, and on *Four Songs* in 1994. In 1993, she was awarded the Nobel Prize for Literature. Then she provided the text for *woman. life. song* by the composer Judith Weir, which was premiered in 2000 at Carnagie Hall, New York. Morrison drew from *Beloved* the libretto for a new opera, entitled *Margaret Garner* (2002), with music composed by Richard Danielpour. It was premiered at the Detroit Opera House in 2005. Six years later, she debuted her third play, *Desdemona,* in Vienna. This new production, consisting of a mixture of music and songs by opera director Peter Sellars and singer-songwriter Rokia Traoré, is based on Shakespeare's *Othello*, but instead of focusing on Othello's jealousy as in Shakespeare's original tragedy, it shifts the attention from the latter to her African nursemaid, Barbary, who is hardly mentioned in the Great Bard's text.

Jack Kerouac (1922-1969), one of the fathers of the beat generation, published several books of poetry and 12 novels in his short life. As reflected in his works, he built up a particular sense for bebop during the long club nights spent listening to Charlie Parker and Dizzy Gillespie, or Billie Holiday with whom he often had a drink. It is not incidental, then, that you can detect traces of bebop in the rhythm of his prose as well as the influence of James Joyce, the writer Kerouac alluded to most in his works, saying that he liked his experimental language and the stream of consciousness technique. Following a request from Allen Ginsberg and William S. Burroughs, Kerouac wrote the article *Essentials of Spontaneous Prose* to explain his method for writing the novella, *The Subterraneans* (1958) in three days. What he says in the article surely applies to his masterpiece *On the Road* (1957), written in about three weeks. He stresses that "no periods separating sentence-structures already arbitrarily riddled by false colons and timid usually needless commas-but the vigorous space dash separating rhetorical breathing (as jazz musician drawing breath between outblown phrases)." The co-protagonist Sal Paradise, together with Dean Moriarty, puts us in the picture, when he is in Chicago, from the beginning of the novel, saying:

> At this time, 1947, bop was going like mad all over America. The fellows at the Loop blew, bun with a tired air, because bop was somewhere between its Charlie Parker Ornithollogy period and another period that began with Miles Davies. And as I sat there listening to that sound of the night which bop has come to represent for all of us.   (Kerouac, New York, 14).

And, when they eventually arrive in San Francisco, he says:

> I looked out the window at the buzzing night-street of Mission. I wanted to get going and hear the great jazz of Frisco–and remember, this was only my second night in town. […]
> Out we jumped in the warm, mad night, hearing a wild tenorman, bawling horn across the way, going "EE-YAH EE-YAH! EE-YAH!" and hands clapping to the beat and folks yelling, "Go, go, go!" "Blow, man, blow!" […]
> Boom, kick, that drummer was kicking his drums down the cellar and rolling the beat upstairs with his murderous sticks, rattely-boom! A big fat man was jumping on the platform, making it sag and creak. The pianist was only pounding the keys with spread-eagled fingers, chords, at intervals with the geat tenormanwas drawing breath for another blast–Chinese chords, shuddering the piano in every timber, chink, and wire, boing! […]
> And finally, the tenorman decided to blow his top and crouched down and held a note in high C for a long time as everything else crashed along and the cries increased […]   (Ibid. 151, 162-3).

Indeed, jazz is part of the background to the story, and there are many suggestive passages showing that he was absolutely passionate about it. Kerouac was a good friend of Jerry Newman, who suggested to Gillespie he should title one of his pieces Kerouac. He loved folk music, Leadbelly in particular, and classical music, especially Bach, Beethoven and Debussy. In turn, he became a forerunner of the hippy movement, and an icon of the beat generation. Indeed, his lifestyle and stories had a strong impact on The Beatles, Bob Dylan, Patti Smith.

Joyce Carol Oates (1933-) is an American writer whose claim to fame is *Where are you going? Where have you been?* (1966), a short story about Connie, a teenager who is infatuated with an older man called Arnold, who holds an increasingly devilish influence on her. Although she is terrified by that, she cannot do much to help it. Her situation is closely based on Bob Dylan's *It's All Over Now, Baby Blue* (1965) which is, in fact, dedicated to the singer. Connie becomes a daydreamer of flirting with boys by listening to songs on the radio. One day Arnold shows up at her house, and then finds out that they like listening to the same kind of music. She is entranced by Arnold and feels that the romance built up in the music she listens to is more alluring than the reality of adult sexuality and seduction. The trouble is that she is unable to see that music, instead of giving her pleasure, is turning into a self-destructive means. With a typical teenage rebellion attitude, Connie has no values; music to her is a substitute for religion and morality. In her fantasy world a dull family life gives her no support at all, while public life is made exciting with music and friends. Music is a "hidden but unmistakable force" in this story as shown by the absolute lack of song titles yet provides an ever-present background. Connie and her friends "listened to the music that made everything so good: the music was always in the background like music at a church service; it was something to depend upon." (Oates, 1966, 1)

World View

If we widen our view all over the world, we find that so many writers and/or musicians have shown a deep interest in music, which would make it very difficult even just to list here. So, with all due respect to everybody, I will mention the most famous ones, and certainly those whose works I happen to be familiar with.

Fabrizio de André (1940-1999), simply known as Fabrizio, a world-famous Italian songwriter and poet, belonging to the glorious tradition of artists such as chansonniers and poets like the Belgian Jacques Brel, the Italian Paolo Conte, the Canadian Leonard Cohen (see below), and the American Bob Dylan. (See Portelli's Essay, 128-135). However, Fabrizio acknowledged strong indebtedness to the French poet and singer Georges Brassens, with whom he shared similar ideals of freedom and justice, and also an immense love for François Villion, the forerunner of 'poèts maudits' ('damned poets') such as Baudelaire and Gautier.

In this short presentation of Fabrizio, and, there again, for the purposes of this essay, I would like to highlight the impact that the *Spoon River Anthology* by the American writer Edgar Lee Masters (1868-1950) had on him. He first read it when he was 18 and was immediately struck by seeing something of himself in that writer and his masterpiece. To start with, he found the common difficulty to communicate which only death can overcome. (Note that only later in his life did he begin to give public concerts, while up to then his songs/poems were sung by others.) All of the 244 characters in the *Anthology*, some imaginary and some real, were dead "all, all are sleeping on the hill" of a Midwestern cemetery. They reveal through their epitaphs on their graves who they were and what they really did, regardless of what their families had written about them. Free from any social convention, they express their real selves in monologues. The Italian novelist and poet Cesare Pavese, an expert on American literature, introduced one of his favourite students, Fernanda Pivano, to the Turin publisher, Einaudi, suggesting that she was the right person to translate Masters' *Anthology*. That excellent, unsurpassable translation, which came out in 1943, triggered Fabrizio's inspiration. What really grabbed his attention were the universal themes dealt with in it: hypocrisy, respectability, outsiders, freedom, rejection of war and materialism, prostitution, suicide, and corruption in every layer of society. Fabrizio picked just some of those topics, which he rendered in an intersemiotic translation, through his music and words: Envy (Un matto, Un giudice, Un blasfemo / A Madman, A Judge, A Blasphemous); Science (Chemist, Doctor, Optician); Love (Il malato di cuore); Freedom (Il suonatore Jones). In fact, he carried Masters' texts across sign systems and typically created connections by offering their embodiments in a different medium. This holistic process is favoured by using non-verbal media, as is the case with conventional intrasemiotic translations, but also by resorting to an auditory channel, that is the very original music, resulting in an outstanding record, *Non al denaro, non all'amore né al cielo* (1971) ("No to money, love, nor to the sky"). The final outcome is best synthesised by Pivano in an interview with Enrico Grassani, where she declares: "Masters' poems presented some very brave ideas for the time, while Fabrizio's songs have a strong poetic content. The true poetry is Fabrizio's." (Interview of Enrico Grassani with Fernanda Pivano "Anche se voi vi credete assolti", Pavia: Edizioni Selecta, 2002, pp. 24-25.

Within the outstanding and long tradition of Italian singer-songwriters, besides Fabrizio, it is surely worth mentioning Branduardi, with his LP, *Branduardi Sings Yeats*, featuring ten ballads based on poems by the Irish poet, which include 'The Fiddler of Dooney' and 'The Swans at Coole'. Francesco Guccini, who took inspiration from literature many times in writing his songs, such as Cervantes' *Don Chisciotte*, Flaubert's *Madame Bovary*, Homer's *Odyssey,* the myth of *Ophelia*, Rostand's *Cyrano de Bergerac*, and his 1983 album, *Guccini*, which includes the song 'Gulliver' where he rewrites the adventures of Jonathan Swift's hero in the eponymous novel.

Leonard Cohen (1933-2016) is no doubt another great poet and musician competing at Fabrizio's level. In his teens he studied music and poetry and was particularly keen on the Spanish poet Federico Garcia Lorca. He expressed all his admiration for Lorca, in an interview with Marco Adria in July 1990, saying: "I think that's what you look for when you read poetry;

you look for someone to illuminate a landscape that you thought you alone walked on." (00) His last volume of poetry, *The Flame*, published posthumously in 2018, shows that he shared with the Spanish poet that sort of insight till the end of his own days, concerned as he really was with contemplation of virtues and sins.

Throughout the 1960s he continued to write both poetry and fiction, until in 1967, being disappointed as a writer, Cohen moved from Canada to the United States to pursue a career as a singer-songwriter and guitarist who used to compose both music and lyrics of his songs, which were widely considered as true poems. His first album was released in that very year and was an immediate hit. In 1993 Cohen published *Stranger Music: Selected Poems and Songs*. His life was characterised by ups and downs during which he focused on music, writing and great tours around the world.

Among the French authors, I have already mentioned above Brassens, but we cannot possibly not refer to one of the most active authors between the 19th and 20th centuries, **Marcel Proust** (1871-1922). He admitted his love for music with the following words: "La musique a été une des grandes passion de ma vie…. Elle m'a apporté des joyes et des certitudes ineffables, la preuve que'il existe autre chose que le néant dans lequel je me suis heurté partout ailleurs. Elle court comme un fil conducteur à travers toute mon eouvre." ("Music has been one of the great passions in my life…. It brought me joys and absolute certainties, the proof that there is something else beyond the void against which I bumped everywhere. It flows like a thread through the labyrinth of my works." - *My translation*) Proust drew freely from musical works in order to graft them onto his fiction. Thus, written descriptions materialise from abstract musical scores allowing one to catch the references. He is particularly interesting here because he manages to transcribe in his outstanding way the understanding of the relationship between music and words. His masterpiece *La recherche du temps perdu*, published between 1913 and 1927, is the very emblem of such an unsurpassable achievement. It would take at least a long article fully dedicated to music and its implementation in Proust's works to make sense of that. Having found the following critical presentation as concise, informative and clear, I am taking the liberty of quoting it below, as I believe it helps to begin to understand the meaning of music to Proust.

> For Proust, music, along with the visual arts, offered a way to expand and enrich the range of his own literary language through figure and allusion. At the same time, he discovered in music a way to explore and challenge the limits of that language as an agent of aesthetic communication. Music as performance, as topic of debate, as catalyst of memory, emotion, and desire, plays an obbligato accompaniment to the interpersonal drama of the

Proustian social world: its hilarity, its pathos, its vacuity, its sensuality, its cruelty. Perhaps the crucial turning point of Proust's work arrives as its narrator listens to a piece of music: the Vinteuil septet, a seminal experience that leads him to the threshold of a life beyond the temps perdu of his youth, a life he enters in earnest at the very end of his work. Few writers have dared to grant music such a pivotal role in a work of literature, even fewer have made such far-reaching claims about the ethical significance of the experience of music, and fewer still have substantiated these claims enough to carry conviction. Proust manages all three. His vision of the potential unity and transformative power of the arts, while Romantic and Wagnerian in inspiration, shaped the European modernist tradition that followed him, and issued in a novel that remains without peer in the literary analysis of musical experience. (ANON. Buffalo, updated 21 Feb 2021)

Milan Kundera (1929-) is a Czech-born French writer, poet, and essayist. He has always manifested his love for music, which he got from his father, a famous pianist and the director of the Music Academy in their hometown, Brno.

In 1982, Kundera wrote the novel, *L'Insoutenable légèreté de l'être* (*The Unbearable Lightness of Being*). It is in this novel, mainly set in Prague between the late 1960s and early 1970s, that he explores the intellectual and artistic life of Czech society. Using Franz as his mouthpiece, he reveals how music is the art nearest to Dionysian experience:

> For Franz music was the art that comes closest to Dionysian beauty in the sense of intoxication. No one can get really drunk on a novel or a painting, but who can help getting drunk on Beethoven's Ninth, Bartok's Sonata for Two Pianos and Percussion, or the Beatles' White Album? Franz made no distinction between "classical" music and "pop." He found the distinction old-fashioned and hypocritical. He loved rock as much as Mozart.
> He considered music a liberating force: it liberated him from loneliness, introversion, the dust of the library; it opened the door of his body and allowed his soul to step out into the world to make friends. He loved to dance and regretted that Sabina did not share his passion.
> (Kundera, 1984, 92-93).

Julio Cortàzar (1914-1984) is one of the major authors of the 20th century. An original novelist, poet, and literary critic, who was born in Belgium, grew up in Argentina, and because he was an anti-Peronist, he had to move to Paris in 1951 where he spent the rest of his life. His masterpiece is *Rayuela* (1963), a novel that is usually considered the Latino-American literary text equivalent to Joyce's *Ulysses* in the European literature of the first half of the twentieth century. This is an anti-novel which does not follow a conventional chronologic pattern, and in this sense is always associated with Cortàzar's love for jazz for its intrinsic feature of disarticulating rhythm, melody and harmony in a wide variety of variations. Apart from many other famous works, there is the lesser-known long story dedicated to jazz, *Las armas secretas* (published as *Les armes sécretes*, [The Secret Weapons], 1963). It deals with the opposition between the brilliant Johnny Parker (in reality Charlie Parker) the great "artist maudit' and Bruno, a music critic infatuated by this living myth in the last days of his life.

The German writer **Thomas Mann** (1875-1955) in *Dr Faustus* (1947) uses music as the object of the agreement between the composer Adrian Leverkühn and the devil. Similarly, we may talk of the musical structure of the sonata form movement in his *Tonio Kröger*, consisting of three main sections, introduction, development, and recapitulation, but there is no plot as such. In the novella *Tristan*, Mann creates textual cohesion through a web of themes, typical of musical structure, making the listener, just as the reader, consider new possible interpretations which cannot be explicitly manifested through work. **Thomas Bernhard** (1931-1989) is one of the most important Austrian authors of the postwar era. A violin, which his grandfather bought him, became an ever-present element in his life, linking him forever with music. He literally used music as the only vital arm to fight the idea of suicide. From the age of 4, his grandfather got him to study music theory and take violin lessons from Steiner, who told him he was a natural music talent. Since he had a good baritone / bass voice, though at such young age, his grandfather asked the singer Maria Keldofer to give his grandson private tuition in singing. In 1983, Bernhard in *Der Untergeher* (*The Loser*, translated in 1991), narrated the devastating impact that the manic power of music and the enigmatic fixation of the sublime interpretation has on three extraordinary pianists. One of them, Glenn Gould, who was incredibly gifted, led the other two to give up their musical careers and do something completely different in their lives.

Roberto Bolaño Avalos (1953-2003) a Chilean novelist, co-authored his first novel with the Catalan A. G. Porta, *Consejos de un discípulo de Morrison a un fanático de Joyce*, 1984, (*Advice from a Disciple of Morrison and a Fan of Joyce*). The title derived from *Consejos de un discípulo de Marx a un fanatico de Heidegger*, a poem by Bolaño's friend, the Mexican poet Mario Santiago Papasquiaro (1953-1998). It is self-evident that Joyce refers to the famous Irish writer, while Morrison refers to Jim Morrison, lead singer of the "Doors", to whom they first thought of dedicating the novel with the title *Flores para Morrison* (*Flowers for Morrison*), but then opted for the current title which refers to both Morrison and Joyce.

Regarding the "Doors," note that the opening of the novel is a quote from their song *The End*:

This is the end, beautiful friend
This is the end, my only friend
The end of our elaborate plans
The end of ev'rything that stands
The end

In addition, I would like to say that Morrison chose the band's name after reading Huxley's *The Doors of Perception* (1954), plucking its title from William Blake's *The Marriage of Heaven and Hell*, reading: "If the doors of perception where cleansed everything would appear to man as it is, infinite. For man has closed himself up, till he sees all things thro' narrow chinks of his cavern." (Blake, 1994, 7).

Murakami Haruki (1949-) is a Japanese writer whose novels are regularly translated into about fifty languages. Many of his titles recall classical music going from Mozart and Schumann to Rossini's *The Thieving Magpie*. Some of his novels are after the titles of songs, such as the Beatles' 'Norwegian Wood' (1987), or "South of the Border" (Down Mexico Way)," (1992), after a popular song by Jimmy Kennedy and Michael Carr with the same title (1939).

Vikram Seth (1952-) is an Indian author who learned to appreciate western classical music and is also an amateur player of violin and flute. One of his earliest works to be associated with music is the libretto for the opera *Arion and the Dolphin* in 1994, which was commissioned by the Baylis National Opera. He is the author of *An Equal Music* (1999), a great novel centred on the tumultuous love-life of a violin player who loves Schubert. From the first page, on reading about the protagonist Michael Holme, who is practicing a Lied by Shubert "The Trout," however incredible it may sound, one has the impression of actually hearing the music which keeps flowing through the words uttered by the narrative voice, the protagonist himself. Holme is a second violin in a famous London string quartet and is particularly close to the precious Italian violin, Tononi, which he is lucky to play. Unfortunately, it does not belong to him, until the elderly, rich lady who lent it to him decides to leave it to him as the only person worthy of owning it for good. There is a co-protagonist, Julia, an outstanding pianist, he meets in Vienna. She introduces him to one of young Beethoven's Trios. They then lose track of each other, only to meet again ten years later. In the meantime, she has been losing her hearing, which is obviously a traumatic experience for a musician. Nobody knows about that except Michael, who coaxes her into playing in his string quartet to substitute the suddenly ill pianist. The concert organisers request that they included 'Trota" in their programme, and so Michael includes her as pianist. Though under incredible tension, they make it, but after that successful performance, she decides to give up playing in public. After a while, she plays Bach's *The Art of Fugue* at Wigmore Hall, London, which is the same piece played in Vienna with the quartet. This is a most moving and dramatic story that musicians and music lovers alike should read.

In conclusion, let me stress that this Introductory essay, or rather the whole book, has been conceived to offer teachers, students, and general readers alike a broad perspective on the key topic of this volume. Unfortunately, many artists and countries deserving to be represented here had to be left out due to lack of space. No doubt my omissions will outrage some, yet I trust that the essays forming this book, written by musicians and literature professors specialising in a wide spectrum of cultural and historic periods, will partially compensate this flaw.

Most importantly, I do hope that we have achieved our main objective of showing how music and literature have reciprocally supported each other throughout their incredibly long-term "marriage." Thus, while enhancing and refining their practical affinity, they have created harmony and melody on the musical front, corresponding to a coherent and alluring narrative structure in the literary world often aspiring, but not necessarily always succeeding, to the musical condition. I think that this is reflected in the formal dissolution of the symphonic form, as it were, when Modernism and Postmodernism meet in the music of the inventor of the dodecaphonic method of composition, Arnold Schoenberg (1874-1951), and his sense of alienation, typical of modern society. On the literary front, his counterpart is James Joyce, with his stream of consciousness narrative technique, which, in turn, broke the rules of Western fiction. These two giants altered the course of classical music and the traditional novel for the centuries to come and have opened up the path to the immediately ensuing postmodernist era of geniuses such as the composers Luciano Berio, Karl Heinz Stockhousen, and writers like Don DeLillo, Italo Calvino, and Thomas Pynchon. (See Hänggi's Essay, 159-168).

Bibliography

Alighieri. Dante. 1912. *Divine Comedy*. Ed. Israel Gollancz. London: J. M. Dent & Sons.

Anonymous. 1643. *The Actor's Remonstrance or Complaint for the Silencing of their Profession*. London: Edw. Nickson.

Austen. Jane. 2000. *Emma*. Introduction and notes Nicola Bradbury. Hare, Hertfordshire: Wordsworth Classics.

Blake, William. 1971. *Songs of Innocence*. New York: Dover Publications, Inc.

Blake, William. 1994. *Marriage of Heaven and Hell*. New York: Dover Publications.

Brontë, Charlotte. [1847] 1983. *Jane Eyre*. Introduction Q. D. Leavis. Harmondsworth: Penguin Books

Burgess. Anthony. 1962. *A Clockwork Orange*. Harmondsworth: Penguin Books.

Byron. 1994. *The Works of Lord Byron*. Ware, Hertfordshire: Wordsworth Editions Ltd.

Chaucer. Geoffrey. 1968. *The Canterbury Tales*. Translated into modern English by Nevill Coghill. Harmondsworth: Penguin Books.

Coleridge. Samuel. 1950. *Select Poetry & Prose*. Ed. Stephen Potter. London: The Nonesuch Press.

Conati, Marcello & Mario Medici Eds. 1994. *The Verdi-Boito Correspondence*. English language edition by William Weaver. Chicago: The University of Chicago Press.

Debussy. Claude. 1987. Monsieur Croche et autres écrits, Paris: Gallim

Freedman. William. 1978. *Laurence Sterne and the Origins of the Musical Novel*. Athens: The University of Georgia P.

Hardy. Thomas. 2002. "The Fidler of the Reels" in *Life's Little Ironies*. Introduction and Notes by Claire Seymour. Ware, Hertfordshire: Wordsworth Editions Ltd.

Hardy. Thomas. 1985. *Tess of the D'Urbervilles*. Introduction by A. Alvarez. Harmondsworth: Penguin Books.

Hugo, Victor, 1880. *William Shakespeare*. 2nd edition. Paris: Hachette.

Huxley. Aldous. 1928. *Point Counterpoint*. New York: New Modern Library.

—. 1957. 'Music at Night.' In *Music at Night and Other Essays* (1931) London: Chatto & Windus.

Keats. John. 1973. *Keats – Poetical Works*. Ed. H. W. Garrod. Oxford: Oxford University Press.

Joyce. James. 1973. *Ulysses* with *Ulysses: A Short History* by Richard Ellmann Harmondsworth: Penguin Books.

Kerouac. Jack. 1955. *On the Road*. New York: Signet Book.

Kundera, Milan. 1984. *The Unbearable Lightness of Being*. Translation by Michael Henry Hein. New York: HarperPerennial.

Leibniz. Gottfried Wilhelm. 2014. Nicholas Rescher. *G.W. Leibniz's Monadology: An Edition for Students.* Ed. Rescher Nicholas. New York: Routledge.

Lutz, Jerry. 1974. *Pitchman's Melody: Shaw about Shakespeare*. Lewinsburg: Bucknell University Press.

Milton. John. 1969. *Arcade* in *Poetical Works*. Edited by Douglas Bush. Oxford: Oxford University Press.

More. Thomas. 1978. *Utopia*. Translation and Introduction by Paul Turner. Harmondsworth: Penguin Books.

Nietzsche. Friederik. 2014. *The Complete Works of Friedrich Nietzsche*, Vol. XVI, Ed. Oscar Levy. Edinburgh, London: O'Gorman. Francis.

O'Gorman. Francis, 2014. Ed. (Nietzsche's quotation in *The Cambridge Companion to Victorian Culture.* Cambridge: Cambridge University Press, i-xvi. (Cambridge Companions Online. Web. 19 November 2014, 101).

Osborne. M. James. 1972. *Young Philip Sidney* 1572-1577. New Haven: Yale University Press.

Pater. Walter. 1986. *The Renaissance Studies in Art and Poetry*, Edited and with an introduction by Adam Philips. Oxford and New York: Oxford University Press.

Pivano, Fernanda. Interview of Enrico Grassani with Fernanda Pivano "Anche se voi vi credete assolti." Pavia: Edizioni Selecta, 2002, pp. 24-25.

Plotinus. 1969. *The Enneads.* Translated by Stephen MacKenna. New York: Pantheon Books.

Prieto. Eric. 2002. 'Metaphor and Methodology in World Music Studies' in *Essays in Honour of Steven Paul Scher and on Cultural Identity and the Musical Stage*. Amsterdam & New York: Rodopi.

Richardson. Samuel. 2018. *Clarissa Harlowe Volume I.* 1st edition. Frankfurt am Mein, Germany: Outlook.

Sand. George. 2004. *La Comtesse de Rudolstadt*. Eds. Nicole Savy and Damien Zanone. Paris: Laffont, 2004.

Schopenhauer. Arthur. 1966. *The World as Will and Representation* (*Die Welt als Wille und Vorstellung*) Vol. Ch. 3, Translated by E.F. J. Payne. New York: Dover Publications.

Sidney. Philip. 2002. *An Apology for Poetry* (or *The Defence of Poesy*). Ed. R. W. Mansen. Manchester: Manchester University Press.
Sterne. Laurence. 1950. *Tristram Shandy*. Introduction Bergen Evans. New York: The modern Library.
—. 1952. A Sentimental Journey Through France and Italy. London: Classics Book Club.
—. 1935. Sterne. Laurence. Letters. Ed. Lewis Perry Curtis. Oxford: Clarendon.
Werfel, Franz & Stefan Paul, 1973. *Verdi the Man and His Letters*. New York: Vienna House.
Werner. Wolf. The Musicalization of Fiction: A Study in the Theory and History of Intermediality. Amsterdam-Atlanta GA: Rodopi B.V., 1999.
Wittgenstein. Ludwig. 1958. *Philosophical Investigations*, Ed. G.E.M. Anscombe and R. Rhees, tr. G.E.M. Anscombe. Second edition, p. 527. Or the 1986, Oxford: Basil Blackwell
Whitall. Arnold. 2010. 'Autonomy / Heteronomy. The Context of Musicology' in AA. VV. *Rethinking Music*. Eds. Nick Cook & Mark Everist. Oxford: Oxford University Press.
Woolf. Virginia. 1977-84. *The Letters of Virginia Woolf.* 6 vols. Ed. N. Nicholson & J. Trautmann. London: The Hogarth Press.
—. 1997. 'String Quartet' Napoli: Loffredo Editore
—. 1993. *To the Lighthouse* Rapallo: CIDEB.
—. 1979-1985. *The Diary of Virginia Woolf,* ed. Anne Olivier Bell and Andrew McNeillie, 5 vols. London: Penguin.
—. 1977-84. *The Diary of Virginia Woolf.* 5 vols. Ed. A. Olivier Bell. London: The Hogarth Press.
Wordsworth. William. 1969. Ed. & Intro by Geoffrey F. Hartman. *The selected Poetry and Prose of Wordsworth*. New York: New American Library.
Young, Julian. 2010. *Nietzsche. Friedrich: A Philosophical Biography*. Wake Forest University: North Carolina

Sitography

Ashiguro. Kazuo. "Biografia di Kazuo Inshiguro".9/11/2018. in *La storia raccontata da Giorgio dell'Arti*
https://www.cinquantamila.it/storyTellerArticolo.php?storyId=5be54ade56a38, (retrived on 25-03-2021)
https://www.theguardian.com/books/2015/mar/15/kazuo-ishiguro-i-used-to-see-myself-as-a-musician

Burgess, Antony. *The Music of a Clockwork Orange*, in International Anthony Burgess Foundation, Manchester, 2021, *The Music of a Clockwork Orange*: https://www.anthonyburgess.org/a-clockwork-orange/the-music-of-a-clockwork-orange/

Cohen Leonard: https://allanshowalter.com/2019/02/16/leonard-cohens-landscapes-of-the-spirit-by-david-peloquin-photomontage-by-martin-ferrabee-part-1-initiation/#footnote_0_22013

Hastings, Patrick. 2016-20120. *A Guide and Resource to Help You Read James Joyce's Ulysses*. http://www.ulyssesguide.com/

Joyce James http://www.ulyssesguide.com/11-sirens (retrieved on 5th April 2021)

Kellaway, Kate, interviews Kazuo Ishiguro.

Morrison. Tony. Brooks Daphne A. 15 Aug. 2019. 'Toni Morrison and the Music of Black Life' In *Pitchfork*: https://pitchfork.com/thepitch/toni-morrison-and-the-music-of-black-life/ (retrieved on 25th March 2021).

Oates. Joyce. Carol. 1966. *Where are you going? Where have you been?* https://www.cusd200.org/cms/lib/IL01001538/Centricity/Domain/361/oates_going.pdf (retrived on 25th March 2021)

Proust, Marcel ANON. "Marcel Proust (1871-1922): Music" (updated 14 Feb. 2021), source: https://research.lib.buffalo.edu/proust/music. University at Buffalo: University Libraries.

Rushdie, Salman. David Fricke, 13-05-1999. "Salman Rushdie" in *Rolling Stone*: https://www.rollingstone.com/culture/culture-news/salman-rushdie-177823/

Thomson, J. Andrew. 2019. 'Setting William Blake to Music.' In Wordsworth Garmere: https://wordsworth.org.uk/blog/2019/02/09/setting-william-blake-to-music/

Self. Will. "Guardian" 5 Oct. 2011. theguardian.com/culture/2011/oct/05/notes-letters-music-modernism-self

Wordsworth William https://www.cusd200.org/cms/lib/IL01001538/Centricity/Domain/361/oates_going.pdf

Translated by Ravindra K Shringy (1978), *Saṅgīta-Ratnākara of Śārṅgadeva: Sanskrit Text and English Translation with Comments and Notes. Vol. 1*, Ed: Sharma Prem Lata, Motilal Banarsidass,

For further reading

Brown. C. S. 1948. *Music and Literature: A Comparison of the Arts.* Athens: University of Georgia Press.

Dubois, Pierre. "Music and Modernity in Laurence Sterne: The Dialectics of Harmony and Dissonance." *XVII-XVIII*, HS3 | 2013, 229-242.

Dubois, Pierre. La conquête du mystère musical dans la Grande-Bretagne des Lumières. Lyon: PU de Lyon - E.L.L.U.G., 2009.

Finney. Gretchen Ludke. 1962. Musical Backgrounds for English Literature: 1580-1650. New Brunswick, New Jersey: Rutgers University Press.

Kramer, Lawrence. 2017. *Song Acts. Writings on Words and Music.* Leiden: Brill-Rodopi.

Handbuch Literatur & Musik. 2017. Edited by N. Gess - A. Honold. Berlin: De Gruyter.

Paterson. Adrian. 2020. "Pound Notes: Modernist Poetry and Music." In *The Edinburgh Companion to Literature and Music.* Edited by Delia da Sousa Correa. Edinburgh: Edinburgh University Press.

Eric, Prieto. 2002. *Metaphor and Methodology in Word and Music Studies.* Amsterdam: Rodopi.

Torabi, Josh. 2020. *Music and Myth in Modern Literature.* New York: Routledge.

Witten, Michelle. 2018. *James Joyce and Absolute Music.* London: Bloomsbury Publishing.

Part I:

English and Irish Literature

FROM THE *BEGGARS' OPERA* TO *THE THREEPENNY OPERA*: A LONG-STANDING RELATIONSHIP OF TEXT AND MUSIC

YURI CHUNG

> Brecht grasped… that 200 years not been able to loosen the alliance that poverty had sealed with vice, but rather that this alliance is as enduring as a social order whose consequence is poverty […] The counter-morality of the beggars and rogues is bound up with the official morality.
> Walter Benjamin in (Hinton, 1990, 144-145)

The Beggar's Opera

Today, when John Gay (1685-1732) is mentioned, one practically ends talking about *The Beggar's Opera*. This work was not only a major hit, documented by the paintings and prints of the time (Fig. 1), but it even inspired renowned artists of the 20th century above all the duo Kurt Weill-Bertolt Brecht. Even though Gay defined his work as a comic opera, it symbolised much more. It reflected his genius but also a career that never took off. Gay always yearned for a place in court since his childhood. It was a strange twist of fate that an opera for beggars and not a court one would bring him fame.

In the 18th century, Italian court opera was the main attraction in England. It made its first appearance in 1705 with Tomaso Stanzani's *Arsinoë*, a work translated into English and then performed at the Drury Lane, London. Even though it had a dreadful translation with the accents placed on the wrong syllables, this did not hinder its success. Furthermore, two years later, the representation of Giovanni Bononcini's *Camilla* obtained the record of twenty-one performances in the same season. Undoubtedly, Italian opera immediately made a great impact. It consisted in an opera sung mostly in Italian and usually divided into three acts with a limited number of singers, generally only six. In each of these acts, the leading artists are expected to sing an aria, a moment in which they dominate the scene. To achieve a more spectacular result, innovative machineries and even animals were used on stage (Montgomery 1929, 417-419). Important English critics like Joseph Addison (1672-1719), the founder of the *Spectator*, and John Dennis (1658-1734), in his "Essay on Opera," expressed at once their aversion to this new "monstrous" and "prodigiously unnatural" product (Dennis 1718, 468). Unfortunately for them, all this was to no avail. The English public just adored the exotism and the nonsensical plots of Italian opera.

Fig. 5: William Hogarth (1697-1764), Engraved print of *The Beggar's Opera* (1728), Victoria and Albert Museum.

In that period, the German composer George Frideric Handel (1685-1759) made his debut on the English operatic scene. In 1710, after becoming Kapellmeister of Prince George, the Elector of Hanover, he got leave of absence to try his luck in London, a fertile city for Italian opera. At his arrival, he was introduced to Queen Anne's court and soon composed the first opera wholly written in Italian on British soil, *Rinaldo* (1711). To the dismay of Addison and Dennis, the opera was warmly received by the public. For this reason, Handel extended further his leave, without permission from Prince George, composing other works: *Il Pastor fido* (1712) and *Teseo* (1713). The sudden death of Queen Anne in 1714 and the immediate declaration of George of Hanover as George I of England initially affected his court aspirations but it was just a matter of time before the king would forget his previous behaviour and re-establish him as the court composer.

A few years after these events, the fall in demand of Italian operas favoured Handel's decision to move to the Cannons in 1717. This was the house of the Earl of Carnarvon, future Duke of Chandos, one of Handel's patrons. The German composer stayed there until February 1719 and, in this period, experimented with other genres making use of the English language. One of these experiments was *Acis and Galatea* (1718), an opera with a libretto entirely written in English. Probably, by undertaking this task, Handel wanted to obtain unanimous acclaim in the island and, for this reason, his encounter with Gay was not fortuitous.

At the time, John Gay was a popular writer of pastorals. His work, *The Shepherd's Week* (1714), combined the style of a great poet of the past, Edmund Spenser (1552-59), with that of a major contemporary poet, Alexander Pope (1688-1744). The latter believed that Spenser's use of a rustic language was old-fashioned and representative only of the lowest classes (Hopes 2017, chap. 1). Even though it was most probably written to mock Ambrose Philip's *Pastorals* (1710), John Gay wanted ultimately to echo his friend Pope by parodying Spenser's language, but, in a good-humoured way (Cumming 2003, 16). In addition, Gay did not solely focus on the British tradition but took also into account its forerunner, the Italian pastorals. In his Proem to *The Shepherd's Week*, he wrote:

> That principally, courteous reader, whereof I would have thee to be advertised, (feeling I depart from the vulgar usage) is touching the language of my shepherds; which is smoothly to say, such as is neither spoken by the country maiden or the courtly dame; nay, not only such as in the present times is not uttered, but was never uttered in times past; and, if I judge aright, will never be uttered in times future. It having too much of the country to be fit for the court, too much of the court to be fit for the country; too much of the language of old times to be fit for the present, too much of the present to be fit for the old, and too much of both to be fit for any time to come.
> (Gay, 1770, 61-62)

Undoubtedly, one of John Gay's greatest abilities was to reckon with the controversies of his lifetime. In these mock pastorals, Gay used parody to raise the awareness of his readers concerning the existing changes. At the same time, he differed from the Italian genre offering a more current and realistic English prototype. By using words and sounds belonging to the common knowledge, he portrayed a world in which his countrymen could finally identify themselves.

This was certainly one of the reasons for Handel's interest in Gay. Previously, Handel had composed an Italian pastoral opera, *Il Pastor fido* (1712), but it turned out a fiasco quite certainly because of the differing principles between the Italian and the English pastorals. The audience felt unquestionably alienated by a work supposedly intelligible to them. Moreover, it was general belief that "a poor libretto reveals the comparative emptiness of the music" (Westrup, 1929, 798). Therefore, John Gay seemed the right choice because he was a member since 1714 of the Scriblerus Club, a group formed by prominent men of letters that included Alexander Pope and Jonathan Swift (1667-1745). In that period, Gay attended the earl of Clarendon as his secretary in his visit to the court of Hanover. The writer was a supporter of the Tories, the ruling party at the time. Unfortunately, when Queen Anne died 15 days after his arrival in London, his hopes to impress at court withered as the Whigs rose to power. To sum up, a collaboration between Handel and Gay must have appeared quite enticing for both because they needed to redeem themselves. On the one hand, Gay might have seen this collaboration as a possibility to revive his possibilities of patronage by writing the libretto for the most renowned composer in England while, on the other hand, Handel hoped to compose a score which could test his newly acquainted understanding of the English audience and help him come out from the existing operatic impasse.

Thus, *Acis and Galatea* (1718) was the outcome of this collaboration. Originally, during his stay in Naples in 1708, Handel had written a pastoral cantata called *Aci, Galatea e Polifemo*. He kept the plot but completely re-elaborated musically this new work creating a short English pastoral opera, very similar to a masque. It was performed privately at Cannons for the Earl of Cannavon, later Duke of Chandos. The absence of potential critics to ditch his work made it certainly a useful test for Handel to fix his previous pastoral failings and create serenely his first opera in English. If the music is solely composed by Handel, the libretto is for the majority written by Gay with contributions by Alexander Pope and John Hughes (1711-1772), a London acquaintance of Handel.

In their collaboration, Handel and Gay exposed the differences between the old and the new pastorals pointing out at the impossibility to re-enact the past in the modern world. It had to undergo a transformation if it wanted to survive the present. The same issue was to be found in the confrontation between the traditional Italian opera and the new ballad work presented in *The Beggar's Opera*. In the ensuing years, Handel acknowledged the innovative qualities of this collaboration and revised the work in 1732 and 1739. It became his most represented opera during his lifetime with more than seventy performances and eight revivals (King, 1989, 4).

Unfortunately for Gay, his collaboration with Handel did not bring the benefits he expected. He did not achieve the long-term economic security he was looking for even though the publication of works like *Poems on Several Occasions* (1720) made him earn some money. Gay's continuous search for economic wealth ultimately led him to a disastrous investment. In 1720, he lost all his money in the South Sea bubble. Due to these economic problems, Gay began to look desperately for a court patronage even though he was disregarded by the men of power, above all Robert Walpole, because of his Tory inclinations. In 1725, he finally believed he had found a way to reach the court via the princess Caroline, the King's daughter-in-law. Under the promise of favours, he wrote some fables for the princess's son even though his friends had advised him to give up this project. These were published as *Fables* in 1727 and brought him great popularity around the continent. In the same year, George II became king and Caroline the new queen. From then on, Gay's expectations to achieve an important post at court were very high and it was appalling for him to discover he was merely offered the role of gentleman-usher to the two-year-old princess Louisa. He sharply declined the offer. This was the final straw for Gay and his first reaction was to produce his greatest work, *The Beggar's Opera*, in which he vented all his frustrations.

In 1727, the choice for Gay to produce an opera seemed quite extravagant. Gay had already written a libretto but this time many changes had occurred in the operatic panorama since his last work. In 1719, the South Sea Company, the main cause of Gay's economic ruin, decided to promote Italian Opera by founding the Royal Academy of Music and placing Handel at its head. The German composer hired foreign singers, like the great castrato Senesino (1686-1758), to perform in Italian Baroque operas including Handel's new compositions. Initially, the performances were highly appreciated for the greater quality of the operas and the singers but, in the long run, the eccentricities of the same singers and the disgraceful actions of their claque discouraged patrons to invest on the project. Handel's attempts to save the Academy from ruin practically failed after the premiere of *The Beggar's Opera* (Montgomery 1929, 424). Ironically, the Italian operatic heyday was put to an end by an opera for beggars.

In truth, Gay was split into two entities: the poet that sought a patron and the one which scorned these seekers. By giving up the idea of a court patronage, he decided to please the theatre audience. (Gay, 2013, xv-xvi). After taking this decision, he could openly report all the wrongdoings he had seen over the years. Anyway, this was not really a novelty because in 1724 he wrote a ballad, "Newgate's Garland." This ballad narrates the story of a thief Blueskin Blake who kills Jonathan Wild, the popular thief-taker. Actually, Blueskin only wounds Wild but Gay interprets the story in a different way concluding that the highwayman is certainly more honest than the gentleman who acts in the shadows. This ballad was considered a direct attack on Robert Walpole, the man who had clipped his ambitions. In any case, the seed was sown and Swift's suggestion, as recounted by Joseph Spence to Alexander Pope, only started a project which was already present unconsciously in Gay's works:

> Dr. Swift had been observing once to Mr. Gay, what an odd pretty sort of a thing a Newgate Pastoral might make. Gay was inclined to try at such a thing for some time; but afterwards thought it would be better to write a comedy on the same plan. This was what gave rise to the Beggar's Opera. He began on it; and when first he mentioned it to Swift, the doctor did not much like the project. As he carried it on, he showed what he wrote to both of us, and we now and then gave a correction, or a word or two of advice; but it was wholly of his own writing. –When it was done, neither of us thought it would succeed. We showed it to Congreve, who, after reading it over, said, it would either take greatly, or be damned confoundedly.   (Johnson, 1840, 218)

Therefore, instead of focusing on another pastoral opera, Gay opted for a ballad, or rather a collection of ballads, even though he officially defined his opera a comic one. The ballad descended from the folksong and had simplicity as its main value. Obviously, this genre was more fit for an English audience compared to the sophisticated and often incomprehensible Italian jargon. This explained its success and also highlighted the fact that Gay belonged to the people. He was the author of "Trivia, or the Art of Walking the Streets of London" (1716), a poem in which he advises his readers the best places to go shopping. He was a Londoner who knew well his roots and the English tradition. If in the theatres, the professed virtues and ethics so magnificently promoted by the Italian culture were in vogue amongst the rich classes, in the London streets the situation was exactly the opposite. The book market was thriving, and the number of books printed per year increased exponentially. However, according to the great authors of that time, the quality was markedly worse. The readers focused mainly on the daily events narrated in the newspapers, especially those concerning crime. During that period, the lack of a true police force favoured the growth of organised crime. As a result, the novels conformed to the general taste of the period and dealt with those topics so popular at the time, namely the stories of rogues and prostitutes.

Gay was a great observer of the London street life and fed the curiosity of the people with all the requested information in *The Beggar's Opera*. It not only talked openly about the topic but mentioned real places where crime took place: St. Giles (a slum full of criminals), Marybone (a gambling house), Covent Garden (a district full of brothels and gin shops), the Moorfields (the home for the underworld) and many others. Moreover, the characters' names fully described their professions. For example, the protagonist Macheath was the son of the heath, a highwayman, Peachum was an informer, Lockit a jailer and Filch a thief. To give an ulterior brush of realism to his work, Gay made his characters speak vulgarly. For example, Mrs Peachum uses the words wench, slut, hussy and jade when she speaks with her daughter, Polly. Londoners could see practically their world, or better the underworld, put on stage.

Theatrically speaking, this was completely new to the English audience. The existing operatic works only talked about unnatural events with mythical heroes. It distracted its audience, mostly the higher classes, from the real-life problems. This was certainly intolerable for Gay. In his view, English society had to open its eyes to the exaggerated opulence of the Italian scenery, the unrealistic characters and the alienating Italian language. Furthermore, he criticised the intricate artificial structure of the Italian opera with its singers performing recitatives and arias ridiculously adorned by excessive virtuosities. For him, these were only sideshow attractions that should not be taken as a model.

However, Gay did not disdain the public's disputable opinion and so gave Italian opera an important role in his masterpiece. His opera included romance, rivalry, jealousy, vengeance, poison, a prison scene, etc. There were all the necessary ingredients to make an ideal Italian opera. At the same time, he also expressed ironically the existing real-life clashes affecting that world. For example, he mimicked Handel when he openly declared at the beginning of his work: "As to the parts, I have observed such a nice impartiality to our two ladies [Polly Peachum and Lucy Lockit] that it is impossible for either of them to take offence." (Gay, 1986, 41). In 1726, during the composition of his opera *Alessandro*, Handel had to be very careful on distributing equally the parts for his two primadonnas, Faustina Bordoni (1697-1781) and Francesca Cuzzoni (1696-1778), to avoid detrimental feuds. Unfortunately for Handel, the rivalry grew to unreasonable levels to the point that the two claques of the respective singers not only ruined the performances with hisses but also encouraged their divas to misbehave on scene to the consternation of the court members. Moreover, violence occurred outside the theatre offering a bad publicity that finally discouraged possible patrons to invest on these shows.

By aping and then displaying these events, Gay could strike while the iron was hot. Not only the portrayal of the well-known rivalry between the two sopranos made the audience laugh but also the subject of their contention. To imagine Senesino, an "eunuch", as the philanderer Macheath was extremely hilarious. But all in all, Gay's intent was not only to entertain the public using parody. He wanted to do social satire by means of his characters. Gay placed himself in his work as the Beggar of the title, granting himself the faculty to speak. This choice was inevitably autobiographic due to a life spent in begging for a court patronship which was never obtained. At the same time, he created an antagonist, the Player, who represented the Italian operatic conventions but at the same time the British social justice as well. In the end, there is a clash between the two and the Beggar justifies his "defeat" by explaining what his true finale would have been:

> Through the whole piece you may observe such a similitude of manners in high and low life, that it is difficult to determine whether (in the fashionable vices) the fine gentlemen imitate the gentlemen of the road, or the gentlemen of the road the fine gentlemen. Had the play remained, as I first intended, it would have carried a most excellent moral. 'Twould have shown that the lower sort of people have their vices in a degree as well as the rich: and that they are punished for them. (Gay 1986, 121)

The Beggar wants poetic justice, the aim of every author, but the Player opposes his decision stating that all operas must end well. Consequently, instead of being hanged for his crimes, Macheath is reprieved and set free to return to his heath lands. If poetic justice is not respected in this work and the same work reflects the actual society, then social justice is definitely challenged. Jemmy Twitcher, a member of Macheath's gang, questions this point in the second act: "Why are the laws levelled at us? Are we more dishonest than the rest of mankind? What we win, gentlemen, is our own by the law of arms, and the right of conquest" (Gay 1986, 68). The underworld fence, Peachum, seems to have the answer:

> Through all the employments of life
>   Each neighbour abuses his brother;
> Whore and rogue they call husband and wife:
>   All professions be-rogue one another.
> The priest calls the lawyer a cheat,
>   The lawyer be-knaves the divine;

> And the statesman, because he's so great,
> Thinks his trade as honest as mine. (Gay, 1986, 43)

The statesman referred to is obviously the omnipresent prime minister, Robert Walpole. He appears also in other forms such as Bob Booty because of the hearsay that he was getting rich at the country's expense and as the same Macheath because of his eye for the ladies. In his opera, Gay models most of his characters to existing people. Not forgetting the primadonnas, he even uses criminals of great renown like Jonathan Wild who is the prime inspiration for Peachum. All of them are depicted realistically through their actions. Peachum, like Wild, works as a receiver of stolen goods denouncing his enemies for money when needed and controlling the underworld by means of blackmail. His ally, Lockit, having bought his place as a Newgate jailor, extorts money from prisoners who want a better treatment. Together, they make additional money by encouraging criminal acts, a practice which really occurred at the time. Treating such troublesome issues without risking censorship implied the use of a form that could allow these facts to be discharged. In this case, opera, thanks to its acceptance at the time as a harmless and unrealistic entertainment, was the perfect solution for this problem. The only difference was that now truth was portrayed.

In the end, Gay's opera consisted in sixty-nine melodies of which twenty-eight came from English ballads, twenty-three from Irish, Scottish and French folksongs while the remaining ones derived from operas by Purcell, Handel and Bononcini. Obviously, John Gay was a brilliant writer but not a true musician. For this reason, one week before the first representation, the impresario, John Rich, asked the German composer, Johann Christoph Pepusch, an old acquaintance of Gay at Cannons, to rearrange and adapt all the various musical pieces of the opera. Besides rearranging this pot-pourri, Pepusch included an original prelude composed by himself in the final score. The premiere took place on January 29, 1728, in Lincoln's Inn Fields in London and it received a triumphal reception. In his notes to *The Dunciad*, Pope wrote:

> This piece was received with greater applause than was ever known. Besides being acted in London sixty-three days without interruption, and renewed the next season with equal applause, it spread into all the great towns of England; was played in many places to the thirtieth and fortieth time; at Bath and Bristol fifty, etc. It made its progress into Wales, Scotland, and Ireland, where it was performed twenty-four days successively. The ladies carried about with them the favourite songs of it in fans, and houses were furnished with it in screens. (Johnson, 1846, 172)

The opera achieved a record of sixty-two consecutive performances in its first season and was on the bill for more than two decades. A sequel was produced immediately after in 1729, *Polly*, but it was never represented due to censorship. In 1737, the Licensing Act suspended the performances of the original *The Beggar's Opera*. Most probably, the authorities, especially Walpole, had grown tired of Gay's satire concerning them. At the same time, also other contemporary authors did not seem to appreciate the work. Daniel Defoe wrote in 1729:

> [...] our rogues are grown more wicked than ever, and vice in all kinds in so much winked at, that robbery is accounted a petty crime. We take pains to puff them up in their villany, and thieves are set out in so amiable a light in the Beggar's Opera, it has taught them to value themselves on their profession rather than to be ashamed of it. There was some cessation of street robberies [...] until the introduction of this pious opera. [...] London, that used to be the most safe and peaceful city in the universe, is now become a scene of rapine and danger. (Defoe, 1729, 9-10)

Threepence Opera

VOICE *off-stage*: What keeps mankind alive?
CHORUS: For once you must try not to shirk the facts: Mankind is kept alive by bestial acts.
           Bertolt Brecht, *Die Dreigroschenoper*. (Brecht ,1979, Act 2)

For the purposes of our book, it must be underlined that, nevertheless, *The Beggar's Opera* was performed for centuries and became a milestone in the English stages. In the 20th century, it inspired various adaptations. The most popular was without any doubt *Die Dreigroschenoper* (*The Threepenny Opera*), a play with music born from the collaboration between two German artists, the playwright Bertolt Brecht (1898-1956) and the musician Kurt Weill (1900-50) in 1928.

In 1920, there was a revival of *The Beggar's Opera* at the Lyric Theatre in London. It was so successful that it set a record run of 1,463 performances from June 1920 to December 1923. (Barlow, 1990, 534). This theatrical achievement did not go unnoticed across the Channel. In Germany, Brecht's secretary, Elisabeth Hauptmann (1897-1973) worked on a German translation of the text after acknowledging the relevance of its message. When the young producer Ernst Josef Aufricht (1898-1971) came to Brecht in search for a new play to promote in Berlin, the playwright offered initially *Joe Fleischhacker*, an unfinished project focused on economic matters which proved too complicated. After Aufricht's firm rejection, Brecht moved on to plan B showing some pages of Hauptmann's translation of *The Beggar's Opera*. Undoubtedly, the fact that it achieved such an enormous success abroad and the strong presence of satire, in vogue at the time, immediately convinced the producer to invest on the project. It should be noted that Brecht did not steal the work from Hauptmann. According to Pamela Katz, "There was a symbiosis there-and it is evident that Brecht was, as Hauptmann herself always insisted, an important teacher and influence on her fiction. He was reaping great rewards from Hauptmann's labor, but from time to time, he returned the favor." (Katz 2015, chap. 6). To produce his play with music, Brecht needed a composer and opted for Kurt Weill. At the time, they were collaborating on the opera, *Rise and Fall of the City of Mahagonny* (1930). Brecht was very slow in the production of the libretto because he had the habit of consecrating his time to more projects simultaneously. Probably, to oblige Brecht, Weill accepted his proposal believing he had to just write some incidental music for a play. Obviously, this was not the case and Weill understood this when Brecht explained to him in detail the project he had in mind.

Like Gay, Brecht's aim was to make satire on artistic, political and social issues. Brecht did not intend solely to adapt Gay's opera, but he wanted to update it and rewrite certain sections. His choice of setting the story during the Victorian era, around a hundred years after the original play, was to make the whole society more familiar to the public. He wanted to "activate the audience" by encouraging "spectators to watch performances critically and alertly, to judge and argue over what they had seen, and to consider its political and social relevance to their own lives." (Bradley, 2016, 1029). The play expressed the hypocrisy of the entire social structure, which was devoted to money and, like *The Beggar's Opera*, it exhibited corruption distributed equally between the bandits and the men of justice. In Brecht's play, the fence, Peachum, became the king of beggars. Human misery was now the new source for making money. As Katz wrote: "In a profit-driven world, misery has indeed been transformed into a commodity. Thus, Brecht turned Gay's opera for beggars into an opera that was about the *art*, and the artifice, of begging" (Katz 2015, chap. 7). To clear their conscience, the bourgeoisie would hypocritically donate some coins to these beggars to save their souls. Furthermore, Peachum was depicted as a very religious man and by doing so, Brecht openly attacked Christianity. After reading Karl Marx's *Das Kapital* in 1926, Brecht's goal was to improve social conditions and create a more just society. But, as Karl Marx (1818-83) stated, religion was the opium of the people and so Brecht found it the main obstacle that he had to eradicate to achieve ultimately social equality. Another important character, Gay's Lockit, was replaced by the policeman, Tiger Brown, a friend of Macheath. Brecht voluntarily emphasised their experience as ex-military comrades, who belonged to the disillusioned youth of the post-war period, to make the plot appear current. The reference to a well-known situation and the strong bond between the bandit and the policeman seem to show how crime and justice have become one. Moreover, Polly, the female heroine, has lost her belief in true love becoming a symbol of bourgeois morality where love is merely a transaction. If the main characters have survived, at times with different disguises, their morality has adapted itself to the deteriorating society.

On the musical hand, Kurt Weill criticised the dominating music of his time, operetta and opera. While Gay was confronting Italian opera, Weill likewise challenged Wagnerism. He did not search for symphonic beauty derived from myths and legends like Wagner but followed a multicultural approach by inserting opera, jazz and German folksongs in his work. With regard to Pepusch's music, he kept only the melody of Air I, "Peachum's Morning Hymn" (Salmon 1981, 70), an echo of the past in the existing world. Similarly to Gay's opera, the spoken dialogue replaced the recitative, a typical operatic device. Furthermore, the performers were singing actors and not opera singers. This gave Weill the opportunity to create a seemingly light tone that could surprisingly include high and low elements together, with the boundaries between the two being continuously redrawn or simply deleted. (Katz. 2015, chap. 7).

The final outcome was a satire on the existing society and its capitalist system. *The Threepenny Opera* questioned the actual status quo depicting all the malfunctions of a society "characterised by the addictive mixture of disillusionment and shamelessness, practicality and sentimentality, always ready to be seduced" that was the Weimar Republic (Böker, Detmers and Giovanopoulos, 2006, 20). The fact that it was a true socialist work, composed in a period of peace and in opposition to the rising Nazi ideals, made it become a symbol of defiance against authoritarianism. If initially Weill and Brecht saw it as an experimental work that would just strike the consciences of the public of their time, it turned out as an inspiration for all the generations. Its musical multiculturalism and prophetic text gained worldwide recognition uniting surprisingly the intellectuals with the mass culture (Böker, Detmers and Giovanopoulos, 2006, 20). The fact that the plot was practically the same as the original *The Beggar's Opera* shows how Gay was ahead of his time.

In conclusion, John Gay demonstrated his ability as a librettist in his first work, *Acis and Galatea*, which became part of the operatic repertory while *The Beggar's Opera* turned out as "cultural repertory of the world" (Gay, 1986, 7). In *Acis and Galatea*, Gay showed a parodic style that could help enhance a genre, the pastoral opera. By offering a modern outlook to the piece, he made it contemporary in all the centuries to follow. Ironically, Gay was also the main person responsible for Handel's operatic demise. After having already demonstrated his literary qualities, Gay, in *The Beggar's Opera*, instinctively mirrored now the people's will. It is important to understand that he was not an enemy of Italian opera although he did write a "burlesque of conventional operatic devices and scenes" (Gay, 2013, viii). Gay merely "studied the bias of the age, found out what the ordinary man wanted to see and hear" (Lejeune 1923, 8). His English light opera, future inspiration to the modern musical and Brecht, was simply an Italian court opera without the artistic and musical embellishments. It portrayed the world everyone knew, everyone commented on but that nobody had the will to represent. Brecht's *Threepenny Opera* only amplified the problem showing how nothing had really changed over the centuries. By 1728, John Gay had reached the bottom of his career. With nothing to lose, he forsook his social restraints narrating the world he actually saw. His view was not dissimilar to Lockit in Act III:

> Lions, wolves, and vultures don't live together in herds, droves or flocks. Of all animals of prey, man is the only sociable one. Every one of us preys upon his neighbour, and yet we herd together. Peachum is my companion, my friend – according to the custom of the world, indeed, he may quote thousands of precedents for cheating me. And shall not I make use of the privilege of friendship to make him a return?   (Gay, 1986, 98-99)

In the world of today where atheism is widespread and the Darwinian natural selection appears as a matter of fact, the words of Lockit seem to echo a veiled but unspoken truth. Nowadays, individual anthropocentrism and personal interests seem to guide the choices of the individuals belonging to our society. Socialism is covertly disappearing devoured by the ravenous jaws of capitalism. If *The Beggar's Opera* is still relevant today, it is because nothing has changed much in the core. Only the current façade has been embellished.

On the music front, it is good to highlight that this opera still arises the interest of contemporary musicians as shown by this transcription of a famous aria, "Through all the employments of life", done by a young Italian musician who arranged it for his *String Quartet Mousiké* (2021).[1]

---

[1] Recordings of *Mousiké* can be heard in the following links:
https://www.youtube.com/watch?v=kFVZ3mpPLLA
https://www.youtube.com/watch?v=Hqagv8q3oQ0
https://www.youtube.com/watch?v=Xr6MyxsQP-k&feature=youtu.be
https://www.facebook.com/giovanni.azzinnari/videos/4048190848586502/

Act One (Air I) Through all the employments of life
THE BEGGAR'S OPERA (1728)

Words by JOHN GAY

Music by Johann C. PEPUSCH & Frederic AUSTIN

Transcription by GIOVANNI AZZINNARI

Works cited

Barlow, Jeremy. 1990. "Published Arrangements of the Beggar's Opera, 1729-1990". *The Musical Times*, Vol. 131, No. 1772: 533-538.
Böker, Uwe, Detmers, Ines, and Giovanopoulos, Anna-Christina. Ed. 2006. *John Gay's The Beggar's Opera: 1728-2004. Adaptations and Re-Writings*. Amsterdam and New York: Rodopi.
Bradley, Laura. 2016. "Training the Audience: Brecht and the Art of Spectatorship". *The Modern Language Review*, Vol. 111, No. 4: 1029-1048.
Brecht, Bertolt. 1979. *Die Dreigroschenoper*. Translated by Ralph Mannheim and John Willett. Vienna: Universal Edition.
Cummings, Robert M. Ed. 2003. *Edmund Spenser: The Critical Heritage*. London and New York: Routledge.
Defoe, Daniel. 1729. *Second Thoughts are Best: or a Further Improvement of a Late Scheme to Prevent Street Robberies*. London: J. Roberts.
Dennis, John. 1718. *The Select Works of Mr. John Dennis in Two Volumes, Vol. 1: "An Essay on Italian Operas (1706)"*. London: John Darby.
Gay, John. 1770. *The Works of Mr. John Gay, in Four Volumes, Vol. I*. Dublin: James Potts.
—. 1986. *The Beggar's Opera*. London: Penguin Books.
—. 2013. *The Beggar's Opera and Polly*. Oxford: Oxford University Press.
Hinton, Stephen, 1990. *Kurt Weill: The Threepenny Opera*. Cambridge: Cambridge University Press.
Hopes, Jeffrey. 2017. "The sounds of early eighteenth-century pastoral: Handel, Pope, Gay, and Hughes", *E-rea*, February 14, 2017. https://doi.org/10.4000/erea.5741
Johnson, Samuel. 1846. *The Works of Samuel Johnson, Vol. II*. New York: Alexander V. Blake.
1840. *Lives of the English Poets: With Critical Observations on Their Works and Lives of Sundry Eminent Persons*. London: Charles Tilt.
Katz, Pamela. 2015. *The Partnership: Brecht, Weill, Three Women, and Germany on the Brink*. New York: Nan A. Talese / Doubleday.
King, Robert. 1989. *Handel's Acis and Galatea*. London: Hyperion Records.
Lejeune, Caroline A. 1923. "Opera in the Eighteenth Century". *Proceedings of the Musical Association, 49th Session*.
Montgomery, Franz. 1929. "Early Criticism of Italian Opera in England". *The Musical Quarterly*, Vol. 15, No. 3: 417-424.
Sadie, Stanley. Ed. 2009. *The Grove Book of Operas, Second edition*. Oxford: Oxford University Press.

Salmon, Richard J. 1981. "Two operas for beggars: a political reading." In *Theoria: A Journal of Social and Political Theory*, No. 57: 63-81.

GEORGE ELIOT AND HER MUSICAL AFFINITY IN *THE MILL ON THE FLOSS*

SANAZ ALIZADEH TABRIZI

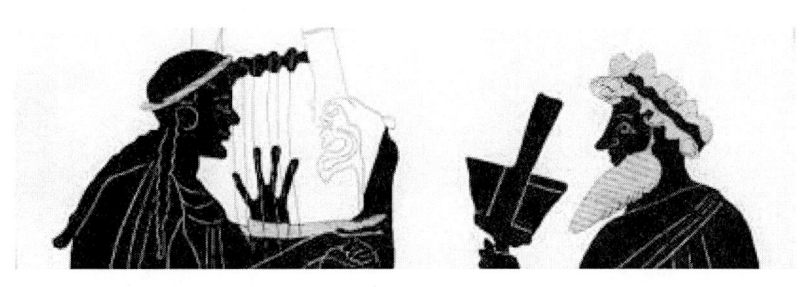

Fig. 6: Image on a Greek vase.

"Poets and musicians are members of one church, related in the most intimate way: for the secret of word and tone is one and the same."
E. T. A. Hoffmann

In *The Birth of Tragedy*, written in 1872, Nietzsche (1844-1900) celebrates the fusion of music and word to turn our focus towards the issues of culture and society by addressing the ancient Greeks as the beholders of the highest form of culture. He theorizes that the absolute articulation of that culture was manifested in the fifth century Attic tragedy, whose deep-seated elements were poetry, music, and dance He conjectures that a tragic culture based on "Wagnerian music-drama" would be the best remedy for the wounds and sorrows of modern society (Nietzsche, 2007, x).

The later-anti Wagnerian Nietzsche considers "Wagnerism" as the only route to salvation which was the upshot of a scrimmage between the two drives of ancient Greek deities: Apollo and Dionysos. Being the representative of "distinction, discreteness and individuality" (ivi, xi), Apollo highlights the ethics of differences, boundaries, and moderation exhibited in literature. (ivi, x). Dionysos, on the other hand, is the epithet of the "transgression of limits, the dissolution of boundaries, the destruction of individuality, and excess," whose purest artistic expression was "quasi-orgiastic forms of music, especially of choral singing and dancing" (ivi, xi).

Nietzsche believes that the two principles co-exist in any human soul, institution, or work of art, yet the creativity would barely transpire because of the tension and the dynamic convergence of both of them. Therefore, the Attic tragedy stage bore the perfect domain for the synthesis of the Dionysiac dancing, singing the chorus and the Apolline reciting, acting (individual) players mainly to save the delicate balance and jape us to enjoy life against the Socratic shift toward reason and its application to gain control of fate; a concept that does shape modern culture. Consequently, Nietzsche argues the urge to return to a state where "tragedy will once again be possible" (ivi, xii). He welcomes Beethoven's music which revived "the Dionysiac" and highlights Wagner's music-dramas which led to the reconciliation of "the Dionysiac power of the modern symphony orchestra to Apolline epic speech and action" (ibid., xii) to dwindle again the pessimism from human life and revive "unity, coherence, and meaningfulness" in a society void of fragmented individuation. Thus, the primary function of tragedy to him is "enveloping [the pessimistic truth about human life and fate] with an illusory appearance which makes it [just barely] tolerable" (ivi, xx), and so helps to rationalize the concept that tragedy is the correlation of Dionysos and Apollo, the alliance of music and words.

Since Nietzsche, scholars have penned on translation or adaptation of literary works. Kristeva and Bakhtin have focused on the theory of *intertextuality* and how texts are interrelated; poststructuralist Barthes and Derrida have studied *intertextuality* in the realm of language, and modern historicists consider it cultural and societal as they credit literary texts "the product of complex social 'exchanges' and 'negotiations'" (Booker, 1996, 138). Nevertheless, in reading and understanding literature, the function of nonverbal art should never be undervalued. In other words, meaning is thoroughly achievable only when the verbal and nonverbal reconcile. Lars Elleström explains that the ultimate understanding occurs when all the necessary conditions of communication are reflected. In other words, "[to] understand things means to interrelate them" (Elleström et all, 2020, 35).

Yet long before intermedial studies and in particular musico-literary relations become the core of interest, in *Word and Music Studies 5*, Steven Paul Scher explains:

> that music and literature share their origin is a notion as old as the first stirrings of aesthetic consciousness. Even a cursory glance at the evolution of the arts confirms that 'histories of both have remained in many ways mutually contingent. (Scher, 2004, 173)

He, however, remarks that "the spectrum of possible parallels between the two arts is vast" (ivi, 174), despite the settled juxtapositions including "music and poetry," "word and tone," and "sound and poetry" regarding the assorted union of literature and music. He values Music in literature and the literary treatment of music aiming at "musicalizing" literature or "verbalizing" music and suggests either a synchronic or diachronic approach to study the relations between the two arts" (ivi, 180).

Thinking through the traditional arrangement of the fine arts, Scher designates that when studying structure-wise, unlike painting, sculpture, and architecture that are matched based on their "visual, spatial, and static nature," music and literature are interpreted as "auditory, temporal and dynamic art forms" since both of them necessitate "to be completed in time" like processes that require "to be decoded" (ivi, 182).

Likewise, Werner Wolf conceptualizes that intermedial studies cover a broad spectrum of arts and phenomena as a milieu for "medial comparisons both from a systematic and a historical perspective" (Wolf & Bernhart 2007, vii). Altogether, the infinite field of intermediality research revolves around the fact that media exist only in connection with each other (Rippl, 2015, 5); a notion that has been evolving since Steven Paul Scher suggested the triadic distinction between "literature in music," "music and literature," and "music in literature" in 1968.

Since the 1980s, "intermediality" has expanded in a wide range of disciplines, including literature. Like Scher, Wolf believes it mainly concentrates on "the participation of more than one medium of expression in the signification of a human artifact" (Wolf, 1999, 1) and underscores the fact that "among the relationship between literature and other media or arts the link with music is especially old" (ivi., 3). He indicates that "whether successful or not" music has been historically entangled "as a shaping element in the signification of fiction," whose analysis would lead to valuable information on individual authors and works of a literary form with the least possibility to be musicalized (ivi., 4).

Hence, like any interdisciplinary approach, the juxtaposition of the two arts of music and literature would shed light on so many paths, but it is more appealing when considering Roland Barthes' remark discussing that interdisciplinary work is "a peaceful operation," as

> it begins effectively when the solidarity of the old discipline breaks down [...] to the benefit of a new object and a new language, neither of which is in the domain of those branches of knowledge that one calmly sought to confront [...]. There now arises a need for a new object, one attained by the displacement or overturning of previous categories.   (Scher, 2004, 475)

That being said, according to Mieke Bal, it is not "a matter of definitions of essences and separation of practices, but of how people communicate: with one another, with the past, with others" (Bal, 2009, 2). Therefore, before I turn to George Eliot, I feel the necessity to take one step backward to briefly observe the development of the two arts and their affinity in the context of the 19th century Europe.

The social and economic transformation at the beginning of this century was the legacy of the French and the Industrial Revolutions, which steered the hegemony of the new social class - the bourgeoisie - and its liaison with the nobility which, of course, aspired "the communal entertainments of parlour or drawing-room in which everyone joined and to which everyone contributed, the vital element of which was music" (Samson, 2001, 239). Despite the Beethoven-Rossini polarization in the general taste of music in the first half of the century and the dominance of Wagner and Verdi in the second, music in general and piano, in particular, played a pivotal role in bridging the cultural diversities and shaping the mindset of the bourgeois family.

While literate gatherings enjoyed sonata or sonata-extract, nocturne, ballad, or song-without-words characterized the favourite genre presenting the piano as an accompanying instrument played by the young ladies in domestic gatherings. Halfway between the drawing-room and the concert hall, salons in more prosperous houses became the perfect setting for "introducing new talent of all kinds, as well as being a good entrée into high society" (ibid., 249), a place in which dance found its aesthetic and symbolic value. (See Ceramella's Essay 'Piano,' 55).

The unification of visual and theatrical effects of grand opera at the verge of the Realist Movement engaged the audience with the conflict of passion, hatred, and sex very much like what most fiction did. Newark conceptualizes that "rendering of operatic storyline, decor, costume, and gesture provided great writers with plenty of material to manipulate in the service of novelistic plot, dialogue, characterization ... to communicate their understanding of the mysteriously unpredictable effect of dramatic music." Hence, "what, the nineteenth-century opera-goer" whether "ideal, professional, inattentive even – or fictional" (Newark, 2011, 12) heard visualizes the social context in which the most remarkable literary and musical pieces were created to capture the hearts and the souls of many generations.

It was at this moment in history when George Eliot (1819-1880) arose to touch the most delicate cultural assets of her society and to wed the two realms of music and literature in her everlasting fiction. Tracing the intermedial connection with music in her work means filling the gaps that have been veiled for long. Moving between the words and the tone in *The Mill on the Floss* (1860) as a microcosm of a broad territory which belonged to a great soul and a genius mind leaves no doubt that Eliot was a perfect observer and interpreter whose authorial techniques were far beyond her time.

The Mill on the Floss

In his review article on Michael Allis's Book, *British Music and Literary Context: Artistic Connections in the Long Nineteenth Century* (2014), Michael Halliwell cites Allis's description of the function of music in the 19th century literary works and the portrayal of musicians and music in these novels as the integral component for their potential to "promote a sense of community and improve education" (Halliwell, 2014,122). He admits that the Victorian fiction was pervaded by the most prominent novelists of the time and George Eliot was one of those few who applied music profoundly and insightfully (ibid., 123) as a result of her "engagement with contemporary science and with German culture" (de Sousa Correa, 2003, 11) and becomes one of the supporters of "Wagner's theories [on] how music and drama should evolve" (ivi, 12). Eliot confirms that she wrote, "as a person with an ear and a mind susceptible to the direct and indirect influences of music" (ivi, 7) which are manifested in the plethora of musical tropes that pass through the body of her works.

She was an adept pianist who esteemed opera performances principally those by Handel, Beethoven, Mendelssohn, apart from those by Liszt and Wagner. In many of her novels, music plays a "narratological and metaphorical" part; "[her] characters use music to communicate emotion and to provoke sympathy in their listeners" and "to communicate and dramatise irreconcilably conflicting claims and emotions (ivi, 111-112). However, she was "critically aware of the musical climate of her age, [wrote] not in a vacuum—using music and composers as simply literary motifs and metaphors to structure her novels [...] but intentionally and even unintentionally engages the larger, social debates on the aestheticism, spirituality, and consumerism of music" (Halliwell, 2014, 123). Halliwell highlights the function of music as it would intensify, combine, and complicate the excited feelings and "exaggerates the loudness, the resonance, the pitch, the intervals, and the variability which [...] are the characteristics of passionate speech" (ivi, 124).

William T. Sullivan (1974, 232) explains that music in *The Mill on the Floss* is presented not only as a metaphor to "define the nature of Maggie's emotional life" but also as illusions to develop the plot. What makes it remarkable is the autobiographical feature of the narrative and the authorial musical taste in the formation of her characters and, in particular, Maggie whose semi-flat character remained unchanged in the course of the story as empathically did the type and the function of music.

The only music that Eliot employs in the early chapters of the novel is Uncle Pullet's musical snuff-box, which was believed would play beautiful tunes due to his "some exceptional talent." It was the melody of this particular source that could soothe the irrepressible rebellious spirit of this young bolshie girl. We read that Maggie could forget the toughness of her brother or perhaps the others'

> […] when the fairy tune began; for the first time she quite forgot that she had a load on her mind, that Tom was angry with her; and by the time "Hush, ye pretty warbling choir," had been played, her face wore that bright look of happiness, while she sat immovable with her hands clasped, which sometimes comforted her mother with the sense that Maggie could look pretty now and then, in spite of her brown skin. (Eliot, 2008, 93)

Here, there is an immediate reference to G. F. Handel's *Acis and Galatea* (1718), whose story comes from Ovid's *Metamorphoses* with a mythical unifying theme of transformation. It is a charming pastoral set by Handel to an English text by John Gay. The simple but emotional dramatic drama recounts the tragic romance of Galatea and Acis. Galatea has been separated from her love Acis and is persuading "the birds to cease their cheerful song as they awaken her desire for him": "Hush, ye pretty warbling choir!"[1] Later, the two lovers are reunited, but the giant Polyphemus aspires Galatea for himself, and upon Galatea's rejection, the jealous Polyphemus kills Acis by hurling a rock at Acis. The mournful Galatea employs her powers to transform Acis's body into a marvelous fountain (see essay on Heroids vs Metamorphosis, 236-247). However, the impact of this exquisite supply is not durable. It moves Maggie to the bone but would disappear and leave her soul "with seven small demons all in again" (ibid., 92-94). This short circuit connects Maggie's story to a future tragic ending: a probable transformation of a particular type.

This motif is linked to Book two, Chapter four, when we read about Maggie's brother, Tom, who is thrilled by Mr. Poulter's sword, wondering that "this is the real sword [he] fought within all the battles." Tom's deep enthusiasm makes him believe that he can surprise Philip, his humpbacked peer since Philip "knows a great deal about fighting … with bows and

---

[1] For further information on the opera, refer to
https://handelhendrix.org/learn/about-handel/opera-synopses/acis-and-galatea/

arrows, and battle-axes." Eliot juxtaposes the crude Tom with the humpbacked but sentimental Philip. It is, in fact, the first time we are led into Philip's private world:

> Tom ran in to Philip, who was enjoying his afternoon's holiday at the piano, in the drawing-room, picking out tunes for himself and singing them. He was supremely happy, perched like an amorphous bundle on the high stool, with his head thrown back, his eyes fixed on the opposite cornice, and his lips wide open, sending forth, with all his might, impromptu syllables to a tune of Arne's which had hit his fancy.
> "Come, Philip," said Tom, bursting in; "don't stay roaring 'là là' there; come and see old Poulter do his sword-exercise in the carriage-house!"
> (ivi, 172)

This comparison of Tom and Philip, who inlaid deep marks on Maggie's soul and character, is very similar to the tunes initially introduced in the tale yet with a twist in characters. Philip is deformed and seems unpleasant to many but owns the discipline that makes him adorable to Maggie. Tom, however, is described to have the desirable expression but lacks the sentiment and the capacity to identify passion, mercy, and tact. The narrator aims to show us Philip's soul is more compassionate and caring than Tom's.

It does not take long when Eliot highlights Maggie's adolescent hood being troubled after her father's bankruptcy that grabbed her "triple world of Reality, Books, and Waking Dreams" (ivi, 276) and led her toward a cheerless life. She remarks that now "(t)here was no music for her any more, –no piano, no harmonized voices, no delicious stringed instruments, with their passionate cries of imprisoned spirits sending a strange vibration through her frame" (ivi, 286). But amid despair, Maggie finds the German-Dutch theologian Thomas á Kempis's *The Imitations of Christ* (1480) as "a strain of solemn music" which mesmerizes her listening to its low voice telling her

> Why dost thou here gaze about, since this is not the place of thy rest? In heaven ought to be thy dwelling, and all earthly things are to be looked on as they forward thy journey thither... Forsake thyself, resign thyself, and thou shalt enjoy much inward peace.... then shall immoderate fear leave thee, and inordinate love shall die. (ivi, 290)

This alternative source could promise Maggie a safe quarter in renunciation, which would lead her to her long-desired satisfaction. She craved happiness but "knew nothing of doctrines and systems, of mysticism or quietism" (ivi, 291) that was in sharp contrast with the good society's "opera and its faëry ball-rooms;" "how should it have time or need for belief and emphasis" (ibid., 291), occupied Maggie's and Eliot's mind. Maggie did not possess the ability to manage her way among conflicting thoughts; "sweet music" would persuade her that maintaining "the bond of friendship with [Philip] was something not only innocent but good; perhaps she might help him to find contentment as she had found it" (ivi, 304). Yet, she could not relinquish the constant "chimes" warning her that "the wrong lay all in the faults and weaknesses of others, and that there was such a thing as futile sacrifice for one to the injury of another" (ibid., 304).

Philip, trying to shed light on other feasible means to reconciliation, advised Maggie that a human being is incapable of fully understanding the reason for every phenomenon or incident. He, who like Maggie, had a keen desire for music and could find solace in it, confesses to Maggie that "certain strains of music affect [him] so strangely; [he] can never hear them without their changing [his] whole attitude of mind for a time, and if the effect would last, [he] might be capable of heroisms" (ivi, 305). Indeed, music bestows him what he lacks. Eliot uses music to draw attention to the affection and the emotional bond between the two. Maggie empathizes with him and admits that "[she] used to feel so when [she] had any music," but then confesses to Philip that "[she] never ha[s] any now except the organ at church" (ibid., 305). Eliot draws a clear sharp line between the two types of music. For Philip could not only sense victorious but also undergo the magic of love through music while Maggie was left with passivity, for she believed that she had to wait patiently and suffer; her credo was to welcome her fate. Philip, like a savior, tries to enlighten her that "[she] will not always be shut up in [her] present lot; [she shouldn't] starve [her] mind in that way … It is narrow asceticism" (ivi, 306) and reminds her of her passion and desire for poetry and art and knowledge, but it is not a facile mission to convince Maggie who is more skeptical than ever. She rejects the offer by uttering "[b]ut not for me, not for me, … because I should want too much. I must wait; this life will not last long" (ibid., p. 306).

It is not implausible to consider that the musical motif which pins all the pieces in the plot in *The Mill on the Floss* together, revolves around Philip's character. From the moment we meet him, the narrative tempo tends to accelerate as Philip's bond with Maggie intensifies. Maggie tells him that she has never had enough of music and asks him to sing something to alleviate. When Philip assures Maggie that they will "be friends despite separation … always think of each other," he touches an old wound. Maggie once again compares him with Tom. She loves Philip but also loves her brother. This deep-rooted uncured lesion engulfs her and her dreams. She cannot free herself from the tentacles that have folded her wings tight, leaving her powerless to soar. She says:

> What a dear, good brother you would have been, Philip, ... You would have loved me well enough to bear with me, and forgive me everything. That was what I always longed that Tom should do. I was never satisfied with a little of anything. That is why it is better for me to do without earthly happiness altogether. I never felt that I had enough music, –I wanted more instruments playing together; I wanted voices to be fuller and deeper. Do you ever sing now, Philip?" she added abruptly, as if she had forgotten what went before.
> [...]
> "Oh, sing me something, –just one song. I may listen to that before I go ..."
> "I know," said Philip; and Maggie buried her face in her hands while he sang ..."
> "Oh no, I won't stay," said Maggie, starting up. "It will only haunt me. Let us walk, Philip. I must go home." (Eliot, 328)

Handel's *Acis and Galatea* is prevailing and seems nostalgic, for Maggie is immediately steered by listening to it. We discussed earlier that Eliot used it to presage a tragic love story and a twist in the male characters. Once more, she reminds us of the giant, the humpbacked Philip, who is the sincerest friend and devotee to Maggie to look into her feelings far more than her brother ever could, to find remedies for healing her.

Maggie has been struggling to pursue a plain passive lifestyle far different from her character and desires. Neither the available books nor the organ can promise Maggie a perpetual peace. Eliot refers to Handel's personal life and trend to shed light on Maggie's case. Handel was a musical genius whose father aspired him to pursue a career in law. However, his secret music rehearsals made him an excellent organist at the age of nine who could soon acclaim the cantor's career, but he left for Hamburg, where he experienced German opera and achieved early success for his *Almira* (1705) once he was only nineteen (Burkholder, 2014, 450). Maggie's self-imposed seclusion and her attempt to find salvation in her new books away from her favorite music taste foreshadow a similar twist in the plot.

In Book Sixth, the reader is invited into "[t]he well-furnished drawing-room, with the open grand piano" at uncle Deane's (Eliot, 363), where Maggie's cousin and her fiancé, Stephen, are talking about Maggie's arrival after her two-year career away from home. Stephen is trying to draw off the scissors and manages a repetition *da capo* (an Italian *musical* term meaning from the beginning/head). Eliot's reference to the grand opera and *da capo* provides adequate inklings for a new but rhythmic plot to happen, especially when we learn that Lucy has required Philip to join them to sing their glees. Eliot constructs her narrative like a *fugue* procedure to seat her four characters to play the love music. However, this four-voice composition is turned into a triple and then a double fugue to meet the climax when Maggie and Stephen are in the boat and spend the night together and then when Maggie and Tom face their tragic ending. The appearance of the four subjects of Stephen, Philip, Lucy, and Maggie around the piano demonstrates a new predicament centering the forbidden love.

Furthermore, Stephen indicates that if Maggie "is to banish Philip, [their only tenor, it] will be an additional bore" (Eliot, 366). To Italian Giovanni Battista Doni (1593-1647), the prime choice for the most crucial roles such as Jesus Christ would be the tenor voice since "tenors equated more to a well-adjusted and perfectly organized body than other voices" (Jocoy, n.d.). This may highlight Philip's magnitude despite his deformed appearance in this cycle. Apparently, Tom's other counterpart and Philip's rival is Stephen, who appears to be a lover of the twisted role in Handel's *Acis and Galatea*. With Haydn's sheet music for *The Creation* open, Lucy and Stephen are at the piano, and Stephen is humming *Graceful Consort* (*The Mill*, 367) but Lucy does not understand why "Philip burst into one of his invectives against *'The Creati'* the other day, [...] He says it has a sort of sugared complacency and flattering make-believe in it as if it were written for the birthday fête of a German Grand-Duke." She thinks Philip is "the fallen Adam with a soured temper" but considers themselves "Adam and Eve unfallen, in Paradise." (ibid., 367). She is so naïve and trusting to question, to ponder beyond her span of imagination. After singing their duet, Lucy requires Stephen to sing "Raphael's great song" because she believes he does "the 'heavy beasts' to perfection" (ivi, 368).

With Lucy's persuasion, Maggie reconciles with music and commences with Purcell (ivi, 383). Soon, after hearing "some fine music sung by a fine bass voice" (ivi, 384), she gains that lost fervor for music that could hasten her temperature and infuse happiness into her long-deprived soul. "Purcell's music, with its wild passion and fancy" dispersed all excuses to "stay in the recollection of that bare, lonely past" (ivi, 385). When she enthusiastically confesses to Lucy that "[she] should have no other mortal wants, if [she] could always have plenty of music. It seems to infuse strength into [her] limbs, and ideas into [her] brain [...] when [she is] filled with music," Lucy tells her that they will "have more music to-morrow evening, [...] for Stephen will bring Philip Wakem with him (ivi, 386).

Once Maggie starts feeling "less haunted by her sad memories and anticipations" (ivi, 401) and embarks on her piano rehearsals, the *da capo* comes about. Now, each one of them is conscious of the presence of the approaching phantom that threatened the transient tranquility and peace, but they longed for it to happen without daring to reflect on the matter or silently ask who can benefit from all that.

Stephen justifies a visit of Maggie by handing things from the 'Maid of Artois' for Lucy upon her absence; 'Maid of Artois' is a story based on *Manon Lescaut* (1893) which is an opera in four acts by Giacomo Puccini (1858-1924) based on *L'histoire du chevalier des Grieux et de Manon Lescaut,* a novel by Abbé Prévost, (1731) with a tragic ending. However, the version that Stephen brings for Lucy and leaves with Maggie finishes happily. So, will terminate the story of Maggie and Lucy. After this point in the novel, the number of references to music accelerates until it reaches a particular moment. Upon their reunion, Philip finds Maggie anxiously unrest, but she tells him that "[she is] too eager in [her] enjoyment of music and all luxuries ..." (*The Mill*, 414). Lucy offers Stephen to "take advantage of having Philip and [her] together" and suggests the duet in 'Masaniello' (ivi, 415). We might prefer to read it a duel rather than a duet, for there will be a struggling incident for Maggie soon, and Eliot requires us to be prepared. Daniel Auber's *La muette de Portici* (1828), is one of the earliest French grand operas and an iconic music work that led to the Belgian Revolution of 1830. French grand opera originally reflects the end of political values in the July Revolution of 1830 and the overthrown of the autocratic Bourbon King Charles X by the middle class. Hence, its plots generally focus on groups of people challenging their oppressors (Frisch, p. 83). Daniel Auber's *La muette de Portici*, written by Germain Delavigne, is an adaptation of Walter Scott's novel *Peveril of the Peak* (1822). It presents the mute sister to the fisherman Masaniello named Fenella, who has been seduced by a member of the Spanish ruling class. Masaniello later leads the Neapolitans to rise and take back the city from the Spanish rulers. However, the fates of Fenella and Masaniello are delicately interlocked as Fenella is driven to suicide by leaping into the lava of the erupting volcano (crater of Vesuvius) and his brother is murdered by his fellowmen whom he led to victory.

Likewise, Stephen is the epitome of domination and is capable of ruling minds and souls but at the same time lacks adequate insight. The disturbed Philip embraces Lucy's offer as he also finds relief in music at that critical moment when complex feelings of "love and jealousy and resignation and fierce suspicion" (*The Mill*, 416) entwined to strike him. He exclaims that singing and painting would help him soothe himself and endure the hardships of life. Nevertheless, Philip's both attitude and taste kindle Stephen's envy. He states that he has no particular facility unlike "men of great administrative capacity" and then either by mistake or intentionally turns to Maggie to tease Philip and asks her view which causes "the answering flush and epigram" saying that [she has] observed a tendency to predominance, ... and Philip at that moment devoutly hoped that she found the tendency disagreeable" (ibid., 416).

It is now the uninformed Lucy who demands something spirited for Maggie. The music tempo harmonizes the narrative pace as the foreseen disaster approaches; Stephen suggests "Let Us Take the Road" (*The Mill*, 417). It is Air 20 from *The Beggar's Opera* (1728) a ballad opera written by John Gay (1685-1732) with music arranged by Johann Christoph Pepusch, using traditional popular ballads and common tunes integrated with political satire in order to criticize the dark side of the corrupt London society, while creating a parody of the conventional Italian melodrama (See Chung's Essay, 2-17) In this specific part of the opera, drums and trumpets accompany the singers:

> Let us take the road,
> Hark, I hear the sound of coaches,
> The hour of attack approaches,
> To your arms, brave boys, and load.
> See the ball I hold!
> Let chemists toil like asses,
> Our fire their fire surpasses
> And turns all our lead to gold.   (Greenblatt, 2012, 2805)

However, while Stephen is looking for the notes for *The Beggar's*, Philip is whispering a tune practicing a melody from *La Sonnambula*[2] (1831), which recounts the story of the innocent Amina who is going to marry Elvino in a marvelous village in Switzerland. Once-engaged to Elvino, Lisa is jealous and devises a plot to foil their marriage by arranging the evidence to prove Amina's betrayal to Elvino. Consequently, he cancels the wedding and enters the church to marry Lisa instead. There, he and the other townmates notice that the sleepwalker Amina was the mysterious wandering ghost in the village, and so are confirmed that she was truly faithful to her fiancé.

In similar fashion, Philip distrusts Maggie, and his rage for Stephen rises to the utmost. He tells Lucy that what he is practicing is "from the 'Sonnambula'–'Ah! perché non posso odiarti.' I don't know the opera," but explains this is the tenor who "is telling the heroine that he shall always love her though she may forsake him…" (*The Mill*, 417). Philip is that tenor! For

---

[2] *The Sleeper* is an opera 'semiseria' in two acts by Vincenzo Bellini (1801-1835) based on a scenario for a ballet-pantomime by Eugène Scribe.
https://www.liveabout.com/la-sonnambula-synopsis-724264

the first and last time, Eliot precisely mentions her aim and tells the reader that "[it] was not quite unintentionally that Philip had wandered into this song, which might be an indirect expression to Maggie of what he could not prevail on himself to say to her directly." (ibid., 417). Then Shakespeare's most lyrical play *The Tempest* is picked as their final choice before Mrs. Tulliver disrupts them to call them to lunch. Not only its name signifies Maggie, Philip, and Stephen's inner commotion and the tumult, but also its motifs of betrayal, repentance, love, and forgiveness accord the scene.

She also practices Wagnerian 'leitmotif' "by which a certain harmony, timbre, or theme would become associated with a character or concept" (Frisch, 2013, 68). Wagner applied Beethoven's symphonic process regarding the absolute music in his compositional principles to create dramatic music which would "have the unity of the symphonic movement" called *leitmotif* or leading motive (ibid., 140). Its focus would be on "two kinds of themes: leitmotifs that recur and accrue meaning throughout the opera, and themes that are local and serve a more immediate structural role" (ivi, 145).

Needless to say, that Wagnerism and Wagner's *Tristan und Isolde* influenced numerous composers all around Europe and had profound intellectual and cultural influence. This widespread phenomenon left a remarkable impact on various forms of art and literature. In the last two decades of the 19th century, the literary Symbolist movement pursued Wagner's legacy since it was "believed that poetry and prose should not depict events, feelings, or objects in a literal way; they should be indirect, suggestive, and allusive" (ivi, 150) or as Jean Moréas defined: "all concrete appearances in this art, ... should be symbolized through sensitively perceptible traces, through secret affinities with the original ideas." Yet, what moved symbolists the most was the usage of actual musical symbols, the 'leitmotifs' (ivi, 151). In addition to this movement, French Wagnerism extremely cherished decadence whose artists supported "a retreat from the real world into what Baudelaire called "artificial paradises" of self-indulgence" (Frisch, 2013, 151).

Hans von Wolzogen (1848-1938) whose focus was on Wagnerian dramas described the trend *leitfaden* ("guideline") a technique through which order can be imposed "on a chaos of impressions." He described it as "a cluster of interrelated motifs" (Bent, 2005, p. 91) or a musical entity that locates a path within a drama, to guide the listener (ivi, 90); also, Wagner had explained it as a 'premonition' when a motif is represented in the orchestra alone before being "actualized in music, word and drama together" which would kindle listener's "desire for that actualization" (ivi, 92).

Indeed, leitmotif presents a broad perspective when meeting the territory of literature. In *The Mill on the Floss*, Eliot devises her narrative plot based on the Wagnerian leitmotif pattern whose signifier is Philip. He symbolizes pure and sincere love despite his deformity. He is the incarnation of the chaos of sensations as his physical complexion and inner soul present differently. Yet, this love motif is interwoven with other motifs and other characters, in particular, Stephen. In Book Six, chapter ten, we see the increasing pace of affection between Stephan and Maggie. At Park House, in "the long drawing-room, where the dancing went forward, under the inspiration of the grand piano" (*The Mill*, 438), Lucy, "who had laid aside her black for the first time" (ivi, 439), glittered like the doyenne of the event in her beautiful white dress. We read that Maggie refuses to dance, but soon after "the music wrought in her young limbs" (ibid., 439), she begins to blank over "her troublous life in a childlike enjoyment of that half-rustic rhythm which seems to banish pretentious etiquette." (ibid.). Agitated by the thought of Maggie and Philip's intimacy, he fosters the desire to "claim her for himself" (ivi, 440).

He finally gathers the courage to dance with Maggie and manages to find her "round the couples that were forming for the waltz" while "her eyes and cheeks were still brightened with her childlike enthusiasm in the dance" (*The Mill*, 439-440). She now seems free from any uncomforting worries of either past or future. He offers Maggie to accompany him "walk about a little" because "[everyone is] going to waltz again, [...] and the room is very warm" (*The Mill*, 440). In the conservatory, he dares to kiss Maggie's arm when she is bending to have "the large half-opened rose" but he is retarded by her. After this apogee, both Maggie and Stephen are driven into a paralysing sense of punishment: Maggie feels guilty "for the sin of allowing a moment's happiness that was treachery to Lucy, to Philip, to her own better soul" and Stephen "[leans] back against the framework of the conservatory, dizzy with the conflict of passions,–love, rage, and confused despair; despair at his want of self-mastery, and despair that he had offended Maggie" which follows another prevailing feeling: "to be by her side again and entreat forgiveness was the only thing that had the force of a motive for him," but her "bitter rage was unspent" (*The Mill*, 441-442).

Once they confess to their mutual love in chapter eleven, Stephen commences paying more frequent visits, whereas Philip turns to be a less frequent company. For a while, he suffices to the mute confessions to Maggie and to sing as an alternative "way of speaking to [her]" (ivi, 459). As she becomes more detached from Philip and her love for Stephen grows, the color of music fades away. The more Philip is pushed aside, the less music we hear. The last time we see them all together, there exists only the instrument. The piano is now silenced forever in Maggie's story. Both lovers are present, each harassed by the other struggling to find a way out of this predicament to win Maggie. Philip is more sensitive to deduce "some double intention in every word and look of Stephen's […] angry with himself all the while for this clinging suspicion, [though]." (ivi, 461). Nonetheless, seeking ways to deepen his hold on Maggie, Stephen approaches her with his back to the piano and whispers "dearest" which makes "Maggie start and blush, raise her eyes an instant toward Stephen's face, but immediately look apprehensively toward" (ibid., 461) Philip who "went home soon after in a state of hideous doubt mingled with wretched certainty. It was impossible for him now to resist the conviction that there was some mutual consciousness between Stephen and Maggie." (ibid., 461). His resentment and agitation are so ground that stop him from boating with Maggie and Lucy and asks Stephan in a letter to excuse him and "fill his place" (ivi, 462); the event which destined Maggie's end.

The ultimate reference to music appears in Philip's letter to Maggie, in which he reveals his deep compassion and devotion for her and his pure trust in her. She reads that "you have been to my affections what light, what color is to my eyes, what music is to the inward ear, you have raised a dim unrest into a vivid consciousness" (ivi, 503).

The Mill on the Floss has been studied as the closest to the autobiography of George Eliot. It is true, for the thematical elements that joined the author with her narrative; from her unapproved love to her atypical life, from her childhood conflicts with her mother and brother to the cultural clashes that she was surrounded by, she left nothing untouched to share with generations to read and to perceive her message, albeit with 'a dim unrest'. Yet, it is her musical affinity that shapes the backbone of *The Mill on the Floss* as a 19th novel written by a female novelist who was fortunate enough to be introduced to circles where word and tone were engaged the most. That Eliot employed music as a key element in her accounts is quite a known fact. That she held it into high consideration for a specific purpose should be assumed through her composition.

Bibliography

Bal, Mieke. and Van Boheemen, Christine. 2009. *Narratology: Introduction to the theory of narrative*. University of Toronto Press.

Bent, Ian. ed., 2005. *Music Analysis in the Nineteenth Century: Vol. 2. Hermeneutic Approaches*. Cambridge University Press.

Booker, M. Keith. 1996. *A practical introduction to literary theory and criticism*. Longman Publishing Group.

Burkholder, J. P., Grout, D. J., & Palisca, C. V. Eds., 2014. *A History of Western Music:* Nineth International Student Edition. WW Norton & Company.

da Sousa Correa, Delia. 2003. *George Eliot, Music and Victorian Culture.* Basingstoke: Palgrave Macmillan.

Eliot, George. 2008. *The Mill on the Floss.* Oxford University Press.

Elleström, Lars., Fusillo, Massimo., and Petricola, Mattia. "«Everything is intermedial»: A Conversation with Lars Ellestrōm", Transmediality / Intermediality / Crossmediality: Problems of Definition, Eds. H.-J. Backe, M. Fusillo, M. Lino, with the focus section Intermedial Dante: Reception, Appropriation, Metamorphosis, Eds. C. Fischer and M. Petricola, Between, X.20 (2020), www.betweenjournal.it

Frisch, Walter. 2013. *Music in the Nineteenth Century: A Norton History.* W. W. Norton & Company, Inc.

Greenblatt, Stephen, and Carol T. Christ, eds. 2012. *The Norton anthology of English literature.* Vol. 1. WW Norton & Company.

Halliwell, Michael. "British Music and Literary Context: Artistic Connections in the Long Nineteenth Century." *Musicology Australia* No. 36.1 (2014): 121-129.

Jocoy, Stacey. "The Rise of the Tenor Voice". Accessed April 2021. https://riseofthetenor.weebly.com/history.html.

Newark, Cormac. 2011. *Opera in the Novel from Balzac to Proust.* Cambridge University Press.

Nietzsche, F. W., Geuss, Raymond, and Speirs, Ronald. 2007. *The Birth of Tragedy and Other Writings.* Cambridge University Press.

Samson, Jim. 'The musical work and nineteenth-century.' *The Cambridge history of nineteenth-century music* 1 (2001): 3. https://doi.org/10.1017/CHOL9780521590174

Scher, Steven Paul. 2004. *Essays on literature and music (1967-2004).* Vol. 5. Rodopi.

Sullivan, William J. "Music and Musical Allusion in *The Mill on the Floss.*" *Criticism* 16.3 (1974): 232-246.

Wolf, Werner & Bernhart, Walter. Eds., 2007. Description in literature and other media (Vol. 2). Rodopi.

Wolf, Werner. 1999. *The musicalization of fiction: A study in the theory and history of intermediality* (Vol. 35). Rodopi.

"THE VOICE OF NETHERMERE"
(A CANTATA)

MALCOLM GRAY & ALAN WILSON

'Fig. 7: Nethermere', the area around Moorgreen Reservoir.

Introduction

In response to D.H. Lawrence's first full length novel *The White Peacock* (1911) and in the creation of their Cantata "The Voice of Nethermere" Malcolm Gray and Alan Wilson, two members of the D.H. Lawrence Society (past and present Chairman respectively) sought to develop the idea that the tragedy of the failed relationship between the two protagonists—George and Lettie— and the sadness of their final years, was the consequence of their failure to hear a voice, the Voice of Nature. This idea that nature has a 'Voice' that speaks to us is not new but for Alan and

Malcolm it took on a greater significance in this age of climate change and ecological uncertainty. In the development of the Cantata the narrative became a forceful allegory for human indifference towards our natural environment. In creating the cantata, the idea was not to impose on Lawrence's text modern theories or ideas which would contradict the sentiment of his work. The musical interpretation becomes an allegory which reflects the author's views. In this essay they seek to explain how the vision came to fruition.

***

The Christian Biblical narrative, and the history of scientific research and understanding over centuries, would seem to suggest that the creation and evolution of our environment has been a structured, ordered and balanced process. The Biblical account in Genesis chapter 1, and Psalm 104, verses 1 to 23, poetically describes this creation and its boundaries suggesting a divine creator, and while many would not accept this specific interpretation there is much evidence to demonstrate an order and balance within the natural world, an order and balance we destroy at our peril. Whatever the time scale, and the expression used in Genesis chapter 1 ("and the morning and the evening were the first day") may be more poetic than literal, much of the evidence available to scientists would suggest that the created world is a world which men may explore but which is in many ways beyond human control, and certainly awesome in terms of its scale, diversity and complexity. The cinema of the night sky gives only some indication of the number of stars, the distance across a galaxy or the mystery of the forces at play, and some would seek to describe what they saw while others would be driven to explain the spectacle. Speaking of Isaac Newton, the Romantic poet Wordsworth described Newton's statue as he saw it in Trinity College, Cambridge as:

The marble index of a mind for ever
Voyaging through strange seas of Thought, alone.
(*The Prelude*, ll. 62-62, Book 3)

Here two minds could meet: the young Romantic poet whose response to the English Lake District and the Fells he knew so well and would respond to in poetic form is confronted by the statue of Newton, the scientist and theologian, who in his time was stirred by the wonder of the world around him and sought to explore and explain the how and why of what he saw.

Scientists may acknowledge the draw of the moon's gravitational pull on our tidal flows, yet despite observation and analysis must recognise that they are very largely hopeless to seek to curb or control such a force, as Canute so clearly showed. The irony of our understanding of the 'stage' that is the backdrop of all human endeavour is that we can explore and research but we have not, as yet, created 'new' from nothing. All the evidence would suggest that we are spectators, some would say mere meddlers, in a drama which time alone unfolds. This sense of our human insignificance within the natural world is hinted at by the naturalist and historian of science Helen Macdonald in her book of essays *Vesper Flights* where she describes moments when she is confronted by 'glimpses' from the world of nature that create for her the feeling of seeing into a world which can be both too big and too small for our understanding. There is there again a voice that speaks to us.

The climax of the Biblical Genesis narrative has it that Man was created as a steward of all that was seen as 'good' within the natural environment, and the unfolding of science and history has undoubtedly given men and women very much such a role, but equally the findings of science and history would suggest that our existence on this stage and within this drama has been very recent: human history for all its fascination is a very late subject for serious study. In more recent times this study of Man's relationship to the Cosmos has all too often high-lighted the fact that this relationship has not always been positive; we have been less than benevolent stewards and more than destructive in our ignorance and greed. The relationship between the natural environment and the aims and ambitions of the human race has always been a complex one. The records of human history show men as hunters, only later settling to sow, to harvest and to graze animals. Cave paintings, pagan fertility rites and 'harvest festivals' all demonstrate that Man has relied on the bounty of the elements for food, for shelter and for clothes.

If scientists and the historians have sought to observe and analyse our natural world then often the artist, the creative craftsman, be it painter, poet, or musician, has sought to describe and communicate the awe, the beauty and 'terror' of where we live and how we relate to the mystery of our solar system. To some extent this has been the case since men first expressed this sense of inter-dependency in cave paintings and other forms of expressive and creative art. The paintings of the Etruscan artists that Lawrence loved so much are surely examples of how men have sought to illustrate what they cannot always understand. It seems only in more recent times that we have become aware that not only has the natural world a 'Voice', and a voice that speaks to us, but that we are in real danger of destroying the very environment and the resources that it provides if we choose to ignore that 'Voice'. Increasingly we are becoming aware that the natural world is a world of complex inter-related links and that at each stage there is a relationship and balance which is essential for our survival and which if broken or disrupted quickly feeds disorder and even extinction.

In his book *The Hidden Life of Trees* the German conservationist Peter Wohlleben explores in great detail the hidden life and 'language' of trees. For him there is no doubt that trees communicate, they 'talk' to each other. Wohlleben's theory is that there can be a connectivity between the trees and that they often work together to ensure the best conditions for survival, and that in some cases they actually send out 'messages' by change of leaf colour or windblown aromas which indicate alterations in their health or in their response to environmental conditions. Wohlleben and others have also suggested that particular species can 'work together' to facilitate the optimum root patterns or the most advantageous conditions for growth in terms of height and spread. Not only have scientists like Wohlleben suggested that trees can 'speak' to each other, but it has also been suggested that they work in conjunction with other organisms to achieve the best conditions to ensure species survival. A tree which is 'forested' and cut down, or areas of forest which are burnt in clearing, leave no goodness in the soil. A tree which falls and is left to rot returns much goodness to the soil and becomes the home for an army of 'creepy crawlies' which in their turn nourish birds and animals further up the chain. It is this diversity and inter-dependence which we are just beginning to appreciate. It seems there is a 'Voice' in the natural world, a voice for survival, and it is a voice that can teach us as human beings if we are sensitive and prepared to listen.[1]

Many artists and creative thinkers have expressed the idea that Nature can and does communicate. Sometimes the landscape becomes almost another 'character' within the narrative, while at other times the mind of the writer is persuaded to a mood or emotion because the very environment creates a feeling that cannot be ignored. Shakespeare has his tragic King Lear cast out upon the blasted heath where he is bombarded by a storm that is so wild that it but mirrors the tempest of his mind. In this instance the elements and the setting emphasise the emotions of the naked King, and in his madness, he draws down the worst that wind and rain can do.

---

[1] A recent magazine article based on a B.B.C. television programme highlighted the idea that trees and plants release chemicals - phytonicides - that actually communicate with human biochemistry to improve our immune system, and the Japanese have had for many years the practice of SHINRIN-YOKU, forest bathing, which is believed to reduce blood pressure - and Lawrence certainly had his favourite tree)

Shakespeare has the elements teach the poor mad King a lesson and in one sense they speak to him. He stands as 'slave' to the elements but will learn from them. And Shakespeare again, on a more positive note, in *As You Like It*—set in the Forest of Arden—has Duke Senior exclaim:

> *This our life, exempt from public haunt,*
> *Finds tongues in trees, books in the running brooks*
> *Sermons in stones, and good in everything.*
> (Act II, sc. 1)

In some cases, the 'Voice' of nature is there in the pattern of a specific episode. The most obvious examples often lie in the lines of the poet where the voice of the environment is caught by the writer and has influence on the thoughts and emotions that become expressed in the verse. Percy Shelley talked about poetry as the unacknowledged 'legislator' of the world. For him if nature had a Voice it was the poet who most often read it and who in turn communicated it within his verse. Wordsworth, the great Romantic poet and son of the Lakeland Fells, could write in book 1 of "The Prelude" (1799) Lines 412—419:

> *Thus, oft amid those fits of vulgar joy*
> *Which, through all seasons, on a child's pursuit*
> *The earth....*
> *And common face of nature spoke to me.*

The claim that Wordsworth's view is so valuable in showing his relationship to nature, and in his references to the fact that he felt it was an essential element in the saga of human development is further emphasised in the recent *Radical Wordsworth: The Poet Who Changed the World* by Jonathan Bate where the author poses the question as to why we should care about Wordsworth's responses today. He gives the answer that suggests that the poet was sensitive to the threat that human carelessness and material greed could do 'potentially irretrievable damage' to the balance that exists between human beings and the environment. If Wordsworth makes this claim in his poetry, it is a claim that is repeated in much of Lawrence's work and which we seek to emphasise in our response in 'The Voice of Nethermere' to Lawrence's first novel *The White Peacock*.

For Wordsworth the elements speak clearly, and he recalls their voice as he describes 'the noise of wood and water and the mist' that he heard out on the hills, sounds which later become associated with memories of his father's death. In the same book Wordsworth makes reference to a specific episode where undoubtedly the landscape of the native Lake-District speaks volumes to his troubled conscience. He recalls a time when he stole a small boat, what he calls 'an act of stealth/ and troubled pleasure'. In his joy as he rows across the lake he is disturbed by a 'huge peak' that seems to rise in censure of his deed and he 'returns homeward' but with 'no pleasant images'. Whatever may have been the young poet's mood as he began to row across the lake there is a 'Voice', and it is a 'Voice' that he cannot ignore. For the young poet it was a foreboding voice that seemed to rise up and rebuke his moment of joy.[2]

What the poet Wordsworth heard as a "Voice" of the natural world so another writer, R.S. Thomas, the poet and vicar of Eglwysfach parish in the remote countryside of N. Wales, caught in similar communication and described in his poem "A Blackbird Singing". For Emily Dickinson, another poet, there was also a "Voice' in the natural world that she describes as 'Harmony', it is for her what we 'hear' and what we 'know'. Within the poem "Nature" Dickinson constructs a dialogue in which she seeks to define Nature through the human senses, what we 'hear' and what we 'see', but she has a second voice define it more as "Heaven' the perfection of all things. The final two lines of her poem are almost mocking as she describes human Wisdom as 'impotent' compared to the simplicity of Nature. She suggests, we think, that sometimes we do not hear the 'Voice' of Nature because we deem it too simple and are arrogant in the confidence of our collected human 'Wisdom' and experience. As the poet, painter, historian and scientist all seem to acknowledge there is in some form a 'Voice' of nature and that it will speak to us if, as the Tiger-lily tells Alice *"There's anybody worth talking to."* [3]

The significance of music in the interpretation of human experiences

For the musician the importance of composition and the 'voice' in terms of musical interpretation became very significant. As a musician the argument regarding the 'voice' within the natural world, and the interpretation of that voice as evidenced in the Lawrence text, was a further field of new development. For me as composer the argument flowed logically that if the poet recognises a 'Voice' within the realm of the natural environment so too does the musician/ composer and this was another aspect of communication

---

[2] A detailed study of Wordsworth's relationship to the world of Nature can be found in chapter 10 'Wordsworth-Nature's Priest or Nature's Prisoner?' in the late Keith Sagar's text *Literature and the Crime Against Nature,* Chaucer Press Pub 2005.
[3] Carroll, Lewis, *Alice in Wonderland,* Ch 2 *'The Garden of Live Flowers'*.

that became significant as we looked at how we might learn from the wisdom of the created world. This was the emphasis that I as a composer sought to emphasise, drawing on some of the ways in which composers have responded to the sound of nature. There is often for them a chance to create a bespoke aural picture, which is generally abstract, and this has then been transformed through the imagination to in turn create a personal tapestry, a tapestry which is often associated with a particular experience or event. Clever and creative use of 'colour', whether it be from the orchestra, choral groups or even a solo instrument can strongly evoke such memories and feelings. One of the best examples is Mendelssohn's Hebrides Overture *(Fingal's Cave)* A personal visit to the cave can readily emphasis what Mendelssohn was inten*ding to describe. The sea is a great source of 'voices.'* Debussy in *"La mer"* captures the waves moving up and down in a particular and powerful rolling way while Beethoven has a stirring storm scene in his *Pastoral Symphony,* followed by utter tranquility. There is even the fragrant smell of rain in the composer's ensuing movement after the storm. In terms of the 'voice' of birdsong it is probably Olivier Messiaen who is the expert in that he recorded such tunes and then reproduced them in his own musical style.

Like poetry it is not just the Romantic or impressionist composers who catch the 'voice'. Vivaldi in his "Four seasons" depicts very vividly the dramatic changes of climate in these concertos, and we learn again of the presence of order and structure in the rhythm of the seasons, a rhythm and order the rural folk of Nethermere would surely recognise, a rhythm which, to some extent, controlled their lives. Several baroque composers (like the keyboard writers Daquin and Francois Couperin) have imitated birdsong and animal noises to great effect and, again, these would be recognised by Lawrence and by his Nethermere folk.

Alan Wilson

So, there is discussion about how and what the world of our environment has to say to us. The Jewish/ Christian theology has a supreme and eternal creator who plans and sustains all that we see around us, there is no element of chance or accident. The purpose of such a creation, the perfect Garden of Eden, by a Personal God was that God and Man might share communion and walk together. Within such a doctrine, the creation directly speaks of the glory of God, as the poet Gerard Manley Hopkins describes it: *"The world is charged with the grandeur of God"* ('God's Glory').

For the secular thinker, or the atheist, there is no God involved and the process of creation is one much more likely founded on the Darwinian theory, the evolution by natural selection to ensure survival. Ironically in his *On the Origin of Species* Darwin did not seek to explain the origin of life, and in a letter to Joseph Hooker in 1863 he affirmed, "*It is mere rubbish*" to think about the origins of life. For the Christian, as for the 'religious' poet, and Lawrence was very much a 'religious writer', there is an acceptance that there is a creative force. Lawrence would call it "*a great urge that had not yet found a body*" but an urge that would come to pass with "*ncarnation.*" Lawrence, like Emily Dickinson, rejected much of the fundamental theology of the Christian faith - and Lawrence undoubtedly read Darwin - but he did recognise that "*where sanity is/ there God is,*" though it may not be the God of Genesis chapter 1 or the opening of John's Gospel. In the same way Dickinson in her "Murmur of a Bee" poem could write "*Take care-for God is here*" (and both give '*God*' an upper case). Dickinson sees the world of nature with awe, almost an old sense of a religious experience.

If the Christian, the 'religious' writer and the atheist see different forces behind the act of creation, and different processes involved in the development and sustaining of the natural environment still there seems to be a recognition that that environment has an order, a structure, diversity and an inter-dependence. The forces at work appear to work together and work together for the benefit and survival of all. For the Christian this is hinted at as a recognition of the 'hand of God' *(See Psalm 104. verses 5—30*, probably a *Psalm of King David)* who imposed 'boundaries' and caused 'the grass to grow'. Here the psalmist speaks of 'He' and 'You' implying a personal God. In his text, *The Hidden Life of Trees* (Chapter 18), Peter Wolleben describes in terms of the eco-system the way in which trees act as a 'water pump'. In a detailed analysis, he explains how the forests of the northern hemisphere influence climate change and 'manage' water even in this vast and complex natural cycle, and he also refers to the habitat stability enjoyed by the freshwater snail (a creature some 0.08 inches long), which is crucial for its existence and survival. He recognises that there is an inter-dependence and balance that ecologists are warning we damage at our cost…and that the health and survival of the freshwater snail is integral to that balance and is an indicator of change and disruption that may occur with time.

For the poet, theologian, ecologist, or scientist to acknowledge that nature has lessons to teach us is perhaps understandable, but that the novelist may explore such truths is less easy to accept. All too often for the novelist sufficiency may remain in an exploration of the narrative, the events, the characters and the relationships, played out across the stage which may be described in more or less detail, but which is, in the end, frequently only a backdrop. Within these parameters some novelists may explore historical events, theological truths or themes and issues beyond the behaviour of the main characters. Thomas Hardy is one example of a novelist for whom the back-drop of the natural world becomes significant in the development of the narrative and the characters, and this is explored in detail in Joanna Cullen Brown's study *Let Me Enjoy the Earth; Thomas Hardy and Nature,* but then, like Lawrence, Hardy is both poet and novelist.[4] In her text *Spirit of Place: Artists Writers and the British Landscape* Susan Owens explores how the creative painter and writer is affected by our landscape in the process of describing/ reproducing the image of that landscape and Lawrence, of course, does the same.[5]

Lawrence's novels *The Rainbow* (1915) and *Women in Love* (1920), first conceived of as "The Sisters, is on one level a family history, a saga of three generations of the Brangwens and their relationship to the land, but through this narrative Lawrence describes the decline of a way of life and the emergence of new social patterns. Very cleverly Lawrence makes a wider social comment and asks us as the reader to learn some lessons from his comment. What is learned at the beginning of the first novel about Tom is that he was reluctant to go to school and 'glad to get back to the farm' and went about farm work 'gladly'. Tom is comfortable on the land and his close companions are the folk around the Marsh. (In the same way George in *The White Peacock* lives easily with the rural folk of Nethermere. It is change that is to be his downfall. Within *The Rainbow* social change is recorded and explored, the landscape and backdrop used by Lawrence almost as a stage on which events are set, but the novel moves from Marsh Farm 'where the Erewash twisted sluggishly' and ends in the snow of the Alps. In the drama of this unfolding almost Biblical saga Lawrence reflects on the fragmentation of the simple relationship that Tom had with the land, and it ends with a death on the frozen Alps. Integral to the narrative of the family history is more than a hint of a lesson, a warning that not all progress, all steps to change and 'modernity', come without cost and social consequences. If Lawrence expounds this idea in his novels *The Rainbow* and *Women in Love,* it is almost as if he has rehearsed it in his first full length novel *The White Peacock*. The novel, often criticised for a weakness in form and structure and the work of a young 'first-time' writer, records a narrative. As well as the narrative the novel also contains very many beautiful descriptions of the area of 'Nethermere,' the area around Moorgreen

---

[4] Pub by W.H. Allen and Co 1990.
[5] Pub Thames and Hudson 2020.

Reservoir that Lawrence knew so well from his walks and his visits to Haggs Farm.

The White Peacock tells the sad story of a failure in a potential relationship, but it was the beauty of the descriptions of the landscape and the importance of the community, which Lawrence describes with a sensitivity that emphasises the tragedy for the protagonists, that first drew our attention to the text and then to the possibility of creating a cantata. The cantata is very much based on aspects of the Lawrence novel and what we have tried to do in creating a musical adaptation is to use music to emphasise the tragedy of materialism, a tragedy which can easily envelope more than just the location and characters which Lawrence used in his text. The cantata is an attempt to bring together the elements of the human social cycle and the significance of the natural environment. Primarily the cantata does not just set the novel to music, but it takes the liberty of using the landscape as a backdrop for a musical exploration of the complexity and the richness of the relationship between the characters and the natural world, and equally importantly to ask questions about the wider issues of how we as human beings can live in such a way that we enrich rather than destroy the complex unity of our human environment. The Prologue seeks to explain the setting of the adaptation 'the beautiful and bountiful Garden of Eden' which is the Nethermere of Lawrence's setting for his novel.

Prologue

This is an allegorical tale of two innocent souls, 'children of the earth'—a sort of modern-day Adam and Eve.
George and Lettie dwell among the folk of Nethermere, a location described in some ways as a bountiful 'Garden of Eden' where choruses of birds sing in rich harmony and plants engage in rhythmic movements and pattens, displaying an array of contrasting colours and shapes. in some ways it is unpolluted where nature and man are all at one in such tender communion. As time goes on, we see this mutual trust being broken, both in terms of the damage to the environment through exploitation and greed, and in the gradual deterioration of human trust within a relationship.

The Nethermere of the tale is home to a tight community of fundamentally rural folk before industrial 'progress' comes to dominate. In this story there are only two human characters, George and Lettie, alongside the voice of nature which plays a pivotal, topographical, and progressive role, a voice which will speak to George in a powerful dream.

Our starting point is in this beautiful garden 'where lovers unite and birds sing—let us rejoice, rejoice for this is our land of Eden.

Alan Wilson

In creating the cantata, we agreed that Nature had a 'Voice' and could speak wisdom if we would but listen. This is not a Pantheistic view, and Lawrence was not a Pantheist…God is not a tree and did not exist in the 'rocky steep' of Wordsworth's buttress that so scared him when he stole the 'elfin pinnace', but we would agree with Alice in her Wonderland that the flowers can speak if we would but listen. The cantata includes clear evidence in the quotations used that Lawrence was a master of language even at a young age, and that he knew and understood the diversity and richness of the rural landscape. It also emphasises the harmony and unity that we believe Lawrence felt existed in the relationship of a Man with the created world, and the danger that creeping materialism might pose if that harmony was broken. In the cantata a fundamental question seemed to arise, and it was one that Lawrence came back to time and again '*How do we fit into the created world and how can we work with it and learn from it before it is destroyed?*'

In Lawrence's text Lettie achieves the new and higher social status that she desired, but she loses her soul, and George is broken in the tragedy of their failed relationship. It seems that Lettie has a vision of new and better things. She becomes less than satisfied with the simplicity of the lifestyle of the simple rural folk of Nethermere. She has ambition and takes almost the Rousseau/Romantic path, she feels herself restricted by the chains that bind her quest for freedom, she is resolved to follow the passions of her inner soul (If a reasonable interpretation of Rousseau's statement that men are born free but everywhere in chains can be accepted then it can be argued that Lettie simply sought a new 'freedom'. For Rousseau "freedom" is most comprehensively achieved by the individual who is free to be free, to make the choices of their passions). In many respects this desire by the women to look out from the land to the world beyond, to look for better things, is hinted at the very beginning of *The Rainbow*: *"The women were different"* and 'wanted *'another form of life'*. By contrast it *was enough for the men that the earth heaved"*. In *The White Peacock* George seems almost content and lacks determination and the resolution to express his love for Lettie, he assumes that she knew it. In the cantata this is expressed in her words and then in the Lament "Vanities of Vanities":

Lettie:

I am so trapped within this world of rural folk with rustic minds who see no further than the plough, the harvest sheaves and routine days. My dreams are more of other worlds and other ways, of moving out to finer things. Yes, I WILL taste of my desires, my heart is set on richer gems, on laughter and on bigger barns, of other men with higher goals whose wealth will feed the joys I'm owed; new pleasures lie beyond I know and I WILL have my dues

Song: 'Vanity of Vanities'

Oh, what piece of art I am
As David to the lesser men,
By subtle use, aspiring goals,
I'm clothed with pride in all I hold,
In finest silk, ambition's gold
With Faustus' mid-night soul
Stand I

Oh, vanity of vanities,
There's nothing new beneath the Sun
What is to gain by all our toil
We cast our bread upon life's sea
And work to gain our soul's desires,

"The Voice of Nethermere" (A Cantata)

A striving after wind.

I'm clothed with pride in all I hold
In finest silk, ambition's gold
With Faustus' mid-night soul
    Stand I
    Stand I.

Malcolm Gray / Alan Wilson

In the cantata George is given a 'dream' where the song of the flowers, 'The Voice of the Plants', speaks to him.
The plants cry out:

O simple man do not stand still on passion's path but take with ardour in your stride the road your heart would set. The lily and the larkspur speak, go listen to the daffodils whose blazing trumpets echo forth giving fresh zeal to life and love with wisdom on the air.

Malcolm Gray/ Alan Wilson[6]

In the cantata George knows his own mind and what he assumes will happen, what he wants, but it is his lethargy which finally destroys him and by the time he comes to admit his love to Lettie (*"But you knew I loved you"*) it is too late. Lettie can hold out her hand and show him her new ring and George is but 'past tense'. Lettie achieves new status and much finery but by the end of the novel she has lost her soul. Some would argue that Lettie is the 'Eve' of the Lawrence text. She is guilty of 'ambition', and it was ambition that Milton described as the deadly sin that saw Satan fall from the courts of heaven. But Lawrence is no misogynist. If Lettie's ambition mars the harmony of this rural setting George's 'Sloth' further feeds the ultimate tragedy.

In chapter VI of Lawrence's novel, a chapter titled 'Pisgah', we see something of the later state of both George and Lettie. Lettie returns to live at Eberwich. She is described as being a good wife and content, but prone to periods of 'torpor', sometimes she feels 'blue', depressed. Her husband is affectionate when he is at home but forgets her when he is busy, as he

---

[6] The concept of a 'dream' in English Lit is not new. In the recent translation of the poem "Pearl" —-pub 2016 by Simon Armitage…a translation of a Middle English poem originally written by an anonymous author; a mourning father falls into a deep sleep. In a dream he is taken to the gates of heaven where he meets again the 'Perle' which is in fact his child. The father is lulled to sleep not by the 'Voice' of Nature but by the 'intoxicating scent of the plants.' Simon Armitage talks in his introduction of the dream vision as being a 'method of religious instruction'. It teaches a lesson.

often is as a mine owner, County Councilor, and member of the Conservative Association. George too in his turn is a man who is unsettled. After his rejection he marries another, becomes involved with the socialists and drinks much. The farm is neglected, and he spends more and more time with his horses and drinking. He too is 'downcast'. Lawrence describes him beautifully as a 'rotten tree'. The symbolism is very powerful. He is a man apart. Lawrence has used the beauty of the 'Nethermere' landscape to enhance the narrative and it is partly the simplicity of the rural setting and the harmony that exists between the farming folk and the bounty of the land that emphasises the tragedy of the failure of the relationship between George and Lettie. The tragedy of the tale, and it is very much a tragedy, is that that harmony is broken by the encroachment of materialism, over ambition, and apathy. The combination of the account of the relationship that might have developed between George and Lettie and the many examples of Lawrence's beautifully crafted descriptions of the landscape have provided a rich source for the musical interpretation of Lawrence's tale. In the interpretation of the tale, we have given George a tragic lament.

George's lament

Sing dark lament and welcome death
The cistern and the well are dry
Come mountain fall
And travail end
My soul must yield to fiery Hell
The seasons' hopes have run their course
My earthly days are done.

Sing dark lament and welcome death
The sail is set, dark oceans call
Cry out, cry out
In anguish wail
The tide of time runs surely on
Flows fast to our oblivion
And earthly loves grown cold.

Sing dark lament and welcome death,
Yet mist the glass once more faint breath,
Alas the silver cord is cut
The windows of the mind are shut
The soul at last takes flight to home
Its harrowing in Hell.

Malcolm Gray/ Alan Wilson.

"The Voice of Nethermere" (A Cantata)

Developing the idea of Lawrence's narrative and creating a cantata posed a number of interesting problems. In terms of the specific use of music the composer Alan Wilson sought to create a piece of work that transcended the facts of the story and moved on to show how an interpretation involving music and the spoken word could emphasise a wider tragedy in the text.

Alan Wilson

Setting Lawrence's words to music is no mean task and I have always shied away from it, as I frequently find that the spoken words themselves create their own musical sound. Lawrence is so brilliant at portraying the sonority and colour of words and I believe that is the musical influence he inherited. However, there are other ways of incorporating music, and that is in using it in the background in a 'Wagnerian' way using 'leitmotifs'. This is where the abstract nature of music can play a great role as it can be very suggestive of mood and even identify itself with a 'character'—in this cantata representing the 'Voice' of nature, portrayed by the cello (and also taken up by the violin), playing an important role in the early pastoral scene, but progressing into more sinister and bruising tragic tones at the end of the work. Obviously, other musical styles and techniques are incorporated into the cantata and that is where Malcolm and I have worked very closely together using arias, choruses and recitatives. Always when we have used the actual words of Lawrence these have remained unchanged. Music has a great power of suggesting mood just as it is used in contemporary films and drama. A good example of this is in the dream sequence where the style of music takes on an 'impressionistic' tone not unlike Debussy.

The most powerful way music is incorporated into this work, though, has to be in the closing chorus. Along with word play, such as *"black crows"* the whole choral setting takes on a dark, threatening and sinister tone, portraying the tragedy of the inevitable downfall of the whole system. But the last word comes from the cello in a heartbreaking unaccompanied lament with its cries plunging deep into one's inner soul, marking that ultimate tragedy, despair and desolation. It was probably in the composition and creation of the final chorus and, especially in the tragic melancholic tones of the unaccompanied cello that the voice of 'music' took on real power. Here the tragedy of Lawrence's narrative of an unfulfilled romance and the brokenness of his two main characters becomes a part of a wider scenario of despair and depression. Music has that way of getting into an emotive depth of the imagination, subsequently taking over where even words are inadequate.

The point of the cantata was to pose the question of how we might work with the natural world to sustain it rather than destroy it. The cantata uses Lawrence's text as a tool. Lawrence the novelist created a romantic narrative while Lawrence the poet set that narrative in a simple environment where the beauty of the landscape and the richness and diversity of the flora and fauna are described in such a way that the significance of the natural world is emphasised by the tragic consequences when the protagonists seek to move out and ignore the harmony and communication of that world. Lettie and George suffer directly, the inter-connection between the characters and their rural setting is fractured. The final chorus of the cantata "Oh Do Not Weep Ye Sons of God" mourns the loss of a social order which is passing. The line "The Love, the labour and the land" suggests a unity which has 'beauty' and has 'rich reward' but 'black crows' and 'brooding clouds' suggest a threat that all this can be destroyed.

Final Chorus: "Oh Do Not Weep Ye Sons of God"

"Oh do not weep ye sons of God
For early days that yielded much,
For Eden's bounty, fruitful store,
Where murmurs of the mill race run
And music of the tumbling brook
Gave reason for the human hymn
As men and earth were one.

So what is gone is lost, is passed;
The love, the labour and the land
That gave so much with early hope
With travail and with rich reward,
In beauty each to each gave birth,
But with the run of cruel time
Life's river bed seems dry.
Oh do not weep ye sons of God
Though black crows swirl o'er waving wheat
Where brooding clouds and landscape meet,
Where corn is cut and sheaves are stacked
Where beauty and the blackened pit
Are backdrop to the toil of men
Where hell and hope are timeless knit
While sorrows' tears still flow.

In the end Lettie, George, Nethermere - all are tarnished and conveyed to an abyss of their own hell.

And the allegory ?
Materialism ?
Climate change ?
Extinction ?
"Where tears of sorrow flow" ?
Hope ? Maybe ?

Bibliography

Author Anon. Translation Armitage, Simon 2016 "Pearl" London: Faber and Faber.
The Bible, New International Version. June 1978. Revised 1983. International Bible Society. Colorado Springs U.S.A.
Bate, Jonathan. 2020. *Radical Wordsworth; The Poet Who Changed the World* London: Publ. William Collins.
Brown, Joanna Cullen. 1990. *Let Me Enjoy the Earth; Thomas Hardy and Nature*. London: W. H. Allen and Co.
Carroll, Lewis. 1865. *Alice in Wonderland*. London: MacMillan.
Dickinson, Emily. 2006. *Selected Poems* Oxford: Oxford University Press.
Lawrence, D. H. 1911. *The White Peacock* U.S.A and London Duffield in U.S.A Heinemann in London. Cambridge Edition of the Works of D.H. Lawrence Pub 1983.
Lawrence, David Herbert 1915. *The Rainbow*. London Secker RE- Pub "The Rainbow" 1926. Cambridge: Cambridge University Press. 1989.
Lawrence, David Herbert 1913 -1921 "Women in Love" Proofs - American Ed. 1920 British Ed. 1921. Cambridge Edition of the Works of D.H. Lawrence Pub 1998.
Macdonald, Helen. 2020. *Vesper Flights*. London: Jonathan Cape.
Owens, Susan. 2020. London *Spirit of Place; Artists, Writers and the British Landscape*. London: Thames and Hudson.
Sagar, Keith. 2005. *Literature and the Crime Against Nature*. London: Chaucer Press.
Shakespeare, William. [1623] 1975. *As you like it*. Ed. Agnes Latham. London: Arden Shakespeare.
Thomas, R.S. 1993. *Collected Poems 1945—1990*. London: J. M. Dent — Paperback Phoenix/ Orion 2000.
Wohlleben, Peter. 2015. Munich *The Hidden Life of Trees*. Pub. Ludwig Verlag / Random House. English translation 2016 by Jane Billinghurst
Wordsworth, William. 1799 version London "The Prelude." London: Penguin Classics.
Magazine Article, BBC Countryfile Magazine Issue 173 February 2021.

'PIANO': SWINGING BETWEEN PAST AND PRESENT

NICK CERAMELLA

The insidious mastery of song betrays me back.
(D. H. Lawrence, 'Piano')

Just knowing the dream, just knowing the song / the tune
Will hold fast in your mem'ry […]

(Opening words of Edvard Grieg's song cycle *Haugtussa*)

Fig. 8: Piano at the Lawrences' in Garden Road 57, the Breach, Eastwood (1887-91).

Introduction

D. H. Lawrence (1885-1930) is hardly known as a music lover mainly because critics have paid very little attention to his enthusiasm for music until quite recently. Therefore, perhaps it is worth noting that Lawrence's great-grandfather, from his mother's side, John Newton (1802-1886), was a choirmaster and organist at the newly established Beeston Chapel, near Nottingham. As early as 1908, when he was a young teacher at Croydon, he wrote a letter to Blanche Jennings, revealing how important music was to him:

> I love music. I have been to two or three fine orchestral concerts here. At one I heard Grieg's *Peer Gynt* – it is very fascinating, if not profound. Surely you know Wagner's operas – *Tannhäuser* and *Lohengrin*. [...]
> (Lawrence, 1979, 99)

Grieg and Wagner had a great influence on Lawrence as far as music, singing, and feelings concerned. I will develop this essay starting from the latter, with a citation by John Worthen, one of Lawrence's leading biographers, who says:

> Wagner's operas successfully brought her [Helen Corke] and Lawrence together. [...] Croydon London had given him far more chance for hearing music and going to opera than Nottingham had; and in October 1909 he had been able to extend his knowledge of Wagner by going to see *Tristan und Isolde* at the Great Theatre, Croydon. [...]
> She passed on her enthusiasm to Lawrence when they began to see each other during the autumn and winter of 1909; he certainly learned about Siegmund and Sieglinde from her. [...]
> (Worthen, 1991, 255)

Helen Corke was Lawrence's fiancée, a lively, cultural stimulus to him. In 1909, she declares that Lawrence's "only experience of Wagner's music had been a performance, in Nottingham theatre, of *Tannhäuser*, when he reacted against the stridency of the Venusberg music' (*DHL Review*, vii, 1974, 231-2). In another article, "D. H. Lawrence as I saw him," she recalls going together to the opera when Lawrence was living in Croydon: "Once we attended a performance of Strauss' *Electra* at the Opera House, climbing endless stairs and sitting on the stone parapet of the gallery steps" (Corke, 1960, 12). (Regarding this episode see also the poem 'After the Opera' (*P 1*, 39). There is no trace of Wagner in Lawrence's first novel *The White Peacock* (1911), which drew on Bizet's *Carmen* instead, and was commended by Nietzsche as 'opposite of

Wagner'. It is from his second novel, *The Trespasser* (1912) that, due to Helen's influence, allusions to the German composer's operas began to appear quite regularly. The protagonist of this novel, a young orchestral violinist, bears the Wagnerian name, Siegmund, which is what she said she called her lover, the pianist H. B. Macartney during the performance of Wagner's *Die Walküre* (*The Valkyrie*, 1870), and he reciprocated her Sieglinde. Two names corresponding to those of the lovers in Wagner's opera. Most importantly, according to Elizabeth Mansfield, in her Introduction to *The Trespasser* says that

> Some things in *The Trespasser* are more deeply Wagnerian than the allusions, which are merely the exchange of references between cultured persons. Siegmund's remark on pp. 98-9 shows a real sense of Wagner's method: 'You seem to have knot all things in a piece for me. Things are not separate: they are all in a symphony. They go moving on and on. You are the motive in everything.' Some of the structural symbolism is also Wagnerian: for instance, the cluster of images (the equivalent of musical motives) [...] which culminates in the thematic and tonal transformation [...] This kind of associated imagery is most developed in the early pages of *The Rainbow*, which are in that respect the most Wagnerian in Lawrence. (Lawrence, 1981, 326-7)

But this is not a one-off reference to Wagner since he appears not only in *The Rainbow* (1915), but also in *Women in Love*, when Ursula says to Gudrun that Gerald looks "like a Nibelung" (Lawrence 1989, 47) while he is swimming in the lake, Willey Water. Actually, according to the Teutonic saga, the name Gudrun, too, has a connection with the daughter of the Nibelung king, Siegfried. Gerald recalls a Wagnerian sort of character, a violent and cruel modern 'warrior,' who, in his dominant position of industrial magnate, has no respect either for people or nature. By contrast, his close friend Birkin is a sensitive and thoughtful man, symbolising a world of serenity and peace, and love for life. He detests modern England which he thinks has been ruined by a false faith in technological progress. Hence, in a sense, and for the purposes of this essay, it must be underlined that Birkin represents the anti-Wagnerian change in Lawrence's attitude to music, when, in a letter to Francis Brett Young of 6 May 1920, he showed his irritation after attending a cello concert at the Greek Theatre in Taormina: 'I can't stand this twisting, squirming, whining modern music. I hated Bach and Shubert and Wagner and Brahms and all the lot of them, [...]' (*L 3*, 514). Even if, as Mark Kinkead-Weekes asserts, Lawrence was irritated for other personal reasons than that, it is true that in those days there was a growing reaction to the predominant high, classical, orchestral music, which had an impact on shaping fiction through the 20th century. (Kinkead-Weekes 1996, 584). In any case, due to the radical socio-political changes, many composers, instead of building on the music of past generations, created new styles and forms. But Lawrence, according to his friend, the novelist Aldous Huxley, among others, after writing *Aaron's Rod*, as he usually did through his life, went his own way and revived an interest in popular songs. We may say that that happened also under the influence of his London friends, the musicians Cecil Gray and Philip Heseltine, who encouraged him to rejoice in Irish and Scottish folk songs. A case in point of how much Lawrence was fascinated by popular music is represented by the essay 'The Dance' in *Twilight in Italy* (1916). He and Frieda, on leaving Gargnano, stopped at the Capellis' in the hamlet of San Gaudenzio, up in the nearby mountain, from 1 to 11 April 1913. Here Lawrence describes a typical evening there:

> Sometimes we had a dance. Then, for the wine to drink, three men came with mandolines and guitars, and sat in a corner playing their rapid tunes, while all danced in the dusty brick floor of the little parlour. [...]
> The three musicians, in their black hats and their cloaks, sat obscurely in the corner, making a music that came quicker and quicker, making a dance that grew swifter and more intense, more subtle, the men seeming to fly and to implicate other strange, inter-rhythmic dance into the women, the women drifting and palpitating as if their souls shook, and resounded to a breeze that was subtly rushing upon them, through them; the men worked their feet, their thighs swifter, more vividly, the music came to almost an intolerable climax, there was a moment when the dance passed into a possession, the men caught up the women and swung them from the earth, leapt with them for a second, and then the next phase of the dance had begun, slower again, more subtly interwoven. (Lawrence, 1994, 167-168)

That experience was a most revealing one as far as the power of music goes. Elgin W. Mellown wrote a most interesting article, touching on both the impact music had on shaping the social standing of some of Lawrence's characters, and about Lawrence's personal rejection of classical music in favour of folk tunes and country life.

> The references to music and theatrical dance in the early novels and letters of D. H. Lawrence serve several important functions. In his personal letters, he appears to use them to reinforce the social positions which he wanted to claim for himself, while in his early novels he often established the social standings of his characters through such references. Some of these musical allusions suggest that at the beginning of his career his attitudes to music may have been influenced by E. M. Foster's novels; but in 1922, in *Aaron's Rod*, Lawrence deliberately turned away not only from

the older novelist's aesthetic beliefs but also from Western, classical music in general, and after that date he rarely ever referred to it in his fiction.
(Mellown, 1997, 49-60)

In fact, Lawrence, as hinted at above, turned his back to western classical music after *Aaron's Rod* (1922) in which the protagonist is a classical flute player and there are references to attending operas by Verdi (Lawrence 1988, 88), Rimsky-Korsakov (Ibid., 136) and Mussorgsky (id.) at Covent Garden, courtesy of Lady Cynthia Asquith who gave the Lawrences a box for the 1917 season. Quite interestingly, this recalls a similar experience at the local Gargano theatre in 1912-13 (see Ceramella 2016, 103-5). As we will see below, on discussing *Women in Love,* such connections showed Lawrence how important they were to find a place in high society and enjoy the advantages coming with them. Indeed, we know that he struggled all his life to fulfill his personal wish to climb the social ladder. Even a name, he thought, could help you do that. (See the novel *Sons and Lovers* in which the use of a French surname, Morel, is meant to give a posh touch to the protagonist family, the author's in the reality.)

Most important, Lawrence's career falls within a period that saw great changes in literature, music, and the visual arts; this made him particularly aware of living in an age of deep crisis which every artist had the responsibility to address. All that pertained to *modernism* and had a strong impact on literature, philosophy, sciences, and even theology. Within certain limits, we can say that Lawrence's production after the Georgian period is modernist in subject matter, although he is not a modernist like Virginia Woolf, James Joyce, T. S. Eliot, or Ezra Pound. However, Anthony Burgess (1917-1993), a modern musician, critic and writer, who knew Lawrence well, maintained that, just like James Joyce, Lawrence enjoyed the musicality of the language; therefore, he could be considered not far from the trend of musical modernism. But, there again, we should bear in mind that Lawrence, like Lawrence, can hardly ever be pinned down to a particular set of beliefs. (See ref. to Burgess, in Intro, lxvii-lxviii).

He was very skeptical of the modernist movement mainly because he felt that experiment mattered more than actual living to many of his contemporaries, while he was very interested in exploring in depth human experience and sought a language to express sensations that often remain beneath the level of articulation. That is where Lawrence's conception of Time plays an important role, which is certainly one of the aspects that modernity brought with it and got him to argue for a radical re-imagining of Time as non-diachronic. Here is how he presented that in *Apocalypse*:

To appreciate the pagan manner of thought we have to drop our manner of on-and-on-and-on, from start to finish, and allow the mind to move in cycles, or to flit here and there over a cluster of images. Our idea of time as a continuity in an eternal straight line has crippled our consciousness cruelly. The pagan conception of time as moving in cycles is much freer, it allows movement upwards and downwards, and allows for a complete change of state of mind, at any moment. One cycle finished, we can drop or rise to another level, and be in a new world at once. But by our time-continuum method, we have to trail wearily on over another ridge. (Lawrence, 2002, 96-97)

Regarding Edvard Grieg (1843-1907) and Arne Garborg (1851-1924), in a letter to Grace Crawford, dated 1910, Lawrence confirms that the two Norwegian artists kept spinning round his mind, "I spend my time humming Grieg and thinking of 'Arne" (ivi, 174). He was fascinated by Grieg's adaptation to music as a song cycle for soprano and piano of Arne's novel in verse *Haugtussa* (1895), consisting of seventy-one epic poems, which is known with the same title, or *The Mountain Maid* (1898).

Much later in his life, their partnership must have intrigued Lawrence and coaxed him to create a musical setting of his play *David* (1926), although he was not a professional musician. First, he composed two songs which were rejected when he managed to have the play put on stage in 1927, but the director, Robert Atkins substituted them with a composition by Richard Austin. Nonetheless, Lawrence composed ten songs altogether, which did not appear in print until the Cambridge University Press edition of *The Plays* in 1999, whereas his score was not performed until 1996 at the Sixth International D. H. Lawrence Conference held at the University of Nottingham. It took the masterly arrangement of Bethan Jones to make Lawrence's music presentable. Here is a comment that this fine musician and Lawrence critic made to stress how hard the job she undertook was:

Lawrence was not an accomplished musical composer and the scoring for the *David* music is in places problematic. He wrote most of the music for scene 15 in C minor, with the vocal line ranging over three octaves, which is unrealistic given the usual range of the human voice. [...] The scoring suggests, in fact, that he was deliberately forcing the voice to the extremes in places, with the intention of creating a sound that was strained and rough; ecstatic and rhapsodic. (Jones, 2012, 163)

Although this quotation shows that Lawrence was far from being a professional musician, his intellectual curiosity and love for music no doubt permeates his works. There are clear signs of that even in the drafts of some of his earliest works, such as the poem 'Piano' (1908), on which this essay is based. Lawrence was really ahead of times since he was already experimenting on the connection between music and words, which led him to try new literary forms. Thus, he anticipated the modernist forthcoming practice of mixing different arts as is also confirmed in his first essay "Art and the Individual" (1908) in which, on referring to Tolstoy, he writes:

> But when the lad told the tale, the words were only as the simple melody running clear through the gestures; and the piece; the art was more likely to be in the tones, the gestures; and the value of song is its music, and its power to call up new pictures; and the value, the beauty of the tale or the song lies in the emotion which follows the music of the tones, the harmony of looks and gesture, the quivering feelings for which there are no words, […] (Lawrence, 1985, 140)

That is when Lawrence began to write of "Art" as "absolute music," a sign of stylistic maturity that he reached in *The Rainbow* (1915) and *Women in Love* (1920). Especially on writing the latter, Lawrence, like other writers in his time, uses music to outline the social and cultural standing of his characters. He was aware that to achieve that aim one needed to acquire culture by going to concerts, theatre, ballets, or, more practically, by buying a painting, or a piano. He learnt that from his mother who was aware that attaining a higher social marker, such as owing a piano in their modest home, was going to help to make that social leap forward and stress the difference in the community. In *Women in Love*, when Birkin says sarcastically to Gerald Crich that a collier would work very hard "to have a pianoforte in his parlor" (Lawrence, 1989, 55), the latter retorted:

> "Don't you think the collier's *pianoforte*, as you call it, is a symbol for something very real, a real desire for something higher in the collier's life?"
> "Higher!" cried Birkin. "Yes. Amazing heights of upright grandeur. It makes him so much higher in his neighbouring colliers' eyes. He sees himself reflected in the neighbouring opinion, like in a Brocken mist, several feet taller on the strength of the pianoforte, and he is satisfied. […]" (ibid.)

This quotation, as we will see, is quite telling as it represents the cultural background to the poem 'Piano,' which is the very focus of this essay. Moreover, in studying Lawrence's writings, it is important to take into consideration not only his personal circumstances, but also the time and place in which he wrote them. He reflected his thoughts and emotions in them as his beliefs changed and developed, including his contradictive, but lifelong attempt, to change his social status.

'Piano'

Now, through a close analysis of the poem 'Piano,' I will try to show how this contrast is reflected in the swinging of time between present and past as mirrors of Lawrence's childhood and adulthood. In brief, what Lawrence meant in practice by that conception of Time considered from the perspective of a creative artist. It is in that privileged position that the awareness of measured Time is lost and replaced with an emotional Time whenever our imagination is engaged. I will argue that what, in my opinion, is the most challenging art – music – has an involving effect on our senses while leading them through a range of past and present time perceptions which move back and forth. In effect, who hasn't experienced the emotion that a certain song provokes on recalling past memories? It is quite likely that most of us would agree with that, although with a variety of individual responses ranging from melancholy to joy. Likewise, we are charmed just to realise that what creates such a magic link is the melody itself, which emerges from music as a particularly conducive element of the past. In agreement with that, Paul Hindemith (1895-1963) calls melody – 'memory' – and explains that we feel the emotion evoked by a lyrical musical line because it triggers the same feeling that we have experienced in the past. This German composer, through his most popular composition, *Symphonic Metamorphosis on Themes by Carl Maria von Weber* (1943), achieves that by taking melodies, mainly piano duets, from various works by von Weber (1786-1826), which he adapts in a way that each movement of the piece is based on one particular melodic theme. Lawrence plays upon the sensibilities of his readers in a similar way when he communicates lyrically with his words. Like a melody invading the present with a continuous reference to the past, the opening line of 'Piano,' "Softly in the dusk, a woman is singing to me; Taking me back down the vista of years…" (henceforth *P* 1, 148) creates a moment for the reader to imagine a melody sweetly sung in the dim light, reminiscent of a bygone experience, suggesting an intimate longing for the past. Therefore, we may say that the poem lends itself to a natural musical exploitation. As I had the privilege to discuss this aspect with my friend, the American musician William Neil, who set 'Piano' to music, I believe that the above is best expressed in his words as I recall them:

In my analysis of the poem, I found that two types of music were needed to effectively interpret the text: a music that was stylistically reminiscent of Lawrence's childhood, and another one that would evoke an emotional association with those memories. In fact, this is realized through the irresistible swinging between the woman's singing with passionate intensity on a piano in the present, and the hymn, sung by his mother, which drags the child with continuous flashbacks to the past, though he tries to resist that temptation.   (from my personal notebook).

This interpretation made me think that this musical approach is inherent to the poem's language and punctuation. Consequently, a question arises immediately regarding the function of that semicolon at the end of the first line. It obviously creates a caesura that, in my view, has a double function: stops the possible smooth rhythm of the poem, and indicates a time shift taking the speaker back to his childhood, due to the singing of a woman. A similar function is that of the many commas which disrupt the flow of lines through the poem, forcing the reader to pause as each image from the past emerges, which is an effect suggested also by the end-stopped lines separating sentence after sentence. Indeed, Lawrence uses sprung rhythm, a system of prosody created by Gerald Manley Hopkins (1844-89), to imitate the natural rhythm of speech, whose musicality is characterized by the juxtaposition of single stressed syllables interrupted by unstressed ones. Sprung rhythms are end-stopped lines which in 'Piano' are often at the end of a longer sentence that stretches across more than one line till the end of a stanza. In correlation with the topic of this essay, it must be underlined that there is a strong tendency with end-stopped lines to read in a sing-song pattern, stressing the metre, stopping and starting in the appropriate note to begin and end each line. Perhaps the risk here is that this kind of poem may sound monotonous and unimaginative, but this is where the *enjambment* itself comes into play to avoid that by creating the perception of a variation which produces a strong aural impression. In brief, it has a flowing effect, almost as if the poet's memory were like an unstoppable flooding river. And this is exactly what we find in 'Piano,' where the effect is favoured by its very structure, consisting of three quatrains, rhymed aabb, ccdd, eeff, resulting in a narrative, lyrical poem portraying, as it has already been stated, two time periods, the present of an adult and the past of a child. On concluding this part, concerning mainly figures of speech, note also the use of paradoxes (i.e., when the protagonist yearns for his happy childhood days, in lines 11-12) and metaphors (i.e., when he says that, however beautiful the singing may be, it cannot satisfy his longing for his wonderful childhood, in lines 9-10). Finally, the whole poem is based on a rather common and direct language. And, now we may as well proceed with a close analysis of each stanza of the poem.

In the **first stanza,** through the repetition of the sibilant sound of words like 'softly,' 'dusk,' and 'singing,' Lawrence creates a soothing tone, characterised by a subtle low-key mood in harmony with the fading lights of the dusk, while engendering a musical language to bring back memories of his long past childhood. Most important, present and past are juxtaposed here. Unusually, the present tense is used to cover both periods in order to create the sensation that the past is as vivid as the present: everything seems to be happening now. We are led to see the scene from the viewpoint of the speaker, who produces a romantic atmosphere enhanced by the singing and playing of a woman. Moreover, note that the use of the first person, with the speaker serving as the protagonist, stresses the lyrical character of the poem and expresses a strong emotion through the use of appropriate imagery which helps to set up the tone for a poem about memory, whose natural function is to link present and past. Again, this is an aspect that Lawrence anticipates by setting the poem 'in the dusk,' at twilight, when, in that typical indefinite faint darkish light, the day is about to become night. This visual image is emphasized by the remembrance of 'the vista of years' (l. 2) where the speaker is carried away down to memory lane and sees himself as 'a child sitting under the piano' and 'pressing' the player's 'poised feet' (l. 4). So, while his mother is playing, he is enjoying being "in the boom of the tingling strings," which suggests that he felt protected there, almost as if he were in his mother's womb. Hence, the music, which should have appealed to him in the present brought him back to entrancing, happy childhood scenes with his mother.

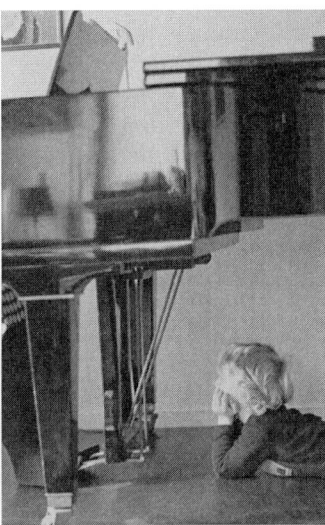

Figs. 9-10: Lucas is enjoying being "in the boom of the tingling strings" while his mum is playing for him.

In the **second stanza**, there is a tone of inner conflict as the speaker, an adult, tells us he engages himself in a forceful fight against his memory which wants to dig down into his past. He is taken by surprise and admits that, although he tries to resist, by making an enormous effort to stay focused on the present, the 'insidious mastery of song' misleads him back, deeper into his memory. This is best explained by Holly A. Laird in a book dedicated to Lawrence's poetry:

> The problem confronting the speaker is not, as we might expect, that he betrays passion for the woman; rather, the passion of her song betrays his childhood emotion. He is a boy shaken into feeling and a man with a profound measure of sentiment, doubly revealed, doubly trapped: […].
> (Laird, 1988, 194)

This indicates also a tone of helpless guilt at ignoring the singer's personal involvement as memory begins to take over. In the last two lines of the stanza, another conventional image, like that in the first stanza, is built. Lawrence offers us an idyllic picture of a middle-class Sunday night in his childhood. It is with a deep sense of nostalgia that he tells us how much he used to enjoy being in the safe and warm atmosphere of those evenings spent at home in a warm and "cosy" parlour, with his mother virtually performing for him only, for her little child, Bertie, as Lawrence used to be called at home. It is self-evident that this is an image in contrast with the outdoor atmosphere: it was a cold, wintry night outside, while the family sang hymns accompanied by a piano, which like a hearth represented the centre of the family's life. Similarly, the piano image takes a living protagonist's role while connecting the first two stanzas of the poem, thus spotlighting the relationship between music and memory. At the same time, Lawrence, through his masterly use of the literary tool of personification, uses music, or rather the piano as a guidance from his childhood to his adulthood.

Fig. 11: Living room at the Lawrences' in Garden Road 57, the Breach, Eastwood (1887-1891).

Fig.12: The Lawrences' in Garden Road 57, the Breach, Eastwood (1887-1891).

In the **third stanza**, the speaker realises that the sudden encounter with his childhood gives him no choice but to plunge into his past as a child, who remembers his mother singing at home on an upright piano. This contrasts with the present time when he, an adult, recalls a woman passionately singing and playing a grand piano during a concert. Nonetheless, much he is attracted to the professional singer, he ends up ignoring her. He is unexpectedly mesmerized by the highly emotional power of his mother's song, which makes him melancholic and sad. This "irresistible attraction" makes one think of the episode of the Sirens, in Homer's *Odyssey*, who did not succeed in alluring Ulysses, this modern "siren" is equally unsuccessful with the speaker. Despite the powerfully dramatic feeling expressed by the climax of her song rising to a crescendo, as suggested in line 9: "[So now] it is vain for the singer to burst into clamour." Surprisingly, her singing produces the opposite of the desired effect by sounding as a "noise" to him more than as a 'loud voice.' While, as a counterpart to the episode in the *Odyssey*, we have a modern Circe in 'Piano,' Lawrence's mother, who is still alluring and enthralling him. This tears his soul apart between a glamorous, innocent childhood and a present tedious adulthood. In the end, it is the child that prevails and finds himself uncontrollably crying for his past innocence. And, while remembering his mother's singing, he forgets he should behave like a man when he acknowledges: 'The glamour of childish days is upon me, my manhood is cast / down in the flood of remembrance, I weep like a child for the past.' (l. 12) Therefore, it seems that the past wins, hence, memory does. Indeed, we know that his mother won. Her love mattered to the writer more than anything else.

'The Piano' vs 'Piano,' a comparison

We know for sure that the idea of writing about his childhood and his close relation with his mother, had been spinning around Lawrence's mind ever since his student days at Nottingham University College, through the years 1905-08. He used to write drafts of some of his early poems in a notebook where he originally entered the academic assignment. According to MS. 1479, No. 14, kept at Nottingham University Library, there is the very first version of 'Piano', which is titled "The Piano" and was most likely first drawn in 1905. As we know, Lawrence typically revised, sometimes even more than once, his writings. Eventually, the poem was published in 1908. Two Professors of the University of Nottingham, Vivian de Sola Pinto and Warren Roberts, throw light to that in their Introduction to Lawrence's *Complete Poems*, reading:

The original draft of the poem, called "The Piano", survives in a manuscript in Nottingham University Library. This early version is diffuse, nostalgic and overcrowded with detail. The words "insidious" and "betray" do not occur in it. It contains five stanzas, as opposed to the three of the printed versions, and it describes the concert singer whose song brought back to Lawrence the memory of his childhood as a "full throated woman... singing ... a wild Hungarian air" with "her arms, and her bosom, and the whole of her soul ... bare." All this is suppressed in the final version and the impression rendered in the concentrated phrase, ... "to burst into clamour. / With the great black piano appassionato.
(Pinto & Roberts, 1977, 7-8)

In relation to the publication of 'Piano,' it is worth recalling that on 9 December 1910, Lawrence's mother passed away and he suffered such a terrible blow that surely represented a turning point in his life, which led him to begin to look at the world more thoughtfully than ever before; thus, making him grow as a man and an artist. Specially with reference to 'Piano,' that is summarised in Holly Laird's words: "Lawrence's power as a poet arose from the antagonistic, yet generative, conflict between the maturing narrator and the eternal child" (Laird, 1988, 195). This is also reflected in the following comparison of 'The Piano' (1908) with the final version of 1918, which we have analysed in this essay. Though less apparent, the original draft lacks that psychological profound complexity that we see in the last version, which shows a more mature man with a more refined artistry. On writing 'Piano' Lawrence's language is more imaginative and original, perhaps he is aware that prosaic language cannot convey his experience effectively. Whichever the case, the piano is the protagonist, whether he refers to the 'great black' (a grand piano) or the 'little and brown' (the upright piano) which Lawrence's mother used to play when he was a child. This is not a secondary aspect because it takes us back to the De Pinto's Introduction mentioned above, where we can see that Lawrence eliminated the last two lines of the third stanza and the entire first and fourth stanzas, reducing the overall number from five to three, and made some thorough revisions of the remaining stanzas as well. Furthermore, as De Pinto says, Lawrence altered his long original conclusion which he rendered in the "concentrated phrase": "[…] to burst into clamour / […] With the great black piano appassionato. […]" Perhaps Lawrence meant to emphasise that the pianist-singer in the original poem so physically attractive as spiritually open (cf. the last stanza 'her arms, and her bosom, and the whole of her soul is bare'), with her very passionate and professional performance, tries violently to supersede his mother's soft singing and playing, but to no avail.

By way of conclusion, as Lawrence himself writes in an essay published in 1908: "The essential quality of poetry is that it makes a new effort of attention and 'discovers' a new world within the known world" (Lawrence, "Chaos in Poetry," 109). Likewise, music has a revealing role in making one swing back and forward between present and past.

Piano (1918)

Softly, in the dusk, a woman is singing to me;
Taking me back down the vista of the years, till I see
A child under the piano, in the boom of the tingling strings
And pressing the small, poised feet of a mother who smiles as she sings.

In spite of myself, the insidious mastery of song
Betrays me back, till the heart of me weeps to belong
To the old Sunday evenings at home, with winter outside
And hymns in the cosy parlour, the tinkling piano our guide.

So now it is vain for the singer to burst into clamour
With the great black piano appassionato. The glamour
Of childish days is upon me, my manhood is cast
Down in the flood of remembrance, I weep like a child for the past.
(*The Poems*, Vol. One, 2013, 108)

The Piano (1908)

Somewhere beneath that piano's superb sleek black
Must hide my mother's piano, little and brown with the back
That stood close to the wall, and the front's faded silk, both torn
And the keys with little hollows, that my mother's fingers had worn.

Softly, in the shadows, a woman is singing to me
Quietly, through the years I have crept back to see
A child sitting under the piano, in the boom of the shaking strings
Pressing the little poised feet of the mother who smiles as she sings

The full throated woman has chosen a winning, living song
And surely the heart that is in me must belong
To the old Sunday evenings, when darkness wandered outside
And hymns gleamed on our warm lips, as we watched mother's fingers glide

Or this is my sister at home in the old front room
Singing love's first surprised gladness, alone in the gloom.
She will start when she sees me, and blushing, spread out her hands
To cover my mouth's raillery, till I'm bound in her shame's heart-spun bands

A woman is singing me a wild Hungarian air
And her arms, and her bosom and the whole of her soul is bare
And the great black piano is clamouring as my mother's never could clamour
And the tunes of the past are devoured of this music's ravaging glamour.
(*The Poems*, Volume Three, 2018, 1399)

Fig. 13: "And her arms, and her bosom and the whole of her soul is bare / And the great black piano is clamouring ..." (ll 18-19, 'The Piano')
Tanja Knežević at her piano recital in Radke Fine Arts Theatre at the University of Central Oklahoma, April 25 2021.

Appendix

(Letter of 19th March 2020 that William Neil wrote to Nick Ceramella, including his score of 'Piano'set for piano and mezzo soprano).

Dear Nick,

thanks for your brilliant article attached to your e-mail. I really enjoyed reading it. And here are my thoughts on my adaptation of D. H. Lawrence's 'Piano.'

I have read Lawrence's *Apocalypse* several times, and I love this idea of time in cycles, cycles that are like the double helix spirals of DNA really. Parallel levels of time that move at different speeds and not the on-and-on-and-on, from start to finish, that you quote in your article. I have actually prescribed to this concept in most of my compositions always trying to reveal what else might be heard beneath the primary level of music that I launch into the air that might further illuminate the meaning of the music from the shadows.

And so in 'Piano,' I was invited literally to employ these enchanting musical techniques in the setting of this poem. It all begins from the first measure of the song and really continues throughout the entire setting. From the very first note of the piano part which serves an introduction to this world, I wanted the listener to be conscious of these parallel worlds of sound. On the first level, the music sounds like a piano accompanying a woman singing in a late romantic style with a very tonal figure in the left hand and the singer on the same lyrical level of the piano music. I imagined that this music would be something that Lawrence might have experienced as an adult and indeed, as a musical event that might have triggered his childhood memory. But also, at the same time, I wanted the piano and voice to sound like what Lawrence was feeling as he remembered this time through his poem. And so, I created these little exit points where the music slips through portals that modulate to different tonal landscapes and back again. For example, in measure 10 of the piece, I set this exit up in measure 9 with the voice leaving the triplet meter of 12/8 and squaring off into a duple figure that lands on a spot where the piano suddenly departs to G major and then back into the original key of E flat. And then again, in measure 13, I use harmonies in G major and G minor to slip out of the original key, but this time, instead of returning to the home key of E flat, I take the listener to E major. So, at any point the listener gets used to the idea that these sonic images have a near-to-home orientation or a faraway distant version of the sound experience. Afterwards, if you go back to the very beginning there is something that may not have been so obvious at first but makes sense after the listener begins to understand the musical language. I am talking about the peculiar off rhythms in the treble notes in the right hand. They are out of sync with the left hand, and occasionally there is a note out of the key of E flat. I wanted it to sound like the notes that Lawrence as a child would have innocently picked out on the piano playing along with his mother, or perhaps when he was alone at the piano after she had left the room. Thereupon, there are techniques which totally destroy the element of continuous time like the speeding up of the piano figures in measure 18. The sound just whirls around and descends down into a rabbit hole of sound. The listener, at this point, loses the original orientation of the piece as a piano accompanying a singer. However, this passage and what follows, works very well to set the listener up for the return home. To this end, the allusion to a rag time piano piece in G major in measure 38, serves to convince the listener that they are looking back into the Lawrences' "cosy parlour", viewing the past from the future.

Piano

D. H. Lawrence
from "Rhyming Poems"
(1928)

William Neil

Copyright 1996 William Neil

'Piano': Swinging Between Past and Present

small, poised feet of a mo-ther who smiles as she sings.

'Piano': Swinging Between Past and Present

eve-nings at home, with win-ter out-side and hymns in the co-sy par-lour, the tink-ling pi-a-no our guide.

a tempo
So now it is vain for the sing - er to
burst in - to cla - - - - mour
with the great black pi -

51
p
f
ap - - - - - - - - pas - sio - na - to.
3
51
6
ff
𝄌
54
p
f
The gla - mour of child - ish days is u - pon me, my man - hood
54
una corda
ppp
fp
fp
58
p
3
is cast down in the flood of re - mem - brance.
58
fp
fp
fp
pp

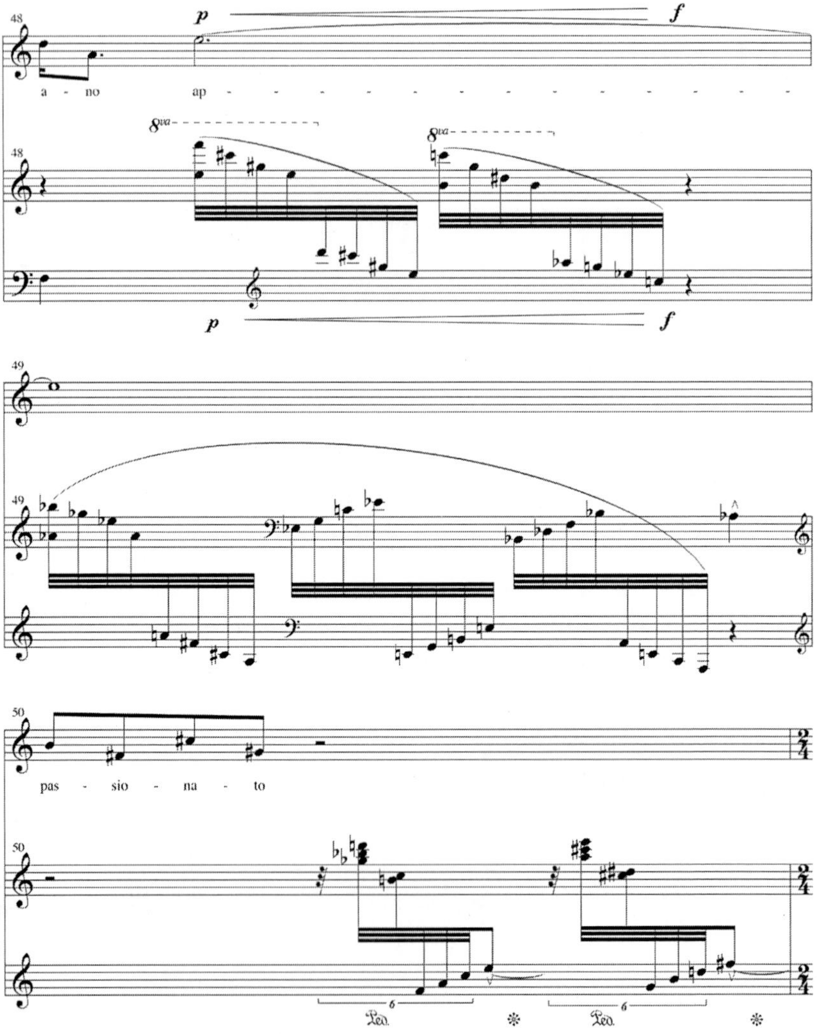
a - no
ap
pas - sio - na - to
8va
Ped.

A recording of this song can be heard on
https://open.spotify.com/album/6422w6dedOcryE5eSLCwxL

Bibliography

Lawrence, D. Herbert. *Apocalypse*, 2002. Edited by Mara Kalnins, 96-97. Cambridge: CUP.

—. "Piano" 1977. In *The Complete Poems of D. H. Lawrence*. Ed. and notes Vivian de Sola Pinto and Warren, Roberts. Harmondsworth: Penguin Books, 1977.

—. *Women in Love*. 1989. Edited by D. Farmer, Lindeth Vasey & J. Worthen. Cambridge: CUP.

—. *The Letters of D. H. Lawrence* Vol. 1. 1979. Edited by James T. Boulton. Cambridge: CUP.

—. *The Letters of D. H. Lawrence* Vol. 3. 1984. Edited by James T. Boulton & Andrew Rob Cambridge: CUP.

—. "Chaos of Poetry." In *Introductions and Reviews*. Eds N. H. Reeve & J. Worthen. Cambridge: CUP, 2014.

—. 1988. *Aaron's Rod*. Edited by Mara Kalnins, 198. Cambridge: CUP.

—. 1994. *Sea and Sardinia*. Ed. Paul Eggert, 167-168. Cambridge: CUP.

—. 2013. *The Poems* Volumes I & II. Edited by Christopher Pollnitz. Cambridge: CUP.

—. 2018. *The Poems* Volume III. Edited by Christopher Pollnitz, 1399, 1529, 1537 Cambridge: CUP.

Jones, Bethan. 'D. H. Lawrence and the 'insidious mastery of song.' In *D. H. Lawrence Studies*, "The D. H. Lawrence Society of Korea" Vol. 20 No. 2 October 2012, 163.

Ceramella, Nick. 2016. "Lorenzo at the Theatre: Meeting Actors and Audience". In *Journal of D. H. Lawrence Studies*, Vol IV, Nr. 2. 98-120. Eastwood, Nottighamshire: *The D. H. Lawrence Society of GB*.

Corke, Helen. "D. H. Lawrence as I saw him." *Renaissance and Modern Studies*, IV, 1960, 12.
Grieg, Edward. 1977-1995. *Haugutussa*. Translated by Rolf Kr. Stang for the Gesamthausgabe. Frankfurt: E. E. Peters.
Kinkead-Weekes, Mark. 1996. *Triumph to Exile 1912-1922*. Eds. James T. Boulton & Andrew Robertson, 584. Cambridge: CUP.
Lair, Holly A. 1989. *The Poetry of D. H. Lawrence,* 194. Charlottesville: University Press of Virginia,
Mellown. Elgin W. "Music and Dance in Lawrence." In *Journal of Modern Literature*, XXI, I (Fall 1997). Foundation for Modern Literature. 49-60.
Worthen. John. 1991. *The Early Years 1885-1912*, Cambridge: Cambridge University Press.

For further reading

Burgess, Anthony. 1985. *Flame into Being: The Life and Work of D.H. Lawrence*. London: William Heinemann.
Moss, Gemma. *Music in Modernist Literature: Politics and Aesthetics in James Joyce, Ezra Pound and Sylvia Townsend Warner*. (Edinburgh University Press, 2021). Contracted.
—. 'Classical Music and Literature'. In *Literature and Sound*, ed. Anna Snaith (Cambridge: Cambridge University Press, 2020).
Reed, Sue. 2019. *D. H. Lawrence, Music and Modernism*. London: Palgrave MacMillan.
Sutton, E. Sophie. 1 Jul 2020, *The Edinburgh Companion to Literature and Music*. da Sousa Correa, D. (ed.). Edinburgh University Press, p. 544-551 8 p. Chapter
Waddell, Nathan. 2017, 'Modernism and music: a review of recent scholarship', *Modernist Cultures*, vol. 12, no. 2, pp. 316-330. https://doi.org/10.3366/mod.2017.0173
—. 2019, *Moonlighting: Beethoven and Literary Modernism*. Oxford University Press, Oxford.
https://doi.org/10.1093/oso/9780198816706.001.0001
Werner, Wolf. 1999. *The Musicalization of Fiction: A Study in the Theory and History of Intermediality*. Amsterdam/Atlanta, GA: Editions, Rodopi.
Witen, Michelle. 2018. *James Joyce and Absolute Music*. London: Bloomsbury.

JAZZ SOUNDS AND STYLES IN THE FICTION OF JEAN RHYS, TONI MORRISON AND ZADIE SMITH

BETHAN JONES

This chapter will briefly examine the early relationship between jazz and literature as reflected in the writings of F. Scott Fitzgerald and Langston Hughes, before considering, in more depth and detail, four later prose works in which jazz music and dance play a fundamental role.[1] These novels and stories – by Jean Rhys, Toni Morrison and Zadie Smith – illustrate how words and sounds can combine powerfully within seminal narratives about racial conflict, exclusion, injustice, desire – and, of course, the transformative influence of jazz.

In the Foreword to her novel, *Jazz* (1992), Morrison defines the 'Jazz Age' as follows:

> The moment when an African American art form defined, influenced, reflected a nation's culture in so many ways: the bourgeoning [*sic*] of sexual license, a burst of political, economic, and artistic power; the ethical conflicts between the sacred and the secular; the hand of the past being crushed by the present. (Morrison, 2005, 85-87)

The 'artistic power' identified here was reflected during the 1920s in the innovatory works of influential modernists such as Pablo Picasso, Igor Stravinsky, Ezra Pound, James Joyce, Virginia Woolf, William Faulkner and Gertrude Stein. In their rejection of conventional modes and methods, these key figures arguably crushed 'the hand of the past', although T. S. Eliot and others also asserted the significance and relevance of tradition. In America, a controversial art form was emerging that responded to, reflected and shaped aspects of modern urban life. Jazz music evolved from ragtime

---

[1] A shorter version of this chapter has previously appeared in the *Yearbook of English Studies*, vol 50, *Back to the Twenties: Modernism Then and Now* (2020), ed. Paul Poplawski, Modern Humanities Research Association, pp. 132-149.

and blues. The latter 'ultimately derived from plantation songs, and may be considered a secular counterpart of the Spirituals popularized in the black church at around the same time' (Cooke 1997, 27). These work songs or 'field hollers' sung by African American slaves usually involved a single vocal line with call-and-response patterns. Improvisation was also a fundamental component and has remained one of the defining features of jazz performance to this day. The end of the nineteenth century witnessed a concentration of freed slaves in New Orleans while Chicago and New York also became crucial epicentres for the dissemination of jazz. In Dixieland jazz (also known as 'New Orleans', 'traditional' or 'hot' jazz), emerging in the early 1910s, instrumentalists took turns in playing the melody, while others in the group wove improvised counter-melodies around the tune. Typical orchestras combined 'horns' (brass instruments and saxophones), banjo, piano, keyboard, double bass, drums, guitar, and often vocals. Big bands emerged during the 1920s, dominating throughout the 'swing era' of the 1930s and 1940s: these musicians played from (or memorized) written arrangements, with some improvisation occurring within the framework of the song.

Kathy J. Ogden writes that 'Jazz was indeed a powerful new music, characterized by syncopation, polyrhythms, improvisation, blue tonalities, and a strong beat. It rose to popularity among strident criticism and extravagant praise' (Ogden, 1989, 7). Significantly, too, jazz evolved in dialogue with literature, as was recognized by F. Scott Fitzgerald with his epoch-defining title, *Tales of the Jazz Age,* chosen for a collection of his short stories published in 1922. This year was, in fact, a crucial one in literature, witnessing the publication of James Joyce's *Ulysses,* T. S. Eliot's *The Waste Land,* Virginia Woolf's *Jacob's Room,* D. H. Lawrence's *Aaron's Rod* and Katherine Mansfield's *The Garden Party and Other Stories.* In jazz, too, 1922 proved an important landmark. Chicago and New York had become the key centres for jazz performance and Paul Whiteman managed multiple jazz dance bands on the east coast. The band of trombonist Kid Ory, based in Los Angeles, made the first recordings of New Orleans jazz played by a black ensemble, while the pianists Fats Waller and William 'Count' Basie made their first recordings. Louis Armstrong moved to Chicago to play with Joe 'King' Oliver's Creole Jazz Band while Duke Ellington arrived in New York, meeting James P. Johnson, Fats Waller and Willie 'The Lion' Smith. The popular blues singer Mamie Smith recorded many songs with her Jazz Hounds, recruiting saxophonist Coleman Hawkins to play with the band. This was also the year in which race records were created, categorizing recordings by the racial origin of the performers. Nonetheless, a number of bands, created by prominent bandleaders such as clarinettist Benny Goodman, included both black and white musicians, impacting positively on race relations at this time (see Hentoff 2009).

Langston Hughes (arguably the creator of 'jazz poetry') poignantly reveals the racial tensions and conflicts underlying jazz. Evoking and addressing 'The South' in the poem with this title, he writes: 'And I, who am black, would love her | But she spits in my face' ('The South': Hughes, 1995, 26-27). This sense of rejection and deep-rooted sadness resonates through his poetry collection, *The Weary Blues* (1926), and is clearly evident in the following stanza:

> O Blues!
> Swaying to and fro on his rickety stool
> He played that sad raggy tune like a musical fool.
> Sweet Blues!
> Coming from a black man's soul. (Hughes 1995, 50)

In the lines that follow, the tune is described as 'melancholy' while the 'old piano moan[s]'. The pianist's swaying paradoxically expresses real feeling while also conveying absurdity ('fool'). Equally, 'raggy' hints at a ragtime style while also complementing 'rickety' and suggesting weariness. Yet this 'bluesy' writing is balanced by more 'jazzy' poems within the collection, one example being 'Jazzonia':

> In a Harlem cabaret
> Six long-headed jazzers play.
> A dancing girl whose eyes are bold
> Lifts high a dress of silken gold.   (Hughes, 1995, 84)

This poem employs 'variation on a theme' and chorus effects, as well as verbal modulations which could be considered to emulate transitions from one key to another. The first two lines quoted here are repeated later but made subject to a subtle alteration. 'In a Harlem cabaret' becomes 'In a whirling cabaret', emphasizing breathless motion — the energy and dynamism of the modernist vortex. The joy associated with this unleashing of vital energy is reflected in the exclamatory couplet: 'Oh, silver tree! | Oh, shining rivers of the soul!' The dance is thus associated both with nature and spirituality, though again the images modulate as they return, chorus-like, at later points in the poem. The 'silver tree' becomes a 'singing tree' then finally a 'shining' tree. The shifting phrases echo the fluidity of the rivers, while the term 'long-headed' describes how wind or brass instruments literally extend from their players' mouths as vital parts of them. The 'silken gold' dress lends the dancer an air of exoticism and luxury.

Many early jazz musicians (including Louis Armstrong and Jelly Roll Morton) performed in cabaret venues, bars, brothels or 'speakeasies.' This contributed to the association of jazz with decadence, sexual licence, rebellion, transgression, and excess. The pejorative connotations of the term 'jazz' at this time are discussed at length by John Lucas: he describes the labelling of this new and controversial form of expression as 'jungle music', 'nigger music' and even 'the devil's music' (Lucas, 1997, 126-28). Such terms highlight the widespread suspicion arising from jazz's so-called 'primitive' origins. Paradoxically, however, others saw jazz as a means for black advancement, facilitating unfettered self-expression within a prejudicial and repressive social context. The *Oxford English Dictionary* definitions of jazz highlight its 'Energy, excitement, "pep"; restlessness; animation [and] excitability': qualities evident, for instance, in Jay Gatsby's vibrant and extravagant parties in Fitzgerald's 'jazz novel', *The Great Gatsby* (1925). The post-war generation sought distraction in the strong, rhythmic drive of Dixieland jazz. The musical liberation associated with improvisatory soloing reflected other freedoms to be found in urban dancing and drinking clubs. In addition, the *OED*'s fourth definition of jazz as 'sexual intercourse' in American slang (a usage dating back to 1918) accounts for the correlation again emphasized by Lucas: 'Sex, drugs, dance music. Signs of the times, elements in the vortex of beastliness' (Lucas, 1997, 117). There was a strong sense among the puritanical that jazz could corrupt and undermine morality. The iconic bandleader, pianist and composer, Duke Ellington, associated the commitment required to perform jazz with extreme forms of risk and even violence: 'Art is dangerous. It is one of the attractions: when it ceases to be dangerous, you don't want it' and 'It's like an act of murder; you play with intent to commit something.'[2] The plot of Fitzgerald's *The Great Gatsby* itself illustrates the way in which both manslaughter and murder can be triggered by sexual intrigue within the fast-paced lifestyle of the 'roaring twenties'.

This novel reflects a society yearning for excess and hedonism. The party-goers experience instant gratification but are shown ultimately to be superficial, without genuine affection for their host. Gatsby is a means to an end for them: at his house they have the opportunity to dance, socialize,

---

[2] According to David Berger, the first of these quotations 'is widely attributed to Ellington, but its source is unclear': see *The Cambridge Companion to Duke Ellington*, ed. by Edward Green (Cambridge University Press, 2014), p. 31 and p. 41, n.1. The source of the second quotation is 'On Jazz', *New York Herald Tribune*, 9 July 1961. I am very grateful to Mervyn Cooke for providing source material and for commenting on a draft of this chapter.

drink, eat and swim. Yet despite this surface glamour the actual experience of his guests in responding to the music provided seems merely sordid:

> There was dancing now on the canvas in the garden, old men pushing young girls backward in eternal graceless circles, superior couples holding each other tortuously, fashionably and keeping in the corners—and a great number of single girls dancing individualistically or relieving the orchestra for a moment of the burden of the banjo or the traps.
>
> (Fitzgerald, 1991, 38-39)

There is a striking contrast here with Hughes's lone dancer in 'Danse Africaine' who 'Whirls softly into a | Circle of light' and whose movements are profoundly natural, 'Like a wisp of smoke around the fire –' ('Danse Africaine': Hughes, 1995, 28). In Fitzgerald's lines above, there is a hint of brutality, or at least clumsiness, in the way in which 'old men' push back the much younger girls, while terms like 'graceless' and 'tortuous' stress the *un*natural, strained quality of this formulaic dance routine. Even the playing of instruments is depicted as burdensome and while 'traps' literally denotes an early drum kit; it still harbours connotations of painful (perhaps disfiguring) restraint. This negative perception is echoed in Fitzgerald's short story, 'Bernice Bobs Her Hair' (1920), in which the superficiality of dancing (and all that it symbolizes) is illustrated through scathing irony and delightful humour. The overriding impression we are given is that 'youth in this jazz-nourished generation is temperamentally restless.'

(Fitzgerald, 1996, 55)

Losing a Song: The Jazz Stories of Jean Rhys

Don't trouble me now
You without honour,
Don't walk in my footstep
You without shame.

Dinah,
With her Dixie eyes blazin',
How I love to sit and gaze in
To the eyes of Dinah Lee! [3]

---

[3] Of the two songs quoted here, the first (unidentified) features in 'Let Them Call it Jazz' and the second, 'Dinah', in 'Tigers are Better-Looking': see Harry Akst, Sam Lewis and Joe Young, 'Dinah', at Lyrics, Stands4 Network LLC, 2001–2019, <https://www.lyrics.com/lyric/6077002/Harry+Akst/Dinah> [accessed 9 April 2021].

In her short stories, 'Let Them Call it Jazz' (1962) and 'Tigers are Better-Looking' (1962), the Dominican/Welsh writer Jean Rhys echoes the melancholy of Langston Hughes's poems within *The Weary Blues*. In these tales the protagonists drink, listen to music, sing, dance and write – nonetheless the pleasure latent in these activities is tainted by loneliness, prejudice, and a sense of loss. If the Creole narrator of 'Let Them Call it Jazz' ever experienced eager anticipation on arriving in London, this has long dissipated as a consequence of poverty and cynicism. Selina's savings have been stolen from her lodgings and she has been evicted by a landlord who is 'drunk already at that early hour' (Rhys, 1987, 158). She is subsequently offered a place to stay by a man named Sims who appears to have housed a succession of young vulnerable women in his London flat. Left alone, Selina allows herself to become thin through lack of food but acquires the habit of buying a bottle of wine most evenings.

Racial prejudice permeates this story. When attempting to reclaim her stolen savings, Selina overhears her landlady saying to the policeman: 'These people terrible liars' (Rhys, 1987, 163). Such injustice extends to Selina's victimization by a neighbouring white couple. Her polite conversational overtures are rejected and the husband 'stare as if I'm wild animal let loose' (Rhys, 1987, 161). The same attitude is reflected by the wife who persistently repeats phrases like '*Must* you stay? *Can't* you go?' in a sweet, sugary voice. (Rhys, 1987, 164). Selina's bewilderment at their unfounded hostility is reflected in the question 'why these people have to be like that?' (ibid.).

In this story, singing provides release and an outlet for self-expression; singing is also used at times as a weapon of defiance levelled against the abusive and bigoted neighbours. Often, the impetus for original composition requires alcohol as a catalyst: 'After I drink a glass or two, I can sing and when I sing all the misery goes from my heart. Sometimes I make up songs but next morning I forget them, so other times I sing the old ones like "Tantalizin"' or "Don't Trouble Me Now"' (Rhys, 1987, 160). Alcohol not only fuels the singing and dancing that take place within the confines of her room but also impacts on Selina's perception of the performance. After taking a number of sleeping pills (though not an intentionally harmful overdose) with two glasses of gin and Vermouth, she believes that the emerging song is 'the best tune that has ever come to me in all my life' (Rhys, 1987, 167). Problematically, however, the drugs and drink curtail inhibition and induce a feeling of claustrophobic confinement. The decision to move outside, still singing and dancing, provokes an altercation with the hostile neighbours in which Selina is made subject to racial and sexual slurs by the enraged wife: 'At least the other tarts that crook installed here were *white* girls' (ibid.). Her inebriation spurs Selina on to uncharacteristic verbal retaliation and, ultimately, the act of throwing a brick through the neighbours' irreplaceable stained-glass window. At this dramatic moment in the story, song, dance, racism and violence converge. At this moment, too, Selina follows an insult hurled at the retreating, 'shameless' neighbours with the song, 'Don't Trouble Me Now' (quoted at the opening of this subsection). The lines 'You without honour' and 'You without shame' have obvious relevance to her situation. The story underlying the song's lyrics is conveyed to us and Selina (associating the song with her grandmother) comments that it 'sound good in Martinique patois too: "*Sans honte*"' (Rhys, 1987, 168). The conjured music thus serves the purpose of evoking memories of the person Selina has most loved and trusted in the past, alongside the familiar language of her Martinique upbringing. Poignantly, however, she abandons singing as her voice sounds 'wrong' and — the following morning — discovers that her own, invented song has flown from her mind.

It is in the last section of the tale that Rhys most explicitly foregrounds jazz. In Holloway prison, Selina feels numb and hardened. There is also a dissociative element to her condition: looking into the mirror she sees a 'strange new person' (Rhys 1987, 172) while other things and people seem oddly distanced. But if music is absurdly the cause of her incarceration – 'I'm here because I wanted to sing' (ibid.) – it also shakes her out of listlessness and depression. Walking through the jail, Selina hears

> a smoky kind of voice, and a bit rough sometimes, as if those old dark walls theyselves are complaining, because they see too much misery — too much. But it don't fall down and die in the courtyard; seems to me it could jump the gates of the jail easy and travel far, and nobody could stop it.
> (Rhys, 1987, 173)

Her initial reaction — one of incredulity — stems from the sense of inertia, nihilism and hopelessness she has come to associate with the jail. It is the pointlessness of the song that astonishes and then inspires her. The tune (she cannot decipher the words) epitomizes her own world-weariness yet represents the ability to transcend it. The song emanates from the punishment block and signifies an attempt to 'tell the girls cheerio and never say die' (Rhys, 1987, 173): it is thus a musical gesture of defiant hope and the will to survive. Selina subsequently conjures up a musical arrangement of this tune in her head – 'One day I hear that song on trumpets and these walls will fall and rest' (Rhys, 1987, 163) – the chosen instrument signifying a revelatory moment of triumph and liberation. Nevertheless, the term 'rest' suggests a paradoxically peaceful cataclysm from which the incarcerated women can walk quietly away. The listlessness of despair is replaced by a sense that 'anything can happen'; that remaining locked up could result in missed opportunities beyond the prison walls. Selina takes the positive steps necessary to regain her freedom.

The story is arguably one of betterment, given that Selina finds a place to live, a decent job, a friend, and a new life. Sill there is a twist towards the end that ironically turns the story against jazz – or at least 'jazz' as understood and interpreted in a certain way. This is not simply because she 'never sing[s] now' (Rhys, 1987, 175): instead, it is catalysed by Selina whistling the 'Holloway song' at a party given by her friend, Clarice. A man there asks to hear the tune again and plays it on an old piano, 'jazzing it up.' (Ibid.). Selina's immediate reaction is to tell him not to play it like that (though the other party guests are impressed): the jazzy version does not match up with the arrangement of the tune she has conjured up in her head. When she receives five pounds as a 'thank you' once the man has sold this song, Selina experiences only a sense of loss and desolation: 'that song was all I had' (ibid.). She articulates this further through the idea of 'belonging', which she has never instinctively felt or been able to pay for, 'But when that girl sing, she sing to me and she sing for me. I was there because I was *meant* to be there. It was *meant* I should hear it – this I *know*' (Rhys 1987, 175). The certainty inherent in the italicized words is stripped from Selina when the song is played 'wrong' – perhaps through transforming it from rough and smoky blues to upbeat, embellished, 'hot' jazz. However, it is also arguable that Selina's objection is not to jazz *per se*, especially given that in her own imagined rendition, the tune is played on trumpets: instruments fundamental to many forms of jazz. Instead, her objection might be to a showy, tame or soulless imitation of 'real' jazz, signalling the misappropriation of black-derived music which (in this case) has its roots directly in pain and suffering.

The tainting of this song leaves Selina with the sense that there is '[n]othing left for me at all'. As with Antoinette in Rhys's *Wide Sargasso Sea* (1966) who is divested of her name, image and flamboyant personality when she is moved to England, life in London deprives Selina of her independence, pride and music. Yet interestingly the tale concludes with pragmatism – Selina buys a pink dress with her money – and a recognition that even her own version of the Holloway tune could not topple the walls of oppression 'so soon'. The story's title is cleverly brought into play almost at the very last: '"So let them call it jazz," I think, and let them play it wrong. That won't make no difference to the song I heard' (Rhys, 1987, 175). The titular phrase can be read with emphasis on 'Let', 'them', 'call' or indeed 'jazz' according to interpretation, highlighting defiance, racial otherness, false labelling or questions of musical genre. A key suggestion seems to be that (white) performers may adapt black-derived music to their own styles, but the tunes still 'belong' to the people and places associated with their origin.

'Tigers are Better-Looking' is partly set in a performance venue attended by Mr Severn and two younger female companions, Maidie and Heather. The only specified orchestra member is 'the mulatto who was playing the saxophone' (Rhys, 1987, 179), hinting at a jazz big band with mixed-race musicians. This instrumentalist 'whoops' and 'titters' at the threesome at various stages of the proceedings whilst they are ignored by the other musicians Maidie's comment on the orchestra is that they 'play so rotten' while Heather's attitude is both more accepting and more cynical: 'The place is packed every night. Besides, why should they play well. What's the difference?' Severn's tailpiece to this dialogue passes judgement through dismissing the music and the debate surrounding it as '[a]ll an illusion' (Rhys, 1987, 179–80). As he becomes increasingly drunk and uninhibited, Severn repeatedly and brazenly demands that the orchestra 'play Dinah!'. This popular song, with music by Harry M. Akst and lyrics by Sam M. Lewis and Joe Young, was first published in 1925 and introduced at the Plantation Club on Broadway. Ethel Waters, The Revelers, Cliff Edwards, Clarence Williams and Fletcher Henderson (with Coleman Hawkins) produced hit versions in 1926, while Josephine Baker also recorded the song during that year. The number of subsequent performances and recordings by high profile bandleaders testifies to the widespread appeal of the song.[4] The lyrics of this tune suggest a southern-belle, Tin Pan Alley style and its performance history illustrates how a jazz standard can resonate through the ages.

The disruptive clamouring to hear this song, coupled with the graffiti doodled on his tablecloth, results in Severn's forcible eviction from the club and a violent *fracas*. The following journey in a police van and attendance at a magistrate's court indicate links with the story by Rhys discussed above. Like Selina, Severn attends to a tune heard in captivity: this time 'Londonderry Air' (with its inherent French punning on London *derrière*) whistled in a 'sexy' (rather than 'smoky') voice. There is also an allusion to escape from restraint: this female singer thinks of growing wings and flying away (although the vision is deflated by a policeman suggesting that she

---

[4] Notable versions were produced by Louis Armstrong (1930), Bing Crosby and the Mills Brothers (1931), Duke Ellington (1932), Cab Calloway (1932; 1945; 1993), The Boswell Sisters (1934), Django Reinhardt (1934), Quintette du Hot Club de France (1934), Fats Waller (1935), the Benny Goodman Quartet (1936), Chet Baker (1952), Thelonius Monk (1964–65) and The Hot Sardines (2011).

might be shot in the process). However, Severn's auditory response lacks the epiphanic significance of Selina's appreciation of the Holloway song.

'Tigers are Better-Looking' is also concerned with the process of writing. Significantly, musical terminology is chosen to express the kind of fluency Severn craves in his journalism: 'He couldn't get the swing of it. The swing's the thing, as everybody knows — otherwise the cadence of the sentence' (Rhys, 1987, 177). In its more colloquial definition, swing in music suggests rhythmic propulsion and a foot-tapping, visceral response. More specifically, it entails the alternate lengthening and shortening of the pulse-divisions in a rhythm, creating syncopation. 'Cadence' has multiple connotations associated with a modulation of the voice – ebb and flow, rise and fall – as well as designating a certain beat, pulse or rhythm. In music, it specifically means the sequence of chords that brings a musical phrase to a close. Throughout the story, Severn finds that a satisfactory rhythm eludes him, as 'Words and meaningless phrases still whirled tormentingly round in his head' (Rhys 1987, 184). The narrative emulates this process through accumulation. Words from a range of written sources – a letter from his companion, Hans, who has left him, graffiti on the walls of a police cell, the placard in front of the newspaper shop opposite his house – all echo in his mind and keep resurfacing in the narrative like riffs or refrains, gathering through a crescendo to this climax:

> Who pays? Will you pay now, please? You don't mind if I leave you, dear? I died waiting. I died waiting. (Or was it I died hating?) That was my father speaking. Pictures, pictures, pictures. You've got to be young. But tigers are better-looking, aren't they? SOS, SOS, SOS. If I was a bird and had wings I could fly away, couldn't I? Might get shot as you went. But tigers are better-looking, aren't they? You've got to be younger than we are …
> (Rhys, 1987, 188)

Here, the narrative achieves a layering effect as these fragments coalesce in stream-of-consciousness style. There is some resemblance to New Orleans jazz in which percussion beats, riffs, melodies, chords and improvised solos produce a richly textured sound. There is freedom in the liberation from strict grammatical structures and (through improvisation) from strictly prescribed sequences of notes. Yet improvised jazz of this kind operates within a strict harmonic framework while Rhys's narrative is discordant – anarchic rather than harmonious. Equally, linear narrative cannot really emulate musical harmony as the effect is always sequential rather than simultaneous. Severn is ultimately freed from the chaos of burdensome echoes and gets into the groove, finding new phrases that are 'suave and slick'. Even so, questions about his confidence and originality remain, while the ellipsis at the very end of the story creates the effect of an interrupted cadence. (Rhys, 1987, 188)

Life Below the Sash: Urban Music and Prose Riffs in Toni Morrison's 'Jazz' (1992)

> I got a new man honey, and he's so much better than you.
> He starts his loving right where yours used to get through.
> So I'm going to blow you a kiss as you leave my door,
> Cause that key ain't going to work in my lock no more
> You got the right key baby,
> But you're working on the wrong keyhole.
> ('You've got the right key baby, but the wrong keyhole': Williams and Green, 1924)

The jazz tune above, written by Clarence Williams and Eddie Green, was recorded for Okey records by Virginia Liston in 1924. This song – and others like it – provoke desire, yearning and outrage in equal measure within the characters of Toni Morrison's *Jazz*. In this novel, set in Harlem during the 1920s, the excitement, allure and danger of jazz are highlighted through the experience of Dorcas Manfred, the eighteen-year-old orphan who embarks on an affair with Joe Trace – over thirty years her senior – and is later murdered by him with a silenced gun after she has broken off their relationship. Lying in bed at night, Dorcas processes the strains of music permeating the city:

> [she is] tickled and happy knowing that there was no place to be where somewhere, close by, somebody was not licking his licorice stick, tickling the ivories, beating his skins, blowing off his horn while a knowing woman sang ain't nobody going to keep me down you got the right key baby but the wrong keyhole you got to get it bring it and put it right here, or else.
> (Morrison, 2005, 814-16)

This passage highlights the way in which musical performance and sex are inextricably bound together through language in this novel. The very act of playing wind instruments such as clarinets ('licorice sticks'), saxophones, trumpets and trombones inevitably involves licking, blowing and fingering, while tickling (piano keys) and beating (drums) hint respectively at sensuality and violence. Coupled with the sexualization of instrumental technique is the citation of lyrics laced with *double entendre*. The Williams and Green song quoted above is about more than a man who returns to the wife he left only to find the locks have been changed — the phallic connotations of the key he pushes in and pulls out are clear. Equally, the

Bessie Smith song, 'You got to keep it...', appears to be about more than just the dime the female narrator demands from her inadequate husband. The women in these songs are strong-willed and even coercive: they assert their independence and their dominance over subservient men, making demands and taking action if their demands are not met. These jazz tunes are associated with female emancipation as well as sexual freedom.

For the young Dorcas, the music signifying 'life-below-the-sash' (817-18) is tantalizing and even comforting: a welcome distraction from the horrific deaths of both her parents as well as a way of finding meaning in her new city life. By contrast, for her puritanical Aunt Alice, who becomes Dorcas's guardian, the music signifies a corruptive force responsible for the restlessness that fuels brutality and depravity in the lives of those around her. Her resistance is partly due to the way in which she is constantly having to repress her own instinctive urge to hear, respond to and interpret the music. While Dorcas revels in the lyrics about phallic keys and dimes, Alice closes windows in order the keep the music out. Ironically, however, lines such as 'When I was young and in my prime, I could get my barbecue any old time' (with the association of meat with sex, common at that time) — words she considers greedy, loose, reckless and infuriating – constantly needle her. (Morrison, 2005, 809-10). Alice also finds herself torn between two opposing sensations stimulated by musical rhythm. On the one hand, she associates the 'cold black faces' (Morrison, 2005, 725) of drummers parading on Fifth Avenue with solidarity and discipline: they provide her with the figurative 'rope' she clings to for support and reassurance in a shifting and immoral world. Yet she cannot completely dissociate this drumming from the percussive impetus underlying jazz tunes and loses her sense of stability when observing the way 'men sat on windowsills fingering horns, and the women wondered "how long"': 'The rope broke then, disturbing her peace, making her aware of flesh and something so free she could smell its bloodsmell; made her aware of its life below the sash and its red lip rouge' (Morrison, 2005, 793-96).

Ultimately, the novel does align jazz-fuelled sexual licence with danger through the murder of Dorcas by her jilted lover. Searching for her on the night of the murder, Joe enacts a kind of primitive hunt modelled on the one undertaken many years ago when searching for his mother (referred to as 'Wild') in the bush. Nonethess musical rhythm is also shown to create, maintain and even rekindle lasting human bonds. On entering the vibrant city for the first time, Joe and Violet stand up to feel their train's pulse, dancing and 'tapping back at the tracks' (Morrison 2005, 444). Much later — after their estrangement, Violet's despair over her childlessness, Joe's affair and the murder of Dorcas – their shared response to music reflects a reconnection: 'Mr. Trace moved his head to the rhythm and his wife snapped her fingers in time. She did a little step in front of him and he smiled. By and by they were dancing' (Morrison 2005, 2688–90).

In her 'Foreword' to *Jazz*, Morrison highlights the paradoxical role of music in her novel, which aims to reflect 'the proud hopelessness of love mourned and championed in blues music, and, simultaneously, fired by the irresistible energy of jazz' (Morrison, 2005, 53). But she also wishes the work to be 'a manifestation of the music's intellect, sensuality, anarchy; its history, its range, and its modernity' (Morrison 2005, 97–99). It is important, then, to consider the way in which novelistic technique emulates musical devices and achieves the kind of self-expression we may associate with improvisatory jazz. Arguably, this is achieved through verbal riffs, repetitions and strongly rhythmic prose: 'There goes the sad stuff. The bad stuff. The things-nobody-could-help stuff' (Morrison, 2005, 159). Such phrases have a musical rather than semantic effect. When obsessed by imagining her husband's intimate interactions with his mistress, Violet conjures an image of Dorcas's hand under the table of a restaurant, 'drumming out the rhythm on the inside of his thigh, his thigh, his thigh, thigh, thigh' (Morrison 2005, 1256), creating in words a strident, repetitive and percussive sequence of beats. Describing blues singer-guitarists taking up their positions on a block, Morrison writes: 'Blues man. Black and bluesman. Blackthereforeblue man. Everybody knows your name. Where-did-she-go-and-why man. So-lonesome-I-could-die man. Everybody knows your name' (Morrison, 2005, 1539–41). In places it is hard to distinguish quoted lyrics from the narrator's verbal play – the voice remains fluid, sliding in and out of jazz and blues riffs and lyrics as it slides in and out of multiple characters' perspectives. In this sense, the narrative emulates the way in which a musical motif or phrase can be altered and developed.

Musical terms – as well as references to instruments and the timbre of voices – permeate the novel. For many city women, sorrow slips 'into a beat of time' (Morrison, 2005, 285), while the 'artificial rhythm of the [seven-day] week' is broken up by the human body, 'preferring triplets, duets, quartets' (Morrison, 2005, 709-10).[5] The abundance of such references means that the reader can scarcely turn a page without being reminded of the pervasive soundscape of the novel. This creates a verbal equivalent of the sounds that unavoidably impact on the characters in their everyday lives. Passing a speakeasy, one will hear a 'clarinet cough'; elsewhere a 'stride piano [is] pouring over the door saddle' while, in party halls, 'music soars

---

[5] In this instance musical terminology is chosen rather oddly: while triplets are divisions of a beat and therefore of time, duets and quartets designate the number of players in a group.

to the ceiling and through the windows'; later it 'bends, falls to its knees to embrace [the dancers]' (Morrison 2005, 861; 870; 2353). These sounds are animate and eclectic: they possess the status of minor characters who come and go, leaving their mark.

The fluidity of Morrison's narrative is also evident in the structure of the novel and in the stream-of-consciousness style redolent of 1920s modernism. Each chapter is designated simply by its opening words followed by an ellipsis, such as 'Sth, I know...', 'Or used to...' and 'Like that day...' (Morrison, 2005, 108; 402; 724). The phrase chosen to begin each chapter serves as connective tissue rather than signalling a clear break between sections. A particularly interesting example is a chapter ending 'But where is *she*?' while the next begins 'There she is...' (Morrison, 2005, 2342–3). Ostensibly the second phrase is a continuation of the first, still on consideration of the context it becomes evident that the 'she' referred to is different in the two phrases; that the time and place have changed though the narrator is the same. The first phrase relates to Joe's search for his mother while the second accompanies his entry into the party venue where he sees his young mistress dancing intimately with a man of her own age. This narrative strategy is symptomatic of the way the novel fluctuates between different scenes and time frames, just as a jazz musician modulates through different keys and moves through different time signatures with a fluency that covers the joins, making the transitions appear seamless. Within and across chapters, Morrison frequently uses modernist free association to convey the wanderings of memory, as exemplified by a description of Violet washing an old woman's sparse grey hair, 'soft and interesting as a baby's', immediately followed by: 'Not the kind of baby hair her grandmother had soaped...' (Morrison, 2005, 291). This progresses into reminiscences of True Belle (Violet's grandmother) and Golden Gray – the infant True Belle helped to raise along with the child's white, single mother. Again, the transition feels instinctive, spontaneous and improvisatory, rather than logical and sequential.

Often, Morrison provides only a partial account of an episode, then – later in the novel – the narrative loops back and describes the episode again in greater detail, or even from a different perspective (a method comparable with William Faulkner's technique in the modernist classic *The Sound and the Fury* (1929). One instance is the relatively early account of Joe asking Wild to extend her hand through dense foliage, as a sign to confirm his belief that she is his mother. This is not a scene we can fully understand until the episode is replayed later with further elaboration, once the reader's cumulative understanding of the characters' lives has broadened. Arguably, this strategy could be related to the musical 'variations on a theme' approach, or simply considered as improvisation around a repeated figure. This is one instance of Morrison's quirky and unique engagement with the jazzy style she wishes to emulate in the novel. For the characters, jazz and blues songs are part of the soundscape of the city: they might provoke revulsion or fear in some, but they also fascinate and compel, like a siren-call. For readers, musical tropes infiltrate many aspects of the narrative style, as though we are listening to – as well as reading – the novel.

Dance, Race and the Rhythms of Jazz: Zadie Smith's 'Swing Time' (2016)

> Like the beat, beat, beat of the tom tom
> When the jungle shadows fall ...
> So a voice within me keeps repeating
> You, you, you ...
> I think of you
> Night and day... ('Night and Day': Porter, 1934)

Zadie Smith's *Swing Time* is steeped in the history, evolution and technique of dance. At the outset, we are presented with a mysterious situation in which the unnamed protagonist has been forced to remain concealed in a neutrally furnished 'luxury condo.' (Smith, 2016, 1). She finally acquires permission to spend an evening outside and Smith provides the following description of her watching Fred Astaire dancing on-screen:

> my feet, in sympathy with the music, tapped at the seat in front of me. I felt a wonderful lightness in my body, a ridiculous happiness [...] I'd lost my job, a certain version of my life, my privacy, yet all these things felt small and petty next to this joyous sense I had watching the dance, and following its precise rhythms in my own body.   (Smith, 2016, 4)

The clip turns out to be one of the dance routines from the movie also entitled *Swing Time*: a 1936 RKO American musical comedy, mostly set in New York, starring Fred Astaire and Ginger Rogers. It is reputed to be one of the greatest dance musicals and one of the best films made by the celebrated pair of dancers. The story is woven around four dance routines, each considered to be a masterpiece in its own right. For Smith's protagonist, the clip derives its power partly from representing one of her favourite films, watched repeatedly during childhood.

While the auditory experience described above clearly provokes uplifting joy, the narrator's visual apprehension of the scene is flawed and partial, as indicated by her reappraisal when she watches it later on her laptop (discussed below). Her role in the novel is often that of an observer, living vicariously and disengaged from life. Much later in the novel (though earlier in chronological time), however, we witness the narrator experiencing comparably intense happiness through her own physical involvement in a tribal group dance. Aimee (the narrator's pop-star employer) has decided to set up a school for girls in an impoverished West African village. As the narrator heads for the river towards Aimee's hotel, her taxi is halted by an extraordinary apparition: a man-sized (though faceless) 'dancing tree' covered in orange leaves, followed by a gang of boys and swathes of dancing women. Conducting subsequent research, she discovers that this 'Kankurang' (a masked individual from the Mandinka ethnic group of West Africa, participating in ritual ceremonies or festivals), is sent to lead the village boys into the bush for circumcision and initiation into tribal rites. She describes this figure as the best dancer she has ever seen and is swept up in the restless writhing of bodies: 'only the present moment, only the dance' (Smith, 2016, 164). Rather like Morrison's Violet and Joe, jigged around by the motion of their train, the protagonist's dancing is initially involuntary: she moves because 'pressed up close to so many bodies' (Smith 2016, 164). The wild energy of the dance subsequently intensifies and is shown by the narrative to be potentially dangerous. With a local villager and teacher named Lamin, the narrator climbs onto a car to avoid the Kankurang's spinning machetes which whirr near to the boys who are daring each other to get nearer to the blades. As the protagonist climbs up onto the car, her sense of elation intensifies and sparks off a kind of epiphany – 'I thought: here is the joy I've been looking for all my life.' (Smith, 2016, 165).

It is within the 'primitive' surroundings of the village, rather than the refined context of Miss Isobel's ballet school which the narrator attended as a child, that she is hailed as an admirable dancer: a crucial attribute for any character of importance and worth within this novel. At a tribal celebration, she achieves success through watching and emulating the extravagant performance of two tribeswomen 'who never lost the beat, who heard it through everything' (Smith, 2016, 417). The narrator's triumph stems from a careful act of attention in which she studies the movements of the women and listens to the 'multiple beats', thus acquiring confidence and self-belief: 'I [...] knew that what they were doing I, too, could do. I stood between them and matched them step for step. The kids went crazy' (Smith, 2016, 417). The instinctive assimilation of the complex rhythms – one that the narrator associates with 'my people' and which transcends a European auditory response – is also reflected in the lines quoted at the beginning of this subsection: 'Like the beat, beat, beat of the tom tom | When the jungle shadows fall.' These lines derive from the Cole Porter song, 'Night and Day', written for the 1932 musical *Gay Divorce* and introduced on stage by Fred Astaire. While this song's assertion of sentimental and all-consuming love seems a far cry from the tangled web of transient, superficial or tainted relationships portrayed in the novel, its relevance is undeniable. When the narrator goes to her first ballet lesson, she encounters 'a very old white man in a trilby [who] sat playing an upright piano, "Night and Day", a song I loved and was proud to recognize' (Smith 2016, 14). Later in the novel the title ironically highlights the unhealthy, obsessive way in which the narrator is required to be 'thinking of Aimee, day and night, night and day' (Smith, 2016, 448). This phrase functions as a leitmotif and resurfaces intermittently within the novel.

The significance of the song also extends to the novel's structure, which is divided as follows: Prologue; Part One: Early Days; Part Two: Early and Late; Part Three: Intermission; Part Four: Middle Passage; Part Five: Night and Day; Part Six: Day and Night; Part Seven: Late Days; Epilogue. Both 'Intermission' (an interval between parts of a performance) and the quotations from Porter's song clearly have performative connotations, while 'Middle Passage' could signify a section within a song or orchestral work – perhaps even the bridge of a jazz tune. Yet 'Middle Passage' also carries obvious racial connotations relating to the transatlantic slave trade. In this context, the recurrence of Porter's lyrics arguably suggests the dichotomy of black and white in terms of skin colour and tribal affiliation. Throughout the novel, racial issues are intertwined with music, as indicated in the following passage where segregation in Harlem infiltrates the narrator's childhood dream:

> One night I dreamt of the Cotton Club: Cab Calloway was there, and Harold and Fayard, and I stood on a podium with a lily behind my ear. In my dream we were all elegant and none of us knew pain, we had never graced the sad pages of the history book my mother bought for me, never been called ugly or stupid, never entered theatres by the back door, drunk from separate water fountains or taken our seats at the back of any bus. None of our people ever swung by their necks from a tree, or found themselves suddenly thrown overboard, shackled, in dark water — no, in my dream we were golden!
> (Smith, 2016, 100)

In this dream, the eleven-year-old narrator attempts to sing but no sound emerges; on waking she finds she has wet the bed. The remedy her mother offers is the perusal of the history of jazz-age landmarks and icons such as the Cotton Club, the Harlem Renaissance, Langston Hughes, and Paul Robeson. Yet the narrator finds more comfort and diversion in reading about the history of dance, while dance rhythms and movements provide a more physical, visceral way to overcome deep-rooted racial despair. As a result of her mixed-race origins (with a white father and Jamaican mother), the narrator admires the aristocratic Astaire and the proletarian Gene Kelly but feels more natural affinity with Bill 'Bojangles' Robinson who 'should really have been my dancer, because Bojangles danced for the Harlem dandy, for the ghetto kid, for the sharecropper – for all the descendants of slaves' (Smith, 2016, 24). Running counter to this argument, however, is the narrator's inherent feeling that a dancer is 'a man from nowhere', without a family or obligations. This sense fuels her love for movies such as *Swing Time*, though in retrospect she recognizes that there are problematic elements within this film. In the dance routine that fills the narrator (even as an adult) with intense and transcendent joy, Astaire has a blackened face and farcical rolling eyes.

The history of racial conflict is seen here as inseparable from the music that has sought to express it. The sadness of this legacy is evident in perhaps the most moving moment of the novel, in which the narrator abandons *her* obligations briefly and gives free reign to her own suffering through her 'lifting' voice:

> it was something I'd released that now rose up and away and escaped my reach. My hands were in the air. I was stamping my heels into the floor. I felt I had everyone in the room. I even had a sentimental vision of myself as one in a long line of gutsy brothers and sisters, music-makers, singers, musicians, dancers, for didn't I, too, have the gift so often ascribed to my people? I could turn time into musical phrases, into beats and notes, slowing it down and speeding it up, controlling the time of my life, finally, at last, here on a stage, if nowhere else. (Smith, 2016, 137)

This is a forthright moment of self-expression for someone who – nameless in the novel – is characterized by her own mother as the kind of person who feeds off the light of others, remaining herself in shadow. Like the ending of Rhys's 'Let Them Call it Jazz', this profoundly expressive moment entails the rejection of a label that is seen to debase African music. As she sings, the narrator thinks of Nina Simone's reference to 'Black Classical Music', rejecting 'jazz' as 'a white word for black people.' (Smith 2016, 137). Despite the ragged bathos of the performance's conclusion, it has been undeniably powerful, as indicated by the perennially selfish Aimee shedding tears and making uncharacteristic enquiries about the narrator's emotional condition. There are hints in the novel, then, that the narrator has a natural talent and ease in performance that Aimee – for all her flamboyance – evidently lacks.

Throughout the novel, the narrator identifies with the pulse of jazz whilst finding herself unable to relate to what Tracey (her closest childhood friend) calls 'white' (namely classical) music. Nonetheless, she is aware that there is something wrong with these clear-cut distinctions: perhaps this is one reason that Simone's hybridizing terminology appeals to her. Even as a child, the narrator speculates that there must be 'a world somewhere in which the two combined' (Smith, 2016, 25). She recollects films and photos with black girls singing alongside white men at the piano, and she yearns to be part of this vision of racial unity through music and dance. Like the other texts discussed in this chapter, Smith uses early jazz as a means to evoke and grapple with racial conflict, injustice, despair and hope, revealing the power and extent of its literary legacy.

Jazz, literature and evolving freedom

The jazz songs whose lyrics preface sub-sections above reveal early signs of progression beyond the 1920s towards more complex modes of expression. 'Dinah' (1925) is simple both harmonically and structurally (with an A1 – A2 – B – A3 form). Contrastingly, 'Night and Day' (1932) is more experimental in harmony, form and metre, opening very unusually with a vocal line of 35 notes, all at the same pitch. The differences between these two songs are symptomatic of a gradual process of evolution through the 20th century and into the new millennium. Different modes have unsurprisingly developed, including bebop, modal jazz, jazz-rock fusion, acid jazz, smooth jazz, punk jazz, M-base and jazzcore. Free (or 'avant-garde') jazz, with its flexible tonality, emerged in the 1950s. Like *vers libre*, it abandoned formal symmetry, metre and beat, also departing from conventional harmonic structures. Free jazz is typically more abstract, experimenting with multiphonics and overtones. It also echoes modernist and post-modernist literature in its referential scope, drawing on musical styles and genres from across the world. The jazz of recent decades has been characterised by pluralism, evident in the appropriation of R&B, hip hop and pop music elements, as well as the incorporation of electronic sounds.

In contemporary jazz – as in new literature – there are differing degrees of innovation and radicalism. Some musicians adhere to avant garde methods while others (such as James Carter) employ experimental elements within a more traditional framework. The prose works of Jean Rhys, Toni Morrison and Zadie Smith discussed above (written between 1962 and 2016) reflect global concerns through a wide range of narrative strategies, though all testify to the legacy of literary modernism. They are characterised by eclecticism, temporal flexibility, free association, symbolic inventiveness and linguistic play. Most strikingly, however – through both explicit engagement and indirect assimilation – these works are infused with the restless, improvisatory, untrammelled energies of jazz.

Bibliography

Akst. Harry, Sam Lewis and Joe Young. 'Dinah'. At Lyrics, Stands4 Network LLC, 2001–2019, <https://www.lyrics.com/lyric/6077002/Harry+Akst/Dinah> [accessed 9 April 2021].

Cooke, Mervyn. 1997. *The Chronicle of Jazz* (London: Thames and Hudson.

Fitzgerald, F. Scott. 1996. 'Bernice Bobs Her Hair'. In *The Diamond as Big as the Ritz and Other Stories*. London: Penguin.

Fitzgerald, F. Scott. 1991. *The Great Gatsby*. Ed. Matthew J. Bruccoli. Cambridge: Cambridge University Press.

Hentoff, Nat. 2009. 'How Jazz Helped Hasten the Civil Rights Movement'. *The Wall Street Journal*.

Hughes, Langston. 1995. *The Complete Poems of Langston Hughes*. New York: Knopf. At *Literature Online* <http://lion.chadwyck.co.uk> [accessed 9 April 2021].

Lucas, John. 1997. *The Radical Twenties*. Nottingham: Five Leaves Publications.

Morrison, Toni. 2005. 'Foreword'. *Jazz*. London: Vintage. Kindle edition.

Morrison, Toni. 2005. *Jazz*. London: Vintage. Kindle edition.

Ogden, Kathy J. 1989. *The Jazz Revolution*. Oxford: Oxford University Press.

Porter, Cole. 1934. 'Night and Day'. An audio-visual version of Fred Astaire and Ginger Rogers singing this tune for the 1934 film *Gay Divorce* is available at <https://www.youtube.com/watch?v=h02OmcR-be4> [accessed 9 April 2021].

Rhys, Jean. 1987. *The Collected Short Stories*. London: Penguin,

Smith, Zadie. 2016. *Swing Time*. London: Hamish Hamilton (Penguin Group.

Williams, C;aremce and Eddie Green. 'You've got the right key baby, but the wrong keyhole'. 1924. Lyrics are available at <https://donniejoemusic.bandcamp.com/track/youve-got-the-right-key-baby-but-the-wrong-keyhole> and the first recording by Virginia can be heard at <https://www.youtube.com/watch?v=4qvpGbzuUl4> [accessed 9 April 2021].

YEATS AND CRAZY JANE: *WORDS FOR MUSIC PERHAPS*

ADRIAN PATERSON

Emblematic of centuries of women scorned as 'fallen', 'distracted', 'cracked', and seen by society as mad, bad, old, dirty, and morally repugnant, 'Crazy Jane' was a surprising, potentially controversial figure for an august male Nobel laureate in his late sixties to adopt as persona. Still, her voice comes to dominate Yeats's 1932 poetic sequence *Words for Music Perhaps*, despite taking direct part in perhaps only seven of the twenty-five poems. This phenomenon has never quite been satisfactorily explained, probably because *Words for Music Perhaps* has always been a bit embarrassing. Embarrassing to the new Irish Free State and its censorship laws because they frankly exhibited a woman of unaccustomed frankness, these poems can be embarrassing to a #MeToo generation for appropriating a woman's voice and ostensibly salivating over her sexuality; and embarrassing to older critics, for whom these apparently throwaway lyrics (with refrains!) mark a retreat from the achievements of 1920s high modernism. Words for music *sans* music, poems pretending to be songs, are anyway to many intrinsically embarrassing, in the way that being confronted by madness is embarrassing. In sum, to be sung at by someone so nominatively determined as Crazy Jane (especially while reading) was always going to provide an awkward encounter, especially if her author supposedly knew nothing of music.[1]

This chapter reasons that just as these embarrassments are interconnected, so too the awkwardness, madness, and musicality these poems present are interconnected: all of them are inextricable from Crazy Jane's spotted history. Neither could they have been conceived nor executed without considerably more musical and historical perspective than is usual to allow Yeats. According to George Yeats the genesis of the whole sequence had direct musical compulsion: her husband "yesterday came dashing along from his cot to announce that he was going to write twelve songs and I had got to purchase 'a musical instrument' at once and set them to music" – an

---

[1] According to Harry White Yeats was "hostile (or at best indifferent) to actual music" and sought its replacement with words (White, 2001, 266).

account born out by an original unambiguous numerologically charged title, *Twelve Poems for Music* (Yeats 2011, 200).[2] Told from a young age he was 'tone-deaf' (an unscientific but surprisingly durable charge), to the poet singing had long been a source of embarrassment, though he knew enough about music to play with twelves and sevens. Doubtfully he remarked the title was "not so much that they may be sung as that I may define their kind of emotion to myself" (1957, 758).[3] He would soon confide "for music is only a name – no one will sing them", and add a half-embarrassed, half-playful, wholly calculated disclaimer *Perhaps* to the title. All the same my reading differs somewhat from Margaret Mills Harper's sense that from the first the poems were "not meant to be set to music" (Harper 2018, 32). For an author who continually asserted "I wanted all my poetry to be spoken on a stage or sung" (Yeats 1961, 529), the initial impulse appears genuine, and affected all that followed. What began (in George Yeats's description) as "songs" of the "most frivolous nature", became as the sequence grew "always keeping the mood and plan of the first poems" sharp, salty, and sexual, borrowing from popular song, while finding a tone of voice and timbre that potentially plumbed a more profound musical resonance (Yeats 1996, 760).[4] No longer precisely songs, they retained distinct features of their originating music.

While these poems were not in the end sung, they claimed the origins of song, its energy and pitch. Through the figure of Crazy Jane, they gathered a piercing sense of the voice and place of their imagined performance. To understand this, the current piece explores Crazy Jane's own embarrassing history in popular literature, from literary poem to stage-song, parlour-song, street-song; examining especially printed broadsides which evidence that astonishing porousness between high and low culture enabled by music. Since her devising in the late eighteenth century, she had become a nineteenth-century 'craze', featuring as principal character in a series of songs, broadsides, and dramatic performances. Crucially, 'Crazy Jane' was almost from the first directly connected with music as well as madness.

---

[2] George Yeats, Letter to Thomas MacGreevy, February 1929. Margaret Mills Harper's reading of this episode finds the suggestion was moot, neither partner being capable of the songs' performance (Harper 2018, 33). But as a sensitive pianist (according to Dorothy Shakespear), her "interests musical, literary, practical" (Yeats 1937, 23), George Yeats may have been amused by this sudden request, but it was not an outlandish one.
[3] W.B. Yeats, Letter to Olivia Shakespear, 2 March 1929.
[4] from Yeats's notes to *The Winding Stair and Other Poems* (1933).

It is worth then spending some time detailing the phenomenon to weigh the effects on Yeats's poems. Examining this history discloses how the poems came to be, awkwardly but precisely, words for music perhaps: less singable, perhaps, but perhaps no less musical. What transpires are not deliberate artsongs, but utterances that give voice to the recalcitrant, scurrilous, pithy energy of curse, delight, and refrain, and the wisdom found in rags, bad printing, sexuality, and scatology. Significantly, they add a vulgar off-key noise to the wider sound of modernist poetry, so often characterized as aloof and elitist. All this required Crazy Jane. Borrowing her voice not only allows her own poems to relish and reverse a marginalized discourse about gender, aging, and disability, but the whole sequence to address a cultural amnesia about words with music.

The Birth of Crazy Jane

Begun in Rapallo, Italy, while Yeats was convalescing from serious illness, *Words for Music Perhaps* returned anew to the landscape and half-ruined buildings of Thoor Ballylee, County Galway. Drawing like his monumental volume *The Tower* on the acerbic songs of the itinerant Irish poet Antoine Ó Raifteirí, these poems by adopting a female persona found particular antecedents in Biddy Early, a wise woman about whose herbal remedies Yeats had sought details on first coming to Ballylee, and 'Cracked Mary', a local satirist of the district with "an amazing power of audacious speech. One of her great performances is a description of how the meanness of a Gort shopkeepers' wife over the price of a glass of porter made her so despair of the human race that she got drunk. The incidents of that drunkenness are of an epic magnificence" (Yeats 1957, 785-6). In remembering these widely forgotten but locally notorious figures Yeats was returning to a source of female wisdom as well as sharp-tongued verve. Cracked Mary could sing, too: she had provided the "words and the air of 'There's Broth in the Pot'" for Yeats and Lady Gregory's play *The Pot of Broth*, and would remain a crucial and acknowledged inspiration, mentioned in the titles of four poems when first published (Yeats 1966, 254).[5] However, according to NLI manuscripts edited by David R. Clark, the name 'Crazy Jane' may have been adopted as early as August 1929 to identify a principal figure in the sequence (1983, 54). Perhaps it became embarrassing to name a real if already half-fictional figure with only local application. Whatever the motives, as the sequence was reworked, expanded, and republished, by

---

[5] in *The New Review*, 12 November 1930.

adopting Crazy Jane instead, Yeats found a more storied and even more intrinsically musical resonance.

Unlike the figures I've named so far, Crazy Jane had the misfortune to be English – but had nonetheless a Romantic history. Her creator was Mathew 'Monk' Lewis, author of the gothic novel *The Monk*, who composed a poem, according to his biographer, after an "encounter with a poor woman" had alarmed his walking companion, Lady Charlotte. Her alarm, and Lewis's exaggerated eye for the main chance, "threw an air of romance over the adventure, which, suffused into the poem, gained for it a degree of popularity scarce yet abated" (Baron-Wilson 1839, 187). Crazy Jane's originator was hardly original, borrowing a familiar trope of an abandoned woman sent out of her wits, discovered suicidal as Shakespeare's Ophelia or sentimentalized in Sterne's Maria. Having been wronged in love, her central characteristic was an endearing pitiable madness: "but the youth I lov'd so dearly | Stole the wits of Crazy Jane". If this pathetic character struck such a chord, it was partly because she was already familiar. William Cowper's 'The Task' featured a sighing, dishevelled former serving-maid "who fell in love | With one who left her, went to sea, and died", concluding frankly: "Kate is crazed" (Cowper 2012, 19). Cowper's own struggles with melancholia let compassion into his narration, but although he also composed hymns and ha'penny songs, his economical blank verse was not singable, or even rhymed. By mobilizing rhyme's empathy Lewis's Crazy Jane might be better compared to the named heroine of many ballads, like the Laura who "wanders this lone grove" shedding "sighs and tears" in 'Henry's Cottage Maid' (whose title conveniently rhymes with "betrayed"), or the 'Lass of Aughrim' whose heroine, carrying her child, beats desperately on Lord Gregory's door, in a song whose vocal performance precipitates the climax of James Joyce's story 'The Dead'.

Notwithstanding Jane's startling confrontation with Lewis, as a poem 'Crazy Jane' is not so startling. It possesses four stanzas of eight lines each, ABAB rhymes, each line four beats and eight syllables. The name "Crazy Jane" which rounds off each stanza in half-refrain may have been chosen for ease in rhyming (with "vain", "again", "brain", "plain"). Such an orderly approach minimizes the disruption of her physical presence, but lends itself to strophic settings:

> Stay fair maid! On every feature
> Why are marks of dread imprest?
> Can a wretched helpless creature
> Raise such terrors in your breast?
> Do my frantic looks alarm you?

Trust me sweet, your fears are vain
Not for kingdoms would I harm you
Shun not then poor Crazy Jane.

"Dost thou weep to see my anguish?
Mark me, and escape my woe:
When men flatter, sigh, and languish,
Think them false — I found them so!
For I loved, Oh! so sincerely,
None will ever love again;
Yet the man I prized most dearly
Broke the heart of Crazy Jane. (Baron-Wilson, 1839, I:188)

Orderly this is, yet it possesses just enough of what Barthes calls the "grain of the voice" to appeal to potential listeners (1977, 177). Lewis evinced considerable interest in madness: his play *The Captive* depicts the ravages of solitary confinement, and his contemporaries evidently intuited real feeling in Jane's situation. Vitally, she speaks her own lines, sympathetically addressing another woman, as well as (implicitly) an imagined audience similarly shocked at her appearance. The ballad's punctuated exclamations, all questions, dashes, and mid-line Oh! with exclamation marks, gives Jane's vocal style an intensity of emotion beneath the decorum. Precisely because of the confluence of all these elements, generic, formal and emotional, the poem was almost asking for music.

Not surprisingly for the period, then, many new melodies were minted. Two musical settings of the original poem, both widespread, make a claim for predominance. As Roly Brown recounts in a comprehensive article tracing the ballad's many incarnations, which came first is hard to know (Brown 2017). John Davy's version featured in gala concerts in Bath, and was quickly published (around 1799) as far away as New York. Harriet Abrams, herself an accomplished singer (Thomas Arne wrote an opera for her, and Haydn accompanied her in concert), produced "Crazy Jane, a favourite ballad, for three voices" with a version for solo singer (**Ill. 1**). Notably this setting by a noted female performer appears to have become more popular. Both melodies actually possess similar features: both had the same key (Bb), the same 6/8 time signature, and similar use of a Scotch-snap, reversing the typical dotted rhythms, though Abrams's melody has more inevitable-seeming phrasing. Both, naturally, were arranged for piano and voice, with Abrams' song allowing the fashionable harp as alternative possibility.

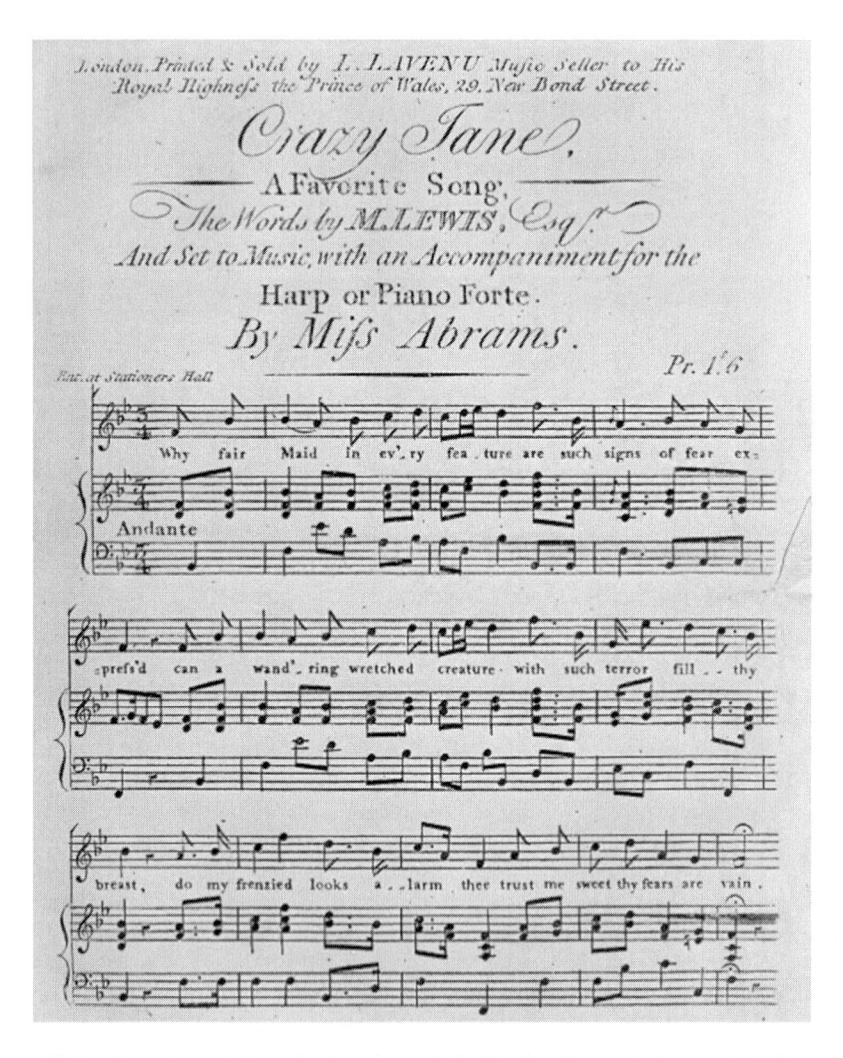

Ill. 1: 'Crazy Jane: A Favorite Song', music by Harriet Abrams (Abrams, ?1798).

Manifestly 'Crazy Jane' became the sensation it did as a "favorite" song for female singers to sing. Part of her appeal was that, like Ophelia in her madness, Jane herself could be imagined singing. For Covent Garden performances of *Semiramide*, *The Woodman*, and *The Siege of Belgrade*, advertisements made sure to mention that afterwards "Mrs Second will sing 'Crazy Jane' in character", presumably played out in artfully dishevelled dress and distracted delivery; later Nancy Storace, Caroline Poole and others performed the "celebrated ballad", sometimes "by special desire" (Brown 44, 2017). The element of role-play in this kind of musical rendition is curious. If Crazy Jane was in some ways a stock character, she possessed a potential energy that given the right performance could transport these verses. All those exclamatory Oh! and sighs, with sympathetic musical setting and in the hands of a skilled singer and actress, could on stage become very effective.

And Crazy Jane didn't stay on stage: she came home with her audience. Supplied with suitable printed music for words the part could be sung oneself. 'Crazy Jane' helped to supply the enormous demand for printed songs to sing with piano accompaniment which occupied the talents of Beethoven, Thomas Moore, and an explosion of music publishing outlets and instrument manufacturers as the new century arrived (see Paterson 2020). This emerging market of often self-accompanying singers was predominantly female. In her own home, pianist and singer could herself become Crazy Jane, voicing her plight and embracing with real empathy her fashionably pathetic situation. Such figures were already closely associated with music, understood to license fellow-feeling. So, for example, Maria's traditional pastoral pipes are here laid aside, implicitly substituted by piano or guitar, the grove by the parlour, the shepherdess by the cottage maid:

> "Ah where can fly my soul's true love,
> Sad I wander this lone grove
> Sighs and tears for him I shed.
> HENRY is from LAURA fled,
> Thy love to me thou didst impart
> Thy love soon won my Virgin heart
> But, dearest Henry, thou'st betrayed
> Thy love with thy poor Cottage Maid" (Henry [?1790).

As a song arranged to a plaintive air for voice and guitar, 'Henry's Cottage Maid', once led astray, can thus politely be taken indoors. In an "alliance of street music and elite parlour fashion" it even became fashionable for women to dress up as 'Savoyards', wandering musicians and ballad sellers, purveyors of street music and portable instruments of all kinds from tambourines and barrel organs to guitars (Page 2020, 101). The piano, though, was queen; and the small pianofortes of the period were more piano than forte, allowing a cottage intimacy it is hard to imagine from a modern concert grand. Just so these songs' open-air encounters were brought into a domestic setting by the growing middle classes through private chamber performance. Their imagined scenarios and the intimate theatre of their playing allowed performers and audience to experience safely a daring frisson of open-air roughness that even the inclusion of dodgy named antagonists like Henry (who featured also in Crazy Jane's story) could not always provide.

Wherever she appeared, then, 'Crazy Jane' was sung. But if her songs fitted conventional generic parameters, they also potentially blurred boundaries. Their publishing and performance can seem to suggest a refined audience only. Actually, like many songs of the period, they had an astonishingly wide reach, as they were sung in concert, on stage, in the home, and on the streets, reaching an audience high and low.

So Crazy Jane became the heroine of a series of dozens of crazily-printed broadside ballads from 1800 onwards, turning up in catalogues and collections for many years. Though the distant origins of broadsides in folk songs and ballads were sometimes rural, it should be remembered that such broadsides were primarily an urban phenomenon, with songs (including 'Crazy Jane') printed in London, Liverpool, Preston, Nottingham, Newcastle, York, Bristol, Norwich, and sold on the streets to all-comers by genuine 'Savoyards' or raucously-singing ballad sellers – reaching an audience across classes, including that vast underbelly of marginalized labourers and working women drawn to the city. This was a brutal marketplace of plagiarized pirate productions selling for farthings and ha'pennies. Songs could be stolen from anywhere, including opera houses, contemporary writers, anonymous sources or folk tradition. They had to adapt to survive, and did not unless they found an audience, some of whom at least had to be able (and persuaded) to pay. As printed ephemera they represent an uneven memorialization of street culture played out in marginalized scraps of paper only occasionally (and perhaps unrepresentatively) gathered and collected. But as a song 'Crazy Jane' clearly appealed, appearing in dozens of different printings up until late in the century. Herself like the broadsides ragged and fugitive, Jane's widespread survival within this culture is telling: and it would have decisive effect on her reception and re-use.

The broadsides were characterized by ragged imprecision and dark energy. With erratic typesetting sometimes eliding gaps between stanzas, their blotted black printing made for stark visual impact, invariably announcing 'Crazy Jane' in bold letters. Most added illustrations. Some few printed a church or flowers with only a bare connection to the ballad. More frequently a figure looms large: even such stock woodcuts tended to feature a recognisably female figure in hat and dress, in one early crude woodcut lying in disarray beneath a tree, in a more refined piece kneeling at a grave (Bodleian 2656, 6673). A maid on a village green before church and cottage indicated a suitable rural origin; sometimes like Cracked Mary she seems to be importuning her listeners in a shop or pub interior; sometimes as for Cowper's Crazy Kate a sea narrative for her lover was suggested by wooden boat and ruined building (**Ill. 2**). In several instructive images Jane is joined by another, male figure: in one of the earliest she encounters him on the road, a tree standing by (Bodleian 5445); in other printings the two actually appear framed by foliage that resembles curtains, as if self-consciously referring to pastoral stage-sets from Jane's theatrical career (Bodleian 18289 and **Ill. 3**). The significance of such disassociated images should not

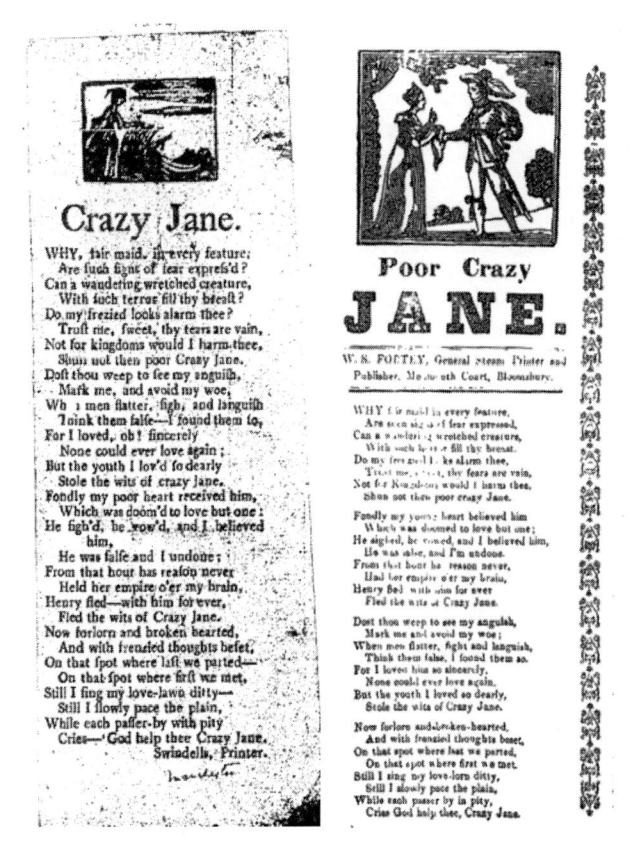

Ill. 2: 'Crazy Jane', Manchester: Swindells c.1796-1853 (Bodleian 17546).

Ill. 3: 'Poor Crazy Jane', London: W.S. Fortey. 1858-1885. (Bodleian 13339).

be overstated. Still, the staging of Jane's madness in these specific locales is revealing of the kind of environs she was expected to inhabit. These discrete scenes open up narrative possibilities in her dialogic meetings, especially as she walks the roads or emerges on stage (surely singing) before an audience. And as with Yeats's poems, through all these songs, her body remained a central iconographical emblem.

Successive broadside printings tended to knock the edges off Lewis's more elaborate poetic diction. So, the grandiose opening "Stay, fair maid!" is almost universally altered to "Why fair maid"; a "wretched, helpless creature" becomes alliteratively "a wandering wretched creature"; "priz'd" becomes "loved", "frantic" becomes "frenzied" and so on – all of which changes give Jane's voice vitality, energy, movement. The final two stanzas are given below with typical variations from the ballads, retained relatively consistently across printings:

"Gladly that young heart received him [Fondly my poor heart believed him
Which has never loved but one [Which was doom'd to love but one
He seemed true, and I believed him, [He sigh'd, he vow'd,
He was false, and I undone!
Since that hour has reason never [From that hour
Held her empire o'er my brain,
Henry fled! – with him for ever
Fled the wits of Crazy Jane.

"Now forlorn and broken-hearted,
And with frenzied thoughts beset
Near the spot where last we parted [On that spot where
Near the spot where first we met, [On the spot where
Thus I chant my lovelorn ditty – [Still I sing my love-lawn ditty
While I sadly pace the plain, [Still I slowly
And each passer by in pity [While each passer-by with pity[6]
Cries – 'God help thee, Crazy Jane!'

(Baron-Wilson, 188)

Rather than printers' mistakes, then, like stones worn by water, the words were worn smooth in the mouths of singers making incremental adjustments towards directness in diction and sense. Such oral transmission 'errors' could be portals of discovery, adding a believable simplicity to her plight. In particular, elements of syntactical and verbal repetition ("On that spot" or "Still I sing") made the song more direct, more singable, and more

---

[6] Variants drawn from 'Crazy Jane', Manchester: Swindells, c.1796-1853 (Bodleian 17546) and from 'Crazy Jane', London: Charles Pigott, 52 Compton Street, Clerkenwell (Bodleian 7333).

immediate. And verses like this were definitely sung, thus validating internal references to their own performance. So, any ambiguity in "chant" is replaced by the determinative "Still I **sing** my love-**lawn** ditty", misspelling taking the song outdoors, implicitly to the roadside grass banks so evidently Jane's milieu.

Surviving for many years in this pirate repertoire, many broadside spin-offs, some featuring Henry's own story, tended to adopt even starker language and sometimes shorter lines. A plethora of song-sequels followed, whether 'The Birth of Crazy Jane', featuring refrain variations ("Drives to frenzy helpless Jane" (**Ill. 4**), an engraved political satire 'Crazy Paul', complete with a chained Russian dancing bear referring to Napoleon's hold on the Tsar (Bodleian 22579), or the maudlin graveyard-set extravagant musical madness of 'Julia's Lamentation: A Pathetic Ballad' ("Thus she sung, and strew'd the flower, | Beat her breast, and wept, and sigh'd", **Ill. 5**).

Closely patterning its verse-form, all these early imitations were composed and sung explicitly "to the tune of 'Crazy Jane'". Their existence suggests the original words' particularity was less important than we might think to the phenomenon. Crazy Jane's name and her music mattered above all. True, broadsides almost never included staff-notation, but this was because the music was assumed to be known by the sellers and their audience: at most, as here, a cue to a compatible tune was referred to by name. But these ballads confirm the survival of a recognisable melody attached to Jane's printed story. Her body and her songs were by such acts irretrievably tied together. The century's continued production of these broadsides declared unequivocally that these were words *for music*, denoting the co-dependence of oral and print culture. So, their survival can be understood by later readers, including the author of *Words for Music Perhaps*.

Primarily then what appeals about these ballads are four things: the compelling central figure of Crazy Jane herself, her direct vocal utterance, her connection with music, and, perhaps, her ragged appearance in print. Indeed, the reach of such songs was astonishing. Crazy Jane gave rise to all sorts of cultural phenomena: hats and racehorses were named after her; real people given the appellation in court cases and newspaper headlines (see Brown 2017). She became the subject of theatre-pieces and even ballets, and later on a powerful watercolour by the Victorian artist Richard Dadd (**Ill. 6**). As the gathering birds half suggest, here she exhibits an outdoor freedom (as well as vulnerability) the artist does not possess: as an inscription attests he himself was held in Bethlehem Hospital, 'Bedlam', a London mental institution. The background ruined castle, like her tattered

The Birth of Crazy Jane.

Tune—*Crazy Jane.*

FRAGRANT is the rose-bud throwing
Sweets ambrosial to the gale,
Gentle as the violet blowing,
Humble daughter of the vale,
In a cot by sweetbriar guarded
From the breeze that fans the plain,
Were her parent's hopes rewarded,
By the birth of lovely Jane.

Not the painted flowers adorning
By their tints the hours of May,
Not the radiance mild of morning,
Gilding autumn's op'ning day,
Boasts a charm so sweetly cheering,
Soothes so well the breast of pain,
As the playful smile endearing,
That adorn'd the infant Jane.

But the vernal flow'ret blowing,
Withers oft in summer's pride;
Oft the morning rosy glowing,
Ushers storms to eventide:
So of childhood's harmless pleasure,
Short and transient is the reign,
And of youth the ripening treasure
Brings distress on lovely Jane.

When the worm insidious preying,
Wastes the chalice of the flow'r,
Soon its silken leaves decaying,
Marks for death its vernal hour.
So true fondness unrequited,
Turns the cup of joy to pain;
So a faithful passion blighted
Drives to frenzy hapless Jane.

Julia's Lamentation:

A PATHETIC BALLAD.

To the Tune of———"Crazy Jane."

Evans, printer, Long-lane, London.

TO the graves where sleep the dead,
Hapless Julia took her way;
Sighs to heave, and tears to shed,
O'er the spot where Damon lay.
Many a blooming flow'r she bore,
O'er the green-grass turf to throw;
And, while fast her tears did pour,
Thus she sang to soothe her woe:

"Soft and safe, thou lowly grave,
Fast o'er thee my tears shall flow—
Only hope the hapless have,
Only refuge left for woe.
'Constant love and grief sincere,
Shall thy hallowed turf pervade;
And many a heartfelt sigh and tear,
Hapless youth, shall soothe thy grave.

"Lighted by the Moon's pale shine,
See me, to thy mem'ry true,
Lowly bending at thy shrine,
Many a votive flower to strew:
But how little do these flow'rs
Prove my love and constancy!
Yet a few sad fleeting hours,
And, dear youth, I'll follow thee!

"Rose, replete with scent and hue,
Sweetest flow'r that Nature blows;
Damon flourish'd once, like you,
Now o'er him the green-grass grow:
Rose, go deck his hallowed grave,
Lily, o'er the green-turf twine;
Honour meet that turf should have,
Beauty's bed and Virtue's shrine."

Thus she sung, and strew'd the flow'r,
Beat her breast, and wept, and sigh'd;
And, when toll'd the midnight hour,
On the green-turf grave she dy'd.
Many a Nightingale forlorn
Sung her knell, while breezes sigh'd;
Haughty Grandeur heard with scorn,
How so poor a maiden dy'd!

Ill. 4: 'The Birth of Crazy Jane'. London: J. Davenport (1800-1802). Bodleian Harding 6028.

Ill. 5: 'Julia's Lamentation: A Pathetic Ballad, To the Tune of "Crazy Jane"' London: Evans, Long Lane (1780-1812). Bodleian Harding 14065.

Fig. 14. Richard Dadd "Sketch of an Idea for Crazy Jane". London: Bethlehem Hospital, 1855.

dress and feathers, appears emblematic of her state of mind, and in the landscape is perhaps encoded a social critique about the decline of old ways, as enclosure drove dispossessed rural women from the land (Humphries, 1990 ff). Yet her studied posture, gender-bending gaze, and intense scrutiny of the viewer suggests a continued unnerving presence. Jane has entered but at the same time resists the asylum's correctional force: such a visible defiance of authority made her a powerful not just pitiable figure. Increasingly perhaps her madness could be seen as dissident, not pathetic, her "wandering" the road a powerful statement. And as she travelled by means of street song, she was never far from music, in a way that both caused and echoed her popularity.

Words for Music Perhaps

Several things therefore were in place to feature in Yeats's sequence: an initial confrontation, a direct address overheard by a listening audience, a distinctive female voice, and body. Adding to this was a long residue in popular memory, a continual association with music, and the metamorphoses made possible by sharper, harder, short-lined song sequels and visual retellings. Many of these cues might be considered a spur for a sequence of answering poems that played anew with music. By choosing Crazy Jane as his title figure Yeats was harnessing many of these traits: it probably even helped that her origins were starting to be forgotten.

Yeats was also, of course, appropriating the figure to suit his own ends. Channelling 'Cracked Mary', his Jane is ribald and unrepentant, remembering one love but among many, as in 'Crazy Jane and Jack the Journeyman'. However, by naming her 'Crazy Jane' an important past is signalled: already she has been possessed by countless singers and printers. Yeats's 'Crazy Jane' poems were themselves essentially pirated sequels. It is obvious from the titles they represented unusual ones. 'Crazy Jane and the Bishop', 'Crazy Jane Reproved', 'Crazy Jane on the Day of Judgment', 'Crazy Jane and Jack the Journeyman', 'Crazy Jane on God', 'Crazy Jane Talks with the Bishop', 'Crazy Jane Grown Old Looks at the Dancers': these titles unlock a metaphysical complexity, just as they insist on a dialogic and raucous spirit. Taking a hint perhaps from her polite importuning of her listeners, and the increasing passion of her approach, Jane's address is unflinching, her madness now strangely cogent, though indecorous and uncomfortably probing.

As far as they travelled, each of these poems remembered their origins as part of a musical culture, as the reference to 'dancers' suggests. Each one retained one or more things conspicuously musical about it: for instance, the simple rhymes, short lines, and repetitions of sung poetry; the extended ballad stanzas or curdling voices of the broadsides; a tissue of specific, sometimes hidden musical references, or nods to street culture; most notably, perhaps, the use of refrains. At the same time, each one in some manner resists, pulls away from something that works concretely or wholly as an actual song, finding some way to shelter from a popular audience's demands for open-air accessibility through a recalcitrant complexity or obdurate unsingability. It is in this kind of tension, just precluding the full vocal release of song, that these poems find and hold their energy.

Such tensions work differently in each poem, so to try to gauge them this piece turns to consider in closer focus three poems from the sequence, all of them spoken or sung as if by Crazy Jane herself. It makes most sense to examine poems certainly composed with Crazy Jane in mind, and 'Crazy Jane on the Day of Judgment' was one of the first.[7] Whatever its precise date, examining its genesis is especially worthwhile, as the grain of her voice is made unusually present through refrain. The pioneer of genetic criticism, Louis Hay, says of manuscripts, 'it is high time we learned to make them speak' (Hay, 1996, 207). Unpeeling the layers of this poem momentarily it is possible to hear how Yeats began to make them sing.

Prose drafts speak of a "Subject for a Crazy Jane Poem", called at an early stage "Crazy Jane and the End of the World" (Yeats, 2010, 246). Increasingly the voice envisaged is plainly Crazy Jane's own, delimited in the end by quotation marks. But in establishing her voice, the drafts disclose a composition process prepared drastically to change semantic direction – and driven to reach that end apparently by reasons of sound. Jane is a demanding lover, provocatively insisting "that you touch all portions of my body", or she will think of "some that might take your place" before a radical compression into short sharp pithy lines reveals vital character as well as metaphysical complexity:

'Love is all
Unsatisfied
That cannot take the whole
Body and soul';
And that is what Jane said.

'Take the sour
If you take me,
I can scoff and lour

---

[7] As noted, from manuscripts David R. Clark dates its beginnings to August 1929 rather than August 1930; in either case before the November 1930 publication in the *New Review* as 'Four Poems' naming 'Cracked Mary'.

And scold for an hour.'
'That's certainly the case,' said he. (Yeats, 1996, 372-3)

The poem thus becomes less about "your" lover's anxiety, and more about Jane's utterances on wider human experience. In her voice the particular and general are constantly inverted. So, an original unplaced refrain "*Love is for wholes | Whether of bodies or souls*" is compressed into the first stanza's ever-unsatisfiable longing. And the drafts' "**Nor** would **my** sweet **display** | For **lack** of **day**" gains an emphatic nominative first person and connective, 'But what can **I display** | **That lack day**', before these sounds cause their own transfiguration:

Naked I lay
The grass my bed;
Naked and hidden away,
That **black** day'
And that is what Jane said. (emphasis mine)

Compressed by the abbreviated line-lengths, under pressure from an accumulated mass of similar syllable sounds and naked emotion, thrust at white heat, words transmogrify, so even parts of speech are altered, from relative pronoun to Yeats's favourite declarative deictic **That.** The original sorrowing **lack** borrows the **b** of **but** to emerge **black**, like some igneous rock. Such changes half-recall the sonically-driven verbal alterations of the broadsides, though here they don't make the poem easier to sing. Rather, for instance, the frankness of "the grass my bed" retains a ghost of Jane's inadvertently punning 'love-lawn ditty'. Potentially, the reader is confronted by Jane's disruptive body, now naked and stripped of all its ragged finery. Yet the word and sense of "display" is actually excluded, "hidden" arriving to work tantalizingly against the repetition of 'naked': there persists a privacy in Jane's presentation, as in such verbal sleights of hand. Nonetheless an element of **play** in display persists into the final draft.

Scrutinizing the philosophical complexities of the sequence, Jonathan Luftig considers its distinctive characteristic "a figure who thus bears witness to love's shattered and shattering character" whose discourse goes so far as to "shatter the 'world' of linguistic reference to pieces" (Lufting, 2009, 1141). If so, this makes Jane a revolutionary linguist. The question is, how? It is a mobilizing song, it seems to me, which sanctions a loosening of linguistic specificity in grammar and semantics, as there the repeatable but mutable nature of sounds plays overtly. In coming to the fore, such 'fore-play' of sounds (if the pun can be forgiven) seems hardly "frivolous". Indeed, the way plays on words survive into the finished poem seems a matter of great weight. So the drafts' rhymed back-and-forth between what is "**known**" and "**shown**", richly suggestive of different forms of knowledge, seems, as so often in Yeats's epistemology, to pit embodied experiential understanding against intellect – as in a late letter declaring "Man can embody truth but he cannot know it" (Yeats, 2002, 7363).[8] The poem's final version instead preserves both kinds of knowledge as fused alternatives, eliminating neat end-rhyming pairs to end its lines with a bare repeat of the same word, **shown**:

> 'What can be **shown**?
> What true love be?
> All could be **known** or **shown**
> If Time were but **gone**.'
> *That's certainly the case, said he.*   (Yeats, 1996, 372-3)

The change shifts emphasis from debating forms of knowledge to the practical impossibility of its discovery – except, in another hopeless longing, outside of Time. If Jane's concluding words seem to call for the title's "day of judgment" and come out against time's continuance, their self-generative energy at the same time expresses its inevitable going on. The "end of the world" is not really nigh: such a time-bound poem expresses an inextricably time-bound world. Finally, although almost entirely stripped down to five lines of two abrupt gnomic questions, one philosophical answer and one dry refrain, the language of this stanza (as the whole poem) registers if anything an increase in complexity as it lets time play with resistant sound-shapes. Even the refrain "*That's certainly the case, said he*" sounds a sly affirmation that undercuts any sense of universal truth, raising the question of voice, and origin, and whom the reader is to listen to.

Because more than anything adopting the voice of Crazy Jane returned refrains to Yeats's verses. Even poems without Jane are influenced by her tone, so 'Her Anxiety' takes on a sharp defiance in refrain:

Prove that I lie.

Five poems out of seven with her name on insist on refrains which are oddly gnomic, redundant, and unplaced:

All find safety in the tomb. […]
The solid man and the coxcomb.
Love is like the lion's tooth.

---

[8] Yeats to Lady Elizabeth Pelham, 4 Jan 1939.

Half-rhymed and barely mellifluous (in 'Crazy Jane and the Bishop' a softer alternating line '*Love is like the lily flower*' disappears from the drafts), gathering all the force of pithy epigrams, these refrains enter the poem with spoken force. Double refrains can be doubly unstable, calling up multiple voices who hardly fit into these short poems:

And that is what Jane said. [...]
That's certainly the case, said he.

With Jane's voice dominant, these unequal italic assertions at least agree in claiming the whole poem as speech. But as firmly as the *he said she said* back-and-forth insists this poem is saying things, it is impossible to tell who speaks its italic commentary, if they are a single entity, or if they are really speaking (they escape the poem's inverted commas). These exterior italic intrusions cannot help but arrive acousmatically, without an obvious point of origin; and anachronistically, with a habit older than the nineteenth or twentieth century. Refrain's conventions go back a long way, and perhaps assume a collective chorus. Given their background in antiphonal choir music, which historians consider may have introduced rhyme into Western verse, double refrains introduce the distant possibility not only of multiply-voiced stanzas but of a genuinely musical antiphony (Winn, 1981, ff). Finally, however they are read, including refrains irresistibly suggests not just saying but song. 'Crazy Jane Reproved' goes so far as to conclude its subtle Latinate verses about subtle making:

Fol de rol, fol de rol.

For a poet not a songwriter to include such nonsense words was challenging – especially to a reader. Consciously playing with (im)"polite meaningless words" shows daring for a modernist poet, as Hugo Ball's Dadaists discovered. Yeats's impulses were not so anarchic, but to employ half or near-empty refrains meant there was music in his madness, borrowed and inscribed though its conscious irrationality was. Embodying quite a departure from sober versifying stanzas, such refrains rejected restraint, sounding an outdoor musical clamour that embarrasses the title's defensive "perhaps".

Such playing with sound spills out from the refrains over whole poems: so, for instance one putative refrain for 'Crazy Jane on the Day of Judgment', "*Time runs on*", emerges in the dance-carol adaptation 'I Am of Ireland'; and "*Love is for wholes | Whether of body or souls*" finds shocking conclusion in the 1931 poem 'Crazy Jane Talks With the Bishop':

> 'A woman can be proud and stiff
> When on love intent;
> But Love has pitched his mansion in
> The place of excrement;
> For nothing can be sole or whole
> That has not been rent.' (Yeats 1996, 375)

Beyond refrains, then, a license for sonic performance, double meanings, and vocal address remembers Jane's ballad history, as well as her places of encounter. "I met the Bishop on the road | And much said he and I" the poem begins, addressing the situation and iterations of 'Monk' Lewis's ballad directly, even as it subverts the initial circumstances of its polite popularity, in favour of an earthy, carnal entrenchment (Yeats 1996, 375). In anal as well as oral suggestion, the poem returns to the road, also a site of "excrement": rubbish, discharge, excreta, the dung of horses and other animals (as well as discarded paper broadsides), before alighting on its central emphatic pun, "rent", meaning torn, ripped (just as the long strips of paper broadsides were separated from larger printed sheets), traded, hired, even bought and sold, something potentially true of both her body and the ballad in this world of street walkers and ballad-sellers. "Fair and foul are near of kin", Jane cries, opposing centuries of church moralising and societal oppression, justifying a liberality in women's sexual choices – which might mirror that of the aging artist. Her affirmation comes close to an idea expressed in Yeats's *A Packet for Ezra Pound* (1929):

> But the Muses are like those women who creep out at night and give themselves to unknown sailors and return to talk of Chinese porcelain – porcelain is best made, a Japanese critic has said, where the conditions of life are hard – or of the Ninth Symphony – except that the Muses sometimes form in those low haunts their most lasting attachments. (Yeats, 1937, 32)

If Crazy Jane can be said in any respect to represent the poet's muse, she is, in this amused telling, likely to be unruly. Crazy Jane is more than a muse who is musical, she is herself, with her own body and mind, her own desires, refusing love's ownership. That Jane herself expresses her creed so bodily, ecstatically, orally, affirms that serious lasting attachments and serious lasting art, including establishment art symbolised by the music of Beethoven's Ninth Symphony, can – perhaps should – remember street walkers and street culture. If this poem's conclusion that in such "low haunts" can be found the "heart's pride" and the grandest of aesthetic conceptions is uncomfortable, it should in turn remind the reader that the marriage of words and music ("perhaps"!) is an "attachment" often disapproved of: an uncomfortable, unfashionable, backstreets arrangement full of distasteful bargains and considerable unfaithfulness on both sides. Yet at the same time it can also represent the most profound, productive, and lasting partnership – something true of Beethoven's Ninth, which itself turns to words, and potentially the broadsides. Like them, she (and her ballad) is "rent", can never be owned – however aggressively it is sold by publisher or street-seller nobody ever quite owns a song, which when learnt by heart persists in the minds and mouths of its audience. With her music now quite forgotten, "My friends are gone", Jane cries. She is out of time, out of luck, out of tune, out of audience, yet (and here she is like her author putting together words for music) defiantly continuing. Jane's contradictory contention seems to be that only when a poem is a song, ripped, rended, rent, for hire, can it be itself alone, and an organic whole.

That Jane's hard-won bodily resistance might be founded in the oral value of song is made plainer in 'Crazy Jane on God', composed sometime in 1931 and first published in Cuala Press's *Words for Music Perhaps and Other Poems* (1932). It is the poem in the sequence closest to Monk's original 'Crazy Jane' ballad, presenting a familiar scenario in four stanzas from the point of view of what the eighteenth-century would describe as an 'abandoned' woman. While its six-line stanzas only present three rhymes, the endline of each stanza acts as a refrain whose pivotal word "*remain*" even makes a rhyme with the title's 'Crazy Jane'. Featuring abrupt changes in topic, the stanzas generate a disconnected, distracted air even as they return obsessively to the central coming of "That lover" – whose departure, if nothing else, is by no means necessarily consensual. Yet overall, the tone is quite different. Instead of lamenting her fate as some passive creature made mad by some aboriginal coupling, having "had wild Jack for a lover", the speaker's voice achieves a glorious indifference as she stakes her survival on song. Certainly, this Crazy Jane has very strange visions in which primal moments of violence are brought to mind. Generically, as well as geographically, the poem travels considerable distances, while the refrain's mantra repeatedly returns to its basis in theology:

> That lover of a night
> Came when he would,
> Went in the dawning light
> Whether I would or no;
> Men come, men go;
> *All things remain in God.*
>
> Banners choke the sky;
> Men-at-arms tread;
> Armoured horses neigh
> Where the great battle was

In the narrow pass:
All things remain in God.

Before their eyes a house
That from childhood stood
Uninhabited, ruinous,
Suddenly lit up
From door to top:
All things remain in God.

I had wild Jack for a lover;
Though like a road
That men pass over
My body makes no moan
But sings on:
All things remain in God.

    The poem travels to some wild places, mobilizing a dramatic stark simplicity in diction and vocabulary. Opening with Jane's taut summary of lovers' meetings, the first stanza suggests nothing so much as a Provençal *alba* or *aubade* (all of which once came with music): the lover's regretful dawn-song recast as curt realist testament. The second, perhaps indebted to Cracked Mary's dream of 'unearthly riders on white horses', rather resembles the dreamlike martial politics of an Irish-language *aisling* poem, except that here male violence is by no means celebrated. Perhaps weirdest of all, the third stanza inserts an unaccountable vision of a lit-up ruined house. This preoccupation resurfaced often in the phantasmagoria of Yeats's later years, often alongside music. His play *Purgatory* figures it in flames as a symbol of the landed destruction of eighteenth-century houses; before this a ghostly vision of a named big house, Sligo's Castle Dargan, features in *The King of the Great Clocktower* with music by Arthur Duff, the lyric published with music as 'The Wicked Hawthorn Tree' in a new series of 1935 *Broadsides* Yeats was editing, including printed music and illustration by Victor Brown. Like some scrap of primal folklore in song, Crazy Jane's version occludes any certainty that she (they? we?) witnessed a house-burning. What remains seems an almost miraculous vision more akin to the "goldfish bowl" of 'All Souls' Night', especially as it is followed by the chime of the refrain, which repeats in a kind of musical as well as philosophical acceptance. But a kind of holy witness, a saintly presence, is always potentially available in ragged wandering figures of the road.

    This is hard to account for: certainly, it is not how early audiences viewed Crazy Jane. But Marsilio Ficino's ideas about *furor*, frenzy or inspired madness, might help interpret Jane's crazed insight. Ficino's philosophy privileged the healing powers of music, particularly of Orphic singing, making it important for Yeats, who found his influential ideas in occult studies of Cornelius Agrippa and Pico della Mirandola. As it happens Ficino's doctrine of the four *furores* matches neatly onto the four stanzas. Ficino recognised four kinds of inspired madness: *furor amatorius*, the ecstasy of the lover, in play in the opening; *furor divinus*, the ravishment of prophecy, which suggests the second stanza denotes an apocalyptic battle yet to come; *furor mysterialis*, the fervour of religious rites, which might account for the third stanza's miraculous light; and finally, the *furor* of poetry, expressed orally in wild shouts but most powerfully of all in singing and songs (*clamor, cantus, carmina*).[9]

Thus, the most frank and insouciant of the stanzas, the last, continues the theme, finding another way to express ecstasy in dissolution. To use the road as central metaphor can't help but associate Crazy Jane's physical presence with the roads she walks and songs of the road she might sing while out walking them. Such songs could recall A.E.'s *Homeward: Songs by The Way* (1894) written by Yeats's friend George Russell, which fascinated him by intimating an ordinariness to their absolute visionary certainty, as if meeting ghosts or ancient heroic figures on the road were an everyday occurrence. As a road walker Crazy Jane's visions have this ordinary power. But Crazy Jane is not just a creature of the road, she is herself a road to be walked on. Becoming in a strange stoic self-abnegation part of others' journeys, she is employed to tell other narratives: so, as in the ballads, she is used, hired, borrowed like the hermit's cloak and thrown away like paper, passed over trodden on like those discarded broadsides themselves. Ignored, soiled, overwritten she might be, but still her song continues: 'My body makes no moan | But sings on' – indeed the more debased she has become the more her body asserts song's survival. For Ficino, poetic *furor* is the lowest of the four *furores*; for Yeats, coming last like this perhaps it rates higher. Certainly, the inspired poetic *furor* his Crazy Jane exudes is refined: expressly it does not feature the clamour of shout or moan, instead taking what Ficino considered its purest form: song. Like the original 'Crazy Jane', she has become a wandering singer, unselfconscious about appearance, aging, or bodily distress. Unlike her, however, she is not doomed but rather inspired to continue the song, which she literally embodies. Rooted in its stubborn persistence, through song her body is translated, transfigured into the piercing theological (in)sanity (not in this case the "artifice") of eternity – or, as this is stated in the refrain, better perhaps to say into a divine eternal recurrence: *All things remain in God.*

---

[9] For more on Ficino's doctrine of the four *furores*, or inspired madnesses, see (Walker, 1958, 12-24).

The curious thing is that, unlike some, if one counts the syllables and stresses metrically, this poem is perversely erratic. Whatever the pronunciation it is difficult to make properly strophic stanzas out of it, so considered as a song it is quite irregular: crazy, in fact, featuring all the defects of the body. Moreover, the many half-rhymes are not helpful for singers who really need matching vowels. These lines are not really singable at all. Probably this is fitting for a poem of such compressed heterogeneity, the irregular areas of its stanzas paved so violently together. Each traverse across the fallen world represented by the off-rhymes **would | tread | stood | road** all make their own weary journey – only to arrive together in the divine, finding a rhyming home in **God**. There is an unlikely seriousness to all this, with a cousin in the original Crazy Jane's "for I loved, Oh! sincerely", the apostrophe "Oh!" nicely suggesting her feeling as well as allowing for the metre. Yeats's poem lacks such direct markers of song. But if on first hearing Crazy Jane's powerful abrupt conclusion "*All things remain in God*" makes an instinctively unmusical refrain, philosophically it suggests a much higher consonance. Crazy Jane's religious sense is hard-won, but sincere: and its implication is momentous. That Jane's claims are holy as well as sexual might appear to wrench her from her origins. But not if the refrain recalls music. Actually, she supersedes the church's sole claim to morality and via similar means: by invoking music, she calls up an ancient authority for irrational insight, *ethoi* (ethical codes), and sonic empathy. Here, as much as in her dialogues with the Bishop, her body, her conviction, her insight, her song (in each of four stanzas) are at once palpable and transfigured; embodying as well as transcending her street origins. Just as her holiness comes from holes as well as wholes, it is plain that her existence as one of the road's ragged wanderers has made her an unlikely modern saint. Moreover, that her divine frenzy or inspired madness, as it did for Ficino, requires music, however debased.

Words For Music?

Yeats noted "in my moments of personal hopefulness—Edwin Ellis's definition of vanity—I begin to think that what my friends call my lack of ear is but an instinct for the music of the twelfth century" (2002, 5229).[10] Old, erratic, improper, at times ugly, yet recklessly sonically-inspired and conditioned by modernity, these poems, perhaps, were words for music of a very old and very new kind. Actual music briefly returned to the sequence when Yeats rehearsed the singer Margot Ruddock for his BBC radio

---

[10] W.B. Yeats, Letter to T. Sturge Moore, 24 March 1929.

broadcasts (see Barnes 1987, Paterson 2011). Instructing her on the *fol de rol* refrain of 'Crazy Jane Reproved' (to return later in 'The Pilgrim') Yeats wrote "I think when you find words like that in an old ballad, they are meant to be sung to a melody, as Partch, the California musician I told you of sings his 'meaningless words' […]. I put [them] at the end of the stanzas in that poem to make it less didactic, gayer, more clearly a song. If you feel inclined to you may put such words at the end of any stanza of any poem where there is not already a burden" (Yeats, 2002, 6134).[11] Harry Partch's setting of Yeats's *Oedipus The King* showed that writing music for words based on speech rhythm and pitch could open up new possibilities for modern music (see Partch 1974). For reasons of propriety, as well as their intricate words or lack of music, *Words for Music Perhaps* would largely remain impossible to broadcast on the new medium. But something changed: taught by the tutelary defiant spirit of Crazy Jane, thereafter *any* poem might be sung, and thumb its nose at decorous semantics. This was revolutionary: and it is hard not to think that it was adopting the voice of Crazy Jane that spurred the later Yeats to play as he did with sound and voice.

Crazy Jane joined a stable of what Daniel Albright calls "vagrants and crackpots", beggars, drifters, mentally unstable marginalized homeless figures populating Yeats's poems. Albright further claims these were "people who are nothing except vehicles of songs" (Albright 1996, 730). Crazy Jane is much more (and less) than this. She was no vehicle, she was vital: though what arrived were no longer songs, her origins almost literally left their imprint. Old and new the poems might be, but they found their feet in the broadsides Jane paced out in the eighteenth and nineteenth century.

Yeats would later claim he sought "a vivid speech that has no laws except it must not exorcise the ghostly voice" of folk song (1961, 537). Jane's distant origins may have been in rural songs of the countryside, and her educated upbringing in Lewis's decorous verses; her inherited madness has an even longer cultural history. But the nineteenth century in more than one sense roughed her up. Jane could take the stage at Covent Garden alongside Rossini, be sung in the parlour, and inspire refined asylum watercolours; but the "proletarianization" of her contemporaries' street life changed her (Humphries, 1990, 17). Through the broadsides Jane was put to work in an urban landscape, part of a displaced rural population subject to vagrancy laws, and the lawless piracy of industrial cities. In her obsessive returns to the same place and insistent singing (as well the printers' disregard of copyright) she repeatedly ran up against authority. Crazy Jane's nature was already changed by the mouths in which she was sung and the places she was printed and policed.

---

[11] Yeats to Margot [Ruddock] Collis, 23 November 1934.

Yeats's poems found Crazy Jane haunting the streets, and co-opted an existing vocal and political energy. Without exorcising the ghosts of her previous lives, they audibly adopt the voice of the broadside sellers' Crazy Jane, who importunes us, addresses us, calls us, sings *at* us in the open air while we go about our business, whether we like it or not. Far from eliciting sympathy, Yeats's Crazy Jane is confronting authority, openly disdaining not just conventional morality but conventional rationality. The poems disdain some conventions of song, too: for these broadsides music was as natural as breathing, so essential it was not necessary to be included. They enabled a kind of verse that sought *not* to be a Victorian parlour piece, but roughly demanded a hearing – which in the modern world, especially in refrain, rudely dares us to join in something awkwardly unsingable, for which the music is long-forgotten, and the poet's muse and musical sense appears cracked. Jane's sharp speech, ragged clothes, aged body, and rough music represents a challenge to our snobbery, which turns up its nose at this kind of song, as well as the nature of the singer. *Words For Music Perhaps* thus confronts readers with unreasoning, unreckonable, levelling irrationality which steals song's unstudied *sprezzatura*, untechnical wisdom, and oral daring, while employing a highly technical command of voices and surprisingly piercing theology. Any embarrassment an audience feels about Yeats's Crazy Jane, therefore, reflects as much our own troubled conscience.

Bibliography

Abrams, Harriet. [?1798]. *Crazy Jane, A Favorite Song, The Words by G.M. Lewis, And Set to Music with an Accompaniment for the Harp or Pianoforte by Miss Abrams*. London [29 New Bond St]: L. Lavenu.
Albright, Daniel. ed. 1992. *W.B. Yeats: The Poems*. London: Everyman.
Baron-Wilson, Margaret. 1839. *The Life and Correspondence of M. G. Lewis*. 2 Vols. London: Henry Colburn.
Barnes, George, 1987. "Account of Yeats at B.B.C." (1940), in *Yeats Annual 5*, 189–194.
Barthes, Roland. 1977. "The Grain of the Voice", *Image Music Text*, ed. Stephen Heath. 179-190. London: Fontana.
Bodleian Ballads Online. Bodleian Library, Oxford. Harding Collection. By accession number. https://ballads.bodliean.ac.uk
Brown, Roly. 2017. "Notes on the Life and Death of Crazy Jane", *Musical Traditions* 44, 308. https://mustrad.org.uk/articles/bbals_44.htm
Clark, David R. 1983. *Yeats at Songs and Choruses*. Colin Smythe: Gerrard's Cross.

Cowper, William. 2012 "The Task". *Romanticism: An Anthology.* Ed. Duncan Wu. Malden: Blackwell, 4th ed. 17-20.

Dadd, Richard. 1855 "Sketch of an Idea for Crazy Jane". London: Bethlehem Hospital.

Davy, John. [?1799] *Crazy Jane: the Original Ballad*: *The Words by G.M.Lewis Esqre, The Music by John Davy*. New York [117 Broadway; Boston, No. 3 Cornhill]: G. Gilbert. Library of Congress: https://lccn.loc.gov/2014568313

Harper, Margaret Mills. 2018 "Crazy Jane and Professor Eucalyptus: Self-Dissolution in the Later Poetry of Yeats and Stevens". *The Wallace Stevens Journal.* 42, no.1. 32-45.

Hay, Louis. 1996. "History or Genesis?" trans. Ingrid Wassenaar. *Drafts*: *Yale French Studies* 89. ed. Michel Contat, Denis Hollier, and Jacques Neefs: 196-207.

Humphries, Jane. 1990. "Enclosures, Common Rights, and Women: The Proletarianization of Families in the Late Eighteenth and Early Nineteenth Centuries", *The Journal of Economic History*, 50 no.1, 17-34.

'Henry's Cottage Maid' [?1790]. Air by Ignaz Pleyel, arranged for English guitar. Dublin: Maurice Hime. Bodleian Vet. Mus. 5 c.79(43).

Luftig, Jonathan. 2009. "Rent: Crazy Jane and the Image of Love". *MLN* 124, no.5. 1116-1145.

Partch, Harry. 1974. *Genesis of a Music.* New York: Da Capo.

Paterson, Adrian. 2011. "Music will keep out temporary ideas: W. B. Yeats's radio performances". In *Word and Music Studies 12: Performativity in Words and Music*, ed. Walter Bernhart and Michael Halliwell. Amsterdam: Rodopi, 43-76.

Paterson, Adrian. 2018. "Stitching and Unstitching: Yeats material and immaterial". *Review of Irish Studies in Europe* 2, No.1 (March).

Paterson, Adrian. 2020. "Harps and Pepperpots, Songs and Pianos: Irish Poetry 1780-1830", *Irish Literature in Transition Vol. 2* ed. Claire Connolly. Cambridge: Cambridge UP.

Russell, George (A.E.). 1894. *Homeward: Songs By The Way*. Dublin, Whaley.

Walker, D.P. 1958. *Spiritual and Demonic Magic from Ficino to Campanella*. London: Warburg Institute.

White, Harry. and Michael Murphy. 2001. eds. *Musical Constructions of Nationalism*. Cork: Cork University Press.

Winn, James Anderson. 1981. *Unsuspected Eloquence A History of the Relations Between Poetry and Music*. New Haven: Yale University Press.

Yeats, W.B. 1937. *A Vision*. London: Macmillan.
Yeats, W.B. 1961. *Essays and Introductions*. London: Macmillan.
Yeats, W.B. 1966. *The Variorum Edition of the Plays of W. B. Yeats,* ed. Russell K. Alspach, assisted by Catharine C. Alspach. New York: Macmillan.
Yeats, W.B. 1996. *Yeats's Poems*. ed. A. Norman Jeffares. London: Macmillan.
Yeats, W.B. 2002. *Collected Letters*. InteLex Electronic Edition. By accession number.
Yeats, W.B. 2010. *The Winding Stair and Other Poems: Manuscript Materials*, ed. David R. Clark. Ithaca: Cornell University Press.
Yeats, W.B. and George Yeats. 2011. *The Letters*, ed. Ann Saddlemyer. Oxford: Oxford UP.

Part II:

American Literature

'SMUDGING THE AIR WITH MY SONG': BOB DYLAN'S *MURDER MOST FOUL*

SANDRO PORTELLI

Strange Day in Stockholm

In this article I will briefly sketch some of the questions raised by the award of the Nobel Prize for literature to Bob Dylan, and then go on to examine an example of his recent work, *Murder Most Foul*, in which he explicitly refers to literary antecedents[1].

There is something uncannily right in the fact that Bob Dylan was awarded the Nobel Prize in literature on the same day of the passing of another controversial laureate, Dario Fo. Both Dylan and Fo are untypical laureates in the lineage of an often stiff highbrow institution. Both – a comedian, a musician – have been labeled as intruders in the precinct of "literature;" yet literature owes a great deal to both of them. By rooting their creativity in the realm of oral, popular, folk cultures, they have changed our perception of language, and reminded us of how indissolubly linked poetry is with sound, voice, body, improvisation, performance, orality. In Dario Fo's *Mistero Buffo* and *The Accidental Death of an Anarchist*, in Bob Dylan's *A Hard Rain's-a Gonna Fall* or *The Lonesome Death of Hattie Carrol* the oral voices of street artists, vagrants and mountebanks from the Italian countryside, of Mississippi Delta field hands and Depression hobos, of Chernobyl survivors and Afghanistan veterans move from the margin to the center of culture and become the new languages of our time.

Alessandro Carrera claims that Dylan's later work is "perhaps the last modernist poem in American literature."[2] Much of his power, however, lies in the relationship between his visionary imagination and his

---

[1] The first section of this paper is based on a section of my book, *Bob Dylan: pioggia e veleno* (Rome, Donzelli, 2017); the second was published as appendix to the Spanish translation of the same book, *Bob Dylan: lluvia y veneno* (La Plata, Argentina, Prometeo, 2019). Both started out as newspaper articles published in the Rome daily *il manifesto*.
[2] Carrera, *La voce di Bob Dylan*, p. 39.

familiarity with the deep history of folk song and folk cultures. Bob Dylan has rooted the languages of the present and the future on the heritage of a centuries-old oral tradition, thus changing the imagination and the life of three generations and more.[3] In Dario Fo, the Nobel Prize recognized the deep seriousness of humor and satire. In Bob Dylan, it recognized a whole world of long ignored and discounted popular arts. The margin seizes the center. In a way, this is a political achievement, too.

Which is why, fortunately, not everyone agrees. Of course, one may legitimately claim that Dylan did not deserve the award because he is not a great artist. In this case, right or wrong, we would only be doing our job as critics. But the claim that he should not have been recognized because his work is not literature is more problematic. In my academic career, I have taught plenty of literature classes that included Bob Dylan and Robert Johnson, the blues and the popular ballad, Woody Guthrie and Bruce Springsteen, and I don't think I have been the only one. The question, then, is not the quality of Dylan's art, but what kind of art it is; whether, in the third millennium, we still think of literature in the same terms as the late-nineteenth-century founders of the Nobel Prize.

For at least a century and a half, since the advent of new "technologies of the word"[4] – cinema, radio, sound recording... – the printed word is no longer the only medium to which we entrust the exploration of language, the invention of visions, the telling of stories, that is, the essential functions of what we call literature. On the other hand, in centuries past and still today, all over the world, orality has been and is the medium in which human beings have told and sung their stories and poems. If there is one thing that we can say about Bob Dylan is that he has bridged over different realms of language and imagination, sustaining a modernist sensibility and a technological imagination on the basis of centuries of oral cultures.

I remember the day the dean of the English and American Studies department of the University of Rome "La Sapienza," where I was working, received a phone call from the Canadian Embassy. A young Canadian poet, whose name was unfamiliar, and he failed to catch, was coming to Rome and they wondered whether we could invite him to speak to our students. To his surprise, on the appointed day, hundreds of avidly

---

[3] My book *Bob Dylan. Pioggia e veleno* is an exploration of the relationship between Dylan's *Hard Rain's a- Gonna Fall.*
and the traditional ballad *Lord Randal* (also known in Italy as *Il testamento dell'avvelenato*).

[4] Walter J. Ong, *Orality and Literacy: The Technologizing of the Word* (London, Rutledge, 2002).

expecting students were climbing all over the walls of the main conference hall. Then the poet stepped on the stage, picked up a guitar and started: "Suzanne takes you down to her place near the river...." His name was Leonard Cohen – another "half breed" artist, here, there, and nowhere. In another song, *A Singer Must Die*, accused of betraying poetry by contaminating it with music, the singer accepts the tribunal's death sentence with humble pride: "And I thank you, I thank you for doing your duty, you keepers of truth, you guardians of beauty; your vision is right, my vision is wrong, I'm sorry for smudging the air with my song."[5]

Dylan, too, smudged our air with his voice. Yes, he does deserve the prize, some critics objected, but it should have been for music, not poetry. I can imagine the protest of "real" musicians – "do you call this 'music'? he's just a pop singer..." And so on. The point, however, is that in order to recognize artists like Bob Dylan we ought not so much add new categories (there is no Nobel Prize for music anyway), but rather rethink the categories that we have, redefine their shape and boundaries, and ultimately question the value of categorizing and parsing knowledge and art into rigidly separate fields. Artists like Dylan do not fit categories, but overstep them, mix them, confound them, take us along the path of doubt and searching – which, after all, is what art and literature are for. Bob Dylan does not belong in literature because we can't lock him inside it. We ought to thank him for challenging us to rethink Jean Paul Sartre's question – "*qu'est-ce que la littérature?*" ("what is literature?") – and leaving the answer to blow in the wind.

Murder Most Foul: History Unlearned

'When will they ever learn?
When will we ever learn?'
                    (From "Where Have All the Flowers Gone?" P. Seeger)

On March 27, 2020, at the height of the Covid-19 epidemic, as his country was becoming the most infected on the planet, Bob Dylan released a 16-minute ballad on the assassination of John Fitzgerald Kennedy that he had composed and recorded at some unspecified time before but never released. This release was followed on April 16, 2020 by another piece, *I Contain Multitudes*.[6] Both pieces, of course, elaborate of classic literary

---

[5] Leonard Cohen, *A Singer Must Die,* from *New Skin for an Old Ceremony* (Columbia, 19 74).
[6] Both pieces are included in Bob Dylan's album *Rough and Rowdy Ways* (Columbia, 2020).

quotes: William Shakespeare's *Macbeth* and Walt Whitman's *Leaves of Grass*.

Murder Most Foul is a lament for John Fitzgerald Kenney and the America he represented, and a search into the meaning and uses of history and memory. As always, Bob Dylan is guided by the sound of music and the sound of language: the obsessive repetition of a deceptively simple, deep musical phrase, and the chain of alliteration rhyme and anaphora, often leading into surprising and revealing connections between apparently disparate elements. The ballad teems with intertextual references and allusions to cultural memory that will keep dylanologists and exegetes busy for a lifetime. The story it tells is one of death, fall, mourning and pain that explains much of our times, and of Dylan's own trajectory. At this time, we can only attempt the beginnings of a temporary, fragile and fragmentary interpretive path, one among many possible ones.

Dylan's Kennedy is more of a universal symbol than the tangible, imperfect human being that we knew; hence, his assassination is more than a run-of-the-mill political murder. "They blew off his head," "they blew out the brains of the king…" Since the revolutionary birth of the nation, American imagination has been haunted by the symbol of the beheading of the king: revolution on the one hand (ghosts of Cromwell's England); and, on the other, the loss of a center, of a reference, of an authority; the vanishing of meaning and order; the absence of a father.[7] No wonder that Dylan's piece hinges on a quotation from *Hamlet*, the story of a king's murder and the absence of a father. Dylan also evokes *Macbeth*, another regicide; and alludes ("a good day to die") to Crazy Horse, another murdered leader of a people.

As in a lysergic hallucination, Dylan projects the scene of the crime as a "human sacrifice" in which – as in archaic hunting rituals – the killers attempt to possess the victim's power by dismembering his body and appropriating his mind and soul: "They mutilated his body and took out his brain…But his soul was not there where it was supposed to be at."[8] Since that day, the soul has been lost. It may be hiding somewhere waiting to return like the mythological buried king[9], maybe it was already dead:

---

[7] I discuss these images in *The Text and the Voice. Writing, Speaking and democracy in American Literature*, New York, Columbia University Press, 1994, pp. 31-7 and *passim*

[8] There is more than a hint of a conspiracy theory in this song: the taking of Kennedy's brain suggests more the autopsy than the murder itself; and it wasn't Oswald who took over Kennedy's power seat.

[9] I discuss the buried king myth in *Il re nascosto. Saggio su Washington Irving* (Rome, Bulzoni, 1979), and "The Buried king and the memory of the future: from

"the soul of a nation been torn away." Like the sovereigns of myth, Kennedy holds in himself the fate of his land. His death is like *le Mort d'Arthur* in the chivalric epic – in fact, wasn't the Kennedy circle known as a modern-day "Camelot"?

How does the land respond to the death of her King? "Hush li'l children, you'll soon understand / The Beatles are coming they're gonna hold your hand ..." The tragedy doesn't teach America to grow up. Like a playful child afraid of the dark – "Slide down the banister, get your coat..." – the country takes refuge in an illusory permanent adolescence. Darkness, however, lurks around the euphoria of the "Aquarian age": the peace and love of Woodstock will soon turn into the blood and violence of Altamont, just like the "home in the valley meets the damp dirty prison" in *Hard Rain* – or perhaps turns into it, or was *contained* all the time, like in a Lovecrat tale. "I contain multitudes," Dylan proclaims, quoting Walt Whitman, in his April 2020 release. "Contain" may mean – as in Whitman and possibly Dylan – an inclusiveness that can accommodate contradiction; but it can also mean (as in Don DeLillo's *Underworld*)[10] the containment of a danger pushing to burst out from underneath of a veneer of tranquility and peace.

Perhaps, this danger, the sweeping of tragedy under the carpet of adolescence, is part of the reason why Dylan no longer felt part of that time. He could no longer be contained in the Kennedy-era folk revival, but he also opted out of Woodstock. He, too, was lost, with no direction home: a "blackface singer or a "white face clown," as in the minstrel-show tradition with which he connects in "*Love and Theft*," or in the mask he wore in the *Rolling Thunder Review*, adrift in America of disguises, deceit and whited sepulchers, searching for his own face through decades of restless change.

Forget the Aquarian Age: "The age of the anti-Christ has just only begun." The theological virtues of "Faith, Hope and Charity died," truth is hidden and lost, there is no difference between "[Vietcong] Charlie" and Uncle Sam[11], and we greet the news with Rhett Butler's immortal words:

Washington Irving to Bruce Springsteen," "The Buried King and the memory of the future: from Washington Irving to Bob Dylan", *Memory* Studies, vol. 13, no. 3, 2020, pp. 267-276.

[10] See my "'We do not tie in twine': Waste, Containment, History and Sin in Don DeLillo's *Underworld*" in Gigliola Nocera, ed., *America Today: Highways and Labyrinths* (Siracusa, Italy: Grafia, 1993), 592-609.

[11] In conversation, Alessandro Carrera pointed out the Vietnam reference in "Charlie." I had been reading it instead as a variant of the "Mr. Charlie" that Black people used to designate arrogant white men, as in James Baldwin's *Blues for*

"Frankly, Miss Scarlet, I don't give a damn." Yet, in this part of the song Dylan begins to evoke another side of reality. "We are living in a nightmare in Elm Street" he sings: a Wes Craven horror movie, but also another part of Dallas, Deep Ellum to black bluesmen, as he reminds us in the next line. Elm Street is the b(l)ack side of Dallas, the red light, dangerous district haunted by Ralph Ellison's (or is it H. G. Wells'?) Invisible Man, the dark face of that sunny November day, the nightmare that Malcolm X saw where Martin Luther King (a symbol of the Kennedy era) saw a dream.

In the third section, Dylan plunges into an exploration of personal and cultural memory, searching perhaps for the runaway soul of the country, and his own. It may be a historical America in which the vision of liberation from slavery in the old spiritual ("Freedom, oh freedom") evolves into the "freedom from want" of Roosevelt's New Deal.[12] Or it may be the America of his adolescence, the radio days of his musical roots: Little Richard's rock and roll, the Everly Brothers' rockabilly, Patsy Cline's country music, the Kingston Trio's folk revival, Louis Armstrong's St. James infirmary – the America of Elvis Presley, another dead King, sexy (*One Night of Sin*) and mysterious (*Mystery Train*), and of its purest dead queen of beauty and innocence, Marilyn Monroe.

But these adolescent Cold War memories also have an underside of danger. The Everlys' Little Susie slept unconscious through it all. Little Richard's Miss Lizzy was dizzy, Tom Dooley died on the gallows, whitened cadavers lay in St. James infirmary, Patsy Cline's greatest hit was "Crazy," and Marilyn Monroe (and Elvis Presley) overdosed. Further back, the work of the New Deal was finished by the War. In a brilliant display of his method of composition, Dylan follows the sound and surfs signifiers to discover unexpected connections among signifieds: the funny men of our childhood movies - Harold *Lloyd*, Buster Keaton, Bugsy Siegel – flow into the outlaw Pretty Boy *Floyd* (who, in another contradictory turn of the screw, sends us back to Dylan's inspiration, Woody Guthrie). This is, indeed, how memory works: spontaneous associations that reveal unforeseen meanings in shards of experience.

So, Dylan keeps searching. Once again, just as he turned to the blues tradition to renew his creativity in the 1990s, Dylan turns to Black consciousness in search of his country's soul – from downtown Dallas to Deep Ellum, as it were. Like Hamlet's Denmark, America is out of joint

---

Mister Charlie. In the polisemy of symbols in this song, the two may not be mutually exclusive.

[12] Roosevelt is evoked in the song's second line: November 23, 1963, like December 8, 1942, is a "day that will live on in infamy."

and, once again, it may be up to the descendants of the slaves to set it right. As the ballad draws to an end, Black voices gradually emerge and prevail – Charlie Parker and Miles Davis, Nat King Cole and Little Richard, Ella Fitzgerald and Jelly Roll Morton, Etta James and Nina Simone ... There are other voices and other names, but these are the dominant ones.

I don't know whether Dylan ever heard a spiritual that the anthropologist Bruce Jackson recorded in the '60s in a Texas prison farm[13]. Improvising antiphonally over a tight tapestry of gospel harmony, the leader begins:

> I wanna tell you about a day, children, wasn't it so sad
> I wanna tell you about November 22 wasn't it sad
> I wanna tell you a long time ago children, wasn't it sad
> When they pushed him on up the hill
> They pushed the man on up the hill
> I wanna tell you about a day you will never forget
> The man was riding down the street
> Ridin' down the street in a long black car
> Oh wasn't it sad, Lord, Lord, Lord

And then another voice takes over:

> One more thing I wanna tell you now children
> I wanna tell you about the woman who was on her dying bed one day
> The same day that they assassinated the president I believe it was...

When they hear that "the President is gone, a great man has passed away," "little children began runnin' and cryin'"; when they realize their mother is dying, her children mourn – "who's gonna wake me up in the morning? who's gonna feed me in the morning?" In the Black consciousness, the murder of Christ, the murder of Kennedy, and the "lonesome death" of a poor Black woman[14] are the same death and leave us equally orphaned. Ishmael's "royal mantle of humanity" falls equally on the shoulders of all[15]. Every murder is foul (in another literary twist,

---

[13] Johnnie H. Robinson, Eddie Ray Zachery, and Group, "Assassination of the President," *Negro Folklore from Texas State Prisons*, recorded by Bruce Jackson (Elektra, 1965).
[14] Bob Dylan, *The Lonesome Death of Hattie Carroll*, in *The Times They Are a. Changin'* (Columbia, 1963).
[15] Herman Melville, *Moby Dick, or, The Whale* (1851: Harmondsworth, Midds.: Penguin, 1992), p. 126.

Murder Most Foul is also an Agatha Christie crime novel); a King's death stands for every death. In a way, the Texas spiritual is the other side of Dylan's elegy: The President represents us all not because he is a King, but because, like Jesus Christ and like Hattie Carroll, he is human.

Throughout his career, Bob Dylan has been warning generation after generation of the impending catastrophe and looming apocalypse – and chiding us for not learning from them and continuing in our "rough and rowdy ways." Most notably, a song like *A Hard Rain's A-Gonna Fall* has functioned as a permanent and evolving tocsin, from the nuclear threat to the environmental disaster to the tragedies of migration and exile. *Murder Most* Foul, unveiled at the time of a pandemic that, at the time of this writing, has killed 2.79 million people worldwide and 555,000 in the United States[16] is another warning in the midst of another disaster.

In the last lines of the song, Dylan returns, in his own ambiguous and cryptic way, to another tragedy whose lesson America has learned only imperfectly, if at all: the Civil War. He had already evoked it indirectly through another literary reference, when he quoted Rhett Butler's final words from *Gone with the Wind*; now, his last request to the disk jockey includes *Marching through Georgia* and *The Blood Stained Banner*: the North's victory song and the South's song of defeat, torn by war, unified by blood, death and destruction. Perhaps, on that November day in 1963 and in the death-ridden spring of 2020, the blood-stained banner may become the symbol of a defeated and wounded nation (and world) that has a lesson to learn but, like Dylan's Mister Jones, may never know what it is.

Bibliography

Carrera, Alessandro. 2017. *La voce di Bob Dylan*, p. 39. Milano: Feltrinelli.

Cohen, Leonard 1974. *A Singer Must Die,* from *New Skin for an Old Ceremony* (Columbia, 19 74).

Dylan, Bob. *The Lonesome Death of Hattie Carroll*, in *The Times They Are a.Changin'* (Columbia, 1963).

Melville, Herman. 1992. *Moby Dick, or, The Whale.* Harmondsworth, Middlesborough.

Ong, Walter J. 2002. *Orality and Literacy: The Technologizing of the Word.* London: Rutledge.

---

[16] https://www.google.com/search?client=firefox-b-d&q=cpovid-19+victims%20world%20wide; https://www.google.com/search?client=firefox-b-d&q=cpovid-19+victims%20united%20states – (both retrieved March 30, 2021).

Portelli, Alessandro. 2017. *Bob Dylan: pioggia e veleno*. Rome: Donzelli.
—. 2019. *Bob Dylan: lluvia y veneno*. La Plata, Argentina: Prometeo.
—. 1994. *The Text and the Voice. Writing, Speaking and Democracy in American Literature*. New York: Columbia University Press.
—. 1979. *Il re nascosto. Saggio su Washington Irving*. Rome: Bulzoni.
—. 2020. "The Buried king and the memory of the future: from Washington Irving to Bruce Springsteen," and "The Buried King and the memory of the future: from Washington Irving to Bob Dylan." In *Memory* Studies, vol. 13, no. 3, 2020.
—. 1993. "'We do not tie in twine': Waste, Containment, History and Sin in Don DeLillo's *Underworld*." In Gigliola Nocera, ed., *America Today: Highways and Labyrinths*. Siracusa, Italy: Grafia.
Robinson, Johnnie H. & Zachery, Eddie Ray, and Group, "Assassination of the President." In *Afro-American Folklore from Texas State Prisons*, (Recorded by Bruce Jackson, Elektra, 1965).
Seeger , 1955. "Where Have All the Flowers Gone?"

A Primal Source of Music

William Neil

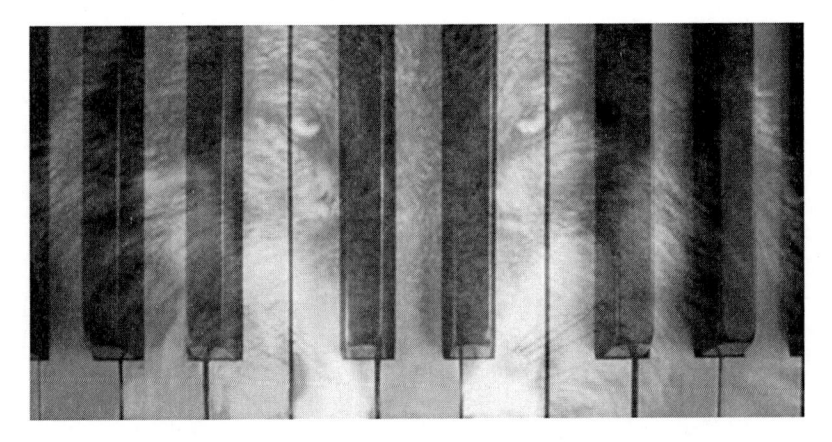

Fig. 15: 'Wolf Keys,' photo image created for W. Neil by Elliot Madow.

The theme of the animal spirit in the wild manifests in Arctic novels by Jack London (1876-1916) and are potent sources of musical inspiration. *The Call of the Wild* (1903) chronicles the journey of a half-breed husky named Buck, who begins as a slave to several cruel owners in Alaska and eventually becomes a sled dog for a loving master, John Thorton. Buck emerges through struggle and primordial instinct as a leader in the wild in an environment that eventually frees him from the bonds of mankind. Throughout the novel, the most important passages that rise above the fundamental quest for survival, describe a primal lure in very poetic and musical terms. Indeed, London's description of the richly soulful howl of wolves that allures Buck, speaks to the very meaning and essence of life and to its cosmic source. *White Fang* (1906), the companion piece to *The Call of the Wild*, chronicles the transformation of a wild animal driven by the hunger to survive from the rewards of being faithful to man. *Love of Life* (1905) places two gold miners returning from the wilderness in the path of a hungry pack of wolves. As their journey progresses, the miners begin to associate the sound of wolves howling with the terrible threat of their demise. These three novels offer numerous transformative passages as sources of artistic inspiration, and this essay will inquire into the musical composition indirectly inspired by the sounds of wolves.

Nature has provided a source of inspiration for artists throughout the ages. In the Romantic era, Beethoven confessed his love of nature when he said, 'How happy I am to be able to walk among the shrubs, the trees, the woods, the grass, and the rocks! For the woods, the trees and the rocks give man the resonance he needs.' (all-about-beethoven.com) These three works of Jack London celebrate the value of animals in nature, which is demonstrated particularly well by the pairing of man and husky in the Alaskan wild for survival. London was personally familiar with the science of seeking food, warmth, and transport in a frozen environment having spent some time in Alaska during the Klondike Gold Rush. London's individual perspective of man and dog as partners in the quest for fulfillment beyond survival is fundamental to the development of the plot in each of these three novels. Jack London's writing is often transformational—it is fueled by something that drives the characters from one state to another.

As a composer, I have been on a similar quest to create a unique musical language that is transformative and effectively expresses the untamed wildness and mystery of nature. The identification with the wolf, both its power and its weakness, led me to an unexpected path of discovery. In my search for a primal source of music, I found in the howl of wolves a seamless integration of passion and the profundity of nature. Before I delve into the passages in London's works which were the impetus to my discoveries, an examination of the science of sound as perceived by the brain will be informative.

'Music is primal. It affects all of us, but in very personal, unique ways,' said Burdette, a neurologist at Wake Forest Baptist Medical Center in North Carolina (Burdette 2017, n.p.). It can be argued that each of our interactions with music are completely different. However, it remains that music has an equally powerful effect on the brain regardless of how each of us interprets it. Fundamentally, music and the emotions that are evoked, stimulate our memories. Our brains can react to music positively or negatively as liked or disliked, but the degrees in between often relate to the intensity of the emotion felt or what is associated with the memory and whether it was a pleasant or unpleasant memory. Moreover, experiencing sound in the natural world elevates this response from being purely emotional to a response that resonates with the spirit. To be moved by art in this context, for example, by the sound of wolves resonating in the natural acoustic, can be astonishing as expressed in this description in the *Love of Life*: '[…] the call, the many-noted call, sounding more luringly and compelling than ever before (London, 1981, 44). The howl of wolves heard in the wild can range unmistakably from awe-inspiring to terrifying particularly as it relates to survival. What then does science say about why and when wolves howl amongst themselves?

Within the last 20 years, extensive, focused research on the howl of wolves has revealed some interesting facts about why and when wolves howl. The primary reason wolves howl is to communicate with one another when they are roaming through vast territories hunting for food. Since howling can be heard for miles, wolves are able to reconnect with the pack when they have been wandering far away in search for prey. Howling can also serve as a reunion call when a pack member has returned. Each wolf produces its own unique quality of sound when it howls, and this can identify them individually (Palacios et al., 2007, 607). When a lone wolf howls and is identified as being a member of another pack it alerts the rival pack that a threat is nearby.

The sound quality of wolf howls has been studied extensively (Harrington, 2000: n. p.) and has revealed some interesting observations about the range of frequencies in the howling. When wolves howl together in a chorus, they are able to modulate the frequencies in such a way as to create a more complex sound that tricks a rival pack listening into believing there are more wolves present. This phenomenon is called the Beau Geste Effect (Harrington, 2000, n. p.) and provides evidence of a collective defense intelligence among wolves. Wolf packs each have a specific range of frequencies among them that identifies them as a group. When a rival pack trespasses on their territory, the defending pack will howl at a lower pitch indicating to the intruders that they are ready to fight. Outside of communicating with other pack members, wolves often howl on their own in what appears to be purely for their pleasure and individual expression. It is this phenomenon that humans most identify with as the wolves appears to be expressing themselves and declaring: 'I am' or 'I'm howling because I can.'

Indeed, this fascination has inspired literature and folk tales through the ages. In folklore, wolves are often portrayed as conniving and evil. The timeless stories, Aesop's Fables, which are believed to have been written in the mid to late sixth century, portrayed the wolf in over two dozen moral tales. For example, The Lamb and the Wolf, and The Nurse and the Wolf depict the wolf as a threat; The Shepard and the Wolf, as cunning; and The Wolf and the Crane, as defiant (Aesops, 1999: n. p.). This stereotyping of wolves as malevolent beasts has its roots in the Christian New Testament: 'Beware of false prophets, which come to you in sheep's clothing, but inwardly they are ravening wolves' (King James Version, Gospel of Matthew 7: 15). One of most dramatic allusions is found in *Dracula* by Bram Stoker (1847-1912):

> There seemed a strange stillness over everything; but as I listened, I heard as if from down below in the valley the howling of many wolves. The Count's eyes gleamed, and he said: -'Listen to them–the children of the night, what music they make.!
>
> (Stoker, 1997, chapter 4, 4)

In my own region of Wisconsin, USA, Robert E. Gard and L.G. Gard's book, *Wisconsin Lore,* and *The Beast of Bray Road* by Linda S. Godfrey the wolf is profiled as a large wolf or doglike creature with human features that was first reported as sighted in Elkhorn, WI, in 1949. The story describes this creature as a beast that stands up on its hind legs and has been spotted eating with its front paws turned upward like human palms. Tales like these and the classic conflict between farmers and predators has continued to demonize the wolf in this region. An American survey conducted in the years 2001-2009 found that '656 of the respondents had an increasing fear of wolves despite years of conservation efforts with the state of Wisconsin' (Treves et al., 2013, 320). However, a rising awareness of the importance of wolves in stabilizing the natural ecology has brought the wolf into the spotlight as a partner in keeping nature in balance. Perceiving the wolf as an important part of the fabric of nature versus a singular demon reflects London's vision in his literature, which highlights the romantic bond between man and the wolf through the common quest for survival in the wild. In this way, literature can change the way we perceive ourselves in the universe creating an opportunity to understand ourselves through the inspiration of the writer.

London's word-paintings remind me of the work of the American artist Andrew Wyeth. Portraits of the people in his life, and the settings that he paints them in, show equally the dreams of the sitters and the painter himself. London's writing in *The Call of the Wild* similarly incorporates the dreams of his main characters, Thorton and his husky, Buck. Throughout the novel the most important passages that rise above the fundamental quest for survival describe, in graphic terms, the mysterious environment that man and wolf find themselves in together, simultaneously describing the rich sonority of the howls and the man's interpretation of the howl as a sad song. A sad song in a minor key-the most natural of tonalities that resonates with the past so well and certainly the sadness and lament of a world that is still and frozen:

With the aurora borealis flaming coldly overhead, or the stars leaping in the frost dance, and the land numb and frozen under its pall of snow, this song of the huskies might have been the defiance of life, only it was pitched in minor key, with long drawn wailings and half-sobs, and was more the pleading of life, the articulate travail of existence. It was an old song, old as the breed itself-one of the first songs of the younger world in a day when songs were sad. (London, 1981, 15)

In *White Fang*, the theme of sadness, one that is arresting in the silence, gives a special meaning to the darkness in nature:

"A long wailing cry, fiercely sad, from somewhere in the darkness, had interrupted him. He stopped to listen to it: then he finished his sentence with a wave of his hand toward the sound of the cry, "—one of them?'"
(London, 1981, 3)

Is it only man who interprets the sound as sad? Do these same intervals and timbres heard by the wolf have the same effect on its brain that evokes sadness? Perhaps what man interprets as sad, the wolf registers as loss, as in the memory of a pack member that died or some game that got away. What, then, are the more fundamental common responses by man and wolf to the sound of howling? In *The Call of the Wild* there is a passage that expresses a primal quest to connect with our ancestors that is common to man and wolf:

And when, on the still cold nights, he pointed his nose at a star and howled long and wolflike it was his ancestors, dead and dust, pointing nose at star and howling down through the centuries and through him. And his cadences were their cadences which voiced their woe and what to them was meaning of the stillness, and the cold, and dark. (London, 1981,12)

London then develops the theme in these descriptive passages from purely emotional and sensorial to examining the impetus behind the howling as an expression of ecstasy for life at its peak.

In *The Call of the Wild,* London suggests that wolves in the wild, besides howling to communicate, are howling in agony of pain, or because they are hungry, or howling because they know they are alive as this passage suggests:

There is an ecstasy that marks the summit of life, and beyond which life cannot rise, and such is the paradox of living, this ecstasy comes when one is more alive, and it comes as a complete forgetfulness that one is alive. This ecstasy, this forgetfulness of living, comes to the artist, caught up and out of himself in a sheet of flame; it comes to the soldier, war-mad on a stricken field and refusing quarter; and it came to Buck, leading the pack, sounding the old wolf-cry, straining after the food that was alive and that fled swiftly before him through the moonlight. He was sounding the depth of his nature, and of the parts of his nature that were deeper than he, going back into the womb of Time. (London, 1981, 18)

In a similar passage in *White Fang* the effect of the call of wolves has a similar effect on man as they perceive a desperate vitality in the wolf's cry:

An hour went by, and a second hour. The pale light of the short sunless day was beginning to fade, when a faint far cry arose on the still air. It soared upward with a swift rush, till it reached its topmost note, where it persisted, palpitant and tense, and then slowly died away. It might have been a lost soul wailing; had it not been invested with a certain sad fierceness and hungry eagerness. …A second cry arose, piercing the silence with needle like shrillness. Both men located the sound. It was to the rear, somewhere in the snow expanse they had just traversed. A third and answering cry arose, also to the rear and to the left of the second cry. (London, 1981, 2)

In both of these descriptive passages it is important to note that silence is the paramount element in rendering the howls as uniquely expressive. What makes the sound of wolves howling in nature so dramatic and spellbinding is the manner which it penetrates the silence. Equally dramatic are the passages in London's novels that pair the envelopes of sound and silence with light and darkness. For example, in these passages in *White Fang:*

Cry after cry, and answering cries, were turning the silence into a bedlam. From every side the cries arose, and the dogs betrayed their fear by huddling together and so close to the fire that their hair was scorched by the heat. …At once began to rise the cries that were fiercely sad-cries that called through the darkness and cold to one another and answered back. …At midday the sky to the South warmed to rose-colored, and marked where the bulge of the earth intervened between the meridian sun and the northern world. But the rose-colored swiftly faded. The grey light of day that remained lasted until three o'clock, when it, too, faded, and the pall of the Arctic night descended upon the lone and silent land. (London, 1981, 4)

In the final section of *The Call of the Wild*, London underscores the final transformation from domestication to animal in the wild by defining the distant howl as a beckoning that must be answered.

So peremptorily did these shades beckon him, that each day mankind and the claims of mankind slipped farther from him. Deep in the forest a call was sounding, and as often as he heard this call, mysteriously thrilling and luring, he felt compelled to turn his back upon the fire and beaten earth around it, and to plunge into the forest, and on and on, he knew not where or why; nor did he wonder where or why, the call sounding imperiously, deep in the forest. (London, 1981, 34)

The multi-faceted descriptions of wolves howling in the wild found in London's Arctic Tales, *The Call of the Wild*, *White Fang*, and *Love of Life* illuminate the transformative themes of courage, resourcefulness and strength from human beings in the form of the wolf and half-breed in the wild. These passages illuminate the transformative themes from four perspectives. Emotionally, as a sad song in the wild; physically, as the wolves drive from one state of existence to another; spiritually, as they express ecstasy for life at its peak; and naturally, as in the way sound is rendered in silence. For some time as a composer, I have been pursuing an approach to composing that embodies all of these characteristics in one style of composition. These aesthetics were foremost in my mind when I composed a work for string quartet and digital acoustics composed of the sounds of wolves crying, whining, growling and howling both solo and in chorus. The piece *Canis Lupus-Nocturne*, is part of a larger work, *Sacrum Creaturae* (Sacred Creatures) and is inspired by three species at risk in the natural world: wolves, dolphins, and birds. A recording from the premiere of *Canis Lupus-Nocturne* can be heard on my website: williamneil.net. A description of the music follows.

The piece opens with a tremolo minor chord that is played so softly as to emulate the pure murmuring of sound in the wilderness. The minor triad embodies a universal tone of sadness that colors the unfolding chorus of wolf howls in this movement. A single howl is heard in the distance and then a second wolf joins in the chorus. In my studio, each of the individual wolf calls were digitally tuned to a single note. The tension than rises over time as they howl in and out of tune with one another, rising and falling from the silence. A solo violin enters over the wolves calling in chorus. The chorus builds as the sound moves closer into to the foreground. The violin solo slowly oscillates over chorus of violin, viola and violoncello of the quartet and together the two parallel choruses of wolves and strings begin rising in volume and density. The music pauses and the space is silent for a moment. A violent and loud interruption in the quartet breaks the silence. When the wolves return, their chorus is at its peak, the quartet begins to fade away. This passage ends with a compressed succession of minor triads in the string quartet capsulizing the sadness expressed by the minor chord and the minor third interval prevalent in the howl of the wolves. With the wolves now absent, the quartet develops this opening music in pure musical terms. The wolves return in a cacophony of growls and barks that underscores the primal fire in these animals, passionate in their will to survive. At the very peak of the movement all of the primal elements, the agony of survival, and ecstasy for life are unleashed. The simple chorus of wolves is now magnified digitally into a thunderous chorus of sound accompanied by the string quartet in unison and octaves. And then, in a descending cascade, all of the voices dramatically unwind in a counterpoint of cries, whining and howling that diminishes to a quiet murmur. Finally, the sad minor chord from the beginning returns and is softly struck and fades into silence.

The success of this premiere performance has opened up the possibility of further exploration in this genre of blending sounds from the wild within a musical composition. Just as London has conjured a story of life's origin from the perspective of the wolf, I look forward to continuing to develop a unique musical language that can tell this story of primal being in musical terms. In closing, Jack London should have the final word regarding pursing one's passion: 'I'd rather sing one wild song and burst my heart with it, than live a thousand years watching my digestion and being afraid of the wet.'

Bibliography

London. Jack. 1981. The Call of the Wild. Ed. Andrew Sinclair. London: Penguin Books

London. Jack. 1981. White Fang. Ed. Andrew Sinclair. London: Penguin Books

London. Jack. 1981. Life of Life. Ed. Andrew Sinclair. London: Penguin Books

Burdette. Jonathan. 2017. Wake Forest Baptist Medical Center in North Carolina. 2017. Science Daily. Source:
https://www.sciencedaily.com/releases/2017/04/170412181341.htm

Palacios, V., Font, E. and Márquez, R. (2007), 'Iberian wolf howls: Acoustic structure, individual variation, and a comparison with North American populations', *Journal of Mammalogy*, 88: 3, pp. 606–13.

Harrington, F. H. (2000), 'What's in a howl?',
http://www.pbs.org/wgbh/nova/wolves/howl.html.
Accessed 11 September 2015.

Aesop. (1999). The Lamb and the Wolf. In D.L. Daily (Ed.)

Aesop. (1999). The Nurse and the Wolf. In D.L. Daily (Ed.)

Aesop. (1999). The Shepard and the Wolf. In D.L. Daily (Ed.)

Aesop. (1999). The Wolf and the Crane. In D.L. Daily (Ed.)

Stoker, B. 1997, *Dracula*. Eds. Nina Auerbach & David J. Skal. New York: Norton Critical Editions.
Gard E. Robert & L. G. Gard. 1962, *Wisconsin Lore*. Madison: Wisconsin House Ltd.
Godfrey. Linda S. 2014, *The Beast of Bray Road*. Amazon Kindle
Treves, A., Naughton-Treves, L. and Shelley, V. 2013, 'Longitudinal Analysis of Attitudes Towards Wolves'. In *Conservation Biology* Vol. 2, Nr. 27, 2013.

ELUSIVE TUNES:
JAZZ AND POPULAR SONGS
IN *THE GREAT GATSBY*

GIANFRANCA BALESTRA

Summing up the sadness and suggestiveness of life in new tunes.
(F. Scott Fitzgerald, *The Great Gatsby*).

Fig. 16: Jazz Age Rage.

The Great Gatsby, published in 1925, has in time acquired the status of canonic American novel and universal masterpiece, beyond epochal representation. However, it retains its quality of iconic novel of the Jazz Age, a definition that Fitzgerald contributed to establish with his early novels and short stories, including a collection aptly named *Tales of the Jazz Age* (1922). But what was the writer talking about when he talked about jazz? In "Echoes of the Jazz Age" (1931), an article that gave an insider's view of the decade and its cultural manifestations, he wrote that "the word jazz in its progress toward respectability has meant first sex, then dancing, then music" (Fitzgerald 1993, 13). What is particularly revealing in this statement is his preoccupation with respectability and the process through which jazz achieved it. What is significantly missing is the connection with African American culture, an implication that surfaces later when he mentions in passing the "bootleg Negro records with their phallic euphemisms that made everything suggestive" (Fitzgerald 1993, 18). This is the only oblique reference to the African American origin of jazz, and the racially labeled connotation of sexual permissiveness that scared conservative white America and had to be removed to make it "respectable." According to jazz historians, the transformation happened mainly through a diluting of the original musical innovations rooted in blues and traditional black music. The music of the Harlem Renaissance, characterized by improvisation, new rhythms and syncopated patterns, influenced mainstream popular music and was taken over by big symphonic orchestras, making it more acceptable to white audiences.[1] In his fiction, and in particular in *The Great Gatsby*, Fitzgerald represented this appropriation and incorporated various styles of popular music that at the time could be loosely grouped under the category of "jazz", only vaguely alluding to its social and racial implications.[2]

Keeping in mind this cultural context, this essay will explore the use of music in *The Great Gatsby*, which raises interesting questions in terms of its cultural impact as well as its contribution to the modernist style of the novel. The discussion will take into consideration the relationship between literature and music, the power of music to symbolically express meaning and the power of language to describe the sound of music. Recent critical studies provide useful material for this discussion, and not accidentally two of them carry in their titles references to Keats's famous lines about "heard"

---

[1] See, among others: Shaw; Gioia; Ogren; and Anderson.
[2] Henson convincingly argues that "in the 1920s, "jazz" emerged as a multivalent term that encompassed a range of musical styles and alluded to a whole worldview or lifestyle," so that it would be more accurate to speak of jazz-influenced music in the case of Fitzgerald (Henson, 50).

and "unheard melodies", that is about real sounds and their artistic representation.[3] (See Intro., xlviii).

"There was music from my neighbor's house through the summer nights."[4] With these words Nick Carraway, the internal narrator, remembers and establishes the pervasive sound of the novel. It is at the beginning of chapter III, when he first attends one of Gatsby's parties, a pivotal moment for the explosion of music. He describes the orchestra as "no thin five piece affair but a whole pit full of oboes and trombones and saxophones and viols and cornets and low and high drums" (hereafter cited as *GG*, 33). The narrator conveys the idea of Gatsby's grandeur in providing a big orchestra to entertain his guests and signals the cultural change that has intervened from the original small jazz band composed of black musicians to the lavish ensembles that included both classical and jazz instruments. They play at first "yellow cocktail music," a beautifully ambiguous definition that uses synesthesia, mixing color and sound, perhaps suggesting a danceable, softer type of music, and possibly a racial connotation.[5]

There is dancing in the garden. At one point a girl dances alone on the platform, moving like a famous jazz dancer, and "the orchestra leader varies his rhythm obligingly for her" (*GG*, 34). This episode introduces improvisation, which is a characteristic feature of jazz, by adapting and modifying rhythms in a carefree style. There are fashionable couples "holding each other tortuously," "and a great number of single girls dancing individualistically or relieving the orchestra for a moment of the burden of the banjo or the traps" (*GG*, 38-39). The description continues in a fantastic sequel of scenes and images, stunts and performances, which contribute to the excitement and confusion, while "a celebrated tenor had sung in Italian and a notorious contralto had sung in jazz," mixing different types of music, opera and jazz, with Broadway musical songs. Above what the narrator calls the surrounding "echolalia," comes the announcement of the orchestra leader that, at the request of Mr. Gatsby, they are going to play "Vladimir Tostoff's Jazz History of the World," a work which caused a big sensation at Carnegie Hall (*GG,* 41). His words are pronounced in a condescending tone and are received with laughter, while at the end of the performance Nick confesses

---

[3] The essays I refer to are Berret, *Music in the Works of F. Scott Fitzgerald: Unheard Melodies*; and Graham, "The Literary Soundtrack: Or, F. Scott Fitzgerald's Heard and Unheard Melodies".

[4] Fitzgerald, *The Great Gatsby* 1991, 33. In the quotations, the novel will be hereafter referred to as *GG*.

[5] Colors are very important in the novel and they form an intricate pattern of symbolic meaning. Yellow is always related to gold and wealth, but here it could also refer to skin tone gradation, of light brown.

that the nature of this composition eluded him. Since no other clues are given about this "sensational" composition, it would elude also most readers, who are left only with a fictitious title and a well-known auditorium used mostly for classical music but where some works of serious jazz were also performed at the time. Most critics cite as a possible model Paul Whiteman's *Experiment in Modern Music* played at the Aeolian Hall in New York in February 1924 and later at Carnegie Hall.[6] This performance, which had great resonance in the newspapers, took place after the action of the novel, which is set in the summer of 1922, but while Fitzgerald was at work on it. It was considered a history of jazz and featured George Gershwin playing his *Rhapsody in Blue,* a famous combination of jazz and classical music. Apart from these scarce exterior elements, critics have based their hypotheses and analyses on important textual evidence: a long description that was present in the early draft of the novel and was erased by the author from the final version. This deleted passage was the most extensive attempt in the novel to describe music and make it resound by the creative use of language. In a letter of 20 December 1924 to his editor Maxwell Perkins, Fitzgerald wrote: "I thought that the whole episode (2 paragraphs) about their playing the Jazz History of the world at Gatsby's first party was rotten." (Fitzgerald 1964, 192-93). The writer had tried to put two distinct arts into productive dialogue with each other, and apparently felt he had failed. Was the decision based on purely aesthetic grounds or were there other cultural, racial, political reasons for this choice? It is worth looking into this excised musical passage, which is available in manuscript and as facsimile,[7] and has received a lot of critical attention.

Without reproducing the whole text, we can highlight some of the most significant elements. The narrator describes the four different movements that compose this musical piece, here titled "Les Epstien's Jazz History of the World," as well as its effect on him and the audience. The first movement starts "with a weird, spinning sound that seemed to come mostly from the cornets, very regular and measured and inevitable" and turns into a "sort of dull beat" until something tremendous happens, and the spinning becomes "all awry" while a distant bell comes alive. In the second movement there are a "muted violin cello and two instruments (he) had never seen before" that try to establish a sound through monotony and repetition, and suddenly seems "to lurk all around." The third part, according to Nick, was full of an even stronger emotion: "There would be a series of interruptive

---

[6] Breitweiser, 370; Henson, 133 n3. Together with Whiteman's concert, Berret mentions as a possible influence Richard Strauss's *Also Sprach Zarathustra,* following Darrel Mansell's suggestion (Berret 2015, 125).
[7] Fitzgerald, *The Great Gatsby: A Facsimile of the Manuscript*, 1973, 54-56.

notes that seemed to fall together accidently and colored everything that came after them until before you knew it they became the theme and new discords were opposed to it outside," producing "a ghastly sense that it was all a cycle after all." The last movement, which intends to mark the last stage of musical evolution, "had recognizable strains of famous jazz in it – Alexander's Ragtime Band and the Darktown Strutter's Ball and recurring hint of The Beale Street Blues." These three pieces mixed different genres and racial connotations (Henson, 52) that might be culturally disturbing to Nick, who significantly considers this part weaker, differentiating himself from most of the audience who seemed to like it best. However, he confesses of being curiously moved by some of the music, which stayed in his head, so that "Whenever I think of that summer I can hear it yet."

The narrator's response to this performance is troubled by conflicting impulses. He is fascinated but also disoriented by the "Jazz History," he tries to make sense of it without completely understanding it. He admits that he knows "so little about music that (he) can only make a story of it – which proves I've been told that it must have been pretty low brow stuff – but it wasn't really a story." Nick's conclusion that this composition must have been pretty low brow stuff, according to other people's opinion, characterizes the disputable status of jazz in the early 1920s and his feeling of superiority in terms of social and racial identity. Perhaps the narrator's uneasiness reflects Fitzgerald's anxiety about social hierarchies and racial mingling embodied by jazz, according to some readings of this passage and its erasure. Perhaps Nick's confessed little knowledge of music and his difficulty in turning it into narrative corresponds to the author's dissatisfaction with his literary representation of music, as well as his fear of producing low brow material instead of the artistic work he was envisioning. Moreover, the writer might have considered this long passage too intrusive and distracting from the main concentration on the characters. More subtly, as Breitweiser maintains, jazz fractures and discontinuities represented a threat to a unified cultural vision and especially to an organic cohesive form of art Fitzgerald was pursuing in his novel.

In any case, most critics see Fitzgerald's decision to remove the long passage about the "Jazz History" as a significant suppression in the text, be it for stylistic, cultural, social or racial reasons. In particular, the suppression of the African American origins of jazz signals a racial problem that surfaces in other parts of the novel and has been stressed in recent criticism. If the prototype of "The Jazz History of the World" was, as suggested by some, Whiteman's concert titled "An Experiment in Modern Music," we have to remember that this was already an example of the process of appropriation and legitimization of jazz on the part of big white orchestras toward a more symphonic form of art with pseudo-classical arrangements of pieces. (Gioia, 85) According to Kristin Henson's study, music's symbolism in literature and the Jazz controversy in Twentieth-century American fiction document the difficult ways that cultural boundaries are continually negotiated. In the case of Fitzgerald, allusions to jazz-influenced popular music would suggest an anxiety over the cultural amalgamation that permeates American modernism. (Henson, 37). Even so, I would argue that Fitzgerald's attempt to find words to describe music succeeds in depicting the disruptive quality of jazz, the unfamiliar discordancy of notes, even the improvisation at its core. Breitweiser considers this passage "one of the first perceptive reactions to jazz performance among white American writers," and argues that "were Fitzgerald to have left the excised fragment in, would have put on view a rather fabulous cultural reversal, jazz per se reviving or breaking out at the heart of an event staged to curtail jazz and to appropriate its aura, not only an overturning of Whiteman's pretension but also an exuberant betrayal of the aesthetic norms governing the book in which it would have been enclosed" (Breitweiser, 371).

In spite of the erasure of this important description of jazz, *The Great Gatsby* resonates with music, even if by allusion rather than description. In fact, the novel is interspersed with references to real popular songs that contribute to situate it in the cultural context of the 1920s, but also function to set moods and comment on the action at crucial moments in the plot. Specific songs are named or quoted in each of the following chapters, to the point that Berret suggests *The Great Gatsby* resembles a musical play, with the "Jazz History" as an overture introducing the various themes that will be expressed later by these popular songs,[8] perfectly suited to the scenes and emotions they accompany either by similarity or counterpoint. These musical pieces were obviously recognizable by contemporary audiences but are less easy to decipher in their meaning and melody in a twenty-first century context. However, as Graham convincingly argues, "listening to long-outmoded but still audible musical literature" does not undercut its universal potential but rather reinforces the sense of being out of tune that pervades the novel (Graham, 537). So that paradoxically the introduction of popular culture – in this case time bound music – which is part of Fitzgerald's modernist strategy, works to create a sort of literary soundtrack that "seems to indicate that musically inspired emotions are perfect only insofar as they are temporary and fleeting, escaping listeners even as they are possessed of them" (Graham, 537).

---

[8] Berret 2015, 127. Catherine Kunce and Paul M. Levitt, instead, argue that the novel is patterned after a vaudeville show format.

Let's now briefly examine the popular songs that constitute the literary soundtrack of *The Great Gatsby*. The first is "The Sheik of Araby," sung by children in Central Park, with lyrics quoted in the text:

I'm the Sheik of Araby.
Your love belongs to me.
At night when you're asleep
Into your tent I'll creep—(GG, 62)[9]

The song was such a hit, played on phonographs and by dance orchestras everywhere, that most probably contemporary readers could "hear" its melody and rhythm. Although it has acquired the status of jazz standard song, it remains "unheard" for present-day readers, unless we search for it in the internet where different versions are available, from the original to an unexpected 1962 cover by the Beatles. In this case, more than the musical effect, the purpose of the quotation resides in the words themselves and what they refer to. This 1922 jazz song was inspired by *The Sheik*, a romance novel by English writer E. M. Hull and the 1921 film adapted from it, starring Rudolph Valentino. It is an orientalist text that tells the story of an English girl who is kidnapped in the desert and raped by an Arab Sheik. In spite of the violence, the girl eventually falls in love with him and they marry. In the end, she discovers that he has British aristocratic blood in him, so that class and racial differences can be happily overcome. In "Echoes of the Jazz Age," Fitzgerald mentions *The Sheik* together with other novels representative of contemporary sexual mores and considers it an example of how "even rape often turns out well." (Fitzgerald 1993, 17). This cynical comment is based on Fitzgerald's opinion that *The Sheik* was "written for children in the key of *Peter Rabbit*," and because of this "the erotic element did not one particle of harm" (Fitzgerald 1993, 17).

Why did Fitzgerald quote from "The Sheik of Araby" and does this have any implications in terms of the plot and imagery of *The Great Gatsby*? We have to remember that this quotation arrives at the end of chapter IV, after Nick has gathered some information about Gatsby's past. Among the improbable episodes of his life, Gatsby recounts that he "lived like a young rajah in all the capitals of Europe – Paris, Venice, Rome - collecting jewels, chiefly rubies," with phrases that evoke for Nick "no image except that of a turbaned 'character' leaking sawdust at every pore as he pursued a tiger through the Bois de Boulogne" (*GG,* 52). Moreover, in the same chapter Nick learns from Jordan Baker about his earlier love affair with Daisy and

---

[9] "The Sheik of Araby," lyrics by Harry B. Smith and Francis Wheeler, music by Ted Snyder.

his dream of conquering her back through his wealth and impressive mansion. The exotic images of Gatsby associate him with the sheik, even if, as Curnutt notes, Gatsby's idealized sense of romance contrasts sharply with the rapacious sexuality of Hull's male protagonist. (Curnutt, 642). I would argue that *The Sheik* is one of the many hypotexts on which Fitzgerald constructs his novel, transforming its plot, reversing some of its values, and finally turning it from a rather childish popular romance into a mature and complex masterpiece.

The citation of this popular song works at various levels: to evoke music through its lyrics, to situate the novel in its time and enrich it with popular cultural products, including a successful film and the original best-selling novel, and finally to foreground exotic images and underline a plot that invites comparison. Fitzgerald uses the same method throughout the novel, inserting pieces of popular music carefully selected to fit the situation, as we shall see in a brief overview of the rest of the musical references. In chapter V we find two songs that represent different visions of love and life, and highlight the inner contradictions of Gatsby's dream: "The Love Nest" and "Ain't We Got Fun?" While the first song celebrates romantic love that can find happiness in a modest environment, the second one glorifies reckless pleasure in spite of economic problems and social inequality. The two pieces are played on the piano by a house guest of Gatsby when he takes Daisy to visit his impressive mansion and try to win her love back. Of the first instrumental performance only the revealing title is given, with no words quoted, but the popular refrain would resonate with its common wisdom: "Better than a palace with a gilded dome, / Is a love nest/ you can call home."[10] Although the lyrics are not rendered in the text, Berret argues that they reflect the subtext of the scene and comment on the theme of wealth by contrasting different types of houses. Moreover, this popular song comes from *Mary*, a 1920 musical that also reflects some concerns of the novel, and could have served as a model and source, as Berret demonstrates in a detailed analysis" (Berret 2013, 296). In the second case, some of the lyrics are reproduced:

In the morning,
In the evening,
Ain't we got fun—

and

---

[10] "The Love Nest," 1920 song; music by Lewis A. Hirsch, lyrics by Otto Harbach.

One thing's sure and nothing's surer
The rich get richer and the poor get – children.
In the meantime,
In between time— (*GG*, 75) [11]

They represent in a humorous tone the irresponsible pleasure seeker of the decade, those Fitzgerald referred to in "Echoes of the Jazz Age" as "a whole race going hedonistic, deciding on pleasure" (Fitzgerald 1993, 15) This lively and jazzy foxtrot has become indelibly associated with the 1920s but the words show a certain awareness of the poverty contrasting the overspread prosperity and even foreshadow impending disaster.

The chapter closes with a different music, that of Daisy's voice, in Nick's words: "I think that voice held him most with its fluctuating, feverish warmth because it couldn't be over-dreamed --- that voice was a deathless song" (*GG*, 75). Maybe, after all, the real and metaphoric music of the novel is Daisy's voice, that recurs and becomes a central trope. In fact, in the next chapter, "Daisy began to sing with the music in a husky, rhythmic whisper, bringing out a meaning in each word that it had never had before and would never have again. When the melody rose her voice broke up sweetly, following it, in a way contralto voices have, and each change tipped out a little of her warm magic upon the air" (*GG*, 84). We do not know what music she is singing to, since no song has been named so far, but the melody of her voice becomes magic and gives new meaning to unknown words. She is at one of Gatsby's parties, where they dance together and Nick is "surprised by his graceful, conservative fox-trot" (*GG*, 82). When she and Tom are leaving, "Three o' Clock in the Morning," a neat sad little waltz of that year, was drifting out of the open door" and "seemed to be calling her back inside" (*GG*, 85). The lyrics are not quoted, but they are almost too obvious in their reflecting the situation, "It's three o'clock in the morning / We've danced the whole night through / and daylight soon will be dawning / just one more waltz with you / That melody so entrancing / seems to be made for us two/ I could just keep on dancing forever dear with you."[12] These romantic lines stress the passing of time and the desire to hold it forever, one variation on the central theme of the novel: time, the illusion of holding it or even, in the case of Gatsby, "repeating the past." T. Austin Graham analyzes also the grandiosity of the music, pointing out its "heroic

---

[11] "Ain't We Got Fun?", 1921 popular song; music by Richard A. Whiting, lyrics by Gus Kahn and Raymond B. Egan.
[12] "Three o' Clock in the Morning." Julian Robledo composed the music for piano solo in 1919, and two years later Dorothy Terriss wrote the lyrics. Paul Whiteman's 1922 instrumental recording became an extremely popular hit.

arpeggios," "the occasional acrobatic leap" and "other flamboyant touches", and considers it "too flashy, too extravagant, and, above all else, too literal for what is otherwise a brooding and ambiguous scene" (Graham, 539).

While throughout the novel the music of Daisy's voice has a romantic idealized quality, when reality takes over the dream Gatsby pronounces the final famous definition of it: Daisy's voice is full of money. Although Nick agrees, he continues to use musical metaphors: "it was full of money – that was the inexhaustible charm that rose and fell in it, the jingle of it, the cymbal's song of it…" (*GG*, 94). This realization comes before the showdown at the Plaza hotel, which marks the end of the dream, and is accompanied by "the portentous chords of Mendelssohn's Wedding March from the ballroom below" (*GG*, 99)[13] This music reminds Daisy of her marriage with Tom, an engagement she will not be able to break in order to start a new life with Gatsby. Mendelssohn's "Wedding March" is the only classical piece mentioned in the novel, but it is followed by a "burst of jazz" that opens the dances after the ceremony.

Memories of the past are evoked again in chapter VIII, and recount Daisy's life in Louisville after Gatsby had left to go to war, and she is waiting for him to come back. Once again it is left to music to denote the atmosphere and emotions: orchestras "set the rhythm of the year, summing up the sadness and suggestiveness of life in new tunes. All night the saxophones wailed the hopeless comment of the 'Beale Street Blues' while a hundred pairs of golden and silver slippers shuffled the shining dust" (*GG*, 118). Fitzgerald beautifully succeeds in expressing the mood and the sad sound of music, through alliterations and masterly choice of words, and an instrument like the saxophone which was rising in importance in blues, ragtime and jazz in general. The mention of this particular blues – already present in the deleted passage of the "History of Jazz" – reveals the African American origins of jazz, which remained equivocal in other pieces. In fact, blues is a musical form which originated in the South of the United States and had roots in African musical traditions and African American spirituals. W. C. Handy, the composer and lyricist of "Beale Street Blues," was responsible for transcribing and publishing this orally transmitted music, which became a strong influence on mainstream culture and was amalgamated in popular jazz. Written in 1916 and named after a famous club street in Memphis, Tennessee, "Beale Street Blues" actually combines a blues tune with a fairly conventional popular song. In any case, according

---

[13] This is the most famous piece of music from Mendelssohn's *A Midsummer Night's Dream*. Berret comments on both the title and the plot of the play, and underlines similarities with *The Great Gatsby*. (Berret 2015, 139-140).

to Berret, "it is the only song in *Gatsby* with a background of race, segregation, slavery, and Africa." (Berret 2015, 142.)

The last song quoted in the novel is "The Rosary,"[14] ironically whistled by a Jewish gangster who refuses to attend Gatsby's funeral. It evokes death and the cross, but it is not a funeral hymn. Rather, it uses a symbol of Catholicism to develop an analogy with romantic love, since the lyrics express love, loss and the passing of time, bringing together some of the major themes and images of the novel. With the death of Gatsby, and the careless desertion of Daisy, no more jazz music is possible since, as we have seen, most music is related to him, and Daisy. In an earlier draft, Fitzgerald even had Gatsby compose his own song, "a vague compendium of all the tunes of twenty years ago," which he sang to Nick "in a low unmusical baritone" (Fitzgerald 1973, 162 and 177). The song reminded Nick of something, "an elusive rhythm, a fragment of lost words, that I had heard somewhere a long time ago" (*GG*, 87). But only this vague memory remains, moved to the end of chapter VI, as a reaction to Gatsby's "appalling sentimentality." The conclusion is silence, his lips "made no sound and what I had almost remembered was uncommunicable forever" *(GG*, 87).

In this and other reflexive moments, silence prevails over the noise of the "Roaring Twenties," the other famous label for the decade, and even over the pervasive music of the Jazz Age that characterizes the novel, its parties, the general atmosphere of the times, and the individual emotions of the protagonists. Fitzgerald perfectly integrates his musical allusions in the text, with words that are themselves musical, with exact timing of a reference or a quote. Even if in his substantial rewriting during the editing process he eliminated his most important attempt to describe music, this absent presence proves a complex interplay between Fitzgerald and jazz. We have taken in consideration various possible explanations for this erasure, from his artistic concerns to his racial and cultural anxieties, but the music still resonates in the text and contributes to creating the context. Perhaps, as suggested by Goldsmith, Fitzgerald "sublimated difference to the level of style, engaging with the racially and ethnically diverse popular culture of his day through textual allusions and stylistic innovations" (Goldsmith, 463). From this perspective, the discourse becomes aesthetic, the presence of popular music together with other forms of popular culture is part of a textual strategy that characterizes his version of literary modernism. Fitzgerald did not subsume the dissonance and improvisation

---

[14] Written in 1898, words by Robert Cameron Rogers and music by Ethelbert Nevin, "The Rosary" was popular at the turn of the century with opera singers.

of jazz, he did not turn it into a form of literary experimentalism by adopting the new idiom for his narrative technique, like some writers of the Harlem Renaissance did[15] – and something that will be done by Toni Morrison in her novel *Jazz* (1992), which explicitly wants to reclaim both jazz music and the African American experience that created it. However, his engagement with popular music is significant, he incorporated it in *The Great Gatsby* as an element of a complex cultural collage that meets his goal to write something new and "intricately patterned." This is the kind of modernist narrative he was writing, under the influence of new modes of music and other art forms, which called for the inclusion of popular culture and songs.

Bibliography

Anderson, Maureen. "The White Reception of Jazz in America." *African American Review,* 38, no.1, (Spring 2004): 135-45.

Berret, Anthony J. 2015. *Music in the Works of F. Scott Fitzgerald: Unheard Melodies.* Madison, NJ: Farleigh Dickinson University Press.

—. "Broadway Melodies". In *F. Scott Fitzgerald in Context*, ed. Bryant Mangum, 293-301. Cambridge: Cambridge University Press, 2013.

Breitweiser, Mitchell. "Jazz Fractures: F. Scott Fitzgerald and Epochal Representation." *American Literary History,* 12, 2000: 359-81.

Curnutt, Kirk. "*The Great Gatsby* and the 1920's." In *The Cambridge History of the American Novel*, eds. L. Cassuto, C. Eby, and B. Reiss, 639-52. Cambridge, UK: Cambridge University Press, 2011.

Fitzgerald, F. Scott. 1993. *The Crack-Up*. Ed. Edmund Wilson. New York: New Directions.

—. *The Great Gatsby.*1991. Ed. Matthew J. Bruccoli. Cambridge: Cambridge University Press.

—. *The Great Gatsby: A Facsimile of the Manuscript.* 1973. Ed. Matthew J. Bruccoli. Washington DC: Microcard.

—. *The Letters of F. Scott Fitzgerald.* 1964. Ed. Andrew Turnbull. Harmondsworth: Penguin Books.

—. *Tales of the Jazz Age.* 2002. Ed. James L. W. West III. New York: Cambridge University Press.

Gioia, Ted. *The History of Jazz.* 2011. New York: Oxford University Press.

---

[15] Ogren mentions Langston Hughes and Claude McKay as examples of Harlem Renaissance writers who used jazz aesthetics as a model for stylistic innovation in terms of language and narrative structure (Ogren, 151).

Goldsmith, Meredith. "White Skin, White Mask: Passing, Posing, and Performing in *The Great Gatsby.*" *Modern Fiction Studies*, 49, no. 3 (Fall 2003): 443-68.

Graham, T. Austin. "The Literary Soundtrack: Or, F. Scott Fitzgerald's Heard and Unheard Melodies." *American Literary History,* 21, no. 3 (Fall 2009): 518-49.

Henson, K. Kristin. 2003. *Beyond the Sound Barrier: The Jazz Controversy in Twentieth Century American Fiction.* New York: Routledge.

Kunce, Catherine, and Levitt Paul M. "The Structure of *Gatsby*: A Vaudeville Show, Featuring Buffalo Bill and a Cast of Dozens." *The F. Scott Fitzgerald Review*, 5 (2005): 101-28.

Ogren, Kathy. 1992. *The Jazz Revolution. Twenties America and the Meaning of Jazz.* New York, Oxford: Oxford University Press.

Shaw, Arnold. 1989. *The Jazz Age: Popular Music in the 1920s.* New York, Oxford: Oxford University Press.

PYNCHON, WEAVER OF MUSIC AND WORDS

CHRISTIAN HÄNGGI

Thomas Pynchon, born in 1937 and to all appearances still alive, is respected, sometimes feared, for his complex and multilayered novels. His writing oscillates between historical precision and the imagination of alternative histories, between poetry-like prose and adolescent puns, between philosophical discussions of high-culture topoi and snide remarks on popular culture (or the other way round). Oftentimes labeled encyclopaedic, his historiographic metafiction spans at least 250 years of American and world history, both the history of ideas and politics as well as that of the sciences and the arts. In all this, he displays an unwavering allegiance with the disinherited, the lost, and the love-lorn, or, in his terminology, the Preterite, the passed-over.

One intuits the importance of music in Pynchon's work by looking at some figures I put together. In his seven novels, one collection of short stories, and miscellaneous writings, I counted 940 mentions or allusions to historical musicians or works of music as well as to 130 different musical instruments (Hänggi, 2020, 233–237), not including uncounted mentions of all sorts of combos, choirs, bands, and orchestras. Pynchon's work also includes well over 200 song lyrics he penned himself, possibly to an existing tune in mind. While these figures alone are quite impressive, particularly when keeping in mind that music is by far not the only thing Pynchon is interested in, close readings and the characters' musico-philosophical discussions reveal how well-informed the author is and how intricately he spins it all together.

It is little wonder, then, that since the beginning of Pynchon Studies some years after the 1973 publication of his groundbreaking novel *Gravity's Rainbow*, many a reader has noticed the importance of music in his work. Fine scholarly contributions on the topic have appeared in various places but never exceeding the length of an article or a book chapter. Only in 2020, nearly sixty years after his first novel, *V.* (1963), did a somewhat systematic study in the form of a monograph on the topic appear, my *Pynchon's Sound of Music*. In what follows, I will first briefly touch upon the various ways in which Pynchon brings music into his prose, mostly by ways of brief examples, and then offer a synthesis that attempts to paint in broader strokes the role music plays in Pynchon's writing.

Beginnings and Endings, Dedications and Epigraphs

Starting with *V.*, almost every single novel and many short stories have a musical reference on the first, and many also on the last pages: *V.* opens with an old street singer and his guitar. *Gravity's Rainbow* is dedicated to his late friend, the musician and novelist Richard Fariña. It opens, if not with music, with the sound of a V-2 rocket, "A screaming comes across the sky," and it ends with another rocket descending on a cinema as the moviegoers and possibly the readers are invited so sing a hymn. His 2006 tome *Against the Day* has an epigraph attributed to jazz pianist Thelonius Monk ("It's always night, or we wouldn't need light") and, shortly before the end, the narrator compares the skyfarers' announcements of their pregnancies to a "canonical part-song" (Pynchon, 2006, 1218). *Vineland* (1990) is epigraphed by a song by blues musician Johnny Copeland ("Every dog has his day, and a good dog might just have two days") and it ends with the family dog Desmond "thinking he must be home" (Pynchon, 1990, 385). The name of the dog could either hint at jazz alto saxophonist Paul Desmond or at The Beatles' "Ob-la-di, ob-la-da." *Inherent Vice,* his 2009 novel on the closure of the hippie era, has a reference to Country Joe & The Fish on the first page and it ends with the protagonist singing along to The Beach Boys' melancholic "God Only Knows." With these opening lines and paragraphs, his dedications and epigraphs, Pynchon sets the tone for and extends an invitation to read his novels through the lens of music.

Musical Forms as Structuring Device

More important than just setting the tone is a tendency of Pynchon's to use forms of music to structure his tales. As with other writers, for instance Aldous Huxley in *Point Counter Point* or James Joyce in the Sirens episode of *Ulysses*, it is the fugue that caught Pynchon's attention early on. His 1960 short story "Entropy" (Pynchon, 1984, 79–89) is structured like the literary analogue of a fugue as convincingly shown by Robert R. Redfield and Peter Hays in 1977 and Carmen Pérez-Llantada Auría in 1991. It ends with the words: "[T]he hovering, curious *dominant* of their separate lives should resolve into a *tonic* of darkness and the final absence of all motion" (Pynchon, 1984, 98; my emphasis).

Bénédicte Chorier-Fryd compares the overall structure of *Mason & Dixon* to that of a minuet, and she finds support for this interpretation in the dialogues of the novel too (Chorier-Fryd, 2008). The tripartite minuet structure is not uncommon in other Western musical forms; something similar happens, for instance, in the standard sonata form. More importantly perhaps, this structure—which has an exposition in the tonic, moves on to the development in a number of keys, oftentimes the dominant, and returns to the "home" key in the tonic again—is, by analogy, a common narrative form, thinking, for instance of Homer's *Odyssey* or, in some sense, of Freytag's pyramid.

The four-part structure of *Gravity's Rainbow* can either be read as following a parabolic shape (analogous to the flight of a rocket) or, as Steven Weisenburger prefers, a circular structure (Weisenburger 2006, 9). One character in that novel complains: "You were never immune over there from the simple-minded German symphonic arc, tonic to dominant, back again to tonic [...]" "Teutonic?" (Pynchon, 1973, 450). Similarly, a few pages before the end of *Mason & Dixon*, the narrator says: "[I]t is a musickal piece returning to its Tonick Home. Nothing more would be expected of [Mason] now, than some quiet Coda" (Pynchon, 1997, 762). Published nine years later, *Against the Day* has a four-part structure where the last part, entitled "Rue de Départ," in fact functions as a quiet coda. Thus, while structures such as departure–adventure–return (narrative), exposition–development–recapitulation/final entry (sonata form/fugue), or, more generally, tonic–dominant–tonic (much of Western music) are not uncommon, Pynchon makes his awareness of it explicit and has his characters and narrators comment upon it.

Musicians, Works of Music and Musical Events as Plot Devices

While Pynchon employs generalized musical forms mainly to lend his stories an overall structure, he frequently uses references and allusions to existing works of music to comment on or foreshadow the plot. David Cowart noted: "Pynchon does not [...] decorate his fiction with the first opera title that comes to mind. He selects the one that resonates with his own theme and characterization and foreshadows subsequent developments in the novel" (Cowart, 1980, 69). One example is a string of references and allusions to songs sung by the child actor Shirley Temple in a *Gravity's Rainbow* episode that has graphic descriptions of child abuse. There, Pynchon appears to hint at Graham Greene's allegation of Shirley Temple movies catering to an audience of male pedophiles (Greene, 1995,

233–35). Another example of a cluster of allusions is what is often referred to as the Charlie Parker passage in *Gravity's Rainbow* (Pynchon, 1973, 63–72). In that dreamlike episode, a flashback or fantasy, of sorts, the protagonist Tyrone Slothrop recalls or imagines the night in 1939 when alto saxophonist Charlie Parker discovered bebop, and he intuits Parker's early demise in 1955 (which he already mentions in *V.*). Throughout the episode, one can find titles of Parker tunes woven, at times almost imperceptibly, into the narrative: "that was 'sho nuff,' Slothrop?" ("Shawnuff"), "a pound of salted peanuts" ("Salt Peanuts"), "Cherokee."

Particularly in his earlier novels where Pynchon appears to have had a greater interest in opera and modernist music, the motif of *Liebestod,* love-death, can be found in various forms, oftentimes accompanied by allusions to operas by Wagner and Puccini and, in the case of *V.*, a re-imagination of the opening night of Igor Stravinsky's *The Rite of Spring* (Wagner is the most frequently referenced composer in Pynchon's work, mainly owed to the earlier novels, particularly *Gravity's Rainbow*; he alludes to no less than eight of his operas). Another reenactment or re-imagination of the opening of a new chapter in the history of music, scandalous in its times, can be found in *V.*: Ornette Coleman's 1959 debut and his discovery of free jazz and new ways to improvise collectively. In the novel, McClintic Sphere, who has traits not only of Coleman but also of Thelonius Monk, blows a hand-carved ivory alto saxophone. This instrument only exists in Pynchon's and, by extension, his readers' imaginations, but it appears to be a clever mash-up of Coleman's white plastic Grafton sax and the ivory flutes that Belgian instrument maker Adolphe Sax made early in his career before inventing the saxophone. This fictional instrument furthermore connects to other themes in *V.* related to ivory and colonial exploitation, and black jazz musician characters in general allow Pynchon to muse on and expose racial and racist prejudices and both racial and sexual anxieties of white men.

Rhythmic Qualities of Prose

William Wordsworth once wrote that "some of the most interesting parts of the best poems will be bound to be strictly in the language of prose, when the prose is well written" (Wordsworth 1997, 676). Perhaps the opposite is true too. If the best prose is written in the language of poetry and, by extension, in the melody and rhythm of song, then Pynchon's careful prosody offers a great number of those gems. Bénédicte Chorier-Fryd, who has a remarkable ear for rhythm, writes: "Though this is narrative prose, it evinces a number of identifiable poetic schemes which come into play with plainly linguistic prosody—the rhythm of ordinary language" (Chorier-Fryd 2015, 259). At times, Pynchon openly invites for such rhythmic reading when characters speak a beat late or wait a beat, or a perfect beat and a half, when they are quite upon their beat, or when there is a beat of silence.

One, to my mind, particularly striking passage is in the already mentioned Charlie Parker passage, two long sentences starting with "Down in New York, drive fast maybe get there for the last set—" and ending with "the saxes downstairs getting now into some, oh really weird shit" (Pynchon, 1973, 65). When read out loud, but particularly when recorded and sped up to make it sound like a "Munchkin voice" (Pynchon, 1973, 65), these 17 lines of free indirect discourse emulate the rhythm and some of the melodic qualities of bebop that Pynchon writes about ("32nd notes demisemiquavers"), ending, like a number of Parker tunes, on a quarter triplet and a quarter note. What is more, that passage thus recorded would turn out to correspond in length to what Parker was able to do with one lungful of air. Such passages tend to be overlooked in the thematic and linguistic opulence Pynchon's work offers but when one pays closer attention, it becomes evident how good an ear the author has when composing his lines.

Musical Interludes

One of the first things that catches a reader's attention, even just leafing through the novels, is Pynchon's use of song lyrics. Occasionally out of nowhere, occasionally with a long build-up, those indented songs are a signature of every single one of Pynchon's novels, though less frequent in later works. Sometimes they come with time signature, tempo or genre indications, or even choreography. As such, the lyrics or songs interrupt the story briefly, bringing a moment of respite, introspection, or plain fun to the characters, a function or effect not unlike that of showtunes or musicals.

It is possible that the lyrics Pynchon wrote are all based on existing tunes but, with a few exceptions (Weisenburger, 2006, 52), scholars and fans alike have had a hard time identifying those tunes. Some of the songs follow an easily identifiable verse and rhyme scheme that can be modeled on many existing tunes. When recording "Dream Tonight of Peacock Tails," a twisted lullaby from *V.*, Tyler Burba of the band Visit and I were inspired by The Beatles' "Good Night" because it follows the same structure and rhyme scheme (Visit 2020). After listening to Visit's interpretation, conductor Michael Zlabinger pointed out to my sister that Pynchon's lyrics may well have been inspired by the ending of Shakespeare's *A Midsummer Night's Dream* (Shakespeare, 1967, 121–122). Other lyrics are not so straightforward and require the stretching of syllables and the insertion of bridges and rests in order to be performed.

Over the years, a number of scholars have attempted to classify the songs Pynchon penned. Kathryn Hume and Thomas J. Knight (1986), for instance, categorize them into three different levels of dealing with reality or escaping from it. Anahita Rouyan (2017), on the other hand, focuses on the disparity between oral and written language and looks at how, graphically and in terms of meta-language and transcription, they appear in the text.

While there is not one function that all of Pynchon's lyrics fulfill, most of them do offer a moment of relief to the characters, readers and, perhaps, author alike. William Vesterman writes: "[W]e can be sure song is a very serious issue precisely because of the frivolity with which it is treated. [S]ongs do act like a magic cape in Pynchon's books by concealing not the characters but their author: they protect the author's ability to acknowledge, display and enjoy complexity without being dominated by it" (Vesterman 1976, 103). Seeing the differences in where the songs appear, their metric structure and rhyme schemes, what function they fulfill for the characters and readers, and how they are introduced or not, perhaps Charles Clerc was most to the point in his broad characterization: "[T]hey both interrupt and bolster the action; they change mood and focus; they comment or expand upon an incident; they render protests or pay tribute; they show the lighter side of a sad or tragic event; they show rifts between illusion and reality; by making fun, they affirm the necessity of laughter and joy" (Clerc, 2000, 116).

Character Names

Pynchon is known for giving his characters funny and absurd names. In a novelistic microcosm with several hundreds of characters, it is no surprise that some of them appear to be inspired by or derive from musicians' names or musical terms. McMingus, Miles, or Lester may be nods to jazz musicians Charles Mingus, Miles Davis, or Lester Young. Andrea Tancredi, Jessica Swanlake, and Eddie Pensiero appear to have received their names from Rossini's opera, Tchaikovsky's ballet, and Verdi's "La donna è mobile" from *Rigoletto* ("Muta d'accento / E di pensiero"). However, as Patrick Hurley's book on Pynchon's character names demonstrates, there is a very unreliable relationship between *nomen et omen*, between the characters' names and their personalities, roles, or fates (2008). As Terry P. Caesar notes, "the characters are often discontinuous with their names" (Caesar, 1981, 6). Music encoded in the characters' names is undeniably there and it further points to Pynchon's love for and engagement with music, but such naming does not appear to carry a deeper meaning.

Musico-Philosophical Discussions

Every so often, Pynchon has his characters engage in discussions about the history and philosophy of music. These are among his richest and densest music passages, allowing for extended close readings, and they demonstrate a depth and precision worthy of a musicologist. Similar to what Cowart (1980, 69, see above) remarked on musical allusions in general, these discussions are never there in the service of name-dropping or to simply adorn the stories; they always relate to the broader themes of the novels.

Against the Day deals, among other things, with the labor struggles of the turn of the 19th/20th century, many of which were fought by anarchists. Fittingly, in a New Orleans saloon, a group of black musicians of nascent jazz discuss this new idiom with some of the saloon's patrons (Pynchon, 2006, 416–417). The discussion revolves around questions of anarchist organization which is likened to jazz improvisation. On the one hand, the patrons and musicians at the table display a sense of international and interracial friendship and solidarity characteristic of the international outlook of the labor movement. Pynchon, however, does not leave it at that. He constructs the dialogues themselves so that they actually perform the improvisation and the interchange they talk about.

Mason & Dixon deals with the birth of the American Republic and is set in a transitional time between an age of mysticism and superstition and an age of science and reason. In 1786, the reader is witness to an extended family discussion centering around an English drinking song, "To Anacreon in Heaven," a song which later, with only a minor shift in the melody line (a minor third, in fact) and new lyrics turns into the "Star-Spangled Banner." The philosophical backdrop of this discussion spanning almost five pages (Pynchon, 1997, 261–265) is Plato's admonition in Book III of *The Republic* that nowhere are the laws of music changed without changing the most important civil dispositions. This is a theme which, less explicitly, runs through several other discussions of music in Pynchon's work. In *Mason & Dixon,* it allows the author a quick run through the history of the American musics of the future, from hymns to anthems to jazz and pop music, for the most parts by hints, intimations, prophecies, and puns ("Surf Music!" [Pynchon, 1997, 264]). This political reading shows how music, particularly when fictionalized as Pynchon does or through the lens of Jacques Attali's essay *Noise* (1985), can indeed serve as a harbinger of revolutionary change, particularly in how it announces an ever-widening expansion of civil rights and the inclusion of formerly disenfranchised people in the political realm.

In *Bleeding Edge,* there is a young Asian-American rapper, Darren, who performs a song of his for the novel's protagonist Maxine on a Roland TB-303 bass line synthesizer (Pynchon 2013, 282–283). He spins a web of references that, much like clever hip-hop lyrics and much like Pynchon's own work, continuously refers to other webs of references by means of mash-up, remix, borrowing, juxtaposing, quoting, and throwing in meta- and intertextual references. Although there is not really an in-depth discussion on the history and nature of remix culture and its position in capitalist music industry taking place, Pynchon is giving the careful and diligent reader enough hints and snatches of dialogue to be able to reconstruct a fairly precise image of it, starting with the TB-303, an instrument of early acid house, to the rap lyrics and, finally, appalling capitalist Chandler Platt by remix culture's practice of giving away CDs for free: "It strikes at the heart of Exchange itself" (Pynchon. 2013, 283).

Foreign and Domestic Agents: Musical Instruments

Rather unique, to my mind, is the way Pynchon has musical instruments almost take on a life of their own that endows their players with a certain set of characteristics deriving from the instrument's social and political history. He references clearly identifiable musical instruments as many as 720 times. These references can be broken down into 130 unique instruments in about 70 categories (such as "percussion" or "saxophone"). Four instruments he is particularly fond of and most elaborate about are the toy-like kazoo, the harmonica, the ukulele, and the saxophone. Since Sean Carswell (2015) has already done an insightful reading of the ukulele, I concentrate on the kazoo, the harmonica, and the saxophone in *Pynchon's Sound of Music* (Hänggi. 2020). Each of these instruments has a unique history of being embedded in power struggles and international cooperation and warfare, of being ridiculed and commended. More than once, in Pynchon's novels, do they take on a subversive function: a supposed Haydn Kazoo Quartet disquiets the Nazis at a dinner party (Pynchon 1973, 725–25), the harmonica and the tambourine unnerve a character modeled on Richard Nixon (Pynchon, 1973, 772), and the saxophone, much like in Billy Wilder's *Some Like It*

Hot (1959), is connected, among other things, to the theme of going into hiding. Pynchon treats his favorite instruments not just as media that are "extensions of man," to use Marshall McLuhan's famous subtitle, but as somewhat active agents. There is always an interplay of resistance and discovery between the instrument and its player, resonating with the notion that we shape our media and then our media shape us.

Yes, But What Does It All Mean?

The above sketches should give the reader an overview of how Pynchon employs music in his prose. It is something like a catalogue of different ways of letting music speak in a medium that has fundamentally been silent since the Middle Ages or so. Enumerating those different techniques and approaches may give a somewhat disjointed impression: at times he does this, at times he does that. It is important to note, however, that the richest passages display many of those techniques simultaneously. Like a fractal, the reader can zoom in on a detail, for instance a part of a sentence or even a word, and then zoom out and see the same concerns, themes, and qualities replicated at each scale: paragraph, chapter, novel, and, finally, the sum of Pynchon's writing. In order to tease out such an understanding, close readings are necessary, and those close readings may even be augmented by distant readings.

The question remains if there is a thread that runs through these diverse means of alluding to, referencing, discussing, or simply making heard music in Pynchon's novels?

The main insight, I believe, is that Pynchon attributes transformative powers to music, be it personal or political. While he is aware that music can be appropriated, reappropriated or co-opted by oppressive or reactionary forces, and occasionally hints at it, for instance in a discussion reminiscent of Nietzsche's later Wagner pieces in *Gravity's Rainbow* (Pynchon, 1973, 634) or in the mention of the "Horst-Wessel-Lied" (Pynchon, 1973, 450, 666, 731), he clearly focuses on the hopeful, liberating, and emancipatory powers of music. The author has hundreds of characters, many of which are musicians, professionals as well as amateurs, or everyday people who happen to break out in song at one point or another; barring oversight, not one of them is clearly in the service of sinister forces (the "Elect" in Pynchon's reversal of Calvinist or Puritan terminology). Thus, whatever appropriation of the art of music has taken place before, Pynchon's worlds of fiction reappropriate it.

Most clearly visible in the musical interludes—the indented lyrics—is another point Pynchon makes time and again: cybernetic or neoliberal ideology and technology structures, predetermines, and solidifies much of our world and our lives, our *Lebenswelten*. While we may not be able to change that, music allows us to break loose from those structures from time to time in order to get a moment's respite, to enjoy life more innocently, to form communal bonds, to regain energy either to simply live on or to resist and fight back. Music, in this reading, speaks a language that the Elect are not attuned to and cannot parse. Significant, too, is the fact that Pynchon has so many amateur musicians appear in his novels, which seems to make the point that music is there for the common man, woman, and child, and that it does not require formal training to be enjoyed or to be meaningful. Music is a life technique in the service of the Preterite, the passed-over, and it is something that can bring about karmic adjustment.

In all this, Pynchon has intimate knowledge of the history of—predominantly Western—music and the ability to offer concise interpretations, be it in elaborate discussions or side remarks dropped almost imperceptibly. Just as important in a literary context, however, is the ways in which he weaves it all together. At first sight, most of the musical allusions, references, and discussions, appear to simply be there, oftentimes scattered and without much of a connection to one another. Only on a second or third reading does his writing reveal the complex structures of meaning, the multilayered, inter- and metatextual dimensions that make the diverse references remarkably consistent, both in terms of the philosophy and politics of music and in terms of how they add to and bolster the broad themes of his novels—from a 1261 hymn by St. Thomas Aquinas to twenty-first century hip-hop.

Much more could be said on the subject. What has entirely been left out is Pynchon's other writing, a biographical sketch as it relates to music, the manifold ways in which technology plays a role, the interplay between film and music, a statistical analysis of the references I compiled, or music that was inspired by Pynchon's work or set to his lyrics. For some of this, the reader is referred to any of the scholarly essays and articles on the topic or to my monograph. Or better yet: to do his or her own readings and share it with the scholarly community.

Bibliography

Attali, Jacques. 1987. *Noise: The Political Economy of Music*. 1985. Trans. Brian Massumi. Minneapolis: University of Minnesota Press.
Caesar, Terry P. 1981. "A Note on Pynchon's Naming." *Pynchon Notes* 5 (February 1981): 5–10.
Carswell, Sean. 2015. "Thomas Pynchon's Ukulele." *The Journal of American Culture* 38:3 (2015): 205–17.
Chorier-Fryd, Bénédicte. 2008. "Mason & Dixon, 'a Novel in Musick' – syncopes de la Révolution chez Thomas Pynchon." Mélanges offerts à Bernard Vincent. *Source,* 2008 (automne): 205–15.
—. 2014. "'A Beat Late'—Rhythmical Oddities in Thomas Pynchon's *Mason & Dixon*." *Thomas Pynchon*. Ed. Gilles Chamerois and Bénédicte Chorier-Fryd. Montpellier: Presses universitaires de la Méditerranée, 259–70.
Clerc, Charles. 2000. *Mason & Dixon & Pynchon*. Lanham/New York/Oxford: University Press of America.
Cowart, David. 1980. *Thomas Pynchon: The Art of Allusion*. Carbondale and Edwardsville: Southern Illinois University Press.
Hänggi, Christian. 2015. "'Harmonica, kazoo—a friend.' Pynchon's Lessons in Organology." *America and the Musical Unconscious*. Eds. Julius Greve and Sascha Pöhlmann. New York/Dresden: Atropos Press.
—. 2017. "Pynchon on Record, Vol. 4." 28 September 2017. Web. 12 June 2018. https://thomaspynchon.com/thomas-pynchon-inspired-music.
—. 2018. "The Pynchon Playlist: A Catalog and Its Analysis" (including the Pynchon Playlist as an Excel file). *Orbit: A Journal of American Literature* Vol. 6 issue 1 (2018). Web. 12 June 2018. https://doi.org/10.16995/orbit.487.
—. 2020. *Pynchon's Sound of Music*. Zürich/Berlin: Diaphanes.
Hume, Catherine Hume, Kathryn and Thomas J. Knight. 1986. "Pynchon's Orchestration of *Gravity's Rainbow*." *Journal of English and Germanic Philology* 85 (July 1986): 366–85.
Hurley, Patrick. 2008. *Pynchon Character Names: A Dictionary*. Jefferson, NC: McFarland & Company.
Joyce, James. 1922. *Ulysses.* London: Penguin Classics, 2000.
McLuhan, Marshall. 1964. *Understanding Media: The Extensions of Man.* Cambridge: The MIT Press, 2002.
Pérez-Llantada Auría, Carmen. 1991. "Beyond Linguistic Barriers: The Musical Fugue Structure of Thomas Pynchon's 'Entropy'." *Cuadernos de Investigación Filológica,* 17, no. 1–2 (1991): 127–40.

Plato. 1930. *The Republic*. Trans. Paul Shorey. New York: Putnam's.
Pynchon, Thomas. 1963. *V*. London: Picador, 1975.
—. 1965. *The Crying of Lot 49*. New York: HarperPerennial, 1999.
—. 1973. *Gravity's Rainbow*. 1973. New York: Penguin, 2006.
—. 1984. *Slow Learner: Early Stories*. London: Vintage, 2000.
—. 1990. *Vineland*. Boston: Little, Brown and Company.
—. 1997. *Mason & Dixon*. London: Vintage, 1998.
—. 2006. *Against the Day*. London: Vintage, 2007.
—. 2009. *Inherent Vice*. New York: Penguin.
—. 2013. *Bleeding Edge*. New York: The Penguin Press.
Redfield, Robert, and Peter L. Hays. 1997. "Fugue as a Structure in Pynchon's 'Entropy'." *Pacific Coast Philology*, Vol. 12 (Oct. 1997): 50–55.
Rouyan, Anahita. 2017. "Singing Thomas Pynchon's Gravity's Rainbow: Interfaces of Song, Narrative, and Sonic Performance." *Partial Answers: Journal of Literature and the History of Ideas*, Vol. 15, No. 1 (January 2017): 117–33.
Vesterman, William. 1976. "Pynchon's Poetry." *Mindful Pleasures: Essays on Thomas Pynchon*. Eds. George Levine and David Leverenz. Boston/Toronto: Little, Brown and Company, 101–12.
Visit. 2020. *"Now Everybody—" Visit Interprets Songs by Thomas Pynchon*. Existential Hymns.
Weisenburger, Steven C. 2006. *A* Gravity's Rainbow *Companion*. 2nd ed. Athens and London: The University of Georgia Press.
Westerath, Gerhard. 1987. "Pynchon's Parker Passage: A Source and Sound Analysis." *Pynchon Notes* 20–21 (1987): 109–14.
Wilder, Billy. 1959. *Some Like It Hot*. United Artists.
Witen, Michelle. 2018. *James Joyce and Absolute Music*. London: Bloomsbury Academic.
Wordsworth, William. 1997. "From the Preface to Lyrical Ballads." *The Arnold Anthology of British and Irish Literature*. Ed. R. Clark and T. Healy. London: Arnold, 673–77.

Part III:
German Literature

GEORG ANTON BENDA:
A GLOBAL COMPOSER AND HIS SINGSPIEL
ROMEO UND JULIE (1776)

CHRISTA JANSOHN

These days, emigration, taxation, and "globalisation" are common topics of conversation. They are also problems which could just as easily apply to Bohemia and Moravia in the seventeenth and eighteenth centuries, and which were important for the work of many of the period's artists. One consequence of this was the increasingly dire work situation for the artists who lived there, in spite of the often-exceptional training which they had received. It was thus mainly for economic rather than political or religious reasons that many practising musicians (choirmasters, organists, singers, instrumental musicians, virtuosos, conductors), composers, instrument makers and music instructors left their homeland and went on to be celebrated in various European countries – often under a naturalised version of their name, more often than not Germanified.

As is so often the case, there is more than one side to this development. Whilst for some, this emigration meant a heavy cultural loss for their home country, for others it represented a great opportunity for the individual artists, or as Jiří Voskovec put it: "These people lost their home, but gained the world".[1] Without doubt, the Benda family can be counted amongst the most successful of these, particularly the two brothers Franz or František and Georg Anton or Jiří Antonín Benda, whose works were cited very early on in Leipzig's book fair catalogues.[2] The Benda family is known as the 'Bach family of Bohemia' and today – fourteen generations later – the so-called Benda Musicians, whose roots go back to Franz Benda's family, still exist. Nevertheless, it cannot be denied that, nowadays, the name Benda

---

[1] Jan Vičar, "Echoes of Czech Music in America," *Acta Universitatis Palackianae Olomucensis, Facultas Philosophica. Philosophica – Aesthetica*, Vol. 24 (2001): 193-197 (193).

[2] Klaus-Peter Koch, "Böhmische Musiker waren in Sachsen des 18. Jahrhunderts nicht nur in Dresden. Anmerkungen zur böhmischen Musiker-Migration," n. p. (unpublished paper).

Fig. 17: Jiří Antonín Benda (1722-1795), Czech composer, violinist and Kapellmeister.

means something to only very few of us. Furthermore, their works are as good as absent from today's repertoire and amongst non-music scholars the name often meets with ignorance, even if the two Benda brothers were once honoured on two Czech postage stamps.

Nevertheless, one can still talk of a certain 'revival' in the past few years, in particular of Georg Anton Benda's *Romeo und Julie* opera. For instance, several performances have taken place in Austria (Innsbruck, Linz, Vienna), the Czech Republic (Prague), France (Clermont-Ferrand), Germany (Bremen, Kassel, Pforzheim, Potsdam, Gotha)[3], and Switzerland (Geneva), as well as in Sweden (Stockholm) where, in 2010, Johann Adolph Hasse's opera *Pyramus and Thisbe* and Georg Anton Benda's *Romeo und Julie* formed a double bill at Vadstena Castle, reflecting the tragic fates of the lovers through two widely diverse temperaments and styles.[4] In 1994 and 1998 two CD recordings of a performance in Gotha (1993) and in Bremen (1997) were released[5], which are unfortunately no longer available, and the opening performance in Britain in the summer of 2007 by the small Bampton Classical Opera House, which specialises in Baroque music, met with great acclaim. It is only too understandable that, 231 years after its first actual performance, many English critics admitted that they had "never [...] heard a note of Benda".[6] Thomas Kahlcke, in his article accompanying the CD, cites substantial reasons for this and also attempts to place the composer Georg Anton Benda within the period's musical history. Kahlcke writes:

> Sometimes it seems as if there was only a sudden musical vacuum in the period between the baroque and classic. A look at today's concert and record repertoire does indeed leave the impression that, quite simply, nothing at all was composed subsequent to the ethereal late work of Johann Sebastian Bach and prior to the intensive phase of the trio of Haydn, Mozart, and

---

[3] See Horst Koegler, "Julchen sollte sie heißen," *Opernwelt*, No. 1 (1996): 43 (on the Pforzheim production, premiere on 8 November 1995), and Wolf E. Martinsen, "Nach 200 Jahren aufgeweckt," *Opernwelt*, No. 12 (1993): 46 (on the Kassel production premiere on 17 July 1993).
[4] Stephan Mösch, "Romeo und Julia auf dem Lande," *Opernwelt*, No. 9/10 (2010): 29-31.
[5] Boris Kehrmann, "Väter und Söhne," *Opernwelt*, No. 7 (2014). He compares the Gotha CD (Gotha version 1776) with the later version (Mannheim version 1784), which is also available on CD (cpo 999 496-2). See also: Gabriele Buschmeier, "Jiří Antonín Benda und Christoph Willibald Gluck. Ihr Beitrag für das europäische Musiktheater." In *Symposiumsbericht: Gluck und Prag, Nürnberg, 20-22. Juli 2012*, ed. Thomas Betzwieser and Daniel Brandenburg (Kassel: Bärenreiter, 2016), 201-216.
[6] Michael Church, "Superb": Review of Benda's *Romeo and Juliet. The Independent*, September 20, 2007, accessed March 6, 2021, available at https://www.bamptonopera.org/operadetail.htm?event=56.

Beethoven. In the meantime, almost nothing is known nowadays of the unbelievably diverse works of men such as Stamitz, Richter and Holzbauer, Canabich, Wagenseil or the Bach sons. The description of this era as "preclassic" shows clearly that people are hardly prepared to acknowledge the originality of their works. And if Mozart, whose music only became possible as a result of the achievements of "preclassicism," acknowledged "that Benda was always my favourite among the Lutheran conductors," then most of us will have to admit: Benda?[7]

In the following, I would like to discuss Benda's Singspiel *Romeo und Julie*, the libretto of which written by the then highly acclaimed Gotha poet and playwright, Friedrich Wilhelm Gotter (1746-97). The discussion seeks to shed light on the influence his work had on the development of opera and its significance for the reception of Shakespeare's work.

1. Georg Anton Benda's *Romeo und Julie* (1776)

Shakespeare's plays have been an inspiration for most of the great opera composers of all musical periods, and there are several hundred operas based on his work.[8] And yet, the *Romeo und Julie* opera by Benda and Gotter was, alongside Gottfried Schwanenberger's eighteenth-century *Romeo e Giulia* with an Italian libretto by Giulio Roberto Sanseverino (1722-?), not only the first to set the *Romeo and Juliet* material to music[9], but was one of the first ever Shakespeare operas. After the enormous success of Benda's *Romeo und Julie*, other operas were to follow, almost all of which finished with a *lieto fine* ("happy ending"). Amongst others, there

---

[7] See the leaflet with Thomas Kahlcke's article, "Georg Benda, *Romeo und Julie*" (Teatro Musicale, 3). 2 CDs (Neumünster: Canterino Musikproduktion, 1994): 3-4 (4). The libretto (in German, English and French) is also accompanying the CD, 18-40.

[8] See Bryan N. S. Gooch and David Thatcher, *A Shakespeare Music Catalogue*. 5 vols (Oxford: Oxford University Press, 1991); Wilson, Christopher R. "Shakespeare". In *The New Grove Dictionary of Opera*, 4 vols, ed. Stanley Sadie (London: Macmillan, 1992), vol. 4, pp. 338-347; and Winston Dean, "Shakespeare in the Opera House," *Shakespeare Survey*, Vol. 18 (1965): 75-93 (including a survey of "Operas based on the Plays", 88-93).

[9] In the same year, Gottfried Schwanenberger composed the opera for the court at Braunschweig (1776). The libretto, which, alongside the two lovers, only Benvolio as the third character sings, had been written three years earlier and departs considerably from the original: thus, the lovers survive and marry in the finale. See Bernd Kaven, ed., *Johann Gottfried Schwanenberger. 1737-1804: Ein Wolfenbütteler Komponist* (Wolfenbüttel: Herzog-August-Bibliothek, 1988).

were three operas with French libretti, namely by S. von Rumling (Munich, 1790), Nicolas-Marie Dalayrac's *Tout pour l'amour, ou Roméo et Juliette* (Paris, 1792) and Daniel Steibelt's opéra comique, (Paris, 1793), as well as Italian versions by Luigi Marescalchi (Rome, 1789) and the highly successful version, admired by Napoleon, *Giulietta e Romeo* by Niccoló Zingarelli (Milan, 1796 and Paris, 1806), and by Pietro Guglielmi, which celebrated its premiere in London in 1819. These were followed, amongst others, by Stephen Storace's *Gli equivoci* (*Comedy of Errors*, Vienna, 1786). E. W. Wolf's *Die Zauberirrungen* (*A Midsummer Night's Dream*, Weimar, 1785) and A. Salieri's *Falstaff le tre burle* (*The Merry Wives of Windsor*, Vienna, 1799), as well as several versions of *The Tempest*. Many years later saw Vincenzo Bellini's *I Capuleti e i Montecchi* (Venice, 1830, Libretto: F. Romani), which is not based on Shakespeare, however, but on Luigi Scevola's drama (1818), which in turn draws on one of Shakespeare's sources, namely Luigi da Porto's version (1530); finally, we have C. Gounod's *Roméo et Juliette* (Paris: 1867, Libretto: J. Barbier and M. Carré) and Hector Berlioz's "dramatic symphony", *Roméo et Juliette*, op. 17 (1839),[10] which was conducted at the Shakespeare celebrations in Prague in the "New Town Theatre" (Novoměstské divadlo) on 22 April 1864 by no less a figure than Bedřich Smetana.[11]

It is important to note here in the context of the musical reception of Shakespeare's plays in Germany that these took place both on the musical stage – in the form of opera versions – as well as spoken theatre, and here in the form of incidental and stage music.[12] These examples of incidental music have – if at all – only survived in manuscripts and were published in very few cases. It is only in the last few years that they have become an increasing focus of research.

---

[10] On its composition and reception see Julian Rushton, *Berlioz: Roméo et Juliette* (Cambridge: Cambridge University Press, 1994). See also Riethmüller, Albrecht. "'She Speaks, Yet She Says Nothing: What of That?' *Romeo and Juliet* in Hector Berlioz's and Leonard Bernstein's Adaptations". In *German Shakespeare Studies at the Turn of the Twenty-First Century*, ed. Christa Jansohn (Newark: University of Delaware Press, 2006), 128-143.

[11] Otakar Vočadlo, "Shakespeare and Bohemia," *Shakespeare Survey*, Vol. 9 (1956): 101-110 (108).

[12] See Dieter Martin, "Deutsche Shakespeare-Opern um 1800," Goethezeit Portal, accessed April 7, 2021, http://www.goethezeitportal.de/db/wiss/epoche/martin_shakespeare_opern.pdf, 1-13 (2). (First published [in French]: "Shakespeare et l'opéra autour de 1800". In *Le monde germanique et l'opéra. Le livret en question*, ed. Bernard Banoun und Jean-François Candoni (Paris: Klincksieck, 2005), 297-316.)

2. Friedrich Wilhelm Gotter

Apart from the three aforementioned works by Benda, *Ariadne auf Naxos*, *Der Jahrmarkt* und *Medea*, it is *Romeo und Julie* in particular which had great significance for the development of musical-dramatic aspirations in the eighteenth century. The premiere of *Romeo und Julie* took place on 25 September 1776 at the Gotha Court Theatre, where it saw nine repeat performances, a clear indication of the production's success. The sheet music was never printed, even though this would clearly have been in keeping with Benda's wishes.[13] The surviving handwritten musical score of 1776, kept in Gotha, has the title: *Romeo u. Julie, | Eine Oper | mit gesprochenen Dialog | oder | Ein Drama mit Gesang | in | Musick gesetzt | von | Georg Benda.* [Romeo and Julie, | An opera | with spoken dialogue | or | A Drama with singing | set to music | by | Georg Benda].[14] In the piano score, which was published later, it is simply called 'an opera'.[15] In 1784, Benda revised the music significantly; this handwritten score is housed in the Berlin State Library.[16] To date, thirty-seven manuscripts or part-manuscripts of the music score have been identified, and these reflect the wide circulation of the work in the eighteenth century.[17] In these handwritten scores the play is usually called "an opera" or "a serious Singspiel". The term 'serious' is here presumably meant to be understood as the counterpart of 'seria' from the Italian 'Opera seria' and hence refers to the music. The publisher's Dykische Buchhandlung also published the libretto in 1779 under the title "Romeo and Julie. A Play with Singing in

---

[13] See the letter of 8 October, 1786 to Gotter, which can be found re-printed in Fritz Brückner, "Georg Benda und das deutsche Singspiel," *Sammelbände der Internationalen Musikgesellschaft*, Vol. 5, No. 4 (1904): 571-621 (616).

[14] University and research library Erfurt/Gotha; class mark: D-GOl/ Mus.4|o 44b/10a. See also Thomas Bauman, ed., *German Opera 1770-1800 – A Collection of Facsimiles of Printed and Manuscript Full Scores*, Librettos 5: Georg Anton Benda: *Romeo und Julie*, and Joseph Schuster: *Der Alchymist* (New York & London: Garland Publishing, 1986), 1-128. In this article all translations from German into English are my own.

[15] *Klavierauszug | von | Romeo und Julie, | einer Oper in drey Akten. | In Musik gesetzt | von | Herrn Kapelldirektor Benda. | [etching] | Zweite Auflage. | Leipzig, | im Verlage der Dykischen Buchhandlung. | 1784. | [at the end:] Leipzig, gedruckt bey Johann Gottlob Immanuel Breitkopf.* Hans-Sommer-Archiv, Berlin, Berlin; Signatur: D-Bsommer / Mus.pr. Benda G.A. 2.

[16] Staatsbibliothek zu Berlin – Preußischer Kulturbesitz, Musikabteilung, Signatur *D-B/ Mus. 4|o 44b/10a.*

[17] On this see the entries in the international database of the RISM ("Répertoire International des Sources Musciales").

Three Acts"[18], a clear indication that the theatre was the starting point for Gotter's project and that, in his capacity as unofficial theatre poet for the Gotha-based Seyler troupe, he reckoned on finding good actors to perform the work.

In terms of its genre, the work has the formal features of a Singspiel[19] since it does not use any sung recitatives but spoken dialogues to join the arias and ensembles together. What is innovative about the play is the composer's decision to have his librettist Friedrich Wilhelm Gotter based his work on an ambitious text, unusual for Singspiele up to that time. In the intellectually and culturally volatile atmosphere of the *Sturm und Drang* [Storm and Stress] period, Shakespeare's plays had only just been discovered and translated for German audiences. To set a text by this author to music – albeit in some parts heavily changed and given a *lieto fine* (happy ending) – was in itself a new challenge for the genre; it also represented a commitment to cultural progress and, at the same time, a challenge to the musically creative powers. It may well have been his reverence for the composer as well as a justification for this innovative approach which caused Gotter to defend his work against the critics and at the same time to distance himself from any of its predecessors. Thus, he wrote in the foreword to the libretto:

> Benda's music may be my writ for protection for those who regard it as a profanation to put a subject from the muse of tragedy onto the opera stage. But have not more lyric poets taken similar liberties? And is it not the fate of masterpieces in all the arts to be copied and imitated? The following Singspiel has almost nothing but name and story in common with the famous German tragedy of the same name. But the name and story belong to Shakespeare.[20]

In Gotter, Georg Benda had chosen an experienced, albeit, as far as the literary innovations of the time were concerned, a rather conservative poet, whose career nevertheless bears witness to the breadth of his talents and

---

[18] Printed as a facsimile in Bauman, *German Opera 1770-1800*, 7-64.
[19] On the Singspiel, see Chapter 5 of Bodo Plachta, *"Ein Tyrann der Schaubühne?": Stationen und Positionen einer literatur- und kulturkritischen Debatte über Oper und Operntext im 18. Jahrhundert* (Berlin: Weidler Buchverlag, 2003), 119-138.
[20] Friedrich Wilhelm Gotter, "Vorrede". In Gotter, *Romeo und Julie: Ein Schauspiel mit Gesang in drey Aufzügen* (Leipzig, Dykische Buchhandlung, 1779), 7-9 (7). Bauman correctly points out that Gotter often stays closer to the English original than Weisse. See Thomas Bauman, "Opera versus Drama: *Romeo and Juliet* in Eighteenth-Century Germany," *Eighteenth-Century Studies*, Vol 11, No. 2 (1977-78): 186-203 (193).

interests. He had already written the libretti of Benda's monodramas *Ariadne auf Naxos* and *Medea* and produced a translation of Rousseau's *Pygmalion* for Benda's piece.

Gotter came from a distinguished family from Gotha, studied law in Göttingen (1763-1766), and while he was there, he fostered lively connections with various actor troupes.[21] In 1766 he became a registrar in Gotha, and a year later legation secretary at the Imperial High Court in Wetzlar, where he kept company with, amongst others, Goethe, and his friends. From 1772 until his death on 18 March 1797, Friedrich Wilhelm Gotter was the ducal privy secretary in Gotha where he founded a private theatre. His debut – a performance of Goldoni's *Wolhtätiger Musskopf* on 27 January 1773 – was enthusiastically received and he went on to be one of the most frequently performed authors with a reputation outside of Germany.

In addition to his position at the court, Gotter wrote more than forty plays, numerous poems, and romances, translated, or adapted from French, Italian, and English (including Thomas Gray and Oliver Goldsmith), and he co-edited and wrote for H. C. Boie's *Göttinger Musenalmanach*. As an outstanding authority on the theatre, and as an actor, author, and director, he was frequently sought out for advice. His friends included A. W. Iffland, Johann Wilhelm Ludwig Gleim, Goethe, and the young play director in Hamburg Friedrich Ludwig Schröder.

Without doubt it was as librettist that Gotter was most successful and together with Georg Benda he conquered many theatres in Germany and abroad for several years. He returned to Shakespeare as his final big project a few years before his death (1797) and in the years 1790-1791 he worked on turning Friedrich Hildebrand von Einsiedel's text into a *Tempest* opera (1778). His libretto *Die Geisterinsel: Eine Oper in drei Akten* ("The Island of the Spirits: An Opera in Three Acts") was, however, only published in Schiller's *Horen* (1797)[22] after Gotter's death. Mozart, who was meant to write the music for it, died before he could do so. In 1798 and 1799 it was set to music and performed simultaneously on a number of occasions by,

---

[21] The following discussion is based on: Kai Agthe, "Friedrich Wilhelm Gotter," *Palmbaum: Literarisches Journal aus Thüringen*, Vol. 5, No. 17 (1997): 77-83 (79). Agthe rightly points out that there has been no collected edition of his works since the Gotha edition of 1802; there is also no recent biography. See here Christoph Köhler, "Friedrich Wilhelm Gotter (1746-1797) zum 200. Todestag," *Gothaer Museumsheft* (1997): 39-50; and Rudolf Schlösser, *Friedrich Wilhelm Gotter: Sein Leben und seine Werke. Ein Beitrag zur Geschichte der Bühne und Bühnendichtung im 18. Jahrhundert* (Hamburg & Leipzig: Leopold Voß, 1894).

[22] *Die Geisterinsel. Ein Singspiel in drey Akten, Die Horen*, Vol. 3 (1797), St. [part] 8: 1-26, and St. [part] 9: 1-78.

amongst others, Johann Friedrich Reichardt (Berlin: Theater am Gendarmenmarkt [National Theatre], 6 July 1798), Johann Rudolf Zumsteeg (Stuttgart: Court theatre, 7 November 1798), Friedrich Wilhelm Haack (Stettin, 1794), and the Meining composer Friedrich Fleischmann, which was performed in Frankfurt am Main in the 'National Theatre' in 1792 and in Weimar on 19 May 1798.[23] Audiences were not impressed with the music and the libretto, in particular, as a result of its sparse metaphorical language, banal metaphors, superficial dialogue, and the static scenes with no action. Gotter's method of simplifying the story, his approach of "the more human, the more appealing", fell flat with audiences.[24]

This may well be one reason why Gotter's libretti are nowadays barely known. Another reason is no doubt the – for us – utterly foreign style of the language which he used with great precision either wittily or sentimentally depending on the theme, and was characterised by his friend Goethe in his *Dichtung und Wahrheit* as follows: "His mind was gentle, clear and mirthful, his talent practiced and controlled; he cultivated French elegance and enjoyed the part of English literature which deals with moral and pleasant subjects."[25] Another contemporary once said something similar about Georg Benda, and it may be this congeniality between composer and librettist which brought them together and was responsible for their success:

> But the dreadful and the horrible do not quite fit in his world. He therefore would not be much good at setting all of Shakespeare's works to music. His imagination is not wild but subject to the sceptre of reason. His wit does not vie for the audience's applause through harlequinades, rather it manifests itself only in the charming execution of his musical ideas. The atmosphere he creates is not blinding, but utterly charming and warm like his heart. His portrayal of the naïve is exceptionally successful, only the grotesquely comic always fails.[26]

---

[23] See Huesmann, Heinrich. "Gotter-Fleischmann: Die Geisterinsel". In Huesmann, *Shakespeare-Inszenierungen unter Goethe in Weimar* (Graz: Hermann Böhlaus Nachfolger 1968), 212-222. See also Thomas Bauman's chapter in his *North German Opera in the Age of Goethe* (Cambridge: Cambridge University Press, 1986), 310-322. On its genesis see also Werner Deetjen, "Der Sturm als Operntext bearbeitet von Einsiedel und Gotter," *Shakespeare Jahrbuch*, Vol. 64 (1928): 77-89.
[24] Huesmann, "Gotter-Fleischmann: Die Geisterinsel", 213.
[25] Translated from Johann Wolfgang Goethe, *Dichtung und Wahrheit: Zwölftes Buch* (Berlin: Aufbau-Verlag, 1976), 574. See also 586-587, where Goethe speaks about the two translations of Goldsmith's poem "Deserted Village".
[26] Christian Friedrich Daniel Schubart, *Ideen einer Aesthetik der Tonkunst*. In Schubart, *Gesammelte Schriften und Schicksale*, Vol. 5 (Stuttgart: J. Scheible's Buchhandlung, 1839), 122.

Apart from these obvious shortcomings, it is also important to point out that the two artists – like eighteenth-century translators – were not aiming to produce a faithful translation of Shakespeare: rather, they were more concerned, among other things, with its usefulness so that they could provide their own native national theatre with new plays, especially since there were only "a few good originals with largely mediocre translations of foreign, and mainly French, plays".[27]

Gotter's play also has to be seen in this context. The libretto in three acts is not only based on Shakespeare's original but also the then very popular adaptation *Romeo und Julie* in five acts (Leipzig, 1767) by Christian Felix Weisse (1726-1804)[28], who was also a well-known writer, playwright, and excellent librettist – and known most of all for the Singspiele by Johann Anton Hiller. Both Gotter and Weisse were also familiar with David Garrick's version. Gotter may also have had access to Giulio Roberto Sanseverino's libretto for Schwanenberger's opera, which was published in its second edition in Berlin in 1776[29], and, like Gotter's and Garrick's versions, also ends happily.

They tread similar paths in their adaptations which are characteristic of their period in their attempt to find a middle way between the passionate plays from England, with their often unrestrained language, and French plays with their concern for order and regularity, which also distinguished themselves in the "respectability of the morals, the correct relation of the parts to the whole, the chastened and fine language of the court, of courtship and of love". "With such a combination", as Weisse wrote in a letter to Ramler on 15 January 1766,

> we would avoid the bombast and exaggeration of the one and the emptiness and the dullness of the other, the English's lack of restraint, their irregularity and frequent degeneration into wildness and the laughable, the gallant, the coquettishness and triviality of the French.[30]

---

[27] Christian Felix Weisse, "Vorbericht", in: Weisse, *Trauerspiele*, Vol. 1 (Karlsruhe: Christian Schmieder 1778), ii-vii (iii).

[28] General overviews of this can be found in Simon Williams, *Shakespeare on the German Stage*, Vol. 1: 1586-1914 (Cambridge: Cambridge University Press, 1990); and Roger Paulin, *The Critical Reception of Shakespeare in Germany 1682-1914: Native Literature and Foreign Genius* (Hildesheim: Olms, 2003).

[29] Oscar George Theodore Sonneck, *Catalogue of Opera Librettos Printed Before 1800*, 3 vols (Washington, DC: Govt. Print Office, 1914), Vol. 1, 949.

[30] Quoted in Walter Hüttemann, *Christian Felix Weiße und seine Zeit in ihrem Verhalten zu Shakespeare* (Duisburg: Buschmann, 1912), 60. See also Renata Häublein, *Die Entdeckung Shakespeares auf der deutschen Bühne des 18.*

In Weisse's adaptation, as in Gotter's libretto, there was a determined attempt to bring together the merits of both theatrical traditions and to adapt them to contemporary audience tastes. Comical elements, typical of the Singspiel genre, are absent from the text and the music. These had already been eliminated in Weisse's version for, as he argued, the original was "overloaded with many trivial, superfluous things irrelevant to the plot", and the humour "in some places spilled over into the childish".[31] Hence, in both versions there are no puns or crude figures of speech, particularly as they were deemed inappropriate for the tragic context. Capulet's irate tone in Gotter's text is, in comparison with Weisse's adaptation, toned down even more, and in the libretto the audience encounters a language which resembles the original wording only slightly. Unlike Weisse's prose version, Gotter wrote his in prose as well as in verse, in iambic and trochaic metre, but in spite of this his language is, as most critics pointed out, only rarely convincing.[32] One of the texts which were heavily criticized is Romeo's song "Hoff und liebe! Lieb und Hoffnung" (Act 1, scene 3, CD, p. 22) which runs:

> Hope and love! Love and hope
> Defy all adversity.
> Gaze after my ship's flight
> With steadfast free heart!
> True love is at the helm,
> Bold hope swells the sails,
> Wishes of warm friendship jest
> At my side and ahead of me,
> And conjure up wind and waves.

Jahrhunderts: Adaptation und Wirkung der Vermittlung auf dem Theater (Tübingen: Max Niemeyer, 2005), 43.

[31] Christian Felix Weisse, "Vorbericht" (235-237 (236)). The text is quoted in Christian Felix Weisse, *Romeo und Julie: Ein bürgerliches Trauerspiel in fünf Aufzügen*. In *Die Aufnahme Shakespeares auf der Bühne der Aufklärung in den sechziger und siebziger Jahren*, ed. Fritz Brüggemann (Darmstadt: Wissenschaftliche Buchgesellschaft, 1966), 234-306. See also the review "Romeo und Julie, nach Shakespeare, frey fürs deutsche Theater bearb.," *Neue allgemeine deutsche Bibliothek*, Vol. 30 (1797): 370. "Additions and changes were necessary as were the omission of some pointless word plays about which even the warmest and keenest admirer of the English poet would not speak in public. One of the author's most noble efforts was therefore the alleviation and equalisation of the language and in this he was fairly successful."

[32] See here the discussion in Thomas Bauman's *North German Opera in the Age of Goethe*, 125; and his essay, "Opera versus Drama: *Romeo and Juliet* in Eighteenth-Century Germany," 195.

It was argued that:

> On the whole, the poetry shows a backward step. Whilst "Walder"'s dialogue does demonstrate an unenjoyable sentimentality this here, in the light of such a model, is even more unforgivable. The backward step is clearly a result of its dependence on Italian operatic poetry. Romeo's first song may well have been taken directly from an Italian example. The combining of metaphors of ship, sea, wind, sail, rudder with personified love in a single image is typically Italian.[33]

In Weisse's and Gotter's versions the unity of time and place were also changed as a result of their decision to limit the settings to two or three locations, namely a hall in the Capullet's palace (in Weisse's with several rooms) or Julie's room (Gotter), the Capulets' grave (Weisse) and the graveyard (Weisse and Gotter).[34] The unity of time is also preserved, as the

---

[33] See Brückner, "Georg Benda und das deutsche Singspiel," 595. The German text of Romeo's song reads (CD, p. 22):

Hoff und liebe! Lieb und Hoffnung
Trotzen jedem Ungemach.
Sieh mit standhaft freiem Herzen
Meines Schiffes Fluge nach!
Treue Liebe sitzt am Ruder,
Kühne Hoffnung schwellt die Segel,
Warmer Freundschaft Wünsche scherzen
Mir zu Seite, vor mir her,
Und beschwören Wind und Meer.

[34] See the stage direction at the beginning of the play: "The setting in the first four acts is a hall in the Capellets' palace and the final the Capellets' grave." and the stage description in the Fifth Act: "The setting depicts a churchyard. One side shows the wall and the gate leading to it; the wall near the gate is tumbling down so that it can be climbed over. There is a flying buttress in the background." See Weisse, *Romeo und Julie: Ein bürgerliches Trauerspiel in fünf Aufzügen*, 235 and 292, and Gotter's instruction at the beginning of the first act ("Juliet's room; including a table with cups on it; three doors, of which one leads off to the side into the garden." (11)): "Julie's Zimmer; unter anderen Möbeln ein Tisch, auf welchem Tassen stehen; drei Türen, von denen eine zur Seite nach dem Garten führt." See the direction for the Third Act ("A grove of cypresses, tapu trees and Babylonian willows. To the rear, the vaults of the Capellets, open and illuminated, inside several coffins, including the latest, next to the entrance, Thebaldo's. Before, Juliet's open coffin, resting on the bier.", 45): "Ein Hain von Cypressen, Tapussen, babylonischen Weiden. Hinten das Erbbegräbnis der Capellets, offen und erleuchtet. Innerhalb desselben verschiedene Särge, unter welchen der frischeste, nächst am Eingange, Thebaldos

action in both works takes place in just a few hours. Weisse opens with Julie's utterance "schon schlug die Glocke zwölf" ("the clock has already struck twelve") and ends at about midnight.[35] In Gotter's version, as well, we are told in Act 1 Scene 2: "It is midnight", and when Juliet takes the sleeping potion, we are told that she will wake again towards midnight (Act 2, Scene 6). This time is once again skilfully integrated into the final monologue of the Second Act in Julie's fearful speech (Act 2, Scene 7, CD, p. 32), through which the urgent and highly dramatic unfolding of the events is re-emphasised:

> Wohl denn! sei
> Willkommen, Rettungstrank! Doch wie? – wenn beim Erwachen
> Romeo nicht erscheint? wenn mein Schrein
> Nicht zu Lorenzos Ohren dringet? –
> Um Mitternacht! – allein! – in einem Sarg! – umringet
> Von meiner Väter Gräbern! –

> So, be
> Welcome, oh drink destined to save me.
> But what of, when I awake
> Romeo should not appear?
> If my cries
> Do not reach Lorenzo's ears?
> At midnight! Alone! In a coffin! Surrounded
> By my ancestors' graves! Heaven help me!

In contrast to Weisse, Gotter reduces the *dramatis personae* even further. Whilst Weisse limits his adaption to eight characters, three of whom only appear on stage sporadically[36], Gotter creates an even smaller cast, a

---

Sarg andeutet. Vor dem Begräbnisse Juliens offener Sarg, auf der Baare ruhend." Quoted in Gotter, *Romeo und Julie: Ein Schauspiel mit Gesang in drey Aufzügen.*

[35] Christian Felix Weisse, *Romeo und Julie*, I.i. (237) and V.iii (297): "Romeo: '[…] Das Gift fängt langsam an durch meine Glieder zu schleichen: bald, bald wird es in dem innersten Verhältnisse meines Lebens sein! […] Um welche Zeit ist's' – Pietro (der nach der Uhr sieht). 'Halb zwölfe.'" ["Romeo: 'the poison is starting to move slowly through my limbs: soon, soon it will be in the innermost part of my life! […] What time is it' – Pietro (who looks at the clock). 'Half eleven.'"]

[36] These are Pietro, Romeo (only in Act I and V) and Montecchio (Act 5, 6. Szene). See also the "Dramatis personae"; ibid., p. 237: "Montecchio and Capellet: the two heads of the most distinguished families in Verona, Romeo: Son of Montecchio, Julie; Daughter of Capellet; Lady Capellet; Laura: Julie's confidante, Benvoglio: a Veronese doctor; Pietro: old servant to Romeo."

decision based on the available actors and singers in Gotha. In total there are just four soloists: Julie, her confidante Laura – both soprano –, Romeo (tenor) and Capellet (baritone / tenor), a speaking role for Father Lorenzo and finally five solo voices for the grave scene at the beginning of the third act and the final song. The other roles, such as those of Benvolio, Mercutio, Tybalt, and Lady Capulet have all been cut; and an encounter with Count Paris, who in Gotter's version is called Lodrona according to the pre-Shakespeare source, does not occur. There is also no nurse, but a soubrette, the friend Laura "who is a bit of a moralising pain, plus a mysterious aunt Camilla, from nowhere in Shakespeare, who seems to be the eminence not just *grise* but gruesome".[37] Departing from his source texts, Gotter uses male and female choruses in the graveyard scene which, following classical tragedy, deliver samples of general worldly wisdom. After the male chorus has praised death as the saviour from this earthly life, a chorus of girls comes forward who, alternating with Laura, sing that Julie's fate is to be envied since the dead are removed from all earthly worries. The male chorus repeats the same words and appears again after Capellet and his daughter's reconciliation with the reminder that the hostility should be forgotten, and peace should prevail in Verona. An alternating song between the count and the chorus in which the benefactions of peace are celebrated ends the play.[38]

Many contemporary critics saw in the happy ending, which harks back to the Italian tradition of the *opera seria*, a pure concession to contemporary audience tastes. Heinrich Leopold Wagner wrote that Gotter had "criminally misappropriated Shakespeare for the sake of deteriorating tastes"[39], and even Carl Friedrich Zelter, who otherwise had a very high opinion of Benda's opera, wrote: "The end of the play was utterly distasteful to me, in fact I hated it. To watch the rapid transformation from the most profound pain caused by death into wild, exuberant joy was for me more damaging than the death itself."[40] However, perhaps the happy ending was simply

---

[37] Roderic Dunnett, "Brilliantly engaging": Review of Benda's *Romoe and Juliet*. *Music & Vision*, September 2, 2007, accessed April 7, 2021, available at https://www.bamptonopera.org/operadetail.htm?event=56.

[38] Artur Sauer, *Shakespeares "Romeo und Julia" in den Bearbeitungen und Uebersetzungen der deutschen Literatur* (Greifswald: Julius Abel, 1915), 63-74.

[39] Heinrich Leopold Wagner, *Briefe, die Seylerische Schauspilergesellschaft und Ihre Vorstellungen zu Frankfurt am Mayn betreffend* (Frankfurt am Mayn: Eichenbergische Erben, 1777), 12th letter: 3 June, 1777, 179.

[40] Johann-Wolfgang Schottländer, ed., *Carl Friedrich Zelters Darstellungen seines Lebens* (Weimar: Verlag der Goethe Gesellschaft, 1931), 120. Zelter continues: "I complained about this to Professor Engel, who said nothing more than that the entire poem was not worth tuppence." Further contemporary critical opinions are quoted in the article by Dieter Martin, "Deutsche Shakespeare-Opern um 1800," 7-8.

nothing more than a pragmatic decision, following reports of a performance in Hamburg of Shakespeare's *Othello*, where there were supposed to have been "fainting fits after fainting fits", as the audience were unable to cope with the "overly tragic tragedy".

Performances today still apparently mistrust the ending, if not the entire libretto, as is shown particularly clearly by the performance in the Palace Theatre of the new Sanssouci Palace (Potsdam, 16 November 1996). The stage set, a bare, almost completely empty, room with Julie's steel bed is, from the beginning, reminiscent of a jail. At the outset, Julie's room is presented in dark blue, like a Chagall painting. Later, the gloomy house of Julie's parents is shown in patchy olive green and in the third act, the crypt is flooded in a harsh neon light. Julie is not the fervently loving and suffering heroine, nor is Romeo the romantic pursuer. From the beginning she seems much more childish and, at the same time, suicidal when in front of her threatening father she climbs onto a staircase which breaks off in the middle of the room. With this, Julie's love from the outset seems doomed. At the beginning, in the middle of her child's world surrounded by dolls, rocking horse and cradle, she is put into a wedding dress, the arms of which are too long – by her father which he laces up into a straitjacket. Although in the end the lovers fall into each other's arms, the stage contains another bed hanging on chains from the ceiling over them with a dead Julie in it. While on stage the reconciliation drifts into burlesque, a second Romeo and Julie pair act out in pantomime the tragic ending of Shakespeare's version.[41] Whilst this interpretation might have touched a nerve of our times, it misses the highly sensitive and lyrical style of Benda's opera which so delighted his contemporaries. Thus, for example, Carl Friedrich Zelter, writing about a rehearsal led by Georg Benda, recalls that the music moved him so much that "sitting in the orchestra with my violin in my hand I wept bitter tears of compassion […] I could not get rid of Julie's image as it has buried itself inside me through Benda's music; I lived and suffered; I lay in the coffin with her".[42]

Let me return in this final section to Gotter's libretto. Alongside the aforementioned changes to the original and the adaptation, there are others to mention which Gotter took over from Weisse, and which are expressed even in the subtitle of his version in his description of the drama as "a bourgeois tragedy". "Bourgeois" here is meant "in the sense of human-private-moral-emotional", and unlike "high tragedy", it does not address a

---

[41] See Stephan Mösch, "Bürste statt Pinsel," *Opernwelt*, No. 2 (1997).
[42] Schottländer, *Carl Friedrich Zelters Darstellungen seines Lebens*, 115.

particular status, but general human experiences[43], which were meant to allow the audiences to identify with the characters and to concentrate attention on them. For this reason, Weisse and, after him, Gotter only take the basic constellation of Shakespeare's drama:

> [T]he couple as the children of two enemy families, the banning of Romeo from the city as a consequence of Tybalt's murder, Julia's marriage to Paris planned by her parents, her feigned death and the suicide of the two lovers in the Capulets' crypt.[44]

Weisse and, to a certain extent, Gotter then concentrate their focus completely on the father-daughter conflict. At the centre, therefore, is not the drama of the two enemy families but Julie's dilemma of not complying with her father's wish that she should marry Paris.[45] Thus, Julie's anguished condition determines the drama from the beginning to the end, in which Romeo develops into a responsible, "gentle, young man" who stabs the "arrogant, fierce and proud" Tybalt in self-defence. The equally highly sensitive mother cares lovingly about her daughter, while the tyrannical father forces his daughter into a marriage with the Count of Londrona (Act 3), and at the end admits his errors. This balance between the characters in Weisse's adaptation is absent from Gotter's. As previously mentioned, the character of the mother was cut completely, and the roles of the father and Romeo are substantially shorter, while that of Julie is so dominant in the first two acts that the opera could simply be called *Julie*. In one of the handwritten music manuscripts, it is in fact referred to as *Julie und Romeo*.[46] Without doubt, Julie is the protagonist of the play, followed by Laura. Since little action takes place on stage, the focus falls completely on the characters and the music. This is encouraged by the markedly unostentatious libretto with its simple verses, which inspired the composer to write "the best most moving songs". Benda is reported to have said: "I have unmusical verses to thank for my best, most moving songs, as they forced me to collect myself

---

[43] Karl S. Guthke, *Das deutsche bürgerliche Trauerspiel*, 5th edn (Stuttgart: J.B. Metzler, 1994), 54, quoted in Renata Häublein, *Die Entdeckung Shakespeares auf der deutschen Bühne des 18. Jahrhunderts*, 44-45.
[44] Renata Häublein, *Die Entdeckung Shakespeares auf der deutschen Bühne des 18. Jahrhunderts*, 47.
[45] Following da Porto's source, in Weisse's version he is called Pariade von Londrona.
[46] *Julie und Romeo: Eine Oper in drey Aufzügen. Von Georg Benda.* Handwritten musical score of 1810 from the provenance of the Royal Theatre Library, Staatsbibliothek zu Berlin – Preußischer Kulturbesitz, Musikabteilung, Signatur *D-B/ Mus.ms. 1354/1*.

completely in order to improve the poet." Here he quotes a verse from his beautiful aria "Meinen Romeo zu sehn" [To see my Romeo]:

> Alle Gedanken verlieren sich
> In den Wonnegedanken:
> Meinen Romeo zu sehn usw.
>
> [All thoughts are lost
> In the blissful thought:
> Seeing my Romeo]

> He ran to the piano and sang the magnificent aria with such inner emotion that clear tears ran down his cheeks and everyone standing around was moved to tears in spite of his ugly voice, his broad Bohemian accent, violent gesticulations, and facial expressions.[47]

It is obviously precisely this talent as a composer which contemporaries admired Benda for. Clearly, he succeeded in realising precisely what Jean Jacques Rousseau describes so vividly in his musical dictionary:

> In the hand of the composer, the text becomes an orange which he squeezes for so long until the last golden drop is squeezed from it; this has hardly been shown any better than by Tomelli and Benda. […] It is thorough, free from pedantic accuracy, high and low, serious, and funny; […] His melodious songs are like silk to every educated ear […].[48]

3. Musical Analysis

The audience at the first performance would have heard the voices of very young actors. The role of Julie was played by the then seventeen-year-old Franziska Koch[49], a pupil of Benda, who had already played the female leading role in his musical comedy *Walder*, performed in Gotha seven months earlier. Julie's confidante Laura was sung by Benda's daughter

---

[47] Friedrich von Schlichtegroll, "Georg Benda: Herzogl. Sachsen-Gotahischer Kapelldirektor (30. Juni 1722–6. November 1795)", in: *Musiker-Nekrologe: Joh. Chr. Friedrich Bach, G. Benda, J. J. Ch. Bode, M. Gerbert, W. A. Mozart, F. Ch. Neubauer, E. W. Wolf, J. R. Zumsteeg*, neu herausgegeben von Richard Schaal (Kassel: Bärenreiter, o.J.), pp. 13-40 (29).

[48] Schubart, *Ideen einer Aesthetik der Tonkunst*, 120.

[49] Benda also mentions Ernst Dauer. See his article in *Dreihundert Briefe aus zwei Jahrhunderten*, ed. Karl von Holtei, Vol. 1, repr. edn (Bern: Herbert Lang, 1971), 31. See also Richard Hodermann, *Geschichte des Gothaischen Hoftheaters 1775-1779 nach den Quellen* (Hamburg & Leipzig: Voß, 1894), 4-8.

Justina in her debut role, and Romeo was sung by Johann Ernst Dauer (1746-1812), who later played the role of Pedrillo in the first performance of Mozart's *Die Entführung aus dem Serail* (1782) in Vienna.[50] The parts of Julie, Laura, and Romeo in particular are very rewarding, technically extremely challenging as a result of their virtuosity and extreme coloraturas. The work also requires all the soloists to be competent prose speakers.

The entire opera lasts for around 90-100 minutes and hence is considerably longer than most other musical comedies of the period. This meant that the then usual practice of staging a Singspiel both before and after the opera was called into question, and indeed was no longer feasible. Quite simply, Benda's opera fills up an entire evening. It is not just its length, however, but also the 'serious' nature of *Romeo und Julie* which would have made the performance of a serious Singspiel followed by a serious opera within a single evening programme unthinkable.

Benda's opera consists of an introductory overture with brief concertante sections for flute, oboe, and violin.[51] The opening instrumental movement flows over into an 'accompagnato' sung by Julie. This is followed by seventeen songs which are separated by relatively short dialogues, meaning that the songs follow quickly on from each other: in total there are eleven arias, four duets, a soloist ensemble, and the final song. To have the opera begin with music was fairly uncommon for Singspiels of the period, and this also underlines the deliberately serious character of the work. The opera's three acts are divided into eighteen entrances in total (three in the first act, seven in the second and eight in the third act). The setting of the first two acts is Julie's room; the third act is set in a grove in a cemetery and initially

---

[50] F. L. Schröder's appraisal of J. E. Dauer was not very enthusiastic: "He touched the heart in neither serious nor comic roles. His manner was a little cold and remote; his movement somewhat wooden." (Otto Michtner, *Das alte Burgtheater als Opernbühne: Von der Einführung des deutschen Singspiels (1778) bis zum Tod Kaiser Leopolds II (1792)* [Vienna: Böhlau, 1970], 369, 521.)

[51] On this see also Brückner's remarks on Gotter's Singspiel "Walder": "All the texts of Singspiels by Benda begin directly with music. This is different from the Singspiel music by other composers. This is all the more important to note since of course Benda introduces as few songs as possible, whilst the French trend suffers from an excess of highly unnecessary 'epigrams'. Nevertheless, we see here that a song was inserted before the original text by Benda. How can this be explained? Simply by the reason that the German Singspiel is more concerned with development, that is with the audience's compassion, than with the catastrophe and its more often than not obvious consequences. That this is by no means a result for example of aesthetic insight is irrelevant to the form of the Singspiel, and the guilt must lie with the poet." See Brückner, "Georg Benda und das deutsche Singspiel," 590.

shows Julie laid out in an open coffin. No fewer than five of the totals of eleven arias are allotted to Julie, whilst the other soloists each sing two. As well as this, Julie also takes part in three of the duets: two with Romeo and one with her confidante Laura. A further duet is sung by Capullet and Laura.[52] If we include the final song, Julie is part of more than half of the songs in the opera.

It is characteristic of Benda's opera that it follows a musical-dramaturgical concept, which shows or incorporates several features which would later be significant in the reform of opera. The fluid transition from the overture to the first scene as the curtain opens is as much a part of this as the attempt to use the music and drama to create longer scenes, in which arias are joined with 'accompagnati' to form interrelated dramatic episodes, although as a rule the arias are no longer 'da capo'. An example of this is the end of the second act, a significant solo scene for Julie which shows her taking the supposed poison with which she will feign her death. The solo scene begins with an extended 'accompagnato' which is interspersed with numerous 'arioso' sections. It opens with a string adagio in piano in G-major to which the flutes are soon added. The adagio then moves quickly into an Allegro assai moderato as the idea of taking the poison begins to take root in Julie's mind: "Welch ein Gedanke drängt sich ungestüm mir zu! – Ha, wär es Gift?" ("What kind of thought is pressing itself urgently towards me! Ha – would this be poison?"). At this point the flutes fall silent again. After a few bars the tempo once again moves into an adagio and the flutes re-join the strings. This fluid alternation between 'accompagnati' and aria sections is characteristic of the whole work and indicates Benda's attempt to compose directly alongside the text, as it were, and specifically with the means that seemed suitable to him: through shifts in tempo, momentum, and key and equally through the detailed use of instruments. The orchestra in *Romeo und Julie* has an important share in the dramatic events. Julia's expressive solo scene with her in parts dramatic and in others lyrical passages ends with the string-accompanied aria "Wo bist du, Romeo?", ("Where art thou, Romeo?"), at the end of which she drinks the poison: "Romeo! – Dies trink dir zu!" ("Romeo! – this I drink to thee!"). The second act concludes with a short instrumental finale without 'da capo'. The traditional three-part form of the aria is also abandoned elsewhere in the opera, as this form could not be reconciled with the dramatic action.

---

[52] This was the case in the first performance in Gotha. In later performances in Hamburg the scene was clearly altered and instead of Laura, a 'mourner' sang the duet with Capellet. An additional duet was added for Laura and a female soloist. See Thomas Bauman, *North German Opera in the Age of Goethe*, 126.

While the first and second acts consist mainly of solo passages as well as a duet in each, with the change of setting in the third act the musical character changes completely. As previously mentioned, the setting is the cemetery at Julie's grave and begins with laments by Julie's father and fellow mourners. This atmosphere is echoed in detail by the music in a longer interrelated scene which consists of choral and solo parts.[53] This is introduced by a funeral chorus in C-minor which begins with an instrumental overture played largo. In the first performance the chorus must have been sung by a soloist quartet behind the stage. It is probable that the curtain initially remained down and was only raised after a few bars in order to heighten the dramatic impression made by the entrance of mourners with Capulet at the centre. In musical terms, the soloist choir begins with a descending arrangement in unison, which in triad moves down an entire octave. This is followed by a contrapuntal section evocative of church music forms. The slow and solemn C-minor chorus is followed by an expressive duet by Julie's father and Laura, who attempts to console him in E-flat major in andante. As the mourners are leaving the stage, the C-minor soloist chorus sings once again and ends the scene. With his composition of this entire grave scene, Benda places himself in a tradition dating back to Gluck's *Orfeo ed Euridice* of 1762, the 'azione teatrale' (theatrical action) of which famously opens after the overture with a lamentation of the dead, also sung in C-minor by a chorus positioned symmetrically on the stage.

Let me now turn from the musical structure of Benda's work and conclude by touching briefly on a problem in the German Singspiel tradition which Benda recognised and to which he frequently referred in his writings, namely the way the prose always interrupts the atmosphere created by the music.[54] In an open letter, "Ueber das einfache Rezitativ" ("On the simple recitative"), published in 1783 in Cramer's *Magazin der Musik*[55], Benda thanks his librettist Gotter for having written the dialogue in prose and not in verse. However, it is clear from his own reasoning that he is not entirely convinced himself:

---

[53] Thomas Bauman has already referred to the later changes to or expansion of this scene in "Opera Versus Drama: Romeo and Juliet in Eighteenth-Century Germany," 199-200.

[54] On the nature of the recitative, see Friedrich-Heinrich Neumann, *Die Ästhetik des Rezitativs: Zur Theorie des Rezitativs im 17. und 18. Jahrhundert* (Strasbourg & Baden-Baden: Éditions P.H. Heitz, 1962), 9-16; and on Georg Benda (21-22).

[55] Georg Benda, "Ueber das einfache Recitativ," *Magazin der Musik*, Vol. 1, No. 2 (1783): 750-755. See also Thomas Bauman, "Benda, the Germans, and Simple Recitative," *American Musicological Society*, Vol. 34 (1981): 119-131.

> You are surprised, worthy friend, that I did not set the dialogue in *Romeo und Julie*, an entirely serious drama which has all the structures of an opera, into music. I confess to you sincerely that I am much indebted to the author that he did not put the dialogue in verse. In doing so he saved me from the risk of weakening the plot of this moving play through operatic language which is often stripped of its force by singing or natural declamation, and most of which is not understood.

And he goes on:

> I am very far from scrapping this simple recitative. In oratorios, cantatas and other pieces dedicated to music and singing, it has its place. Even in Singspiels it can have a positive impact in some places; it is only no good when it is meant to replace all of the dialogue and to represent the natural speech necessary for discussing a particular theme. Nevertheless, the dialogue converted into verse in an opera and the heroic nature of the subject seems to require musical accompaniment.[56]

Four years after the publication of this open letter, however, Benda entertained the idea of having the prose dialogues of *Romeo und Julie* translated into Italian and setting them to music as recitatives. Thus, he wrote in a letter to Gotter: "The easiest thing, which would however create a lot of work for me, would be to set the dialogue put into verse to music."[57] The project failed, as the already existent French version of the libretto, which was meant to serve as a basis for the translation into Italian by the court poet Verazi, could not be found.[58]

---

[56] See the copy of the open letter in Brückner, "Georg Benda und das deutsche Singspiel," 611-613.

[57] See the letter of 21 March 1787 to Gotter; reprinted in Brückner, "Georg Benda und das deutsche Singspiel," 617.

[58] Ibid., 617: "In Mannheim, I spent the two months, January and Feb., most happily thanks to the Wendling house, where I presented myself every day. Gustel Wendling hopes to spend next winter in England and is most keen to see Romeo und Julie translated into Italian, keeping my music. This is all too easily said but almost impossible to realise. The court poet here, Verazi, who does not understand German, is supposed to translate it. And because she now knows that I am in possession of the opera in French translation, she asks and asks that I engage you to go to Ohrdruf and to look for it amongst my papers and to send it here. I do not need to tell you of the difficulties which all this trouble and tortuous proceedings would cost and in vain. Even if Verazi wanted to take on the translation, I would have to be there constantly, and there would still remain the question of whether we would manage it." See also Benda's letter to Gotter from Mannheim, between April and June 1787

The fact that Benda only published his comments "On the simple recitative", which he possessed in an earlier version[59], in 1783, might also have something to do with the fact that in that same year, seven years after its premiere, he was invited by August Wilhelm Iffland to direct a performance of his opera *Romeo und Julie* at the Mannheim National Theatre himself and to organise "the music of *Romeo and Julie* according to the requirements of the Mannheim stage".[60]

For this purpose, Benda thoroughly revised the work he had written eight years previously. He reduced the plot to the most essential elements and cut all ornamental extras such as 'coloratura' and the embellishments in the arias. His reworking of the extended accompagnato-recitatives was particularly intensive so that the music would be at the forefront of this opera. Michael Dißmeier has compiled a list of the main changes which give the version of 1784 a "more rounded and sonorous sound as well as slight shifts in the periodic":

- For the overture, Benda composes a new quick middle section. This dynamic moment which reflects the drama of the action complements the loving depiction of nature of the original entrance. The two concertizing violins of the first version have been removed.
- The accompagnato-recitative before the first Julie-aria has been extensively recomposed. Benda succeeds in creating a clearer and more fluid dramatic dialogue between the singer and the orchestra. The declamation is more natural.
- Capellet's aria "Schwere Amt, ein Kind zu retten" [Difficult task, saving a child] (originally the second musical number in Act II) has been dropped.
- In the aria "Wo bist du Romeo" Benda does without the wind pedal tones from the bassoons and horns, the aria is now accompanied by violins only.
- The mourning song at the beginning of the third act is now in four parts, rather than five. (This music quickly became incredibly famous. It was performed for example at Lessing's memorial

---

(ibid., 619): "With a heavy heart she [Wendling] will abandon the idea of seeing Romeo translated into Italian. I would of course do something if this were possible."
[59] Written between late 1776 and early 1777. Published in von Holtei, *Dreihundert Briefe aus zwei Jahrhunderten*, 29-33.
[60] Letter from Iffland to Benda of 24 October 1783. Quoted in Michael Dißmeier, "Die Mannheimer Fassung (1784)", theatre programme for the performance in Potsdam on 16 November 1996 (Palace theatre in the Neues Palais [Hans Otto Theater]): 11-15 (13).

ceremony on 24.2.1781). In the instrumentation, a solo-oboe replaces flutes and bassoons. Benda leaves out the closing section and in the following duet with Capellet and the coffin bearer leads from the prelude directly into the song. In doing so he leaves behind rigid divisions between musical numbers and makes a step towards scenes blended seamlessly together.
- The duet between Laura and the coffin bearer (between the preceding duet and the reprise of the mourning song) is dropped.
- The accompagnato-recitative from Romeo's aria "Ihr trennet uns" [You are separating us] has been extensively recomposed. In the aria, the coloratura has been dropped in order to not clutter up the aria's simple and touching statement.
- The Julie-Romeo duet was originally followed by an adagio section which contained a prayer of thanks. This section has been dropped completely.[61]

After its first performance in Gotha in September 1776, *Romeo und Julie* was performed in the following years (1777 and 1778) by the Seyler Troupe in Dresden, Frankfurt, and Hamburg. There were further performances towards the end of the eighteenth century in various cities including Amsterdam, Bonn, Bremen, Graz, Kassel, Königsberg, Leipzig, Lübeck, Mannheim, Munich, Prague, and Riga; indeed, there are even records showing that a performance took place in Odensee. It was only at the beginning of the nineteenth century that the opera fell into obscurity, and it was not until 1931 that it was performed again at the Prague Conservatory.

The opera met with a very positive initial reception. There were critical voices mainly concerning Gotter's libretto, which no doubt can be explained by the language used, which "no longer served the ideas in their richness of tone and beauty" but rather was subordinate to the demands of the music. Another critic who found fault with the conventionality of the libretto wrote:

> If only the poet had not so irresponsibly reduced the material to a well-mannered quotidian opera! On the occasion of Alceste [by Christoph Martin Wieland], we talked a great deal about the usual gratifying conclusion of tragic operas: and here the subject is such that one really cannot understand how the father does not furiously stamp upon the little games that are being played with him. Even if the poet should want to change the ending, let it be as it is in Shakespeare and Weiße![62]

---

[61] Ibid., 14-15.
[62] Reichardt, quoted in Martin, "Deutsche Shakespeare-Opern um 1800," 7-8.

By contrast, Johann Joachim Eschenburg, who himself translated *Romeo and Juliet* into prose, voices few objections to the libretto, instead acknowledging its aesthetic features, which would be central to the further development of opera in the ninteenth century. In his review of the text edition in 1780 he summarised:

> We know the music which Benda composed, and which has been in print for some time, and the tone was certainly not unworthy of this masterful composition. For in most of the arias a gentle purity and captivating lightness dominate, alongside the noble choice of earthly expression, all of which Herr Gotter, more so than any similar poets, has made so eminently his own. The arrangement of the play itself much to recommend it, primarily the rapid unfolding of the plot, often all too rapid, but which was presumably necessitated by the musical treatment, which left little space for dialogues in between. How much more objectionable by contrast are the many scenes which drag on in plays which come under the name of tragedy in Germany? We do not have anything against the happy ending we find here; but perhaps the scenes of reconciliation added at the end were not essential to this conception. However, presumably the author was keen to gather all performers on the stage at the end in order to end the play with a chorus.[63]

4. Conclusion

It is typical of eighteenth-century musical culture that it needs to be seen in a European context and can accurately be regarded as a commercial enterprise. A dense network of contacts amongst artists, in which members of the Benda family were active and thus represent a characteristic feature of Czech music of the eighteenth century. Through their musical achievements they also contributed to the profiling of other (that is, non-Czech) cultural centres and schools. In their lifetime, the Bohemian composer was naturally a "global composer", or at the very least a European one. He did not have to define his identity according to nationality – he was a highly valued citizen of the world, a composer without borders, for whom surely the quotation from the Bohemian-Austrian poet Rainer Maria Rilke's poem "In dubiis" seems fitting:

> Der erscheint mir als der Größte, […]
> weil er vom Teil sich löste,
> nun der ganzen Welt gehört.[64]

---

[63] Eschenburg, "Singspiele von Friedrich Wilhelm Gotter," 162.
[64] "He seems to me the greatest, / […] because he detached himself from the part, / now belongs to the whole world." German quotation from: Rainer Maria Rilke, "In

Bibliography

Agthe, Kai. "Friedrich Wilhelm Gotter." *Palmbaum: Literarisches Journal aus Thüringen*, Vol. 5 (1997): 77-83.

Bauman, Thomas. "Benda, the Germans, and Simple Recitative." *American Musicological Society*, Vol. 34 (1981): 119-131.

Bauman, Thomas, ed. 1986. *German Opera 1770-1800 – A Collection of Facsimiles of Printed and Manuscript Full Scores*. New York & London: Garland Publishing.

Bauman, Thomas. 1986. *North German Opera in the Age of Goethe*. Cambridge: Cambridge University Press.

Bauman, Thomas. "Opera Versus Drama: *Romeo and Juliet* in Eighteenth-Century Germany." *Eighteenth-Century Studies*, Vol. 11, No. 2 (1977-78): 186-203.

Benda, Georg. *Romeo und Julie*. 1994 (Teatro Musicale, 3). 2 CDs. Neumünster: Canterino Musikproduktion.

Benda, Georg. *Romeo und Julie: Eine Oper in drey Aufzügen. Von Georg Benda*. Handwritten musical score of 1810 from the provenance of the Royal Theatre Library, Staatsbibliothek zu Berlin – Preußischer Kulturbesitz, Musikabteilung, Signatur *D-B/ Mus.ms. 1354/1*.

Brückner, Fritz. "Georg Benda und das deutsche Singspiel." *Sammelbände der Internationalen Musikgesellschaft*, Vol. 5, No. 4 (1904): 571-621.

Brüggemann, Fritz. 1966. Ed. *Die Aufnahme Shakespeares auf der Bühne der Aufklärung in den sechziger und siebziger Jahren*. Darmstadt: Wissenschaftliche Buchgesellschaft.

Buschmeier, Gabriele, "Jiří Antonín Benda und Christoph Willibald Gluck. Ihr Beitrag für das europäische Musiktheater." In *Symposiumsbericht: Gluck und Prag, Nürnberg, 20-22. Juli 2012*, edited by Thomas Betzwieser and Daniel Brandenburg. Kassel: Bärenreiter, 2016, 201-216.

Church, Michael, "Superb": Review of Benda's *Romeo and Juliet*. *The Independent*, September 20, 2007. Accessed March 6, 2021. Available at https://www.bamptonopera.org/operadetail.htm?event=56.

Dean, Winston. "Shakespeare in the Opera House." *Shakespeare Survey*, Vol. 18 (1965): 75-93.

Deetjen, Werner. "Der Sturm als Operntext bearbeitet von Einsiedel und Gotter." *Shakespeare Jahrbuch*, Vol. 64 (1928): 77-89.

Dubiis." In: *Sämtliche Werke*, edited by the Rilke-Archiv in Verbindung mit Ruth Sieber-Rilke, besorgt durch Ernst Zinn. Frankfurt am Main: Insel-Verlag, 1955, Vol. 1, 42-43 (43).

Dißmeier, Michael. "Die Mannheimer Fassung (1784)", theatre programme for the performance in Potsdam on 16 November 1996 (Palace theatre in the Neues Palais [Hans Otto Theater]): 11-15.
Dunnett, Roderic. "Brilliantly engaging": Review of Benda's *Romeo and Juliet*. *Music & Vision*, September 2, 2007. Accessed April 7, 2021. Available at https://www.bamptonopera.org/operadetail.htm?event=56.
Eschenburg, Johann Joachim. "Singspiele von Friedrich Wilhelm Gotter. Erstes Bändchen. Leipzig, bey Duk. 1779." *Allgemeine Deutsche Bibliothek*, Vol. 39 (1780): 162-163.
Goethe, Johann Wolfgang. 1976. *Dichtung und Wahrheit: Zwölftes Buch*. Berlin: Aufbau-Verlag.
Gooch, Bryan N. S., and Thatcher, David. 1991. *A Shakespeare Music Catalogue*. 5 vols. Oxford: Oxford University Press.
Gotter, Friedrich Wilhelm. 1779. *Romeo und Julie. Ein Schauspiel mit Gesang in drey Aufzügen*. Leipzig: Dykische Buchhandlung.
Guthke, Karl S. 1994. *Das deutsche bürgerliche Trauerspiel*. 5th edn. Stuttgart: J. B. Metzler.
Häublein, Renata. 2005. *Die Entdeckung Shakespeares auf der deutschen Bühne des 18. Jahrhunderts. Adaptation und Wirkung der Vermittlung auf dem Theater*. Tübingen: Max Niemeyer.
Hodermann, Richard. 1894. *Geschichte des Gothaischen Hoftheaters 1775-1779 nach den Quellen*. Hamburg & Leipzig: Voß.
Holtei, Karl von, ed. *Dreihundert Briefe aus zwei Jahrhunderten*. Vol. 1. Repr. edn. Bern: Herbert Lang, 1971.
Huesmann, Heinrich. 1968. *Shakespeare-Inszenierungen unter Goethe in Weimar*. Graz: Hermann Böhlaus Nachfolger.
Hüttemann, Walter. 1912. *Christian Felix Weiße und seine Zeit in ihrem Verhalten zu Shakespeare*. Duisburg: Buschmann.
Kahlcke, Thomas. "Georg Benda, *Romeo und Julie*" (Teatro Musicale, 3). 2 CDs (Neumünster: Canterino Musikproduktion, 1994), 1-6.
Kaven, Bernd et al., ed. *Johann Gottfried Schwanenberger. 1737-1804: Ein Wolfenbütteler Komponist*. Wolfenbüttel: Herzog-August-Bibliothek, 1988.
Kehrmann, Boris. "Väter und Söhne." *Opernwelt*, No. 7 (2014), 26-27.
Klavierauszug | von | Romeo und Julie, | einer Oper in drey Akten. | In Musik gesetzt | von | Herrn Kapelldirektor Benda. | [etching] | Zweite Auflage. | Leipzig, | im Verlage der Dykischen Buchhandlung. | 1784. | [at the end:] *Leipzig, gedruckt bey Johann Gottlob Immanuel Breitkopf.* Hans-Sommer-Archiv, Berlin, Berlin; Signatur: D-Bsommer / Mus.pr. Benda G.A. 2.

Koch, Klaus-Peter. "Böhmische Musiker waren in Sachsen des 18. Jahrhunderts nicht nur in Dresden, Anmerkungen zur böhmischen Musiker-Migration." n. p. (unpublished paper).
Koegler, Horst. "Julchen sollte sie heißen." *Opernwelt*, No. 1 (1996), 43.
Köhler, Christoph. "Friedrich Wilhelm Gotter (1746-1797) zum 200. Todestag." *Gothaer Museumsheft* (1997), 39-50.
Martin, Dieter. "Deutsche Shakespeare-Opern um 1800." Goethezeit Portal. Accessed April 7, 2021. http://www.goethezeitportal.de/db/wiss/epoche/martin_shakespeare_opern.pdf, 1-13.
Martin, Dieter. 2005. "Shakespeare et l'opéra autour de 1800". In *Le monde germanique et l'opéra. Le livret en question*, edited by Bernard Banoun und Jean-François Candoni. Paris: Klincksieck. 297-316.
Martinsen, Wolf E. "Georg Benda: Romeo und Julie: Nach 200 Jahren aufgeweckt." *Opernwelt*, No. 12 (1993), 46.
Michtner, Otto. 1970. *Das alte Burgtheater als Opernbühne: Von der Einführung des deutschen Singspiels (1778) bis zum Tod Kaiser Leopolds II (1792)*. Vienna: Böhlau, 1970.
Mösch, Stephan. "Benda: Romeo und Julie: Bürste statt Pinsel." *Opernwelt*, No. 2 (1997), n. p.
Mösch, Stephan. Romeo und Julia auf dem Lande." *Opernwelt*, No. 9/10 (2010), 29-31.
Neumann, Friedrich Heinrich. 1962. *Die Ästhetik des Rezitativs: Zur Theorie des Rezitativs im 17. und 18. Jahrhundert*. Strasbourg & Baden-Baden: Éditions P.H. Heitz.
Plachta, Bodo. 2003. *"Ein Tyrann der Schaubühne?": Stationen und Positionen einer literatur- und kulturkritischen Debatte über Oper und Operntext im 18. Jahrhundert*. Berlin: Weidler Buchverlag.
Riethmüller, Albrecht. 2006. "'She Speaks, Yet She Says Nothing: What of That?' *Romeo and Juliet* in Hector Berlioz's and Leonard Bernstein's Adaptations." In *German Shakespeare Studies at the Turn of the Twenty-First Century*, edited by Christa Jansohn. Newark: University of Delaware Press, 128-143.
Rushton, Julian. 1994. *Berlioz: Roméo et Juliette*. Cambridge: Cambridge University Press.
Sauer, Artur. 1915. *Shakespeares "Romeo und Julia" in den Bearbeitungen und Uebersetzungen der deutschen Literatur*. Greifswald: Julius Abel.
Schlichtegroll, Friedrich von, "Georg Benda: Herzogl. Sachsen-Gotahischer Kapelldirektor (30. Juni 1722–6. November 1795)", in: *Musiker-Nekrologe: Joh. Chr. Friedrich Bach, G. Benda, J. J. Ch. Bode, M. Gerbert, W. A. Mozart, F. Ch. Neubauer, E. W. Wolf, J. R. Zumsteeg,*

neu herausgegeben von Richard Schaal (Kassel: Bärenreiter, o.J.), pp. 13-40.

Schlösser, Rudolf. 1894. *Friedrich Wilhelm Gotter: Sein Leben und seine Werke. Ein Beitrag zur Geschichte der Bühne und Bühnendichtung im 18. Jahrhundert.* Hamburg & Leipzig: Leopold Voß.

Schottländer, Johann-Wolfgang. 1931. ed. *Carl Friedrich Zelters Darstellungen seines Lebens.* Weimar: Verlag der Goethe-Gesellschaft.

Schubart, Christian Friedrich Daniel. 1839. *Ideen einer Aesthetik der Tonkunst.* In Schubart, *Gesammelte Schriften und Schicksale*, Vol. 5. Stuttgart: J. Scheible's Buchhandlung.

Sonneck, Oscar George Theodor. 1914. *Catalogue of Opera Librettos Printed Before 1800.* 3 vols. Washington, DC: Govt. Print Office.

Vičar, Jan. 2001. "Echoes of Czech Music in America." *Acta Universitatis Palackianae Olomucensis, Facultas Philosophica. Philosophica – Aesthetica*, Vol. 24, 193-97.

Vočadlo, Otakar 1956. "Shakespeare and Bohemia." *Shakespeare Survey*, Vol. 9, 101-110.

Wagner, Heinrich Leopold. 1777. *Briefe, die Seylerische Schauspilergesellschaft und Ihre Vorstellungen zu Frankfurt am Mayn betreffend.* Frankfurt am Mayn: Eichenbergische Erben.

Weisse, Christian Felix. 1778. *Trauerspiele*, Vol. 1. Karlsruhe: Christian Schmieder.

Williams, Simon. 1990. *Shakespeare on the German Stage*, Vol. 1: 1586-1914. Cambridge: Cambridge University Press.

Wilson, Christopher R. 1992. "Shakespeare". In *The New Grove Dictionary of Opera*, 4 vols, edited by Stanley Sadie. London: Macmillan, 338-347.

SCHUBERT'S *WINTER JOURNEY* IN "SPACE-TIME": THE POWER OF SOLITUDE

CHARLOTTE STOPPELENBURG

Fig. 18: Portrait of Franz Schubert (source: unknown)

As a listener and musician, how do you comprehend Schubert's *Winterreise* (1827; *Winter Journey*)? The song cycle, composed by Franz Schubert (1797-1828) on texts by the poet Wilhelm Müller (1794-1827), is about a male character who takes an inner, wintery journey of solitude in 24 songs, embracing bitter reality more than false appearance. The main character is isolated from society, love and human contact, the worst that can happen to a human, a social being. The work has the same status in the song repertoire as Bach's *St. Matthew Passion* in the realm of oratorio. Millions of listeners can interpret *Winterreise* in countless ways: as a farewell to childhood dreams in order to consolidate them into adult life, or perhaps as a description of a phase of life and its issues that relate to *Winterreise*. (See ref. in Ceramella's Essay, li).

Some time ago, I was asked to perform *Winterreise* in a translation singable in English. As a professional mezzo-soprano singing in English, my rendition would differ greatly from the traditional performance practice for *Winterreise* – a baritone or tenor voice singing in German. A performer considering the relationship of text and music must first contemplate the marriage of Müller's poems and Schubert's compositions. Schubert's setting of Müller's poems not only gave them musical voice, but an audience and acclaim far beyond what the poems might have received on their own. During my master's degree in German Studies at the University of Amsterdam, my own contemplation of the unity of language and music intensified when I came across the "spacetime" theory (chronotopos) by the Russian language philosopher Michael Bachtin (1895-1975). Bachtin's theory states that space and time are indivisible and that each (literary) world view has its own chronotopos (Bachtin, 2008). An analysis of a story in chronotopoi asks about *where* and *when* and their symbolic relationship. What environment is chosen and how is it embedded in the story? How does the narration deal with space – through travel, circular motion or stillness? How do the characters of the characters relate in space? How do the sequences of events, the observations of the characters and their movements in space relate to each other? A knightly novel, for example, has a completely different chronotopos than an autobiography. Vocal pieces of music are partly literary. The literary part can therefore be analyzed in chronotopoi, but a vocal work also represents a unity of text and music that, as the whole, leaves an impression on the audience. *Winterreise* has more layers than the eye meets. The possibilities for analysis in the light of chronotopoi are numerous and can help to better understand these sometimes very subjective, elusive experiences from music practice. It should be noted that music is ultimately an abstract 'art of time,' as the composer Arnold Schönberg (1874-1951) stated (Stukenschmidt 1974: 286), and that the literary part has the advantage that it uses language in an artistic form. In short, can Bachtin's spacetime shed new light on *Die Winterreise*, this epitome of art song?

The "space-time" of Franz Schubert and Wilhelm Müller: The cultural climate after Napoleon and the Restoration

While the Viennese composer Franz Schubert and Berlin-based poet Wilhelm Müller lived in virtually the same "spacetime" of the early 19th century, the two artists never met. Müller's poetry bridged the spatial distance to create a spiritual encounter between them during their brief lifetime. Both artists lived at the time of the *Deutsche Bund*, which was founded in 1815. In that period, the sentimental conservatism of the *Biedermeier* era dominated until the revolution broke out in 1848. Censorship was exercised as a result of anti-terror laws, including in Schubert's native country, Austria, where about 2,000 intellectual agents were tasked with enforcing cultural laws (Hufschmidt, 1993, 50). Operas and political romances and poetry were constantly examined, as was Wilhelm Müller's overtly political *Lieder der Griechen* (1821).

However, *Winterreise* was in no danger of censorship due to its introverted nature. It may be that the texts are deliberately rendered in an encrypted, perhaps even autobiographical language, for example when an artist 'could not become a man on the way to adulthood' (Vollmann, 1975, 184). Other commentators emphatically distance themselves from the purely autobiographical vein in *Winterreise* and point to a secret interpretation of general (political) discontent in that early Romanticism. Other disparate visions of *Winterreise* have been seen over the ages: total disintegration (Mustard, 1946, 87-89); complete separation from society (Baumann, 1981, 67); the elimination of the 'lyrical self' (Stoffels 1987, 143); and a contemplated abandonment of the inner world of experience (Stoffels, 1987, 143). These are just some examples from the extensive critical reception of this work. All these visions do not seem far removed from the idea of chronotopos, or spacetime, in that inner winter journey. Such a journey may also reflect the influence of Müller's Freemasonry and its corresponding development of the self, as we see in Mozart's *Die Zauberflöte* (1791, *The Magic Flute*).

During the *Biedermeier* period, the political German poet Heinrich Heine (1797-1856) proved to be a dominant factor with his *Buch der Lieder* (1827). Wilhelm Müller was important to Heine for being a great example as a political critic. At least in the French capital, the Jewish cosmopolitan who had fled to Paris could safely criticize his own countrymen and contemporaries, such as his literary colleagues 'of the still water': Ludwig Uhland (1787-1862), Gustav Schwab (1792-1850) and Justinus Kerner (1786-1862).

Heine was fond of the folk song-like tone, rapid variation in lyricism and natural German style of Müller, who remained faithful to town (Dessau) and country his entire brief life. Müller was weakened by whooping cough and heart failure and died at age 32 in 1827. Schubert died one year later from complications relating to syphilis at the age of 31. Both creators of *Winterreise* were already old at an early age.

Fig. 19: *Wilhelm Müller* by Johann Friedrich Schröter (1770-1836). Engraving ca. 1830.

Wilhelm Müller (1794-1827)

Wilhelm Müller was born in 1794 in Dessau, a city in the eastern German state of Saxony-Anhalt. The son of a tailor, he ultimately died in Dessau as well. He studied in Berlin and became involved in the literary world of Brentano, De la Motte Fouqué, Berger, Von Arnim and others. An unrequited love for the charming and spiritual Luise Hensel was the inspiration for *Die schöne Müllerin* (1816). Encouraged by Carl Ludwig Berger (1777-1839), a musician who Müller described as a "like-minded soul-mate" (Müller, 1903, 5), the poems were finally published in 1820 in his hometown of Dessau. Schubert composed his song cycle of the same name in 1823. However, his best-known collection of poems became the *Sieben und siebzig Gedichte aus den hinterlassenen Papieren eines reisenden Waldhornisten* (1821). It opens with *Die schöne Müllerin* and *Winterreise*, written in the first years of his marriage (1822-23) for Adelheid Basedow (1800-1883). Müller was also called the "Greeks-Müller" because of his identification with Lord Byron in his fight against the Turks. Müller's own military experience came as a soldier in the Prussian army against Napoleon. In Italy, he was briefly a member of an artists' colony that included Friedrich Rückert. In his 'wanderlust' ('strong longing to travel') he later met Goethe, Uhland, Tieck, Von Schlegel, Schwab, Kerner, well-known names in German artistic circles. The popularity of Müller's poems among musicians may have resulted from the song-like structures found in his *Reiselieder, Tafellieder* and *Griechenlieder.* Müller was acquainted with musicians such as Felix Mendelssohn (1809-1847), Carl Maria Von Weber (1786-1826), and Carl Friedrich Zelter (1758-1832). Zelter was a Berlin-based composer and conductor who also served as musical counselor to Johann Goethe (1749-1832). Müller wrote "I can't play or sing, but I still sing, and I also play. But, comforted, maybe there is a like-minded soul who takes tunes from the words and gives them back to me." (Müller, 1903, 5). These words turned out to be prophetic when Schubert used Müller's texts for *Schöne Müllerin* and *Winterreise*, among others.

Franz Schubert (1797-1828)

Fig. 20: *A Schubertiade at Ritter von Spaun's* (Schubert and the singer Johann Michael Vogl at the piano). Oil sketch, 1868 by Moritz von Schwindt.

Would the musicians of Müller and Schubert's time have understood Schubert's through-composed, early romantic songs? In any case, when Schubert's friend Joseph von Spaun sent several of Schubert's settings of Goethe to the great poet himself, no response forthcame. It can be said of Franz Schubert that he was considerably underestimated by his contemporaries. Schubert became a choirboy at the Imperial Court Chapel in 1808 and received instruction from Antonio Salieri (1750-1825) at the

Royal College. The Italian-born Salieri had been an important figure in Vienna's musical life since his days as an operatic rival of Mozart.

Schubert's large oeuvre is in inverse proportion to his short life. He left behind a great deal of chamber music, operas, nine symphonies, masses and more than 600 songs. Reluctant to follow in his father's profession as a teacher, Schubert relied heavily on the support of his friends. Schubert's social circle enjoyed the gifts of the young composer in many an evening gathering that came to be known as Schubertiads (see above Fig. 19). The Sonnenleither family and poets such as Johann Mayerhofer (1787-1836) and Franz von Schober (1796-1882) provided Schubert with texts that ultimately appeared in songs at their many salons. The high baritone Johann Michael Vogl (1768-1840), in the years after his career as an opera singer at court, was the first important champion of Schubert's music and introduced the composer's songs to the aristocracy and public. Another friend was Moritz von Schwind (1804-1871) who made illustrations for Schubert songs, such as for *Erlkönig*, *An Schwager Kronos* and *Der Schatzgräber*.

Brief history of the *Winterreise* and its text / music ratio

Winterreise as a collection of poems was created in two parts, a form replicated in Schubert's cycle. Twelve poems were first published in the magazine *Urania* in 1822. Schubert adopted these texts, assuming that the cycle was complete (Stoffels, 1987, 103). However, in 1823 Müller produced ten more poems noting that they belonged to the previously published poetry series *Winterreise*. Schubert was probably not aware of this intermediate publication (Stoffels, 1987, 174). In 1824 the entire cycle of poems in the second volume of *Sieben und siebzig Gedichte aus den hinterlassenen Papieren eines reisenden Waldhornisten* was published and expanded with two more poems. Schubert worked on the cycle until 1827, the year before his death. He incorporated a few of the poems from Müller's second publication but modified the order to suit his own purposes. In the autumn of 1827, at the home of his friend Schober, Schubert performed "these terrible songs" (Deutsch, 1957, 160), with the composer both singing and playing the piano. Schubert was 'melancholic' and 'appalled' in the process of creating *Winterreise* (Ibid., 160). Perhaps the first listeners would have shared Schubert's feelings, noting his departures from the traditional "art song" genre. After all, didn't simple poems just call for a simple verse song, the form that dominated the entire 19th century? A special sound – in several respects – comes from the famous baritone Dietrich Fischer-Dieskau (1925-2012), who met the need for introspection in the German-speaking territory by dusting off Schubert's art songs. Of particular interest were Fischer-Dieskau's performances of *Winterreise* during the *Trümmerzeit* and *Wiederaufbau* after the Second World War, a time not unlike the period following Napoleon. Fischer-Dieskau and his distinguished accompanists, brought a highly level of attention and acclaim not only to *Winterreise*, but to German art song in general.

Winterreise's poems have withstood the test of time thanks to Schubert's music, with further support from the performances and reflections of Fischer-Dieskau, who in 1971 published his book *Auf den Spuren der Schubert-Lieder: Werden-Wesen-Wirkung*. Müller's poems are sometimes treated negatively in critical commentary. For example, one writer speaks of an "appallingly childlike naiveté" of Müller's texts (Vollmann, 1975, 183). In general, Müller's poems have a reflective character and song-like lyrics that lend themselves readily to musical setting. Conversely, texts conveying complex thought constructions are more difficult to set to music. Fischer-Dieskau notes this as well when in discussing the history of *Winterreise,* he says 'at that time the music was still able to take care of the pale (Biedermeier) thoughts unimpeded' (Fischer-Dieskau, 1971, 46). He believed that one cannot be a *Schubertianer* if one completely rejects Müller at the same time. (ivi, 197).

As mentioned in the introduction, the question of the relationship between text and music is intriguing. The difference in quality between the two art forms, which belong to different disciplines, is part of this. Schubert often used poems from friends or artists that he just happened to meet. This is also the approach of Fischer-Dieskau when he states that Schubert was not concerned with the determination of value between the two arts (ibid.), but only with the usefulness for himself and his special musicality in anticipation of what the poets found. Furthermore, Fischer-Dieskau rightly says: 'We just have to ask ourselves what Bach with his cantatas or Beethoven with *Leonore* and also Schubert with *Die Winterreise* offered to us.' (ibid.).

Schubert's own dramaturgy

Even if Schubert's friend Joseph von Spaun had succeeded in getting Goethe to look at Schubert's songs, the great poet would surely not have been accustomed to such nuance and elaborate interaction between text and music. *Neun Wanderlieder von Uhland* (1818) by Conradin Kreutzer (1780-1849) was more well-known during this time than *Winterreise* - Schubert once said he wished he had composed the work himself (Deutsch, 1957, 21, 115), though *Winterreise* is clearly of higher quality.

In noting the different poem orders followed by Müller and Schubert, musicologists Hans Joachim Moser and Günther Baum have compared the two series and found a difference in character. In short, Müller's evokes a sentimental mood while Schubert creates intense drama (Fischer-Dieskau 1971: 294). Thus, the song *Die Post* ended up at the beginning of the second part, as a reminder of better times. Schubert also repositioned songs from Müller's initial twelve poems to the back, such as *Frühlingstraum*, creating an extended reminder of unrequited love. The Schubert sequence leads more to a sense of alienation at the end. Schubert chose to precede *Der Leiermann* with the static wintery atmosphere of *Nebensonnen,* whereas Müller had the courageous *Muth!* before *Der Leiermann.* Schubert followed Müller's original sequence for the first five songs up to and including the famous *Der Lindenbaum*. Set in E-major, *Der Lindenbaum* is notably lighter in contrast to the rest of the cycle. Schubert clearly made his own "terrible" story, so that it could astonish the world.

Chronotopoi of the *Winterreise*

The time elements

Dietrich Fisher-Dieskau characterizes *Winterreise* as a wintery journey by a person disappointed in love and ideals (Fischer-Dieskau, 1971, 201). The protagonist distances himself literally and figuratively from society and wanders ultimately to absolute loneliness. The time elements that are so important to Romanticism are death (or the desire to die) and the "*wandern,*" the wandering, eternal search. Nature is hereby the outer mirror of the inner self, a concept that extends from the German Romantic philosopher Johann Gottlieb Fichte (1762-1814) to our time.

The tenses used by the main figure are the ordinary verb of past, present and future. But in the poems, they do have their own meanings. Where the past often turns out to be the idealized world, the present is the harsh reality of winter, and the future contemplates death or worse, absolute isolation. The day and the night are also symbolic, where the day represents facing reality, in short, disillusionment. Night is dream time, as also shared by the romantic German poet Novalis (Georg Philipp Friedrich Freiherr von Hardenberg, 1772-1801) in his *Hymnen an die Nacht* (1800). In *Winterreise*, however, dreams are rather deceptive and are always overtaken by the day, the reality. The seasons are also symbolic: Winter, the harsh, depressive reality, versus Spring, symbolic for everything that is optimistic such as love, fertility, light (or enlightenment), hope, idealism and warmth.

The places (or *"space"*)

The location of the people (the city, the village) is paradoxical. At first, locations represent disappointment in love, but also beautiful aspirations. The protagonist closes the door behind him after his departure in *Gute Nacht*. He sets off on the "cheerful paths" (*Wasserflut*) that are roads connecting towns and cities, making him feel rejected. In the village, the main character finds a community asleep (*Im Dorfe*), which can only realize its wishes while dreaming at night. Perhaps this reflects Müller's own critique of society? Even the graveyard (*Das Wirtshaus*) is an inn where all the rooms are already occupied. The locations are also linked to characters, such as the unreliable girl, in which the main character is so disappointed. Or the girl's mother, who represents social affirmation (*Gute Nacht*).

There are also portrayals of the protagonist himself: As a pseudo-old man (*Der Greise Kopf*), a dreamer (*Frühlingstraum*), and a fool (*Muth!*). At last, a real person appears, the famous *Leiermann* (*Der Leiermann*). One can wonder if the main character recognizes himself in *Der Leiermann*. *Winterreise* ends with the protagonist asking the Leiermann "Curious old fellow, Shall I go along? Will you grind your organ, only to my song?" (Singable translation: Jeffrey Benton).

Animals are part of the landscape in *Winterreise*. Crows (graveyard birds), ravens, roosters and dogs (guards of people) belong to the human environment, while larks and nightingales belong to the wished-for world of Spring (*Frühlingstraum*). The *Winterreise* chronotopos also includes the typical winter light effect of the 'mock suns' (*Nebensonnen*), the interpretation of which has still to be discussed. Does it symbolize the demise of memory (Stoffels, 1997, 115)? Or does it go deeper? Is the changing worldview upon, or do the three suns represent the Christian trinity: faith, hope and love (Hufschmidt, 1993, 115), in which the main character wishes that the last sun, hope, also sets? Without hope, there is no more pain and disappointment. The ground beneath the feet and the water of the brook are inaccessible to the protagonist and frozen, buried under snow and ice. He is even afraid that his heart will be frozen by the disappointment of Winter (*Erstarrung, Auf dem Flusse*). From top to bottom, inside and out, the main figure is locked in Winter, with limbs and hair frozen and inundated by snow. Does God belong to an outer spacetime? Or has the conception of God, as experienced in Schubert's times, partly as a result of the Enlightenment, already turned from the outside to the inside? In an attempt to rescue himself, the main character encourages himself in "*Muth!*: *Will kein Gott auf Erden sein, sind wir selber Götter!* If there are no Gods on Earth, Gods we will be together!" (Singable translation Jeffrey Benton).

The main character in *Winterreise* has a strong inner space, which projects the introspective outward. The interplay of dark and light are also important. The Enlightenment gave elucidation, certainly, but Romanticism often sought out the darkness of introspection. Darkness references reality in *Winterreise*, while the light is a wandering light, an illusion (*Irrlicht*). It is striking that dreams in the first part of *Winterreise* increasingly make way for the harsh reality of the second part. While the main character in the first part still had one leg in the illusion, in the second part, he sinks deeper and deeper into the winter abyss.

Musical chronotopoi

Musical space

A more artificial leap is the naming of space and time in music, especially if the theory comes from a philosopher of language. Yet you can speak of important "spaces" in music, but these can only be discussed on the basis of concepts from other disciplines, so for example with the help of language to describe it or with the help of a script to describe the music. The most important in the case of *Winterreise* (but probably with all music) is the harmonic space: The keys and the relationships between them. The space of melody, the mood and emotional value that the harmony can express is a world in itself. These values change over time. In Western culture, during the Classical Enlightenment (18th century), various ancient church modes were "secularized" to the two main types of major and minor, defined by the tertian interval (the third, the major, and the minor) in the middle of the triad. The characterization of modes and keys was described by Christian Schubart (1739-1791) in his *Aesthetics* (Schubart 1806) and is representative of 'classical music.' Schubert was aware of these concepts and wrote several songs based on Schubart's literary texts, such as *Die Forelle*.

Schubert's choice of keys reflected his awareness of Schubart's theories and Schubert's own fairly high tenor voice. Johann Michael Vogl, the first "Schubert singer" who had already sung *Die schöne Müllerin*, had more or less the same voice type: a high baritone.

The choice of keys for the various songs was thus related to Schubert himself and the moods that the poems evoked in him. However, the songs are often performed in other transpositions, including a widely adopted lower version utilized by Dietrich Fischer-Dieskau and pianist Gerald Moore (1899-1987) recorded just after the Second World War. The remarkable thing is that the character of the original keys is more or less preserved in the lower version, perhaps because the intervals between the notes are the same. This is also true of other higher versions for female voices, such as by Brigitte Fassbaender (b. 1939), Christa Ludwig (b. 1928), and Nathalie Stutzmann (b. 1965). In considering performance space, Schubert's songs were originally performed in the intimate setting of a salon.

Musical time

Musical time can be understood to mean time signature, tempo indication, nature of the musical flow, agogic accents and rhythm. Musical time relates to the songs themselves, though the duration of the song cycle also plays a role. Let us now examine how rhythm and harmony are linked as an unbreakable chronotopoi and together form the entire chronotopos of *Winterreise* as a song cycle.

Analysis of the songs in their musical and textual chronotopoi

The tempo of walking is often found in *Winterreise,* not as a cheerful excursion but more reminiscent of meandering (Feil 1975: 101) which corresponds to Müller's tone of disappointment. The tempo indications reflect the mood of introspection: 'Mäßig' (moderate) found in *Gute Nacht, Lindenbaum, Rast,* and *Der Wegweiser,* and slower indications such as 'Langsam', 'etwas Langsam', 'nicht zu langsam' or 'sehr Langsam' found in *Gefrorne Tränen, Wasserflu*t, *Auf dem Flusse, Irrlich*t, *Einsamkeit, Der Greise Kopf, Die Krähe, Im Dorfe, Das Wirtshaus,* and *Der Leiermann.* Occasionally the tempo indications are faster, though not to an extreme: "Ziemlich geschwind" ("moderately quick"), "ziemlich schnell" ("moderately fast"), "Nicht zu geschwind" ("not too quick"), "etwas bewegt" ("rather agitated"), "etwas geschwind" ("rather quick") found in *Die Wetterfahne, Erstarrung, Rückblick, Frühlingstraum, Die Post, Letzte Hoffnung, Der stürmische Morgen,* and *Täuschung.* It is striking that, in most cases, these faster songs represent the illusions of the world. Embedded in the walking movements are representations of stumbling (*Gute Nacht*), inward sobbing (*Erstarrung*), raindrops (*Gefrorne Tränen*), and stinging pain (*Rückblick*). These effects are achieved by accenting the weak beats in the piano part. Conversely, accents in the vocal line, for example in *Gute Nacht,* express the ironic, light-hearted farewell to the beloved, while the piano part reveals the suffering behind the irony. The piano part seems to tell its own story, creating a double layer.

The movements in triple time represent unreliability (*Wetterfahne*), desire (*Erstarrung*), illusionary Spring (*Der Lindenbaum, Frühlingstraum*), warm sadness (*Wasserflut*), memory, whether or not of better days (*Auf dem Flusse, Rückblick, Frühlingstraum, Einsamkeit*), illusionary light (*Irrlicht*), desire (*Die Post*), deception (*Der Greise Kopf, Täuschung*), the false companion of the crow (*Die Krähe*), last hope (*Letzte Hoffnung, Die Nebensonnen*) and false dreamers (*Im Dorfe*). Trills and arpeggios suggest the trembling of the main character, or are used as a recitative accompaniment (*Der Greise Kopf*) to make the wind blow unexpectedly (*Die Wetterfahne*). They are also used to finish a song, or to serve as a transition to the next song (*Auf dem Flusse, Frühlingstraum*).

With the song cycle, tension is derived from the contrasting aspects of inner stillness (frozen heart and world) and inner movement (desire, illusion).

Beginning with the opening song, minor keys are predominant in *Winterreise*. Minor represents the sad, hopeless present while major looks back on better times. (Dittrich 1991: 115). However, the major keys have a double meaning. They are not only memories, but represent self-deception, idealizations, desires of the protagonist and the deceiving world. They convey a longing that cannot be fulfilled. In *Gute Nacht*, for example, the fourth verse goes to major at the farewell to the beloved. Ingeborg Gürschig-Pfingsten has written "For the worst pain that can no longer be expressed in words, a minor is created outside the minor, a super minor, which is also outside the usual meaning of the tonal genders and sounds like a major" (Gürschig-Pfingsten. Musica 1984, 22).

Given Schubert's familiarity with Schubart's theories, I tried to connect the songs with the following character descriptions. The terms "masculinity" and "femininity" would no longer be chosen today and should be understood here as "decisiveness" versus "passivity."

1. The first song *Gute Nacht* is in D-minor, an objective, serious key, but feels gloomy and foggy as well. It takes some time to fully absorb the nuance of the four verses. Gerald Moore, Fischer-Dieskau's accompanist stated that "the cycle must be set up generously and not consist of a series of miniatures" (Moore, 1978, 106). Almost all the songs have a minor character, in accordance with the character of the poems. The minor tuning is regularly alternated with a major one but conceived as "super minor."

2. In the second song, *Die Wetterfahne*, the weathervane spins violently in all directions, a symbol for the unreliable girl. The song is in A-minor, the key of femininity and passivity. Trills, rising and falling motifs and arpeggios in the accompaniment suggest wind gusts in rapid 6/8 time while vocal line reproaches the behavior of the girl.

3. The third song, *Gefrorne Tränen* is in F-minor which has a character that is milder and sad, regretful and pitiful. The walking motif returns but not in an even rhythm as in the first song as it is now interwoven with a dripping tear motif. At the end, there is a sudden burst of emotion.

4. The fourth song, *Erstarrung* is in C-minor, a key of tragic passion, love, and longing. Continuous triplets suggest the growing snowdrift. It is one of the most exciting songs because it simultaneously evokes both warm memories and disappointment. The highest note of the entire cycle is in the phrase *'mit meinen heißen Tränen.'*

5. *Der Lindenbaum* ('Tree of the Germans'), a kind of folk song, moves us to E-major on the other side of the circle of fifths. With its four sharps, E-major is a delightful key for lyricism, laughter and love. In this song, one of the few in a major key, Schubert conjures up playful tone garlands that contrast with a passage of cold wind in E-minor. From its premiere onward, *Der Lindenbaum* has been recognized as a pinnacle of Romantic art song.

6. *Wasserfluth* is a kind of funeral march with a dotted ostinato: Teardrops fall in the melting snow. Occasionally we hear emotional accents with strong dynamics in E-minor, a reference to the previous song.

7. *Auf dem Flusse* is in the same complaining key of E-minor. The stream along which the main character runs is covered with ice, while underneath the water flows furiously. The brook is an emblem for the wounded heart.

8. *Rückblick,* one of the most hectic songs, is in the key of G-minor, that of anger and discomfort. While both hands drum on the keyboard, the singing voice sounds in ascending phrases. The song ends with a climax in a major key, as if the main character longs again to stand in front of his lover's house.

9. The quasi-indifferent melody from *(Irrlicht)* draws us '*in die tiefsten Felsengründe',* into the darkest depths. The song is in B-minor (with two sharps), which according to Schubart's *Aesthetics* is a key of fate.

10. As the main character finds respite in the house of a poor coal burner (*Rast*), the continuous motion of eighth notes undermines the sense of rest. The key of C-minor, the same as in the fourth song (*Erstarrung*), again reflects tragic passion but now feels slow and lethargic.

11. *Frühlingstraum* begins in the love key of A-major and has the feeling of a swaying gondola song. It is abruptly disturbed by roosters crowing in the earthly two-quarter time. Static octave changes refer to ice crystals on the window, mocking the memory of better times. *Wann halt ich mein Liebchen in Arm?* The final chord in A-minor conveys hopelessness.

12. In *Einsamkeit*, the trek continues in the elegiac key of B-minor. The icy cold, the silence, the light. Misery is worse than the storms of life. This first part of the cycle thus comes to an end.

13. *Die Post*, beginning of the second part, is in E-flat major, a key suggesting faith and love, and also associated with horns. The main character longs for a message from the town girl, but none is forthcoming. The music contrasts an earthy duple feeling with a more lyrical and lilting triple-time, enhanced by horn motives. The protagonist could return to town to ask (obviously in minor) why he was rejected in the first place.

14. In *Der greise Kopf*, somber musings continue in C-minor. The movement feels like a forlorn sarabande with second beat accents alternating between the voice and piano parts. His hair has turned white with frost, making him look old and ready to die. But when it thaws, his hair turns black again, revealing his youth. "My grave how long you taunt me?' he asks. (Singable translation Jeffrey Benton).

15. *Krähe* continues in the gloomy key of C-minor. The crow is a "perverted image of loyalty" (Just, 1964, 471), who has followed the main character from the city and does not leave him. The black crow continues to circle over him in triplet motifs. The protagonist expresses hope that the crow will be faithful to him until the end.

16. With *Letzte Hoffnung* we return to E-flat major. With its three flats, E-flat is often associated with the Holy Trinity, though in this song, feelings of desperate hope contrast with those of love and reverence.

17. *Im Dorfe* is cast in D-major, a key of triumph. Throughout music history this key has been used for overtures, marches and festive chants. The association at first seems out of place, unless it refers to the smug, safely sleeping and dreaming residents, guarded by chained growling dogs – the bourgeois "victory," so to speak. The monotonous growling accompaniment in the bass part keeps the wanderer at bay.

18. *Der stürmische Morgen* modulates to D-minor. This song is at once the shortest of the cycle, and one of the most thrilling. The gentle seriousness with which the cycle began has returned, but now with seething motifs and violent staccatos that suggest cloudy skies and threatening weather.

19. *Täuschung* is in A-major and dualistic in nature. It can be seen as expression of innocent love, youthful cheerfulness and trust in God, but also one of displeasure and anger. The walker encounters the beguiling charm of morning light, based on the 'Cloud Girl' from Schubert's own opera *Alfonso und Estrella* (1822), in a lovely 6/8 time and in that seemingly innocent A-major.

20. In *Der Wegweiser* is in G-minor, a key suggesting unease and failed plans. The walker moves on, but at a slower pace than before. This specific sequence of modulations evokes a feeling of inescapable fate and anticipates the next song.

21. With *Das Wirtshaus* and the key of F-major, there is a sense of comfort and tranquility. This funeral march in a major key portrays the cemetery as an inn and shelter. Welcoming though this illusion may be, we find the rooms are already occupied: Even a cemetery is a place in society, and again, there is no room for the protagonist.

22. We return to the tragically hopelessness of G-minor with *Muth!* By exclaiming 'If there are no Gods on earth, Gods we will be together!' the protagonist hopes to give himself some courage to numb his pain, but it's not enough to help him.

23. The penultimate song, *Nebensonnen,* is in a hopeful and trusting A major. Of the three "mock suns," perhaps a symbol for faith, hope and love, two have already gone down (faith and love). The last one (hope) must also go, because truth reveals itself in the dark, in giving up. Again, there is an unyielding sarabande rhythm as encountered in the fourteenth song, *Der Greise Kopf.*

24. *Der Leiermann* appears to be a kind of *Doppelgänger* (a poem by Heinrich Heine, also set to music by Schubert). Here we see an image of the alienated self, a literary motif often encountered in the literature of German Romanticism. This particular song and *Der Lindenbaum* are the most well-known songs from *Winterreise*. The key of A-minor in this case suggests a passive and gloomy atmosphere, representing lost love. Originally Schubert composed this song in B minor, the key of fate. So why would the first publisher print the song in A minor? Was it just a bit too high for Vogl, or did it have something to do with the rising of pitch during the 19th century? B-minor would evoke acceptance, whereas A-minor according to Schubart, points to pious femininity and softness of character. Does the protagonist identify with the old organ grinder – also an outcast? *Winterreise* ends with that question. Whatever it was, softness of character or passivity, Schubert brilliantly elevates it into musical expression of profound sensitivity, of an existential crisis, made timeless in music.

Conclusion

The power of *Winterreise* is enhanced by the paradox between beauty and bitter truth. The tension between these elements causes the main character to focus increasingly on his inner self and to seek reflection. In other times, this deep inner search was often associated with the monastic life of Lutheran Pietism, or the 18th-century *Empfindsamkeit*. But even in our own time, we can relate to this search. Loneliness, alienation and a real sense of time versus a subjective experience of it can be elements of everyone's life. Even though we are far removed from Schubert's time, the deep inner world of his music transcends time and space, chronotopos par excellence. Listening to or performing *Winterreise* can be a transcendental experience.

Unfortunately, interest in art song, including performances of *Winterreise*, is waning. This is curious given that the themes of the work are so beautiful and timeless. The strong inner world and authentic expression of *Winterreise* are in sharp contrast to our time, where outward appearances reign. Concrete, visual elements are highly preferred above imagination.

Performances today are often very operatic, or are striving for an overly academic rendition, polished to perfection but bland in expression. Several elements can be attributed to this: the rise of electronic media, which raised pop music (once referred to as folk music) to the status of established culture, and the phenomenon of 'art religion' where the artist got a semi-religious status. These factors contributed to changing classical music to an art form for the elite and for institutions that are increasingly irrelevant (James, 1997, 317). Future audiences will also be poorly educated in classical music because little or no attention is paid to it in schools. Also pertinent to *Winterreise* would be that German language and culture lost importance and popularity after the Second World War. This was one of the reasons for me as a performer to offer the work in an English translation.

Initially, *Winterreise* did not have a large audience – the work was created in a very modest setting. The song cycle is a clear exponent of European culture of that time. In Schubert's days, people were accustomed to living in the paradoxical combination of the rationality of the Enlightenment on the one hand, and Romanticism with its mysticism and celebration of the great unknown, on the other. Politically, common people had very little power.

After the Second World War, when Germany was at its lowest in material goods and moral, and highly introspective, Fischer-Dieskau found an audience for *Winterreise*. The song cycle originally emerged from cultured intellectuals, who, though in a position of political weakness, were able to create remarkable works of art that celebrated a rich inner life. Such works resonated with the post-WW2 audience. But these remarkable artists, such as Schubert, were often lonely in their eloquent expression of deep inner worlds.

Today many artists, instead of being swept in all possible directions, such as is represented in *Wetterfahne,* find respite in inner profundity.

Schubert embodies a special part of the European heritage, opposite to the artificiality of our current culture. This music, so replete with beauty and truth, offers comfort and healing. *Winterreise* rewards our attention, remaining both unique and indispensable.

Works cited

Bachtin, Michail. 2008. *Chronotopos*. Berlin: Suhrkamp.
Baumann, Cecilia. C. Wilhelm Müller. 1981. *The poet of the Schubert Song Cycles: His life and Works*. University Park and London: The Pennsylvania State University Press.
Benton, Jeffrey. (2021, March 29). *Schubert. The Winter Journey* (Die Winterreise). English translation. Retrieved from https://www.jeffreybenton.co.uk/winterreise.
De La Motte-Haber, Helg. 1990. *Musik und Bildende Kunst*. Laaber-Verlag, Laaber.
Deutsch, Otto Erich. 1957. *Schubert. Die Erinnerungen seiner Freunde. Gesammelt und hg. von O.E. Deutsch.* Leipzig.
Dittrich, Marie-Agnes.1991. *Harmonik und Sprachvertonung in Schuberts Liedern*. Hamburger Beiträge zur Musikwissenschaft. Ed. Constantin Floros. Hamburg: Verlag der Musikalienhandlung Karl Dieter Wagner.
Cassirer, Ernst.1929. *Philosophie der symbolischen Formen*. Berlin: Bd.3.
Feil, Arnold. 1975. *Franz Schubert. Die schöne Müllerin. Winterreise. Mit einem Essay "Wilhelm Müller und die Romantik" von Rolf Vollmann.* With 88 Notes. Stuttgart: Philipp Reclam jun.
Fischer-Dieskau, Dietrich. 1971. *Auf den Spuren der Schubert-Lieder. Werden-Wesen-Wirkung.* With 76 illustrations. Wiesbaden. F.A. Brockhaus.
Gürschig-Pfingsten, Ingeborg. *Dur und Moll als musikalische Ausdrucksmittel.* In: *Musica* 38 (1984).
Hufschmidt, Wolfgang. 1993. *Willst zu meinen Liedern deine Leier drehn? Zur Semantik der musikalischen Sprache in Schuberts Winterreise und Eislers Hollywood-Liederbuch.* Saarbrücken: PFAU-Verlag.
Just, K.G. *Wilhelm Müller und seine Liederzyklen.* In: Zeitschrift für deutsche Philologie 83, 1964.
Jamie, James. *De muziek der sferen. De parallelle geschiedenis van muziek en wetenschap; van hemelse harmonie tot kosmische dissonantie.* Dutch edition: Bres BV, Amsterdam 1997.
Moore, Gerald. 1978. *Schuberts Liederzyklen. Gedanken zu ihrer Ausführung. Gemeinschaftliche Ausgabe.* Kassel- Basel-Tours- London: Bärenreiter-Verlag. München: Deutscher Taschenbuch Verlag

Müller, Wilhelm. 1903. *Diary and Letters of Wilhelm Müller.* Ed. Ph. Sch. Allen; J.T. Hattfield. Chicago.

Mustard, H. M. 1946. *The Lyric Cycle in German Literature.* In *Columbia University Germanic Studies*, n.s., No. 17). New York: King's crown Press.

Schubart, Christ. Fried. *Dan: Ideeën voor een esthetica van de toonkunst uitgegeven door Ludwig Schubart Koninklijk Pruissisch Legationsraad.* Wenen: J.V. Degen Boekdrukker en boekhandelaar 1806.

Schubert, Franz. 1928. *Schubertalbum. Gesänge für eine Singstimme mit Klavierbegleitung. Nach dem ersten Druck revidiert von Max Friedlaender.* Band I. *Ausgabe für mittlere Stimme.* Leipzig: Edition Peters.

Schubert, Franz. 1966. *Die Winterreise. Faksimile-Wiedergabe nach der Originalhandschrift Franz Schubert.* Kassel: Bärenreiter.

Stoffels, Ludwig. 1987. *Die Winterreise I. Bd.1: Müllers Dichtung in Schuberts Vertonung.* Bonn: Verlag für systematische Musikwissenschaft.

—. 1991. *Die Winterreise II: Bd.2: Die Lieder der ersten Abteilung.* Bonn: Verlag für systematische Musikwissenschaft.

Stoppelenburg, Charlotte. *Winterreise (1827): ein Weg durch die Chronotopoi.* (Universiteit van Amsterdam: Master's degree Graduation thesis).

Die Texte des Liederzyklus Winterreise (Wilhelm Müller und Franz Schubert) im *Licht der Chronotopos-Theorie des Michail Bachtin analysiert.* Universiteit van Amsterdam. 2010.

Stukenschmidt, Hans Heinz. 1974. *Schönberg – Leben, Umwelt, Werk.* Zürich und Freiburg.

Vollmann, Rolf. 1975. "Wilhelm Müller und die Romantik". In: Arnold Feil: *Franz Schubert. Die schöne Müllerin. Winterreise.* Stuttgart: Philipp Reclam jun.

Part IV:

Italian & Latin Literature

THE LIGHT BETWEEN THE LIMINAL SPACE: ITALO CALVINO'S INVISIBLE CITIES AND THE MUSIC OF INDIGENOUS AUSTRALIANS- ARCHIE ROACH, KUTCHA EDWARDS, AND CHRISTINE ANU

JEMA STELLATO PLEDGER

Fig. 21: 'Guerriero donne', Stradbroke Island, Queensland, Australia.

Music is one of the most universal ways of communicating and exists in the everyday lives of people across generations and cultures globally (Mehr et al., 2019). Similarly, literature has influenced humanity's cultures, beliefs, and traditions for centuries. "Perhaps one of the most important qualities that binds music and literary reading and differentiates them from a number of other cultural artifacts is that both unfold in time, offering a kind of 'narrative' that can be followed" (Omigie, 2015, 1). Together, music and literature are a powerful combination which have been handed down through the ages by our ancestors. This interconnection has long fascinated me, particularly in relation to Italians and Indigenous Australians in terms of their commonality of the human experience shared fusion of storytelling traditions, dance, and music.

I will draw on Italo Calvino, a northern Italian storyteller who writes some of the most extraordinary stories that engage the fantastical to address reality—stories that literally sing across the page. These stories meet Archie Roach, a Gunditjmara/Bundjalung[1] man, Kutcha Edwards, a Mutti Mutti[2] man and Christine Anu, a Torres Strait Islander[3]; their haunting music and lyrics tell stories of Indigenous culture that transport the listener from the Dreamtime to the Stolen Generation.

Socio-political elements will inform this paper as much of the artists' works reflects past and contemporary issues. I will position the relationship between music and literature from the perspective of the liminal space and belonging. In turn, I will formulate a sample performance to reflect the music and literature connection focusing on Calvino's *Invisible Cities* infused with music from the three First Nations people.[4] These consummate storytellers speak to the audience, in lilting tones with accents on the most essential elements, of cultural heritage and socio-political issues, creating rhythmic brush strokes to produce moments that hang within the space between time and memory.

Liminality or the 'in-between' is understood to be a space of transition. For Van Genepp (1909), a liminal phase is a state of uncertainty when a person is standing on a threshold of a new life, and simultaneously leaving the old life or phase of life behind. This could be marriage, death, or migration. Liminal people are those not easily positioned into a specific category of existence. Artists could be characterised as liminal beings "as they embody the semi-autonomous borders of the social world" (Frank 1977, 8). Artists across disciplines are in spaces of transitions particularly in periods of great creativity. Indigenous people globally could also be

---

[1] People from South western Victoria and North East Coast of NSW and the Southern Eastern coast of Queensland.
[2] People from Southern Murray Basin and includes the centres of Balranald, Robinvale and Euston. NSW.
[3] Torres Strait islands are the only Australian islands that share a border with another country. They are located between mainland Australia and Papua New Guinea.
[4] I was unable to get permission to use the lyrics in the body of the essay in time. Therefore, I have provided links to lyrics and music in foot notes where applicable.

considered liminal beings as they continue to experience a transition, away from their traditional life and culture brought on by colonisation (King, 2006). In this context for indigenous communities, and migrant, exile or refugee, liminality is a way of life where the desire to belong means they remain in the life's waiting room.

During liminal periods, social order maybe overturned or temporarily disbanded, and the continuity of traditions becomes uncertain, and expected future outcomes are thrown into confusion. Turner (1967) expanded Van Genepp's initial concept of liminality "to represent the unlimited possibilities from which social structure emerges" (La Shure, 2005 3). These can be difficult periods due to lack of connection to this structure within the world. (Stellato Pledger, 2017).

When I read Calvino (1923-1985) and listen to Roach (1956-), Edwards (1965) or Anu (1970-) I am drawn to their social conscience; their stories and music take their audience on a journey, leaving them with more questions than answers. Though diametrically diverse, they have one thing in common: the ability to allow an audience to live in the moment and be held in a liminal space. In the process of questioning, we are in a place of transition, waiting and not knowing. These can be moments of great personal change, where time stands still, a pivotal point, on the edge of a precipice, prior to a leap.

McShane (1983) notes that:

> Calvino's attitude has enhanced his popular appeal because unlike so many others he does not try to offer solutions to public issues. Rather, by asking questions, he lets his own obsessions run loose and thereby liberates the feelings of his readers. (3).

Similarly, Roach's music and lyrics *Took the Children Away*, ask questions allowing the listener to determine their own answers, Edwards has a comparable approach, though softer, leaving the audience held in a space of ancestral memory as seen in his latest song *We Sing*. Anu's, beautiful voice rings out the plight of her people and there is a sense of belonging in Neil Murrays, *My Island Home*. There is an intimacy in the works of all three that is both gut wrenching and beautiful, that compels audiences to listen and go on a journey that has fought and won extraordinary challenges in a bid to hold a sense of belonging.

Calvino, Roach, Edwards and Anu come from vastly different life experiences. Calvino was born in Cuba, where his parents worked as botanists. The family returned to Italy when he was quite young. He and his brother Floriano joined the Italian resistance just prior to the WW2. Until the end of the war, he lived and fought in the Maritime Alps (Michel, 2015).

After the war Calvino resumed his studies and worked for leftist papers and wrote more than forty books in his 61 years.

Archie Roach was one of the Stolen Generation. He was born in Victoria in 1956; taken from his parents at the age of two where his language and culture had denied him. He lived in various institutions until he was fostered by a Scottish family. Roach left home at 15 and travelled round Australia for several years. It was during this time he experienced a cultural reckoning in terms of language and a reawakening of his indigeneity (Roach, 2019). Roach married Ruby Hunter, a Ngarrindjeri[5] woman, also a singer songwriter writer. They had two children and fostered others (Marshall, 2019).

Kutcha Edwards (1965-) is an extraordinary songman and storyteller and one of the Stolen Generation. He draws on a "profound sense of all those who have gone before him on this land and his own life experiences" (*Aboriginal Australia*, 2015). He is the ninth of twelve children born to Mary and Nugget Edwards. At 18 months old he and five of his siblings were removed by the government and placed in Orana Methodist Children's Home. "He remembers only a whitened childhood" (Elder, 2015). He was six, when he met his mother and remembers being afraid and perplexed at this strange woman (Ibid.).

Christine Anu is a Torres Strait islander and by all accounts came from a 'normal' background. However, it was not until recent years that she has begun to observe her mother endure years of mental and physical abuse. She advocates against domestic violence particularly in Indigenous communities. Anu worked in a male dominated music industry where for years indigenous women remained in the background. Nancy Bates, curator of the Umbrella Festival Adelaide (2018) discusses the need to change the landscape of indigenous music and hear the voices of the women. Katelyn Barney's (2007) article *Indigenous Peoples, Recording Techniques, and the Recording Industry*, discusses how recording studios and technologies have become a space to create music which in turn sends a message of agency for voices of indigenous women to transition from the liminal into one of power and control.

These short summaries of the lives of Calvino, Roach, Edwards and Anu, demonstrate their unique differences, yet the prose, imagery, and socio-political issues they apply in their stories and songs is where they meet. This is notable in their earlier works, particularly for Roach and Calvino. While the content is different both Roach and Calvino use prose

---

[5] Indigenous Australians from the lower Murray River, western Fleurieu Peninsula, and the Coorong in the southern-central area in South Australia.

that brings forth vivid images while at the same time speaks to social issues that hang in the liminal space.

As an example, Calvino's first novel, *Il Sentiero dei nidi di ragno* (*The Path to the Nest of Spiders*, 1947), tells the story of Pin, an orphan, of indeterminate age. Pin lives with his sister, a prostitute, and spends his time in bars telling sexual jokes and singing bawdy songs he does not understand. He is a child full of bravado desperately in need of a sense of belonging. The recurring theme throughout the book speaks of desperation and the way it shapes a person's ability to be easily bought. The book illustrates the need to belong at any cost, even if it means joining the enemy. Pin exists in an in-between space where a desire to belong is paramount to his survival amidst the cruel world that has taken everyone he loves (*The 1947 Club*, 2016).

In Roach's most notable work, *Took the Children Away*[6], children are the subject. The children are innocent victims of a world that sees them without culture or language, doomed to live under the post-colonial dictates of modern Australia. Roache's prose dances with powerful visual metaphors that allow the listener to be taken to unknown worlds. The language in the lyrics[7] is confronting in its simplicity while the haunting music speaks to ghosts once known, caught within worlds of past present and potential future. Ancestors and spirits hang heavily with reprehensible acts of Australia's colonial past in a beautiful, painful liminality. I could describe this song as Calvino explains Pluto in *The Other Eurydice* (1995) "sometimes a fiery streak zigzags through the dark: it's not lightnings, but an incandescent metal snaking down through a vein" (219). Roach speaks of his experience and relates them to others from the stolen generation and draws on the lies they were told as they took children and babies from their parents. The song is about children being sent to mission schools and points out that they were schooled in the image of the white man while inside they felt black. They experience a hybrid identity and according to Bhaba (1994 & Higgis 2004) "Hybridity refers to the development of identities which straddle two cultures, and are therefore neither one nor the other, while sharing parts of both." He further suggests that hybridity is evident in colonialism, while Higgis (2004) maintains it is the result of post colonialism (2004) and currently (Lupton 1999a) considers it to be one of the results of globalisation. Hybridity is not attempting to blend identity but expresses the continued existence and challenge of a marginalised (i.e., liminal) identity.

---

[6] Link to YouTube *Took the Children Away*
https://www.youtube.com/watch?v=aywDT6yHMmo
[7] Link to lyrics for *Took the Children Away*
https://www.lyrics.com/lyric/4503696/Took+the+Children+Away

King (2006) argues that this is different to multiculturalism and diaspora as these can be seen to be about maintaining cultural identity as opposed to "living together apart" (4) in the dominant culture. *Took the Children Away* speaks to this hybridity and is a tribute to living in liminal spaces created by oppressors. Roach further honours the courage of the children who attempted to find and found, their way back to their families.

Calvino's later work, *Invisible Cities* is an unusual work with each chapter framed in dialogue between Kublai Khan, a fading emperor whose kingdom is coming to an end, and explorer Marco Polo. The book is a dreamlike contemplation, told in prose, on the fate of civilization (Kennedy, 2020) comprising of stories about fifty-five cities, all of which have female names. Each city is more amazing, more inventive, and more reminiscent of Venice, Polo's home, where his sense of belonging resides. The stories are a contemplation on the imagination and the conceivable. They read as parables on death, culture, time and memory and the nature of the human experience (Davis). One of the most interesting elements of the book is the assertion by Marco Polo (Calvino) that "the listener retains only the words he is expecting. It is not the voice that commands the story: it is the ear" (Calvino, 123). In short, it is the listener as opposed to the teller who controls the interpretation of the story. ("Course Hero").

In keeping with this concept, I began to create my own understanding of *Invisible Cities*. This is not a linear book. Rather, it moves in an out of spaces that holds its reader in the 'in between' until you extricate yourself and move on to the next story. Adaptations of *Invisible Cities* have been created in a variety of media. Calvino was not precious about being faithful to the original work, rather he believed that "some things cannot properly be transmitted from the written page" (Pollock, 2002, 3). In 2013 The Industry and L.A. Dance project created an opera of *Invisible Cities*. It was set in Los Angeles' Union Station, whilst it continued to function. Headphones were given to limited audience members to individualise the experience in the public space. Further, audience participation was encouraged, thus enabling them to wander freely through the station and fully immerse themselves in the experience. The 2019 Brisbane Festival in association with Manchester International Festival created *Invisible Cities* as an interdisciplinary work combining theatre, dance, music, architectural design, and projection set in an enormous warehouse with seven loading docks (Delany, 2019), in the Brisbane suburb of Yeerongpilly. When developing Calvino's random, though structured stories into a performance work, Chakrabarti succeeded in respecting the atmosphere, language, and mysticism of Calvino's book (Stewart, 2019).

These were awe-inspiring productions and I pondered how *Invisible Cities* could be crafted as an Italian Indigenous work. I imagined the music would infuse the enchanting cities into a rare piece of magic realism that accentuates the liminal space and simultaneously highlights the plight of Australia's indigenous people and the potential demise of modern civilisation.

The language in *Invisible Cities* is quite intricate, like the particles of liquid glass separating sentences into a thousand meanings. I found the most effective approach is to let the stories wash over you and like Marco Polo in his travels, "you do not stay. You do not really understand; you only arrive, and leave, with traces, memories, thoughts, and dreams." (Savla, 2019). Conversely, the language of Roach, Edwards and Anu's songs is more direct and accessible with symbolism that speaks directly to the heart. I envision Calvino's stories, woven into small vignettes that resonate with the three Indigenous songs.

Invisible Cities exists where memories, thoughts and dreams inhabit simultaneously and separately and echo ideas of magic realism as there is no separation between worlds. This speaks to traditional ideas in Calabrian folklore, which is steeped in magic, where the extraordinary appears conventional and the ordinary, bizarre with an ability to naturalise implausible events (Stellato Pledger, 2017). There is a strong sense that our ancestors and the past walk within the present. This is reminiscent of a short summary explaining The Dreaming, in *Aboriginal Contemporary* website, which states

> The Dreaming is not static or linear. It is the past, but it is also the present and the future. The Dreaming is constantly evolving to explain events and changes today, such as floods, storms and (negative and positive) occurrences in people's lives (1)

Invisible Cities encapsulates these qualities of magic realism, whilst also providing a damning indictment of society. Similarly, Roach's music can bore into the heart of humanity's failings, while Edwards holds a light of hope in his recent song W*e Sing*, and Anu's *My Island Home* is likened to a harbour in a storm. One cannot help imagining parts of the book brought into a different dimension when combining *Invisible Cities* with these story songs. It is important to mention here that a work such as this cannot be produced without the permission and collaboration of the Indigenous communities.

I will now consider an Italian Indigenous work, my sample creation, where songs and music are woven through the *Invisible Cities*. Initially I felt a distinct incongruity when working with the stories of a twentieth century Italian writer and modern Indigenous musicians. Rather, it is this dichotomy that was the ingredient needed for such a collaboration. Furthermore, *Invisible Cities* is not just about cities but rather a dreamscape: about the faraway, the unfamiliar, the majestic, the marvellous and the untamed, unnamed elements of life. The reader is drawn away from the literal meaning of the words to ponder human experience and dreaming which are the essence of storytelling (Salva, 2019). It is at this point I imagine how the songs, music and stories of the cities would come together in a cacophony of language, tones, and hues shaped by the fusion of Indigenous Australians and Italians.

In keeping with the design of Calvino's book, which divides each chapter into eleven categories of cities, I choose one city from three different categories that resonate with the songs. These are *The Continuous Cities 2, City and Memories 4*, and *Cities and Signs 4*.

To give a picture of the intended sample work, I establish my aims, which are to explore how music and literature together can have great affect to bring about social and personal change. The basic framework for the performance space which would be housed in a large unused old warehouse as such a structure has an aura of mystery in respect to stories hidden within its walls. The space would be divided into three triangular sections, each representing a city, with the action taking place in each large triangle. There will be a stage set on a mezzanine floor where Marco Polo and Kublai Khan interact. This will be positioned so it can be viewed from all directions. Given the vastness of the space, there is a significant distance between cities; the space is where the audience move, as travellers from one city to another. There are film projections of each city on three walls that run on a silent loop until the audience, now known as travellers, journey to a given city.

Their first stop is the *Continuous Cities 2*, named Procopia, which exists in a constant state of liminality and illustrates how space can create a city and in time, how it can be transformed to take up so much space, the city becomes unrecognizable. Marco Polo discusses his visits to *Continuous Cities 2,* with Kublai Khan which occur on an annual basis. He always rents the same room in the same hotel on the same street. Every year an increasing number of people sit on the walls outside his room and each year the view changes as slowly, people start taking over the land. The sprawl grows exponentially until the sky disappears. Eventually the people engulf his room. Though luckily most are polite. This is quite a bewildering experience and highlights how difficult it is to find one's bearings in the confusion of the modern world.

In this performance triangle the *Continuous Cities* is projected as a time lapse film of the dessert: the stunning Australian landscapes and oceans, all of which are slowly eaten away by colonisation. The land becomes built up areas, killing off native animals as it encroaches on their habitats. We see a maze of houses, on quarter acre blocks that travel to the horizon. We see a young indigenous man standing in the middle of the time lapse looking on helplessly. We then observe groups of children in "clean white dresses" from Christian Institutions. There are voice-overs of how the land was taken away, how the children were taken away in concert with Marco Polo describing his disorientation in the *Continuous City 2* to Khublai Khan. We hear Roache's strong, plaintive song, *Took the Children Away* which rises above the din until the triangle is in relative darkness with just a performer and a guitar, singing.

Took the Children Away resonates with *Continuous Cities 2* as they both tell stories of irreversible change. In addition, it is reminiscent of Marco Polo in Procopia when his living space was swamped by uninvited guests. From an Indigenous perspective, one can only imagine the country before colonisation. Its vast endless vistas of red sand and lush bushland; places where the land meets the ocean, where the Indigenous Australian nomads roamed unhindered against changing horizons and stunning skyscapes. Throughout colonisation and beyond, land was stolen, indigenous populations were removed to make way for towns. Additionally, cities too often grew on sacred lands without consultation with the original owners, leaving them grief stricken and homeless.

To drive a spear further into the hearts of traditional owners, the Australian Government's assimilation policy[8] (Behrendt 2012), aimed to eradicate a whole culture through systematic genocide by absorbing Aboriginal people into white society through the process of removing children from their families (Find and Connect)[9]. This policy saw children torn from their land, language and culture and placed in institutions or foster homes. The whitening of black children in Australia increased dramatically between 1904 to the early 70s. Thus, their lives were spread out in front of them like

---

[8] The forcible removal of Aboriginal and Torres Strait Islander children from their families was part of the policy of Assimilation, which was based on the misguided assumption that the lives of Aboriginal and Torres Strait Islander people would be improved if they became part of white society. It proposed that Aboriginal and Torres Strait Islander people should be allowed to "die out" through a process of natural elimination, or, where possible, assimilated into the white community (Behrendt, L. 2012).

[9] The Find & Connect web resource brings together historical resources relating to institutional 'care' in Australia. It has been developed by a team of historians, archivists and social workers from the University of Melbourne and Australian Catholic University, with funding from the Australian Government.

the never-ending suburban sprawl, which had literally devoured their country, family, and culture. Then the tormenting feeling of being locked in an unknown space in the relentless reign of cruelty.

> To tell you about Procopia I should begin by describing the entrance to the city. You advance for hours and it is not clear to you whether you are already in the city's midst or still outside it…The question that now begins to gnaw at your mind is more anguished: outside Penthesilea does an outside exist? Or no matter how far you go from the city, will you only pass from one limbo to another, never managing to leave it? (Calvino, 41-42)

The audience then travels to Zora, *Cities and Memories 4*. The projections in the space resemble the six rivers and the mountains a traveller must pass to reach her. She rises like a queen in the mountain mist: unforgettable; mesmerising where images of her cityscape are burned into the traveller's memory. As Marco Polo explains to Kublai Khan "Zora, a city that no one, having seen it, can forget …Zora's secret lies in the way your gaze runs over patterns following one another as in a musical score where not a note can be altered or displaced" (13). While their conversation continues, becoming increasingly distant, the travellers witness the landscape dissolve into a pattern of streets. These are the pathways where its residents walk daily, impregnating the memory of the city further into the cells of their minds. Zora is memory; therefore, she will never be forgotten (Cheng 2020). From this perspective no one can forget her even if they want "which means they could never change anything in their minds, so now when someone walks down those streets, he or she will always see them exactly as they were before" (Calvino, 12).

> This city which cannot be expunged from the mind is like an armature, a honeycomb in whose cells each of us can place the things he wants to remember names of famous men, virtues, numbers, vegetable and mineral classifications, dates of battles, constellations, parts of speech. Between each idea and each point of the itinerary an affinity or a contrast can be established, serving as an immediate aid to memory. (Calvino, 13)

The streets of Zora dissipate into an island and the travellers watch on the screen as one of the Torres Strait Islands slowly rises out of the water. The voice of Marco Polo is heard as he continues to explain Zora to Kublai Khan when a young woman walks into the space and listens to their conversation. They cannot see her as she is a living memory, an image of what is, was and will be. As the conversation dies down there is silence, and the screen is full of a thriving Island. People, busy with their daily lives, walking the streets, laughing, and singing. You can literally touch the happiness and the unadulterated sense of contentment.

Music erupts and the woman breaks into song, taking the audience with her. Zora resonates with Neil Murray's song *My Island Home*[10] (1987), as it speaks to a place that remains the same in memory. As the performer sings of being in a boat on the sea, holding a long turtle spear, one feels a strong spiritual connection to this island that will remain a bright light that shines on every tree, water hole and native animal and their habitats. It is a place that can be returned to again and again in the memory unchanged by time. The song speaks to ancestral belonging surrounded by water that heeds to the spirits of the land and oceans and waits, always with open arms

As the song finishes the space descends into darkness. There is an eerie atmosphere that pervades after such an upbeat song that many Australians identify as another national anthem. That feeling of connection and joy *My Island Home* brings, does not leave, it is suspended forever in the moment[11].

As the travellers find themselves becoming accustomed to the darkness, very slowly signs appear, pointing in various direction to light the way. One sign says Venice, another to Gunditjmara/Bundjalung country, another to Melbourne. The signs are everywhere, and the travellers must follow as if through a maze. Gradually the house lights slowly light the space, becoming brighter until the travellers see a fifty strong choir in the distance. They hum Edwards's song *We Sing.* Photographs of people from different indigenous cultures are projected across the wall. To the back and side, projections from other cities continue to loop. The travellers finally arrive in the *City and Signs 4*, in Hypatia. The projections change to different nationalities speaking in short sharp scenes. Italian, Greek, Arabic, Persian, Guarani Indian and Indigenous Australian languages all spoken together. It becomes a symphony of words and all the while the choir hums in the background. For the travellers, the trick is to allow the languages to wash over you and meaning will become clear. The meaning is personal for each traveller. As the symphony of language dies down, Marco Polo explains his experience in Hypatia to Kublai Khan.

The streets of Hypatia had changed since Polo's last visit. He went to the palace and found convicts instead of philosophers who were now imprisoned. Apparently, there was an outbreak of the plague. He went to the library and found books were now used for children's games. Eventually, he did find a philosopher who told him "signs form a language, but not the one you think

---

[10] Link to Lyrics for *My Island Home*
https://www.lyrics.com/lyric/31852383/Christine+Anu/My+Island+Home
[11] The Youtube link to *My Island Home*
https://www.youtube.com/watch?v=OSFGK9HlEto

you know." (40-41). And so, Marco Polo "understood that travelling to another country or culture it's important not just for us but also our hosts/guests/visitors etc., to try understanding their way of life and how they express themselves differently than we do…" (Cheng 4).

As this conversation finishes, the choir continues to hum, all projections from three triangles with sound, roar in the large space. The travellers are perplexed caught in the in-between. Music, words, and sound paint the space with rhythmic hums until they dissipate into a vibrating bustling whirr before disappearing into silence.

A performer walks in front of the choir. He begins to sing, the choir begins to sing, and the travellers are transfixed as they are carried away by the music that speaks to freedom, justice, and love. The singer calls for a better life for his people and highlights "that black lives matter in terms of people with different complexions, different understandings, different spirit and marginalised spirit" (Edwards, 2020). He speaks about the singers and how the indigenous singers, sing from their spirit and hand that spirit to the listener. It is a gift. The song[12] is about not living in fear, rather about singers being ancestral messengers. It speaks to the signs and symbols from the past and is carried to those who listen. As the song finishes, the travellers have become part of the experience and sing for justice and freedom and change.

Suddenly, the performance stage blacks out for a moment. The house lights slowly fill the space and the journey through three cities has come to an end. For now.

Developing a simple sample performance project gave me an opportunity to understand how the songs and stories sit within liminal spaces that suspend an audience in time and memory while simultaneously calling for social justice. The relationship between music and literature unfolded quite organically, becoming stories within stories. I found uncanny connections between these two diverse cultures through the development of this essay. I am by no means speaking for Indigenous Australians as their voice is loud and clear as the songs testify. This interconnection between music and literature shone a light on the inequities in Indigenous cultures and highlights the failures of 'civilised' society. As Marco Polo said to Khublai Khan that people only hear what they expect to hear, the story never remains the same, I hope listeners hear more than anticipated, and this interpretation will be expanded beyond comfort zones. Ultimately, I hope that the Calvino's cities and Indigenous music are brought to life in a way that illustrates that the music literature relationship can transform and have affect.

---

[12] The Youtube to link for *We Sing*
https://www.youtube.com/watch?v=zxVF7zUD9S0

Bibliography

Aboriginal Contemporary. 2020. Accessed October 31, 2020 https://www.aboriginalcontemporary.com.au/pages/what-is-the-dreamtime-and-dreaming#_ftn1

Aboriginal Victoria. 2020. Accessed October 29, 2020 https://www.aboriginalvictoria.vic.gov.au/kutcha-edwards

Aboriginal Victoria: Kutcha Edwards: "A song man with a message of hope and understanding". Accessed 31/10/2020 https://www.aboriginalvictoria.vic.gov.au/kutcha-edwards

Anu, Christine. "My Island home" Accessed 1/9/2020 https://www.youtube.com/watch?v=OSFGK9HlEto

Barney, Katelyn. "Sending a Message: How Indigenous Australian Women Use Contemporary Music Recording Technologies to Provide a Space for Agency, Viewpoints and Agendas." In *The World of Music* 49, no. 1 (2007): 105-24. Accessed November 1, 2020. http://www.jstor.org/stable/41699742.

Behrendt, Larissa. 2012. *Indigenous Australia for Dummies.* Australia: Wiley Publishing.

Borschmann. Gregg. & Ross. Monique. "From stolen child to Indigenous leader: Archie Roach sings the songs that signpost his life" *ABC News, Radio National* July 12, 2018 7.45 AEST. Big Ideas. https://www.abc.net.au/news/2018-07-12/archie-roach-a-life-in-song/9957168

Boulton, Martin. "Kutcha Edwards and his 100-voice lockdown choir send spirits soaring" *The Age* September 5, 2020, 4.00pm AEST - Music: Culture https://www.theage.com.au/culture/music/kutcha-edwards-and-his-100-voice-lockdown-choir-send-spirits-soaring-20200901-p55rbx.html

Brown, Calvin. 1987. S. *Music and literature.* London; Hanover: University Press of New England.

Calvino, Italo. 1972. *Le città invisibili.* Torino: Giulio Einaudi.

—. *Italo Calvino: Letters, 1941-1985* - Updated Edition. United States: Princeton University Press, 2014.

—. 2016. *The Path to The Spiders' Nests.* London: Penguin Books. Blog: *The 1947 Club.* https://somewhereboy.wordpress.com/2016/10/12/the-1947-club-the-path-to-the-spiders-nests-italo-calvino/.

Cavallaro, Dani. 2010. *The Mind of Italo Calvino: A Critical Exploration of His Thought and Writings.* Jefferson, North Carolina and London: McFarland & Company Inc.

Allen, Cheng. *Invisible Cities Book Summary, by Italo Calvino.* Book Summaries. Accessed 30/9/2020. https://www.allencheng.com/invisible-cities-book-summary-italo-calvino/

Course, Hero. "Invisible Cities Study Guide." January 24, 2020. Accessed September 30, 2020. https://www.coursehero.com/lit/Invisible-Cities/.

da Sousa Correa, Delia; Chornik, Katia and Samuels, Robert . "Literature and music: Interdisciplinary research and teaching at the Open University". *Working with English: Medieval and Modern Language, Literature and Drama*, 5: 50–61. 2009. URL: http://www.nottingham.ac.uk/~aezweb/working_with_e...

Davis, Howard. "A Marvellous Invention - Italo Calvino's 'Invisible Cities.'" In *Scoop Independent news* 28 June 2019, 4:18 pm AES Culture https://www.scoop.co.nz/stories/CU1906/S00341/stop-making-sense-italo-calvinos-invisible-cities.htm

Delany, Brigid. "'Everything could go wrong': Invisible Cities takes over Brisbane warehouse in massive show" 25 Sep 2019 16.35 AEST – Culture. Accessed, 2/9/2020 https://www.theguardian.com/culture/2019/sep/25/invisible-cities-conjuring-up-marco-polo-adventures-brisbane-warehouse

Edwards, Kutcha https://www.youtube.com/watch?v=zxVF7zUD9S0

Elder, John. "Aboriginal singer Kutcha Edwards and his siblings welcomed to country." In *The Age* December 1, 2013, 3.00am AEST. https://www.smh.com.au/national/aboriginal-singer-kutcha-edwards-and-his-siblings-welcomed-to-country-20131130-2yimk.html

Hennessy, Kate. "Archie Roach's Took the Children Away: how one heartbreaking song galvanised a Nation." In *The guardian*. 13 Nov 2020, 03.30 AEST. https://www.theguardian.com/music/2020/nov/13/archie-roachs-took-the-children-away-how-one-heartbreaking-song-galvanised-a-nation

Kennedy, Patrick. "Biography of Italo Calvino, Italian Novelist." ThoughtCo. https://www.thoughtco.com/italo-calvino-author-profile-2207696 (accessed December 2, 2020).

King, Julie. "Personal and social transition and the concept of enforced liminality for Indigenous Australians with adult acquired physical disability." In Proceedings *Social Change in the 21st Century* Conference 2006, Queensland University of Technology.

Koorie. Heritage Trust; Uncle Kutcha Edwards https://koorieheritagetrust.com.au/wp-content/uploads/2020/08/21.-Essay-Uncle-Kutcha-Edwards.pdf

Kutcha, Edwards. *Song Lines Aboriginal Music*. Accessed 27/8/2020 http://songlines.net.au/kutcha-edwards/

McLaren, Aleisha. "Because Of Her, We Can Honours Female Aboriginal Singers and Storytellers for NAIDOC Week" 2018. (Accessed October 27, 2020) https://scenestr.com.au/music/because-of-her-we-can-honours-female-aboriginal-singers-and-storytellers-for-naidoc-week-20180707

MacShane, Frank. "The Fantasy world of Italo Calvino." In *The New York Times*. July 10, 1983 Section 6 https://www.nytimes.com/1983/07/10/magazine/the-fantasy-world-of-italo-calvino.html#:~:text=Calvino's%20attitude%20has%20enhanced%20his,feeling%20so%20of%20his%20readers.

Marshall, Konrad. 2019. "'Music Is The Medicine': Archie Roach On How Song Saved His Soul". In *The Sydney Morning Herald*, 2019. https://www.smh.com.au/culture/music/music-is-medicine-archie-roach-on-how-song-saved-his-soul-20191028-p534xk.html.

McCabe, Kathy. "Christine Anu on My Island Home and the career defining debut record." In *The Daily Telegraph*. May 9, 2015 10:00AEST. Music https://www.dailytelegraph.com.au/entertainment/music/christine-anu-on-my-island-home-and-the-career-defining-debut-record/news-story/369559f5df6e8eb07c90678309633ad7

Meisel, Myron "Invisible Cities: Opera Review." In *The Hollywood Reporter* October 21 2013 PDT https://www.hollywoodreporter.com/review/invisible-cities-opera-review-649834

Lincoln, Michel. "Italo Calvino: The author who did everything. Here's where to start, depending on what you love." In *Oyster Review* 2015 Accessed 27/210/20 http://review.oysterbooks.com/p/6iPBFyWxkpcBWxFF2qMVuX/italo-calvino

Murrey, Neil. "My Island Home" Lyrics. (Accessed 1/9/2020). https://lyricstranslate.com/en/christine-anu-island-home-lyrics.html

Omigie, Diana. "Music and literature: are there shared empathy and predictive mechanisms underlying their affective impact?" In *Frontiers in Psychology*, 6: 1250. 2015. doi:10.3389/fpsyg.2015.01250

Perri Silberblatt Gabriel. "Revising, Re-visioning: Italo Calvino and the Politics of Play." B. Arts diss. Carlton College. 2011.

Perry, Jordan. "'Bittersweet': Survivors of Victoria's Stolen Generations react to announcement of redress scheme" *NITV News*. Updated 18 mar 2020 - 6:29 pm AEST. Accessed September 24, 2020 https://www.sbs.com.au/nitv/article/2020/03/18/bittersweet-survivors-victorias-stolen-generations-react-announcement-redress

Pollock, Adam. "From page to stage" In *The Guardian*. June 29 2002 10.45 AEST https://www.theguardian.com/books/italocalvino/2002/jun/29/all

Roach, Archie. 2019. *Tell Me Why. The Story of My Life and My Music.* Australia: Simon & Schuster.

—. *Took the Children Away* accessed 1/10/2020 https://genius.com/Archie-roach-took-the-children-away-lyrics

—. *Took the Children Away* You tube https://www.youtube.com/watch?v=EA52bupg-BY

Rockman, Lisa. "Christine Anu is a born storyteller who loves to spin a yarn on stage." In *Newcastle Herald* June 23, 2019 - 7:00pm AEST- Music and Gigs. https://www.newcastleherald.com.au/story/6225242/christine-anu-shares-her-words-of-wisdom/

Savla, Freya. "In Visible Cities: Reviewing *Invisible Cities*. Review of *Invisible Cities* by Italo Calvino. In *Yale Daily News*. 2016. Accessed Sept 6 2020 https://yaledailynews.com/blog/2019/09/06/in-visible-cities-reviewing-invisible-cities/

Stellato Pledger, Jema, Anna. "Disturbing the Storm: Narratives from the Liminal Space: Investigating the Commonalities Between Older Afghan Hazara Women and Calabrian Exiles through Theories of Storytelling and Creative Led Research" PhD Thesis, Australian Catholic University 2018. MMS ID 991012836799602352

Stewart, Olivia. "Invisible Cities (Brisbane Festival): A unique experience that's more about the journey than the destination". *Limelight*. September 24, 2019. Accessed 7/9/2020, https://www.limelightmagazine.com.au/reviews/invisible-cities-brisbane-festival/

Tuedio, James A. "Boundaries in Translation at the Margins of Liminal Excess: Calibrating the Voice of Empire to the Ear of Resistance." Empire Conference (CSU Stanislaus: March 2006); published in: Margins CSU Stanislaus Honours Program Journal: 61-65. 2006.

OVID – HEROIDES & METAMORPHOSIS – A MUSICAL JOURNEY FROM J. S. BACH TO A. PIAZZOLLA

MANUELA KUSTERMANN & CINZIA MERLIN

Fig. 22: Poster for Ovid – 'Heroides and Metamorphosis' –

"You could start like this: chance brought us together, and as is often the case, our plans at the time were heading in the same direction.
Cinzia came to talk to me about the release of her first record, 'Metamorphosys', at the time I was studying the letters of Ovid's "Heroides" starting with "Metamorphoses." That's how we combined our projects and came up with a show based on four letters from the Heroides and the music reinterpreted by Cinzia.

The most interesting thing about our performance is that the music creates a world of its own, disconnected from Ovid's prose. The music is definitely not a background to the text. As in a jam session, where each instrument has its own autonomy and follows its own path to then integrate and create a common rhythm, in our show too, our 'instruments', music and prose, integrate perfectly to form a whole while each following their own independent path.

For the performance I chose the letters of Medea to Jason, Penelope to Ulysses, Canace to Macareus, Ariadne to Theseus with an introduction taken from the "Metamorphoses" and the first part of the curse cast by Ipsipile on Medea."

—Manuela Kustermann

"Meeting Manuela was a magical encounter. Our artistic affinity and desire to experiment led us to share our art most naturally and spontaneously, creating this poetic and intense show.

I am a multifaceted and contemporary pianist. I address a repertoire that runs through the history of pianissimo to the dawn of jazz music. In my musical journey, I have always sought beauty. At a certain point, I began to reflect on the possibility of breaking the formal and stylistic rigidity that the classical repertoire often represents, and which I perceived to be a bit narrow for my artistic nature. It was from there that I started to explore new avenues.

I freed the musical forms from their original structure and then reassembled them in a new rhapsodic form that had harmonic connections, searched for new stylistic colours and linked composers far away in time.

From J. S. Bach to A. Piazzolla, I travelled through D. Scarlatti, B. Bartok, S. Prokofiev, C. Debussy up to M. Tisano, a living composer. This is how the 'Metamorphosys' album was born, on 15 April 2019, published by the Fluente Records record label.

Manuela immediately had the sensitivity to grasp this new way of conceiving classical music. So we decided to create this dialogue between music and prose under the aura of Ovid. An innovative exploration of how music and words can merge, blur and lose themselves in each other."

—Cinzia Merlin

The Heroides

The Heroides (*The Heroines)*, written by Publius Ovidius Naso (43BC-17) between 25 and 16 BC, are love letters of famous female figures that myth and history have passed down to us. Imaginary letters addressed to a lover or a sweetheart telling of abandonments, escapes, betrayals sustained and suffered, letters that, even in the marvellous poetry of Ovid, evoke the reality of an ancient female condition made of abuse, solitude, constraints and violence. *The Heroides* are the poetry of suspended time that the imagination fills with memories and desires. By exploring their psyche and humanising these myths, Ovid interprets their passions and hopes and manages to give voice to a female universe evoking a still very relevant condition today.

With *The Heroides*, for the first time in the history of literature, poetic love letters are written in elegiac couplets. They mark the birth of a new literary genre.

Almost in the form of a monologue, each letter explores the psychology of each heroine, announcing her complaints, her passions, and the abuse she has suffered.

The choice of four letters for the performance (Medea to Jason, Penelope to Ulysses, Canace to Macaeus, Ariadne to Theseus) was made to present female models that can still be found in today's society. These are four examples of victims sacrificed because of jealousy, carelessness, opportunism, cynicism and power, which are still the current protagonists of the news of our times. The letters confirm a harsh reality: the role of women has always been one of submission to men.

Medea to Jason

Medea represents the foreigner who has failed to fully integrate into her new homeland and abandoned by Jason out of a thirst for power and opportunism.

After abandoning everything in her homeland and following the man she loves, she is rejected as a wife and mother and disowned so that Jason can marry a new rich wife and daughter of a king.

> *"Having lost my kingdom, my homeland and my home, I am abandoned by Jason, who was everything to me. I have been able to tame dragons and raging bulls, but against one alone, my spouse, I have no such power; I who with wise filters have repelled implacable fires, am unable to escape my own flames.*
>
> *The same spells leave me, and sweet sleep keeps away from me, unhappy, from me, who could put a flame-eyed dragon to sleep!*
>
> *A rival now embraces that body which I saved; she enjoys now the fruit of my labour. And you, Jason, are inventing slanders against my appearance and my manners to brag to your new companion! Let her laugh and rejoice at my faults!*

> *She will cry, and the flames that will burn her will exceed my own!*
> *As long as there are iron, fire and poisonous juices, no enemy of Medea will go unpunished. [...]"*

(Ovid, 2006, Epistle XII. Henceforth adaptation and editing by Manuela Kustermann, unless otherwise stated).

Penelope to Ulysses

Penelope is the woman eternally waiting for her husband confined to the house, abandoned with a heavy responsibility of being the mistress of the house and managing her future. Almost forgotten by Ulysses, she remains faithful to him, bound to her role as his wife. It is the eternal symbol of dedication and absolute fidelity.

> *"This letter, sent by your Penelope, Oh Ulysses slow to return! You need not answer: come yourself!*
> *Troy, you know, fell, Priam and the whole of Troy, were hardly worth such a price! Oh, if then, when setting sail for Sparta, Paris had been submerged by the raging waves!*
> *I would not have lain, cold, in the deserted bridal bed, and I would not in my abandonment have lamented the slow passing of the days, nor while trying to deceive the long night hours, would the pendulous canvas tire my hands.[...]"*

(Ovid, Book I)

Canace in Macareus

Canale is subservient to a domineering father who will drive her to suicide to save her lost honour after giving herself for love to her brother Macareus and bearing his child, betrayed by her own naivety when love and the discovery of eros overwhelm her. An example of a bad sentimental upbringing, Canace represents the woman who is the victim of her father's ignorance, power and cruelty.

> *"I Canace, daughter of Aeolus, send to thee*
> *Macareus, son of Aeolus, the good that she has not.*
> *If some words escape you, obscured by stains, it will be because my blood fell on the letter. The right-hand holds the pen. The other hand grips a weapon and the paper.*
> *This is the image of Aeolus's daughter writing to*
> *her brother: it seems in this way I can*
> *appease our harsh father*
> *I would like him to be the spectator of my death and the action to be carried out under the eyes of him who wanted it: cruel as he is, he would*

look at my wounds with dry cheeks. Surely one does not live in vain with the cruel winds: he sends Zephyrus, Noto, Borea, Levante. He commands the winds, but alas, he does not command the fury of his wrath. Why, brother, have you loved me more than a brother, and have I been for you what a sister should not be? [...]"

(Ovid, Epistle XI)

Ariadne to Theseus

Ariadne is another example of man's indifference and opportunism towards women.

Abandoned by Theseus on a desert island, after having left her homeland, betrayed and sacrificed her own family blinded by love, Ariadne is an example of the brutal cynicism of a man who, after having promised eternal love and protection, unscrupulously leaves his beloved to her fate of death.

"She who was abandoned to the ferocious beasts, cruel Theseus, is still alive, and you, in the face of this, remain unmoved? No one worse than you could have been entrusted with me. What you read, Theseus, I write to you from that shore where the sails carried your ship away without me, where my sleep badly betrayed me, and you with it, you who deceived my sleep.

It was the hour when the earth begins to sprinkle with frost crystals, and under the foliage, the birds begin their wailing.

Only partly awake, in the torpor left by sleep, I moved my hands to embrace Theseus! I retract my hands and try again, moving my arms across the bed: You were gone! Fear shook me from my sleep. I jump up, terrified, and my body leaps out of the abandoned bed. [...]

(Ovid Epistle X)

Metamorphoses

Cinzia Merlin's piano 'Metamorphosys' takes us on a transformative journey beyond time, freeing music from the conventional and giving the classical music repertoire an innovative extension that stems from contemporary influences with an impetus towards new artistic explorations. In a musical act, flowing in rhapsodic form and reflecting the relationship between past, present and future through new aesthetic awareness, the musical patterns create links and connections between composers as far apart as J. S. Bach, crossing D. Scarlatti, A. Siloti, F. Chopin,

F. Schubert, B. Bartok, S. Prokofiev, C. Debussy, A. Piazzolla, up to the living composer M. Tisano. 'Metamorphosys' frees music from the conventional. A profound artistic reflection on the concept of mutation, change and transformation. Reflecting the relationship between past, present, and future, it projects it towards new horizons through new aesthetic awareness. The relationship between the musical art of the past, represented by the classical repertoire, and the new contemporary artistic trends in music, lead to this new and profound reflection on the concept of change and transformation.

'Metamorphosys' aims to express a new interpretative evolution, giving the classical repertoire an innovative aesthetic that stems from new contemporary artistic influences and an impetus towards the future. Through an artistic synthesis between past and contemporary, it wants to reinterpret the classical tradition through an idea of change and artistic contamination as an added value to it.

'Metamorphosys' expresses timeless music, breaking the 'rules' of classical programmes. Interpreting music as an art form that, by crossing time, enriches the past through an awareness of change in the present and projects it into the future. This reinterpretation of the classical tradition aims to break down the barriers of cultured music and open the doors to a wider audience.

In this innovative perspective on music, 'Metamorphosys' could only lead naturally to contamination with other art forms.

The show

"Ovidio. Heroides vs Metamorphosys" is a performance born from the artistic encounter between Manuela Kustermann, an oneiric messenger of words and poetry of the great Latin poet Ovidio and Cinzia Merlin virtuoso pianist. Both engaged in the search for a path of contamination of the arts, and they propose a fusion of music and poetry where the boundaries of one and the other are lost in both artistic pathways, giving rise to an infinite journey of transformations.

Produced by Fabbrica dell'Attore, the show premiered in live streaming from 17 to 29 November 2020 on the stage of the 'Teatro Vascello' in Rome. The sudden decision to premiere the show via live streaming was dictated by the need and impossibility of performing live due to the COVID-19 pandemic. The streaming mode impacted the staging, as it did not allow for more significant scene changes, but the result achieved was a great response from the audience and the critics. The fusion and understanding between music and poetry was successful.

In a scenic space where the intense vocal sounds of the word meet, clash and merge with the hidden meanings of the music narrated by a piano under the aura of the Latin poet Ovid, the performance between poetic and sonorous acts takes place in a black setting where the exception is the faces and bodies of Ovid's heroines interpreted by Manuela Kustermann and Cinzia Merlin's illuminated piano. All this is told in a perfect synthesis of theatre and music in which literary and musical classicism is reinterpreted and renewed towards the new horizons of contemporaneity. After this introduction, it is time to explore this artistic fusion of words and music.

"Ovidio. Heroids vs Metamorphosys" On Stage

The black veil unrolled in front of the stage is about to welcome the projections of images of female statues by Canova immortalised by Mimmo Jodice. The stage space is dark.

> *"To narrate the changing of forms into new bodies, my inspiration drives me. O gods, if these metamorphoses are yours, inspire my drawing so that the song from the origins of the world may unfold to my day.*
>
> *Before the sea, the earth and the sky, which covers everything, there was only one face of nature in the whole universe, that which is called Chaos.*
>
> *There was no Titan to give light to the world, nor Phoebe renewing her white horns; in the midst of the air, governed by gravity, the earth did not hover, nor along the edges of the continents did Amphitrite extend her arms. Nothing had a stable form, and each thing opposed the other because, in one body, cold fought with heat, wet with dry, soft with hard, weight with weightlessness. A god, with the favour of nature, healed these contrasts:*
>
> *from the sky separated the earth, from the earth, the sea and from the dense air marked out the clear sky.*
>
> *And having disentangled the elements out of the formless mass, he reunited those dispersed in space in concordant harmony."*
>
> (Ovid 2005, Book 1)

The performance opens with these words from Book I of Ovid's *Metamorphoses*. Manuela Kustermann's recorded voice echoes in the darkness of the initial stage space. After a few sentences, the music comes on. While a faint light illuminates the pianist, the poetic tale of the origins of the world is wrapped in the purest and most perfect balance of the notes of the 'Prelude in C Major' from the first volume of J. S. Bach's Well-Tempered Clavier, the incipit of Cinzia Merlin's 'Metamorphosys'.

At the end of the word, the musical flow continues without pause. Suddenly, like a rift, the prelude's perfect harmonic peace in C major is shattered by the impetuousness of the 'Prelude in C Minor' from the first volume of J. S. Bach's 'Well-Tempered Clavier,' firm in its obstinate and disruptive rigour. After the 'Prelude in C Minor,' the music is transformed and moves to 'Prelude After Bach' by Massimiliano Tisano, a living contemporary composer. The piece was written specifically for 'Metamorphosys' and, after an incipit of quatrains inspired by Bach's prelude, develops into a brilliant and virtuosic jazz solo at its climax. A double grand glissando in fortissimo concludes the piece. Silence.

Ipsipile's curse on Jason, an anguished omen of misfortune, slices through the stage like a blade from offstage.

Medea enters the scene. The garment alone is in view, illuminated by a sharp light and wrapped in gold embroidery. The heroine's monologue is set to the rarefied harmonies of F. Chopin's 'Nocturne in C# Minor.' Medea unfolds her tale in an increasing flow of pathos and excitement that contrasts with the poignant calmness of the Nocturne. This dramatic climax culminates in the repentance of having given help to Jason, her unfaithful husband, and results in the fiercest anger, pondering enormous thoughts of revenge. At the end of the words, this wrath resounds overwhelmingly in F. Chopin's 'Fantasia Impromtu in C# Minor Op.66.'

An arpeggio on C# prepares the entrance of the recorded chorus of "Ulixe", composed especially for the performance by M. Tisano, whose text is taken from Ovid's original text. The piano accompanies the chorus piece introducing Penelope's scene.

An amber light illuminates the scene. A long table still laden with the remains of food evokes memories of the Procians' banquet. Penelope slumped in the middle of the long royal table, raises her head and invokes her Ulysses, slow to return. In the letter to her beloved, Penelope is fragile, unhappy, abandoned and frustrated by waiting for her husband to return against her father's wishes. A kind of second piano rhapsody accompanies the story. The musical act begins with the melancholic prelude Op. 28 No. 6 by F. Chopin and runs through the purity of the 'Prelude in B Minor' by J. S. Bash/A.Siloti. At the end of the Prelude by J. S. Bach/Siloti, Penelope leaves the stage to make way for the rhythmic impetuosity of A. Piazzolla's sweeping 'Escualo', which, echoing with its virtuosity, concludes Penelope's page.

Tones of red illuminate the scene of Canace lying on the bed. Heartbroken and heartfelt, she recounts and denounces her father's cruelty, Aeolus, the cause of her pain and death, after giving birth to "the burden of guilt laid from her womb", the fruit of incest with her brother Macero and then hidden by her nurse. The 'Funeral March' theme from F. Chopin's 'Sonata No.2 Op.35' accompanies Canace's heartbreaking final words fulfilling her father's wishes. Pierced by her own sword, Canace collapses. As in transmigration of the soul, the music continues, transforms and lives in the notes of A. Piazzolla's 'Milonga de l'Angel.'

The last scene opens with Theseus' invocation of the recorded chorus written by M. Tisano. Wrapped in the whiteness of a white dress, enters Ariadne. Here the unravelling of words and music becomes an extreme game of contamination. The letter of Ariadne and Theseus concerts extemporaneously with F. Schubert's 'Impromptu in G flat,' as a real instrumental duo. The disruptive power of the fusion of the two languages comes to life in an innovative exploration of how music and words can merge, mingle and lose themselves in each other. In the finale, Ariadne leaves the stage, and the music concludes the performance with the harmonic and virtuosic suppleness of 'Prelude' from C. Debussy's 'Pour le Piano.'

The final notes of C. Debussy will echo the voice of Ovid declaimed offstage by Manuela Kustermann:

> "I have now accomplished a deed, which neither the wrath of Jupiter, nor fire, nor iron, nor devouring time can wipe out... and my name shall remain: indelible. And wherever the Roman power extends over the tamed lands, it will be read by the people, and for all centuries,
> thanks to fame, if there is any truth in the prophecies of the poets, it will live on."
>
> (Extract from the end of *Metamorphoses*)

The performance's mechanism is based on two tracks, music and words, revealing a key contrast that is only apparent. This continuous musical sequence, drawn from compositions of several epochs and narrated by Cinzia Merlin's narrating piano, is the musical manifesto that dialogues and alternates with the scansion of these female portraits containing appeals and sufferings of the heroines interpreted by Manuela Kustermann in monologues that almost evoke a musical monodic form. Between harmony and contrast, words and music, visual and sound, and lights, this new fusion of languages comes to life as in a refined Bachian counterpoint.

Bibliography

Ovidio: Eroidi 2006. con testo latino a fronte (with front page text in Latin). Translator L. Koch. Ed. A. Barchiesi Milano: Garzanti.
Ovid: The Heroides. A Complete English Translation. Ed. A. S. Kline, 2001
Ovid. *Metamorfosi.* Testo latino a fronte (front page text in Latin). Vol. 1: Libri (Books) I-III. Milano: Garzanti.

Sitography

The Heroides
 https://www.poetryintranslation.com/PITBR/Latin/Heroideshome.php
Eroidi: https://laprofonline.wordpress.com/letteratura-latina/ovidio-heroides-lettere-damore/

Part V:

World Literature

VINICIUS DE MORAES: A MULTIFACETED BRAZILIAN ARTIST AND THE DIALOGUE BETWEEN LITERATURE AND MUSIC

RITA NAMÉ, IZABEL BRANDÃO & NICK CERAMELLA

Just like the ocean
Is only beautiful in the moonlight
Just like the song
Only makes sense if sung.[1]

Poet, Bossa Nova and The Birth of the Black Orpheus

Vinicius de Moraes (1913-1980) is an icon of the Brazilian artistic scene for many reasons. His bohemian life may appear ahead of anything, but he was much more than that, a Brazilian accomplished diplomat whose soul was tied to his poet's heart as well as his musically minded feelings. An Oxford educated scholar, whose poetry can be seen as quite academic, yet the Brazilian scholarly world was then suspicious of a connection between the academic and the popular, and Vinicius was an artist with an easy transit between both spaces even if some stiff upper lips posed against his works.

This essay is intended to introduce the Brazilian poet and musician Vinicius de Moraes, and discuss the diversity that connects him to the beauty disclosed from his poetic intimacy with the "Musica Popular Brasileira" ("Brazilian Popular Music"; henceforth MPB) of his time as well as see how he is one of the forefounders of bossa nova, the Brazilian rhythm *par excellence*, known worldwide. But we will be discussing this later.

---

[1] "Assim como o oceano/ Só é belo com o luar/ Assim como a canção/ Só tem razão se se cantar." (Moraes, 1998, 562) All the poems by Vinicius de Moraes quoted in this essay are from the 1998 edition of his *Complete Works*. (See Appendix for the poems quoted here.) All translations of the poems are by Izabel F. O. Brandão, and were especially made for this essay.

More specifically, this piece focuses on the relationship between literature and music in Vinicius's works, in that the verbal perspective (literary text, lyrics of a song) is combined with the musical one (rhythmic, melodic and formal) within the scope of musicology. In this research area, this eclectic artist was undoubtedly at ease with because when he entered the Brazilian Popular Music world halfway through the 1950s, he already occupied, as stated by Mário de Andrade (1893-1945), "a place among the greater poets of contemporary Brazil" (de Andrade, 1972, 21). And, with respect to artistic activities in general, his position was that of opening borders and cultivating reciprocal influences, thinking that the dialogue among artistic languages is active and free of hierarchies and ties. Such a dialogue occurs with Vinicius' poetry, according to his own words, reading, "if literature is literary art, the statute of poetry ought to be extended to other genres" (Moraes, 1986, 19). It is not fortuitous that this Brazilian poet is considered an artist of the transition between literature and music, and Affonso Romano de Sant'Anna (1937-) holds him responsible for the aesthetic dignity conferred to the MPB, which is mainly due to the free passage among the multiple paths that he took as an artist, in a process of maturity, rigour and mastery of the Portuguese language.

In his *Poetics I*, written in New York in 1950, Vinicius defines himself and his craft as follows:

> In the morning I darken
> In the day I dusk
> In the afternoon, I get night
> At night, I burn.
> In the west death
> Against whom I live
> From the south captive
> The east is my north.
> Let others count
> Step by step:
> I die yesterday
> I'm born tomorrow
> I walk where there is space.
>   —My time is when.
> (Moraes, 1998, 234)[2]

---

[2] "De manhã escureço/ De dia tardo/ De tarde anoiteço/ De noite ardo.// A oeste a morte/ Contra quem vivo/ Do sul cativo/ O este é meu norte.// Outros que contem/ Passo por passo:/ Eu morro ontem// Nasço amanhã/ Ando onde há espaço:/ – Meu tempo é quando".

In effect, this poem outlines what the poet and songwriter Vinicius represents in Brazilian art in the 20th century, a model of artist who dedicated his life and writings in search of a constant dialogue with various aesthetic languages and moments, trying art and cultural life in an all-encompassing way without rigid borders. The "Poetinha", the "Little Poet", as he was dearly nicknamed by his fans, exerts in an intense way both poetic communicability and social mobility. Thus, he becomes an artist who is cheered in his recitals of poems and songs in Brazil first, the whole of Latin America through the 1970s, and the rest of the world afterwards.

A bohemian spirit, poet, playwright, musician, cinema critic, reviewer, a Law graduate and diplomat, Vinicius never improvised on the stage but had lyrics and music written down in advance. That is because his education is that of a learned man, a scholar, a verbal and aesthetic polyglot who dealt with the Portuguese language with rigour, knowledge, sensibility, and poetic vitality. For a fellow poet, Carlos Drummond de Andrade (1902-1987), a leading figure of Brazilian modernism, Vinicius is the only poet in Brazil who lived and thought coherently as a poet. One cannot dissociate in his life and writings the extraordinary lyricist, the writer, the libertarian, the libertine. Had he not written his literary works, he would nevertheless be part of the MPB history with the songs that have become common currency, as Antonio Candido argues in relation to famous songs, among others, *Serenata do adeus* ("Goodbye serenade"), *Valsa de Eurídice* ("Eurydice waltz"), *Medo de amar* ("Fear of loving"), *Eu não existo sem você* ("I don't exist without you")[3] which were all set to music by Vinicius's best friend, Antonio Carlos Jobim, alias Tom Jobim (1927-1994).[4]

A lesser known feature of such a singular artist – composing both melodic and literary texts – is, nevertheless, a remarkable part of his poetic production. In the songs he wrote, Vinicius attempted different genres, themes, rhythms and melodies. His first book ever, *O caminho para a distância* ("The path towards distance") was his *debut* as a poet, singer and songwriter in the Brazilian scene in 1933. But in truth, his first appearance in the MPB had taken place the year before with *Loura ou Morena*, written in partnership with Haroldo Tapajós (1915-1994), the brother of Paulo (1913-1990), also a close friend of his. It is then that the "Little Poet" begins to work on his future recurrent themes: women, friendship, death, moon, and nature in general.

---

[3] See Rita L. P. Namé (2004), who wrote a doctoral dissertation on Vinicius de Moraes' *Songbook*. See full reference in Select Bibliography. And, in the Appendix, the poems mentioned here which have all been put to music.

[4] See more about their partnership later in this essay.

In the poems appearing in *O caminho para a distância*, he concentrates on typical Christian themes, such as the inner conflicts of the soul, characterising his youth as suggested by the dramatic title of the book itself. He was strongly influenced by the Rio de Janeiro intellectuals and metaphysicians of the time, which is shown by the mystical contents of his poems permeated by a mysterious aura. Biblical long verses found in Christian poets are used, and such a tradition initially serves as a stimulus for him, and gives this collection, from the start, a solemn and sublime tone, as in the poem *Místico* ("Mystical") "the air is fraught with mysterious whispers/ And in the mist of things there is a vague sense of spiritualizing ..." (Moraes, 1986, 61).[5] Later, this religious aura is stripped of its institutional tone and channeled towards sensuality and profane, as in the sonnet *Poetics II* (1960):

> With the tears of time
> And the lime of my day
> I made the cement
> Of my poetry.
>
> And within the perspective
> Of future life
> I've risen its architecture
> in raw flesh.
>
> I don't quite know whether it is a house
> A tower or a temple:
> (A Godless temple.)
> But it is big and clear
> It belongs to its time
> Come in, mine bretheren!
> (Moraes, 1998, 311)[6]

The eternal *liaison* between music and poetry which is the "raison d'être" of our book, is present in Vinicius's masterpiece *Orfeu da Conceição* ("Orpheus of the Immaculate Conception"), a stage play with music, representing a most relevant work in his *oeuvre*. The myth of

---

[5] "o ar está cheio de murmúrios misteriosos/ E na névoa das coisas há um vago sentido de espiritualização...".
[6] "Com as lágrimas do tempo/ E a cal do meu dia/ Eu fiz o cimento/ Da minha poesia.// E na perspectiva/ Da vida futura/ Ergui-me em carne viva/ Sua arquitetura.// Não sei bem se é casa/ Se é torre ou se é templo:/ (Um templo sem Deus.)/ Mas é grande e clara/ Pertence ao seu tempo/ – Entrai, irmãos meus!".

Orpheus, one of the most significant literary themes of western culture, evokes the Greek legend of the man whose melodic words stimulate the collective imaginary love. According to Sant'Anna, Vinicius created the image of a tropical Orpheus. Thus, this Brazilian Orfeu is an updated version of the myth filled with local tones and place. Note that the play *Orfeu da Conceição* has in the name "Conceição", a reference to the popular black character. In one of the opening stage directions, the poet recommends that "all characters ought to be acted by black actors, but, eventually, might be performed with white actors" (Moraes, 1986, 393). This "Tragédia carioca" ("Rio de Janeiro Tragedy"), as is also known, transposes the myth of Orpheus, one of the most emblematic stories of Greek mythology, to a typical Brazilian scenario, Rio de Janeiro. Before proceeding, we believe it is worth introducing this mythical legend to see the link between that world and the modern story.

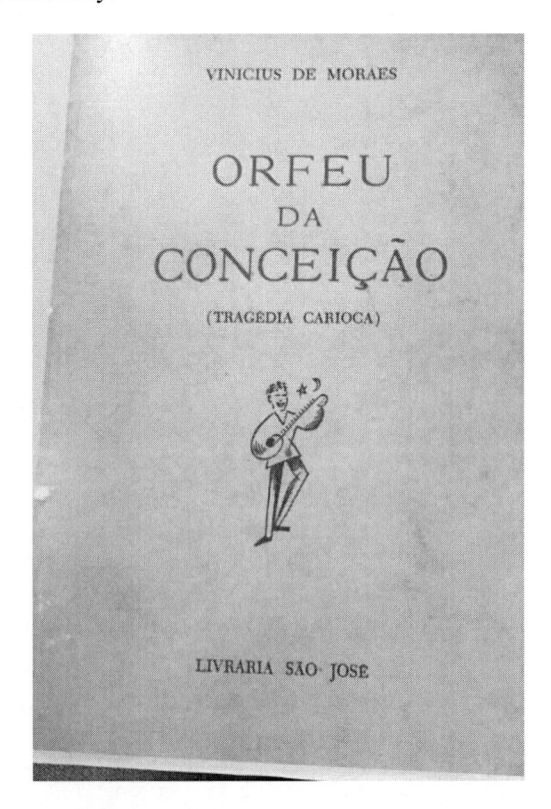

Fig. 23: Front cover of 1st edition, Rio de Janeiro 1956.

In Robert Graves's account of the myth, Orpheus was the son of Oeagrus, a Thracian King, and Calliope, one of the Muses, he "was the most famous poet and musician that ever lived" (Graves, 1988, 111). The God Apollo gave him a lyre and the Muses were his teachers. His unsurpassable ability as a player and singer helped him to enchant whoever came to contact with his music, from wild beasts to trees, and rocks. All moved to follow his divine performing and moved about him in dance. Orpheus visited many places, among them Egypt, joined the Argonauts, and married Eurydice on his return, as Graves tells (Graves, 1988, 112). This wonderful state of bliss was disrupted when one day, Aristaeus, a minor god, pursued Eurydice, who stepped on a viper and died on the spot. Orpheus in deep mourning for his beloved, becomes melancholic, and no longer enjoys life also because he realises that his melodious singing and the divine sounds of his lyre cannot console him on such an immense loss. So, despite his great despair, he descends into Tartarus, the land of the dead, hopeful to retrieve his wife. Such is the unlimited force of love that makes him even challenge death, knowing that he is putting his own life at risk, which may well be the reason why this story has fascinated human beings through the millennia, including us in modern times. Consequently, as a rule, myths usually have many versions, including those with a happy ending as is the case with the anonymous medieval English romance of *Sir Orfeo* (turn of 13th century). Mainly to put things in the right historical perspective here are some further details on the story especially for those readers who might like to go into greater depth. Orpheus' myth originated in Greek mythology, starting from the 5th Century b. C., with the poet Pindar (518-438, b. C.), who says, "from Apollo came that player of the lyre and father of songs, even Orpheus the well-praised." (1945, 41), followed by the playwrights Aeschylus (525-456 b. C.) and Aristophanes (450-385 b. C.). And then, over four centuries later came two of the greatest Latin poets, Virgil (70 b. C.–19 b. C.) first, in *Georgics*, Book IV, (a didactic poem, in the tradition of Hesiod, 29 b. C.), and Ovid (43 a. C. – 18 d. C.) in the Tenth Book of his *Metamorphosis* (8 d. C. an epic-mythologic poem). In the latter's version, even Hades and Persephone cried for the first time ever on listening to the extremely moving and enchanting song that Orpheus played. His sole condition for Eurydice's return from the Underworld was that Orpheus should never turn around to look at her. They have almost made it out and can already see the sunlight, but Orpheus falls in temptation and disobeys by looking at Eurydice who disappears immediately into hell.[7]

---

[7] Graves (1988) also connects Orpheus to Dionysus and Apollo. Both were offended by the poet and musician: he did not pay any homage to the first god (Graves, 1988, 112) who was raised as a girl and demanded that in his homage all had to be dressed

Fig. 24: *Orfeo playing the lyre.* Roman mosaic floor II c. a. D. Palermo Archeological Museum (Sicily, Italy).

With respect to the above, it is useful to know that Vinicius, from the age of 11, attended the Jesuit school St Ignatius in Rio de Janeiro where he was imbued with classical studies which enhanced his sensitivity and interest in the wonderful ancient classical world, and the fascination for myths like that of Orpheus and Eurydice. The idea of transposing it from ancient Greece to a "favela" (slum) in Rio began spinning round the poet's mind since 1942, when he, on accompanying the American poet Waldo Frank (1889-1967) around Brazil, came to contact with the reality, that he did not know himself until then, the world of the Afro-Brazilians. That is

---

as women. Dionysus ordered the Maenads to punish him. He was dismembered and his head ended up to rest in a cave in Antissa, sacred to Dionysus. There it provoked Apollo's jealousy after seeing his temples in Delphi, Gryneium, and Clarus deserted because Orpheus's head (severed by Dionysus' Maenads) was prophesying day and night. This also prompted the god to punish Orpheus by asking the head to stop interfering with his business. (1988, 113) This leads to Orpheus' habit of disobedience, which caused him to lose Eurydice in their return from the Underworld.

when he began to see a comparison between the black people, living in the "favelas", and the tragic Greek heroes of the mythic times. As we know from Vinicius himself, as early as 1942, he was spending a few days at his great friend's Carlos Leão, Cavalão Hill, Niterói, a municipality near Rio, where, while reading a book on Greek mythology, he heard a 'batucada' (a percussive substyle of samba) from a nearby "favela" which got him to discover the Rio samba schools that were rehearsing for the Carnival Festival. It is then that he began to write *Orfeu da Conceição*, and there was virtually the first act of the play. This intelligent re-reading of an ancient Greek myth, looking into the modern social reality, represents to this day a landmark of the marriage between poetry and popular music as well as theatre and song. The play was immediately a top-of-the-bill attraction at the Teatro Municipal in Rio, in 1956. It arose people's curiosity and interest for a variety of reasons, including the enchanting music, and also because Vinicius upheld a revolutionary idea that actors on the stage had to be all black and only exceptionally they could be white. After the song *Monólogo de Orfeu* ("Orpheus Monologue"), a scene of the play's first act shows that

> "Orpheus' guitar already begins to open towards a new melody that the musician resumes. Little by little the samba is unveiled, and in the meantime the words form naturally in the same wave of the rehearsal. Orpheus sings [...]" (Moraes, 1986, 476)

Indeed, Vinicius's brilliant idea to ask Tom Jobim to compose the music for the drama gave an enormous contribution to its success, thus beginning the fruitful collaboration between the poet and the composer. Vinicius argued that he had no idea as to the extent of his request, as illustrated by the song *Se todos fossem iguais a você* ("If everyone were like you"). In the early 1960s, he declares:

> I had no idea that I was giving the young carioca composer – a true native from Ipanema – the starting point for our bossa nova renewal movement, which earned international visibility. Parallel to this, other young songwriters such as Carlos Lyra, Roberto Menescal, the brothers Mario and Oscar Castro Neves would compose individually in the same sense, in a sort of telepathic work that was to be united in a common wave after the birth of Tom Jobim's songs in the LP *Canção do amor demais* ("Song of the too much love") sung by Elisete Cardoso. Here a singer and a guitar player, at the time just known by his most intimate friends, João Gilberto, would accompany Elisete with a new guitar beat, which was to become the rhythmic mark of the modern Brazilian samba. (Moraes, 1986, 685)

From then on, the story is well known, and much has been written and spoken about bossa nova. But, as stated above, this is an aspect which, again, surely deserves to be analysed a little more in depth, given the nature of our book. The partnership of Vinicius and Jobim, embodies the living weavering of word and popular music at its utmost level. Jobim was the first musician to start this new trend with his *Sinfonia de Rio de Janeiro* ("Rio de Janeiro's Symphony", 1955). Indeed, bossa nova is a style of samba which originated in the Afro-Brazilian communities of Rio de Janeiro at the beginning of the 20th century, though the official date of birth of bossa nova coincides with the issue of the record, featuring *Cançao do amor demais* in 1958, a song sung by Elizete Cardoso, composed and played on piano by Jobim, lyrics by Vinicius, and also João Gilberto on guitar in the song *Chega de saudade*. Mainly for the pleasure and satisfaction of those readers who are more into the technical aspects of bossa nova, we will hint at Gilberto's contribution to the creation of bossa nova with his "batida", a typical playing style alternating the thumb on the bass strings while picking the other strings (cf. the forefather of bossa nova Dorival Caymmi), and often tapping with the left hand.

The result is an offbeat rhythm, that does not follow the standard beat which, besides changing the conventional harmonies and chords, introduced also an innovative syncopation, giving birth to the characteristic bossa nova beat. Here is an example of bossa nova progression for piano by the American composer William Neil:

The success of bossa nova, a new musical genre deriving from samba, in the form of *samba canção* was criticised because of the North American influence stretching to "cool jazz" and describing the daily life in Rio de Janeiro. Yet bossa nova eventually spread all over the world and even influenced the American music scene. For example, the American saxophone player Stan Getz and the guitarist Charlie Byrd imported the new Brazilian rhythm into the United States with their record *1962 Jazz Samba*. Meanwhile, bossa nova contributed dramatically to change the stereotyped Hollywoodian view of Brazil by moving the focus from Copacabana Beach to Ipanema with *Garota de Ipanema* ("The girl from Ipanema"), a landmark in the collaboration between Vinicius and Jobim which marked a definite change of the world's approach to Brazilian music and society between 1962-64. It seems that this was mainly due to the "menina carioca cheia de graça" ("the girl from Rio full of grace") who became the symbol of Brazilian beauty. Rumour has it that there was a craze among Brazilian girls who declared that they were Vinicius's muse, but now we know who she really was, a seventeen-year-old girl, known as Helô (short for Heloisa) whose real name Pinheiro, is Heloisa Eneida Menzes Pain Pinto, a former model, now a still very elegant seventy-five businesswoman. As the legend goes, it was 1962, Vinicius and Jobim used to have a drink every morning at the Bar do Veloso (today Bar Garota de Ipanema), situated in Rua Montenegro (today, Rua Vinicius de Morais), where Helô used to live, and they noticed her strolling to go to Ipanema Beach just across the road. They were both struck by her stunning beauty and her samba like allure. In an interview with Lorena Arroyo of BBC Mundo, she declared: "A photographer who had taken some photographs of me for a magazine informed me that he was in a bar when Tom and Vinicius told him they had written a song for me." Only three years later, Vinicius asked the girl's mother if he could reveal the identity of the 'Garota de Ipanema," while Jobim even asked her to marry him.

Today, there is nearby, the cultural centre, Espaço Cultural Toca do Vinicius entirely dedicated to Vinicius and bossa nova. It goes without saying that this place has become a world tourist landmark, which tells us how strong the impact of Vinicius's art still is. Yet, he acknowledged that he did not create bossa nova, adding that it originates from a series of historical, economical and artistic situations in Brazil of the 1950s/1960s where one finds concrete poetry, concrete painting of the late 1950s, the stripped down and crystalline decaphonism and serialism of the concert music of the post-war introduced in Brazil by J. Koellreuter, the intellectualized intimacy of the *Nouvelle Vague* in the cinema, the curved lines of Niemayer's white architecture, the building of the Capital Brasília. According to Vinicius:

> Bossa nova is the modern daughter of the traditional samba that had a fling with Jazz, bringing melodic improvisation and the use of the harmonic fabric that weaves melody with grace and lightness unknown to the old forms of samba that is more anchored in rhythm and percussion. (Moraes, 1986, 685).

Fig. 25: Landmark 'Garota de Ipanema' bar, Rio de Janeiro

Fig. 26: Original score *Garota de Ipanema* at the bar in Rio.

Indeed, the bossa nova movement brought a continuity of the trail of changes that occurred during the 1920s and 1930s, originating as a result of a "mood of change of emphasis," a term coined by Antônio Candido (1918-

2017) and spread during the "Semana de 22."[8] This implies a turn, which is not radical in the body of doctrines that rules a certain moment, for the change of positions occur in a progressive way and new balances appear to replace older aesthetic parametres. We can refer to the example of *Macunaíma* by Mário de Andrade (1893-1945), whose satirical sharpness seems to show already in 1928, the moment of the turning point, stressing alternatively the humorous and melancholy tone of the Brazilian "without a character". On this subject, the musicologist Martha Ulhôa refers to the relevance of bossa nova in the Brazilian historical context:

> The autonomy project of Brazilian music has a distinctive double face, both connected to modernism; a first phase of classical music, beginning with the Semana de 22 and becoming stronger with the modernists around Mário de Andrade, and a second phase, sparked by the Bossa Nova movement and radicalized by tropicalists in the area of popular music. (Ulhôa, 1999, 87)

Regarding the artist who made this profound cultural change possible there is, João Gilberto who is responsible for a new diction in his musical research, in the singing and playing the guitar, whereas Tom Jobim adds new melodic and harmonious possibilities, and Vinicius de Moraes completes such tendencies by bringing his experience as a poet to the lyrics of the songs, having what we call poetic license, to make such a lyrical state colloquial, without forgoing the quality of his verses, as in the song that became a milestone of the movement, *Chega de saudade* ("Enough of longing"). The cultural diversity of Brazilian popular music of that period, which introduced the "samba-canção" from the 1940s, the passionate and romantic thematic, the *baião*[9] by Luiz Gonzaga (1912-89), as well as the 1950s post-ward trends of the western world, alongside the success of Hollywood movies that join the jazz masters, everything works as aesthetic yeast to compose this new musical landscape with the young musicians

---

[8] Translator's note: This term refers to a Brazilian subversive art movement that demarcates a sweeping change in Brazilian art in general, literature and painting in particular. Names such as Mário de Andrade in literature, and Tarsila do Amaral (1886-1973) in painting, are but two of those who contributed to a new air in the country as regards freedom from European influence in favor of a more national tone to the art produced in Brazil.

[9] Translator's note: This musical genre is defined as a kind of choreography conjugated with simultaneous singing that is quite popular in the Northeast of Brazil. It originates in Africa, from one of its "lundu" modes – a musical style generated by the rumbling of the African drums set by the Bantu slaves from Angola who came to Brazil during the slave period. See https://www.infoescola.com/musica/baiao/ acesso em September 20 2020.

from the southern zone of Rio de Janeiro, mostly middle class and university educated. Tired of imports and versions which they simply had to accept, they decided, then, to disrupt this trend and risk a new kind of samba appropriating the jazz procedure as well as other originating from erudite music. From jazz, such an appropriation happens in a quite innovative way, for, while in jazz, the musical specificity is in its harmonic basis and about it improvisation follows, in bossa nova a new conception of improvisation occurs, that is more along the melodical line than with the harmonic. Such a form of innovation, through the melody, is a historical tradition of the popular Brazilian music. As a musical expression, bossa nova was situated rigorously within its own cultural context in that the art borders are deconstructed by creating a new form of expression in all languages. The bossa nova musicians undertook academic studies both at a practical and theoretical level, which allowed them to get along with poets, writers and journalists, thus bringing to the new Brazilian samba a different and more conscious way of expressing itself. We can say that at that moment, the encounter of various cultures is affected by Brazilian popular music, whose analysis had a bearing on the polemic that arose among historians, for, on the one hand, it brings the appropriation of external elements, and on the other, the renewal of the samba. A bridge is also built between the stylistic elements stemming from erudite music that, during the 1920s up to the 1950s, occupied a distinctive place in the Brazilian musical scenario, and popular elements from the music performed in backyards, *terreiros*,[10] and also in the streets. As Ulhôa writes, in the study already quoted above, "the emergence of bossa-nova ended up being accounted for within the pairing tradition-innovation" (Moraes 1999, 88).

It is acknowledged that, the emergence of a renovating attitude, in the sense of opening new ways for old musicians and new talents, is an act that disrupts borders and builds a new poetical-musical paradigm in the Brazilian popular music, having as one of its backbones the poet Vinicius de Moraes who anticipated the tropicalist behavior of the late 1960s, mixing the erudite and the popular music and other arts. It was this poet who gave Brazilian poetry the bossa nova. As a master of the new rhythm, his artistic *oeuvre* now is not only in the books, but also makes room in bars, universities, student movements, in meetings with partners and, despite having changed the tragic with the trivial, and the great metaphysical questionings for little emotions, which is typical of the more popular inviting genre, it is under the lyrical mood that the poet Vinicius de Moraes

---

[10] A place where Afro-Brazilian religious rituals are performed. See https://brasilescola.uol.com.br/religiao/diferenca-entre-candomble-umbanda.htm access 15 October 2020.

continues to carry out his artistic project with the bossa nova. The convergence of these cultural strata constitutes a good pluralistic basis ever open to new experiences. With Tom Jobim, he was a bossa nova man; with Carlos Lyra, he was lyrical and contesting; with Baden Powell, he founded the basis for the Afro-sambas; with Toquinho, he consolidated the exciting popular, traditional samba. Equally important is his double role of songwriter (i.e., poet) and composer of the music of his songs. He united these different features by updating them in twenty-one songs in the condition of a poet who transcended the limits of time and who, in anticipation of his trajectory towards posterity, once wrote: "I walk where there is space/ My time is when" (Moraes, 1986, 277).

Vinicius de Moraes defines bossa nova as follows:

> [...] It is more the loneliness of a street in Ipanema than the agitation of commercial Copacabana; it is more a gaze than a kiss; more tenderness than passion; more a note than a message. [...]
>
> Bossa nova is the pure and lonely song of João Gilberto forever locked in his flat, searching for a more and more extreme and simple harmony in the cords of his guitar and a more and more perfect emission for the sounds and words of his song. [...]
>
> Bossa nova is the suffering of many a young in the whole world, searching in the tranquility of music not for the escape and alienation to the problems of their time, but for the most harmonious way of constituting them. Bossa nova is the new intelligence, the new rhythm, the new sensibility, and the new secret of youth in Brazil. (Moraes, 1986, 645-647)

That Vinicius's masterpiece was going to be an influential work seemed like it immediately. The French film director, Jean Cocteau, after his first retelling of the myth under the title *Le sang d'un poet* ("The blood of a poet", 1930), followed by *Orphée* (1950) – set in Nazi occupied Paris – concludes his "Trilogie orphique" with *Le testament d'Orphé* ("Orpheus's Will"1960). In 1959, another French version, based on Vinicius' play, directed by Marcel Camus, *Black Orpheus* ("Orpheu Negro") which was awarded with the *Palme d'Or* at the Cannes Film Festival,[11] gave a further boost to popularise bossa nova. The film is set in Rio, full of music and dance work, where a couple from a "favela" rambles around the carnival parade harassed by Death. Despite that, Vinicius and Jobim, as well as many Brazilians were not happy that Afro-Brazilian culture was treated like as an exotic attraction rather than capturing the deep meaning of a serious stage play. The good thing, though, is that Vinicius and Jobim became an

---

[11] The movie also won an Oscar for best foreign film in 1960.

unsurpassable songwriting duo, with a soundtrack including international hits as the opening piece *Saudade, Samba de Orfeu* ("Orpheus' samba"), *Manhã de carnival* ("Carnival morning"), and *Chega de Saudade* (also known as "No more blues"), which by becoming classics established the bossa nova standard.

Fig. 27: Film poster *Orfeo Negro*, 1959.

All that happened during a period when other versions of the Orpheus myth such as the ballet dance *Orpheus* by Igor Stravinsky (1882-1971) and another three-act-play by Tennessee Williams (1911-83) were being shown in Europe and America. In recent years, a Brazilian film titled *Orfeu* (1998) has been made and shown in Brazil. It pays homage to some of the music in the original film, while even if is based directly on Vinicíus' play, it is updated to the 1990s. *Gravity's Rainbow* is a 1973 novel by Thomas Pyncheon, an American writer to whom an essay has been dedicated in our book. Finally, in 1999, the Scottish poet Carol Ann Duffy retells the myth from a feminist point of view in the poem "Eurydice". On concluding we cannot but say that if the text (i. e. the poetry of this myth) is important, the myth's legacy lies mainly in music. In fact, the artist who was inspired by the tragic, romantic story of Orpheus and Eurydice, was the Italian Claudio Monteverdi (1576-1643), who composed a true masterpiece in 1607, the first of many musical dramas based on the Greek myth, which paved the path to the *Orpheus* by Christoph Willibald Gluck (1714-87), represented at the Opera House in Vienna, in 1762; *Orpheus in the Underworld* (1858) by Jacques Offenbach (1818-1880). Then in contemporary days, the opera

The Mask of Orpheus (1986) by the English composer Harrison Birtwistle (1934-), and Anaïs Mitchell's Broadway hit *Hadestown*, whose latest version was presented in 2019, which is set in America's Deep South. These either as operas and musicals are among the greatest works to have added to a canon that continues to expand. Such updating and adaptation of poetical sources are a common feature to Vinician dramaturgy through the diving into Brazilian culture. This is also the case with his poems and lyrics, and supports the hybrid construction of this black Orpheus, a metaphor that translates the relationship that the poet carries out with the varied strata which form South American culture at large.

The Vinician space is a multifarious one: his own songs, poems and music get along with songs in partnership, verses with classic metre alongside sonnets and ballads with a popular diction, as in the poem *Operário em construção* ("Worker in progress"). In this poem yet again Vinicius pays a visit to religious myths and turns them into profane ones by using colloquialisms, with the time accent of a 1960s Brazil, suffering from a democratic threat, and that in 1964 endured a military *coup d'état* that lasted for over two long decades. This poem was read, as a homily in a 1 May 1979 mass, in the *ABC Paulista* area, a space for workers, manifesting a cry for freedom and boldness to take action. Below is an extract of the poem:

> It was him who built houses
> Where before there was just ground.
> As a wingless bird
> He rose with the houses
> That sprouted from his hand. [...]
>
> And it was in such way that the worker
> Of the rising building
> Who always said yes
> Started to say no. [...]
> He noted that his packed lunch
> Was the boss's dish
> That his black beer
> Was the master's scotch
> That his jeans jumpsuit
> Was the boss's suit
> That the hut he lived
> Was the boss's mansion
> [...]
> And the worker heard the voice
> Of all his brothers
> His brothers who had died

For others who shall live.
A candid hope
Grew in his heart
And within the soft afternoon
Reason grew larger
In a poor and forgotten man
Reason yet that grew
Inside the worker built
A worker in progress.
(Moraes, 1998, 252-56)[12]

The aforementioned book also contains poems that initially receive musical accompaniment like the *Monólogo de Orfeu* as well as poems whose encounter between word and music, later, are turned into songs, such as *Soneto de Fidelidade* ("Sonnet of fidelity") written in 1939, and put to music by the songwriter Lourenço da Fonseca Barbosa, known as Capiba, from Pernambuco, in 1955. In the 1950s and 1960s, Vinicius is definitely part of MPB, and reveals one more of his interfaces, for as he embraces the popular Brazilian music, he does not shun from the poetic perspective that includes the lyrical trend which always accompanied him. By the 1970s, better known due to music rather than literature, he makes a statement that defines his role as a Brazilian artist: "I'm a poet before anything, and my cultural activity has to be evaluated from thenceforth" (Moraes, 684). Music is thus his newest lyrical adventure ally.

Conclusion

If Vinicius de Moraes lived here in the present Brazilian cultural context, he might say that there is always room for a bossa nova, a new intelligence, a new sensibility, and new human and aesthetic relations. It is little wonder that his poetical trajectory disappoints the purists, for he has started with

---

[12] "Era ele que erguia casas/ Onde antes só havia chão./ Como um pássaro sem asas/ Ele subia com as casas/ Que lhe brotavam da mão...//... E foi assim que o operário/ Do edifício em construção/ Que sempre dizia sim/ Começou a dizer não...// Notou que sua marmita/ Era o prato do patrão/ Que sua cerveja preta/ Era o uísque do patrão/ Que seu macacão de zuarte/ Era o terno do patrão/ Que o casebre onde morava/ Era a mansão do patrão...//... E o operário ouviu a voz/ De todos os seus irmãos/ Os seus irmãos que morreram/ Por outros que viverão./ Uma esperança sincera/ Cresceu no seu coração/ E dentro da tarde mansa/ Agigantou-se a razão/ De um homem pobre e esquecido/ Razão porém que fizera/ Em operário construído/ O operário em construção."

Christian poetry, but he also disappoints Christian poets, for he moves to modernist poetry. Likewise, he disappoints the modernists by embracing the MPB with his bossa nova and, again, he disillusions by composing a hedonist samba, carefree of any trend, looking more like someone in free fall.

It is possible to state that the bases structuring the Vinician poetics are built and fed within this dynamic and renewed dialogue which the author keeps with the diverse poetic sources he uses: at times, the Christian poets with their biblical verses and their metaphysical and sublime preoccupations; at others, the French poets and a more profane vision of poetry; some other times the colloquial tones and the anxieties of Brazilian poetry after the "Semana de 22", thus, taking lessons from Manuel Bandeira, Mário de Andrade, among others, until he found his own way, made up of all these contributions. These bases also set the cultural structure of the musician, and are at the service of Vinicius de Moraes the composer, who, in the 1950s, embraces MPB as one more of his poetical performances.

Vinicius de Moraes takes on the trends from a modern place and time relating a game between feelings of joy and melancholy, from the meeting and misencounter of tradition, contemporary society, and culture.

Concerning that, T. S. Elliot (1888-1965), an Anglo-American poet Vinicius admired, writes, in the literary magazine *The Egoist* (1919):

> Yet if the only form of tradition, of handing down, consisted in following the ways of the immediate generation before us in a blind or timid adherence to its successes, "tradition" should positively be discouraged. We have seen many such simple currents soon lost in the sand; and novelty is better than repetition. Tradition is a matter of much wider significance. It cannot be inherited, and if you want it you must obtain it by great labour. (Eliot, 1987, 2536)

In brief, "tradition" is not inherited in a passive way, copied or repeated, whoever wants it must earn it through a big effort. In this sense, the "Little Poet" appropriates the matrices of Brazilian popular music and, simultaneously, constitutes, what we know as his "Songbook", a new space for creation, putting music to old sounds and creating a new semantics for themes within tradition.

Like Orpheus who, in Greek mythology, is the creator *par excellence* and has his life marked by an aesthetic and a playful sense, and pacifies human beings and impresses the gods, Vinicius' authorial project mobilizes, through songs, the love imaginary of his community, uniting elements of our cultural and aesthetic imaginary. Moreover, as a Brazilian poet, musician and singer, he personifies and brings to the fore the updated Greek myth, as a Tropical Orpheus, a Black Orpheus, an "Orfeo Negro" in Brazilian land. In this connection, it must be underlined that, even if the entire soundtrack of the film is absolutely unforgettable and moving, the "leitmotif," "Manhã de Carnaval," which is heard in the background every now and then, from the opening till the end, was born from the meeting of the musical knowledge with the literary knowledge, which Vinicius through his outstanding artistry managed to transform into a song that forty years after his death is still listened to, studied and admired everywhere. Perhaps only *Garota de Ipanema*, which is sung even in Esperanto, and interpreted by artists going from Sinatra to the jazz version by Stan Getz and Astrud Gilberto, let alone the arrangements of symphonic orchestras, is more popular than "Manhã de Carnaval, / Orpheo Negro." Indeed, *Garota*, in terms of popularity, is second only to The Beatles' "Yesterday."

Saravá, Vinicius de Moraes![13]

GAROTA DE IPANEMA THE GIRL FROM IPANEMA

    Olha que coisa mais linda, *Tall and tan and young and lovely*
    Mais cheia de graça *The girl from Ipanema goes walking*
    É ela, a menina que vem e que passa *And when she passes, each one she passes*
    Num doce balanço caminho do mar.*Goes "a-a-a-h"*

    Moça do corpo dourado*When she walks she's like a samba*
    Do sol de Ipanema *When she walks, she's like a samba*
    O seu balançado *That swings so cool and sways so gentle*
    É mais que um poema *That when she passes, each one she passes*
    É a coisa mais linda *Goes "a-a-a-h"*
    Que eu já vi passar.

    Ah, porque estou tão sozinho *Oh, but I watch her so sadly*
    Ah, porque tudo é tão triste*How can I tell her I love her*
    Ah, a beleza que existe *Yes, I would give my heart gladly*
    A beleza que não é só minha *But each day as she walks to the sea*
    Que também passa sozinha.*She looks straight ahead not at me.*

    Ah, se ela soubesse *Tall and tan and young and lovely*
        Que quando ela passa*The girl from Ipanema goes walking*
        O mundo interinho*I smile but she doesn't see*
        Se enche de graça (Translation by Normal Gibel)
        E fica mais lindo
        Por causa do amor.

---

[13] Translator's note: Saravá! is a welcoming greeting in Afro-Brazilian religions. See https://www.wemystic.com.br/sarava-o-que-isto-significa/ access 6 October 2020.

Fig. 28: In the background: Girl on Ipanema Beach, Rio, 2017, Now as Ever. "Look at this wonderful creature / so graceful / It's she, the girl / who comes and just passes / swinging softly towards the sea."

Select bibliography

Album, Ricardo Cravo. 2010. *Vinicius de Moraes*. Instituto Cultural Cravo Albin/ Faperj/Mec.
Andrade, Mário. 1980. *Pequena história da música*. São Paulo: Martins,
—. *O empalhador de passarinho*. 3rd ed. São Paulo: Martins, 1972.
Arroyo, Lorena. "The authentic Girl of Ipanema." In BBC Mundo, 30 Jan 2012; retrieved on 12 Nov. 2020: https://www.bbc.com/mundo/noticias/2012/02/120130_garota_de_ipanema_helo_pinheiro_lav
Bandeira, Manuel.1977. *Poesia completa e prosa*. Rio de Janeiro: Aguilar,
—. "Coisa Alóvena, Ebaente". 2004. In Ferraz, Eucanaã (org). *Vinicius de Moraes: poesia completa e prosa*. Rio de Janeiro: Nova Aguilar, 87-89.
Brown, Calvin. 1987. S. *Music and literature*. London; Hanover: University Press of New England.
Candido, Antonio. 2008. "Um poema de Vinicius de Moraes". In *Poemas, sonetos e baladas e Pátria minha*. São Paulo: Companhia das Letras, 159-162.
—. "Vinicius de Moraes". 2004. In: Ferraz, Eucanaã (org). *Vinicius de Moraes: poesia completa e prosa*. Rio de Janeiro: Nova Aguilar. 120-122.

Castello, José. 1997. *Vinícius de Moraes: o poeta da paixão*. 2nd ed. São Paulo: Companhia das Letras.
—. 1995. *Livro das letras*. São Paulo: Companhia das Letras.
Chediak, Almir. *Songbook de Vinicius de Moraes*. Vol. I, II, III. Rio de Janeiro: Lumiar, no date.
Chevalier, J.; Gheerbrant, A. 1996. *The Penguin Dictionary of Symbols*. Translation John Buchanan-Brown. London: Penguin Books.
Dufrenne, Mikel. 1969. *O poético*. Translation Luiz Arthur Nunes e Reasylvia Kroepf de Souza. Porto Alegre: Globo.
Eliot, T. S. 1987. "Tradition and the Individual Talent." In *The Norton Anthology of English Literature*, Fifth Edition, NY, London: W. W. Nortin & Co.
Firmino, Carmem Lúcia Zambon. 1985. "A organização do ritmo nos sonetos de Camilo Pessanha." In: Daghlian, Carlos. *Poesia e música*. São Paulo: Perspectiva.
Friederich, Hugo. 1991. *Estrutura da lírica moderna*. Translation Marise M. Curioni e Dora F. da Silva. São Paulo: Duas Cidades.
Garcia, Walter. *"Batucada do samba cabia na mão de João Gilberto" Folha de S.Paulo*, 22 July 2019.
Graves, Robert. 1988. *The Greek Myths*. Vol. 1. London: Penguin Books.
Jairo, Severiano.2009. *Uma história da música popular brasileira: das origens à modernidade*. São Paulo: Editora 34.
Langer, Susanne, K. 1980. *Sentimento e forma*. Translation Ana M. Goldberger Coelho e J. Guinsburg. São Paulo: Perspectiva.
Leal, Ana Maria Gottardi. 1985. "O ritmo fônico nos sonetos de Jorge de Sena." In: Daghlian, Carlos. *Poesia e música*. São Paulo: *Perspectiva*.
Moisés, Massaud. 1973. *O simbolismo*. São Paulo: Cultrix.
Moraes, Vinicius de. 1998. *Poesia completa e prosa*. Rio de Janeiro: Nova Aguilar.
Namé, Rita Luiza Pércia. 2004. *O cancioneiro de Vinicius de Moraes: a construção do Orfeu Moreno*. Doctoral Dissertation. Universidade Federal de Alagoas.
—. 1998. *Poesia e Música em Vinícius de Moraes- ressonância e síntese*. MA Thesis.
Norwood, Gilbert. 1945. *Pindar*. Berkeley: University of California Press.
Oliveira, Solange Ribeiro de. 2002. *Literatura e música*. São Paulo: Perspectiva, 44.
Portella, Eduardo. "Do verso solitário ao canto coletivo." In: *Moraes, Vinicius. Poesia completa e prosa*. Rio de Janeiro: Aguilar, 1986.
Ruwet, Nicolas. 1972. *Langage, musique, poésie*. Paris: Seuil.

Said, Edward. W. 1999. *Cultura e imperialismo.* Translation Demise Botmann. São Paulo: Companhia da Letras.
Sant'Anna, Affonso Romano de. "Morreu Vinicius de Moraes". In: Jornal *Rascunho*, série "Quase-Diário", 9 July 1980.
—. 1978. *Música popular e moderna poesia brasileira.* Rio de Janeiro: Vozes.
Souriau, Etienne. 1983. *A correspondência das artes.* Translation Maria Cecília Queiroz de Moraes Pinto e Maria Helena Ribeiro da Cunha. São Paulo: Cultrix.
Stravinsky, Igor. 1996. *Poética musical em seis lições.* Translation Luiz Paulo Horta. Rio de Janeiro: Zahar.
Silva, Rafael Mariano Camilo da *(2017). Desafinado: dissonâncias nos discursos acerca da influência do Jazz na Bossa Nova (Master) (in Portuguese).* Uberlândia: Federal University of Uberlândia. *2017.*
Tatit, Luiz.1996. *O cancionista* – composição de canções no Brasil. São Paulo: Edusp.
—. "Quatro triagens e uma mistura: a canção brasileira do século XX." In Matos et al. *Ao encontro da palavra cantada*: poesia, música e voz. Rio de Janeiro: 7 letras, 2001.
Ulhoa, Martha T. "Métrica derramada: prosódia musical na canção brasileira popular." In *Brasiliana.* Rio de Janeiro, n. 2, Academia Brasileira de Música, 1999, 87.

Appendix

EU NÃO EXISTO SEM VOCÊ

Eu sei e você sabe, já que a vida quis assim
Que nada nesse mundo levará você de mim
Eu sei e você sabe que a distância não existe
Que todo grande amor
Só é bem grande se for triste
Por isso, meu amor
Não tenha medo de sofrer
Que todos os caminhos me encaminham pra você

Assim como o oceano
Só é belo com luar
Assim como a canção
Só tem razão se se cantar
Assim como uma nuvem
Só acontece se chover
Assim como o poeta
Só é grande se sofrer
Assim como viver
Sem ter amor não é viver

Não há você sem mim
E eu não existo sem você.

MISTICO

O ar está cheio de murmúrios misteriosos
E na névoa clara das coisas há um vago sentido de espiritualização...
Tudo está cheio de ruídos sonolentos
Que vêm do céu, que vêm do chão
E que esmagam o infinito do meu desespero.
Através do tenuíssimo de névoa que o céu cobre
Eu sinto a luz desesperadamente
Bater no fosco da bruma que a suspende.
As grandes nuvens brancas e paradas –
Suspensas e paradas
Como aves solícitas de luz –
Ritmam interiormente o movimento da luz:

Dão ao lago do céu
A beleza plácida dos grandes blocos de gelo.
No olhar aberto que eu ponho nas coisas do alto
Há todo um amor à divindade.
No coração aberto que eu tenho para as coisas do alto
Há todo um amor ao mundo.
No espírito que eu tenho embebido das coisas do alto
Há toda uma compreensão.
Almas que povoais o caminho de luz
Que, longas, passeais nas noites lindas
Que andais suspensas a caminhar no sentido da luz
O que buscais, almas irmãs da minha?
Por que vos arrastais dentro da noite murmurosa
Com os vossos braços longos em atitude de êxtase?
Vedes alguma coisa
Que esta luz que me ofusca esconde à minha visão?
Sentis alguma coisa
Que eu não sinta talvez?
Por que as vossas mãos de nuvem e névoa
Se espalmam na suprema adoração?
É o castigo, talvez?
Eu já de há muito tempo vos espio
Na vossa estranha caminhada.
Como quisera estar entre o vosso cortejo
Para viver entre vós a minha vida humana...
Talvez, unido a vós, solto por entre vós
Eu pudesse quebrar os grilhões que vos prendem...
Sou bem melhor que vós, almas acorrentadas
Porque eu também estou acorrentado
E nem vos passa, talvez, a idéia do auxílio.
Eu estou acorrentado à noite murmurosa
E não me libertais...
Sou bem melhor que vós, almas cheias de humildade.
Solta ao mundo, a minha alma jamais irá viver convosco.
Eu sei que ela já tem o seu lugar
Bem junto ao trono da divindade
Para a verdadeira adoração.
Tem o lugar dos escolhidos
Dos que sofreram, dos que viveram e dos que compreenderam.
  Rio de Janeiro, 1933

SERENATA DO ADEUS

Ai, a lua que no céu surgiu
Não é a mesma que te viu
Nascer nos braços meus
Cai, a noite sobre o nosso amor
E agora só restou do amor
Uma palavra: Adeus
Ai, vontade de ficar mas tendo que ir embora
Ai, que amar é se ir morrendo pela vida afora
É refletir na lágrima, um momento breve
De uma estrela pura cuja luz morreu
Ai, mulher, estrela a refulgir
Parte, mas antes de partir

Rasga meu coração
Crava as garras no meu peito em dor
E esvai em sangue todo o amor
Toda desilusão
Ai, vontade de ficar mas tendo que ir embora
Ai, que amar é se ir morrendo pela vida afora
É refletir na lágrima um momento breve
De uma estrela pura
Cuja luz morreu
Numa noite escura
Triste como eu

VALSA DE EURÍDICE

Tantas vezes já partiste
Que chego a desesperar
Chorei tanto, eu sou tão triste
Que já nem sei mais chorar

Oh, meu amado, não parta
Não parta de novo
Ha na partida uma dor que não tem fim

Não há nada que conforte
A falta dos olhos teus

Pensa que a saudade
mais do que a propria morte
Pode matar-me
Adeus

MEDO DE AMAR

Vire essa folha do livro e se esqueça de mim
Finja que o amor acabou e se esqueça de mim
Você não compreendeu que o ciúme é um mal de raiz
E que ter medo de amar não faz ninguém feliz

Agora vá sua vida como você quer
Porém, não se surpreenda se uma outra mulher
Nascer de mim, como do deserto uma flor
E compreender que o ciúme é o perfume do amor

OPERÁRIO EM CONSTRUÇÃO

E o Diabo, levando-o a um alto monte, mostrou-lhe num momento de tempo todos os reinos do mundo. E disse-lhe o Diabo:
—Dar-te-ei todo este poder e a sua glória, porque a mim me foi entregue e dou-o a quem quero; portanto, se tu me adorares, tudo será teu.
E Jesus, respondendo, disse-lhe:
—Vai-te, Satanás; porque está escrito: adorarás o Senhor teu Deus e só a Ele servirás.
 Lucas, cap. IV, vs. 5-8.

Era ele que erguia casas
Onde antes só havia chão.
Como um pássaro sem asas
Ele subia com as casas
Que lhe brotavam da mão.
Mas tudo desconhecia
De sua grande missão:
Não sabia, por exemplo
Que a casa de um homem é um templo
Um templo sem religião
Como tampouco sabia
Que a casa que ele fazia
Sendo a sua liberdade

Era a sua escravidão.

De fato, como podia
Um operário em construção
Compreender por que um tijolo
Valia mais do que um pão?
Tijolos ele empilhava
Com pá, cimento e esquadria
Quanto ao pão, ele o comia...
Mas fosse comer tijolo!
E assim o operário ia
Com suor e com cimento
Erguendo uma casa aqui
Adiante um apartamento
Além uma igreja, à frente
Um quartel e uma prisão:
Prisão de que sofreria
Não fosse, eventualmente
Um operário em construção.

Mas ele desconhecia
Esse fato extraordinário:
Que o operário faz a coisa
E a coisa faz o operário.
De forma que, certo dia
À mesa, ao cortar o pão
O operário foi tomado
De uma súbita emoção
Ao constatar assombrado
Que tudo naquela mesa
- Garrafa, prato, facão -
Era ele quem os fazia
Ele, um humilde operário,
Um operário em construção.
Olhou em torno: gamela
Banco, enxerga, caldeirão
Vidro, parede, janela
Casa, cidade, nação!
Tudo, tudo o que existia
Era ele quem o fazia
Ele, um humilde operário

Um operário que sabia
Exercer a profissão.

Ah, homens de pensamento
Não sabereis nunca o quanto
Aquele humilde operário
Soube naquele momento!
Naquela casa vazia
Que ele mesmo levantara
Um mundo novo nascia
De que sequer suspeitava.
O operário emocionado
Olhou sua própria mão
Sua rude mão de operário
De operário em construção
E olhando bem para ela
Teve um segundo a impressão
De que não havia no mundo
Coisa que fosse mais bela.

Foi dentro da compreensão
Desse instante solitário
Que, tal sua construção
Cresceu também o operário.
Cresceu em alto e profundo
Em largo e no coração
E como tudo que cresce
Ele não cresceu em vão
Pois além do que sabia
- Exercer a profissão -
O operário adquiriu
Uma nova dimensão:
A dimensão da poesia.

E um fato novo se viu
Que a todos admirava:
O que o operário dizia
Outro operário escutava.

E foi assim que o operário

Do edifício em construção
Que sempre dizia sim
Começou a dizer não.
E aprendeu a notar coisas
A que não dava atenção:

Notou que sua marmita
Era o prato do patrão
Que sua cerveja preta
Era o uísque do patrão
Que seu macacão de zuarte
Era o terno do patrão
Que o casebre onde morava
Era a mansão do patrão
Que seus dois pés andarilhos
Eram as rodas do patrão
Que a dureza do seu dia
Era a noite do patrão
Que sua imensa fadiga
Era amiga do patrão.

E o operário disse: Não!
E o operário fez-se forte
Na sua resolução.

Como era de se esperar
As bocas da delação
Começaram a dizer coisas
Aos ouvidos do patrão.
Mas o patrão não queria
Nenhuma preocupação
- "Convençam-no" do contrário -
Disse ele sobre o operário
E ao dizer isso sorria.

Dia seguinte, o operário
Ao sair da construção
Viu-se súbito cercado
Dos homens da delação
E sofreu, por destinado
Sua primeira agressão.

Teve seu rosto cuspido
Teve seu braço quebrado
Mas quando foi perguntado
O operário disse: Não!

Em vão sofrera o operário
Sua primeira agressão
Muitas outras se seguiram
Muitas outras seguirão.
Porém, por imprescindível
Ao edifício em construção
Seu trabalho prosseguia
E todo o seu sofrimento
Misturava-se ao cimento
Da construção que crescia.

Sentindo que a violência
Não dobraria o operário
Um dia tentou o patrão
Dobrá-lo de modo vário.
De sorte que o foi levando
Ao alto da construção
E num momento de tempo
Mostrou-lhe toda a região
E apontando-a ao operário
Fez-lhe esta declaração:
- Dar-te-ei todo esse poder
E a sua satisfação
Porque a mim me foi entregue
E dou-o a quem bem quiser.
Dou-te tempo de lazer
Dou-te tempo de mulher.
Portanto, tudo o que vês
Será teu se me adorares
E, ainda mais, se abandonares
O que te faz dizer não.

Disse, e fitou o operário
Que olhava e que refletia
Mas o que via o operário
O patrão nunca veria.

O operário via as casas
E dentro das estruturas
Via coisas, objetos
Produtos, manufaturas.
Via tudo o que fazia
O lucro do seu patrão
E em cada coisa que via
Misteriosamente havia
A marca de sua mão.
E o operário disse: Não!

- Loucura! - gritou o patrão
Não vês o que te dou eu?
- Mentira! - disse o operário
Não podes dar-me o que é meu.

E um grande silêncio fez-se
Dentro do seu coração
Um silêncio de martírios
Um silêncio de prisão.
Um silêncio povoado
De pedidos de perdão
Um silêncio apavorado
Com o medo em solidão.

Um silêncio de torturas
E gritos de maldição
Um silêncio de fraturas
A se arrastarem no chão.
E o operário ouviu a voz
De todos os seus irmãos
Os seus irmãos que morreram
Por outros que viverão.
Uma esperança sincera
Cresceu no seu coração
E dentro da tarde mansa
Agigantou-se a razão
De um homem pobre e esquecido
Razão porém que fizera
Em operário construído
O operário em construção.

SONETO DA FIDELIDADE

De tudo, ao meu amor serei atento antes
E com tal zelo, e sempre, e tanto
Que mesmo em face do maior encanto
Dele se encante mais meu pensamento

Quero vivê-lo em cada vão momento
E em seu louvor hei de espalhar meu canto
E rir meu riso e derramar meu pranto
Ao seu pesar ou seu contentamento

E assim quando mais tarde me procure
Quem sabe a morte, angústia de quem vive
Quem sabe a solidão, fim de quem ama

Eu possa lhe dizer do amor (que tive):
Que não seja imortal, posto que é chama
Mas que seja infinito enquanto dure.

SE TODOS FOSSEM IGUAIS A VOCÊ

Vai tua vida
Teu caminho é de paz e amor
A tua vida
É uma linda canção de amor
Abre os teus braços e canta
A última esperança
A esperança divina
De amar em paz

Se todos fossem
Iguais a você
Que maravilha viver
Uma canção pelo ar
Uma mulher a cantar
Uma cidade a cantar, a sorrir, a cantar, a pedir
A beleza de amar
Como o sol, como a flor, como a luz
Amar sem mentir, nem sofrer

Existiria a verdade
Verdade que ninguém vê
Se todos fossem no mundo iguais a você

CHEGA DE SAUDADE

Vai, minha tristeza
E diz a ela que sem ela não pode ser
Diz-lhe numa prece
Que ela regresse
Porque eu não posso mais sofrer

Chega de saudade
A realidade é que sem ela não há paz
Não há beleza
É só tristeza e a melancolia
Que não sai de mim, não sai de mim, não sai

Mas, se ela voltar
Que coisa linda, que coisa louca
Pois há menos peixinhos a nadar no mar
Do que os beijinhos que eu darei na sua boca

Dentro dos meus braços
Os abraços hão de ser milhões de abraços
Apertado assim, colado assim, calado assim
Abraços e beijinhos, e carinhos sem ter fim
Que é pra acabar com esse negócio de você viver sem mim

Não há paz
Não há beleza
É só tristeza e a melancolia
Que não sai de mim, não sai de mim, não sai
Dentro dos meus braços
Os abraços hão de ser milhões de abraços
Apertado assim, colado assim, calado assim
Abraços e beijinhos, e carinhos sem ter fim
Que é pra acabar com esse negócio de você viver sem mim

Não quero mais esse negócio de você longe de mim
Vamos deixar desse negócio de você viver sem mim

'SING OF THE FAMOUS PORTUGUESE / TO WHOM BOTH MARS AND NEPTUNE BOWED': CAMÕES RECURRENCE IN PORTUGUESE MUSIC

LEONOR SANTA BARBARA & LUÍS A.V. MANUEL BERNARDO

Fig. 29: Engraved portrait Luis de Camões.

The poet and the country: history and myth

Luís Vaz de Camões is believed to be born around 1524/1525, in Lisbon, to an aristocratic impoverished family. He, most probably, studied in Coimbra. Scholars have different opinions about the kind of education at the University. According to António José Saraiva he benefited from the renewal of the University; yet J. S. da Silva Dias considers that between 1525 and 1580 – the whole period of Camões' life – the Portuguese University receded to scholasticism, marking a difference towards both the previous century and the other European universities. Probably, during this time he wrote a few plays following Gil Vicente's morality plays. He also wrote letters and different poetic genres, as sonnets and songs. It is usually considered that he returned to Lisbon and frequented the city bohemian life; he was also intimate with several women, some of them noblewomen, which may have caused him some problems. The lack of money and his tendency to get himself into trouble may have been the reasons why he sailed to India in 1553. Besides Goa, he lived in several eastern places, as China, Macau, and the Moluccas. In India he served as a public servant and as a soldier. He lost his right eye in a naval battle at Cetua (Morocco) as confirmed by himself in *The Lusíads*, X.155, 1-2: 'In your service, an arm inured to battle; / In your praise, a mind given to the Muses.' In 1567 he left India back to Lisbon, a voyage that took him about two years: it seems his lack of money made him stay several months in Mozambique. Most part of his famous poem, *The Lusíads*, is believed to have been written while he was in the East. Actually, one of the stories told about him concerns the shipwreck where he lost everything but the poem which he managed to save while swimming. It was published in Lisbon in 1572 and presented to the young king Sebastian, to whom is dedicated. Camões died in Lisbon on the 10th of June 1580, having had a difficult life both because of his choices and some lack of appreciation.

When he was born the Portuguese empire was mostly settled. The Portuguese had managed to arrive in India by sea, establishing themselves in several places such Goa, Malacca and Ormuz and replacing the fully established Genoese trade over there. This was not an easy task for a small country and, according to some, the policies of the Portuguese viceroys were not really welcome in Lisbon. The distance, the animosity of the people and the monsoons may have been the reasons for the court to consider that this commerce did not compensate for all the danger it caused. On the other hand, part of the aristocracy believed that the Portuguese should turn again to the North Africa. Eventually, Sebastian, the young king who succeeded John III, was persuaded by them, and moved to Morocco with his army where he fought the battle of Alcácer-Kebir which ended disastrously. The way this situation was perceived in Portugal led Luís de Camões to write to a friend these words that became famous: 'All will see that so dear to me was my country I was content to die not only in it but with it' (Camões, 2008, X).

This tragic outcome affected the political, economic, and cultural life of Portugal, already in regression since the 15th century, and even more so, due to the Inquisition, in the 16th century. As a matter of fact, even relevant humanists as André de Gouveia, Damião de Góis or Garcia da Orta saw their influence reduced. The Inquisition persecuted the last two and forbade some of their works. According to Silva Dias this situation did not reflect on the poet, whom he considered, literally speaking, a kind of exiled in his own country, instead of adjusting to its reality as did some other contemporary authors, as António Ferreira and Sá de Miranda. Concerning his poetry, Saraiva stresses that he assimilated the Italian poetry of Petrarch, conciliating it with traditional poetry and, therefore, indicating the way to the genre that characterizes the Portuguese 17th century – the Baroque. He also enhances the poet's knowledge of the Portuguese language, choosing polysemous words.

Camões is undoubtedly amongst the major poets in the Portuguese language. When the Castilian King, Philip II, entered Lisbon in 1580, he may have considered *The Lusíads* the ultimate linguistic frontier, preventing the Portuguese to be fully conquered (Picchio, 2012, 77). He recognized not just the importance of the language (almost advancing Fernando Pessoa's statement when he said that his fatherland was the Portuguese language), but the importance of Camões' epic poem. Indeed, though he was a prolific poet, he is celebrated mostly because of *The Lusíads*. Therefore, unlike other figures, the celebrations of the 10th of June, the date of his death, became a day to celebrate the country and the people. This date was celebrated for the first time in 1880, by a King's decree to commemorate the 300 years of his death. But it only became a national holiday in 1919, under the Republic. During Salazar's dictatorship, the date became even more relevant, named as 'The Day of Camões, of Portugal and of the Race' (here meaning the Portuguese stamina). Since 1978 it has been celebrated as the 'Day of Portugal, of Camões and of the Portuguese Communities.' It is noteworthy that, when in 2013, the Portuguese government suppressed a couple of holidays, the 10th of June remained untouchable, while the 5th of October and the 1st of December were temporarily suppressed. These dates, however, refer to important events in the history of the country: the 1st of December commemorates the recovery of the Portuguese independence in 1640 and the 5th of October celebrates the implantation of the Republic in 1910. Moreover, it is also the day when, in 1143, Afonso Henriques and Alfonso VII of Castille signed the treaty of Zamora by which the Castilian king recognized the independence of Portugal.

The relevance of *The Lusíads* rely on the fact that the poem is about the Portuguese, who, now as before, identify themselves with the poem (Picchio, 2012, 77). Carlos A. André, recognizing the influence of the *Aeneid* in the Portuguese poem and all the similarities between both poems, also points out the differences, concerning the hero. First, it is not the one man (*uirum*) sang by Vergil, but the 'matchless heroes' (*barões assinalados*)

Who from Portugal's western shores
By oceans where none had ventured
Voyaged to Taprobana and beyond (*The Lusíads*. I. 1. 2-3)

Camões also goes beyond Virgil, as he refers to an historical hero. This one is meant to surpass historical figures of the past:

Boast no more about the subtle Greek
Or the long odyssey of the Trojan Aeneas;
Enough of the oriental conquests
Of great Alexander and of Trajan;
I sing of the famous Portuguese
To whom both Mars and Neptune bowed. (*The Lusíads*. I. 3. 1-6)

Camões was aware that his poem was not about 'counterfeit exploits,' 'fantasies' invented by the muses (*The Lusíads* I. 11); it includes kings, noblemen, and the anonymous people. (André, 2012, 338). It is also important to enhance that Vasco da Gama's travel to India is just part of the poem. The history of the Portuguese, told by Gama to the sultan of Malindi, as well as the future deeds announced in Canto Ten are the main subject of *The Lusíads*.

Besides the epic poem, it is the character of the poet and his life, that make him so relevant in the country. It became a sort of national myth. Camões is therefore identified with the country, with the Portuguese people, as referred by some scholars. Camões' myth reunites several topics of the Portuguese mythology (Picchio, 2012, 74): the longing, both of the fatherland and of the loved woman; the Portuguese traveller in the East, mainly in India, associated with the castaway; the blind poet (or rhapsode); and the mythic figure of the poet who changed the usual way of classical epic heroes: both in Homer and Virgil, the hero goes from East to West, while in Camões it is the opposite way. Hence, he turned, as Eduardo Lourenço said, into the image of Portugal and not just one Portuguese poet.

Also due to the purposes of this book, we cannot talk about Luís de Camões and his poetry without referring to music in its different aspects. Music and singing are important for the poet. Thus, like in Greek and Roman epic poems, 'singing' is the keyword, even if here there is no musical accompaniment, as there was with the Homeric poems. Besides, João de Freitas Branco (1979, *apud Dicionário de Luís de Camões*, pág. 156, *s.u.* 'Camões e a música') considers that *cantar* (to sing) is the verb used more often by Camões, as we can see from the quotation in the title. (*The Lusíads*. I. 3, 5-6). Most importantly, all along the poem, different musical instruments are mentioned, according to the circumstances: in I. 5. 1-

3 the poet proposes to use the 'battle trumpet' (*tuba*, in the Portuguese), instead of the 'goatherd's querulous piping,' as it is the most suitable to the genre. He also mentions the trumpets in III. 48. 7, when the battle at Ourique's plain is about to begin or at IX. 45. 2, as the instrument accompanying Fame on her acclamation of the Portuguese mariners. The trumpet is used too when Gama is about to describe the battle at Aljubarrota, though here a different kind (*trombeta*, in the Portuguese). If the trumpet seems to be the most suitable for battles and heroic deeds, some other instruments appear in the poem. In IX. 64 the nymphs play zithers, harps, or flutes, while in I. 47, when arriving at Mozambique, the natives play horns.

Other aspects concerning the music are also present in his lyric poetry, as the allusion to the birds and their different sounds (e. g. the sonnet *The pretty, sweet, and wanton little bird*, with 'its soft, bright notes, beyond all measure changing.'). Freitas Branco considers that Camões did not have a particular knowledge of music, using just the regular vocabulary of his time.

The interest of such subject is unquestionable, and some studies intended to deal with it. This is not the case of this essay. We have rather decided to stress the relationship between Camões' poetry and posterior music, focusing on different times and genres.

A memorial of the future

In the first two decades of the 19th century the composition of masses for the dead becomes scarce. The sort of monumental Requiem by Berlioz, Brahms or Verdi only emerges after the Nation-State's matrix stabilizes. Thus, the decision of João Domingos Bomtempo (1775-1842), one of the most prolific and appreciated Portuguese musicians in the European context of that time, to compose his *Requiem*, op. 23, with a civic purpose, has an international relevance.

Prepared during 1818, in France, 'the Requiem was first performed in 1819 at a private concert in the French capital and repeated with great success in London where Bomtempo returned the same year before returning to Lisbon after the proclamation of the Constitution of 1820' (Nery and Castro, 1991, 131). At that time, it was also published by Auguste Leduc with the following specification: *Ouvrage consacré à la mémoire de Camões*. This dedication shows that 'it is integrated in the same revivalist movement of the works of Camões which brought about the famous edition of *Os Lusíadas* by Morgado de Mateus' (Nery and Castro, 1991, 131).

Yet, the reach of this gesture exceeds the cultural context in which the work was created, turning it into an inaugural moment for the entrance of Camões in the Portuguese musical universe. It was the mythicized representation of the model figure from the most glorious time of the Portuguese nation that was considered, not his poems as lyrics. Thus, the way the Requiem works as a kind of hymn of the first Portuguese liberal constitutionalism depends on such a reception of Camões' epic production. Bomtempo intends to enhance the idea of a nation that finds, in the excellence of its past, the resources to surpass the challenges cast into its identity and to prepare the decisive entrance in Modernity. The metonymical effect of the dedication should represent a way to counteract the severe feeling of emptiness and decadence, marking Portuguese culture since the presence of Philips (1580-1640) to the French invasions (1807-1813), and the dislocation of the royal power to Brazil (1807-1821).

Including Camões' name at the entrance of the musical text leads, therefore, to a transfiguration of the conventional sense of the musical composition, depending on a certain reading of the Portuguese History. It confers to the *Requiem* an immanent dimension combined with the religious transcendency, creating a peculiar version of the sense of the liturgy (Eftekhari, 2012). Despite the inexistence of any explanation text to it, the work appeals to a second level of interpretation, whose programmatic lines should elapse from musical orientations. Even if it could appear odd, the choice of a mass for the dead totally fits the expression of this dynamism as it presents a game between death and resurrection, mourning and strife for the continuity of life. The analogy with the desired effect of social, political and cultural regeneration, according to an up-to-date notion of citizenship, emerges almost as natural. The recollection of an idealized genius from the past establishes definitively the historical scope of the memorial and each moment of the liturgy acquires a meaning in the transitory process of the collective, less to a national identity enclosed on itself, than to a new cosmopolitanism related to the one of the Discoveries.

Hence, the musical composition assumes a descriptive dimension. It depicts the hopeful deeds of the Portuguese people in the attempt to get out of the darkness and decidedly entering the European intellectual movement of the Enlightenment. An epic for the new times, present and future, directly identified with the one of ancient times, sang by Camões in *The Lusiads*. This unusual combination contributed for the composition to integrate exequy for the martyrs of constitutionalism, as well as of royal figures, and for his own, until it afterwards entered a period of oblivion, only interrupted lately in the 20th century.

A proof of continuity

Nevertheless, if the work was kept unknown, the matrix of appropriation of Camões' legacy that it staged was meant to remain. This effect lies, probably, in the way that a kind of reading of the national history reverts into the musical scope. Since the absolutism that follows the restoration of the Portuguese independence (1640), an interpretation prevails that places the negativity of the present between two golden moments, one remembered, the other projected, both always idealized. (Bernardo, 2017). As a matter of fact, 'a very significant part of the ideological debate […] of the XIX and XX centuries in Portugal will be precisely in terms of confronting the idea of decadence, accompanied by various attempts and projects of regeneration' (Nery and Castro, 1991, 112).

This schematic way of consecutive generations of Portuguese intellectuals to deal with the feeling of periphery, finds in the Renaissance poet an unavoidable trope. Several marriages of the music with Camões consequently aim at recovering him as the ceremonial backdrop, as if the infinite beauty of a manifold production would not be enough to justify the crossing of two languages, and the giantism associated to it would constrain the necessity of a recurring way of legitimation. Occasionally, the greatness found in the poetic composition makes for an indirect way of symbolic representation, in which Camões acts as the synecdoche of the motherland, rather than for the pure aesthetic appropriation. The combinations follow distinct procedures, some merely evocative, as seen in the previous point, some simply allusive, trusting the presence of Camões in the encyclopaedia of potential listeners, and others using complete poems from his lyric or fragments from the epic poem. The chosen poems differ according to the purpose, though they turn around the suggestion of an imaginary considered to be specifically Portuguese.

In the second half of the 19th century, the obvious difficulties to follow the Industrial Revolution and the loss of geopolitical influence, while still dealing with the trauma of the independence of Brazil, emphasized the feeling of nostalgia of the times when Portugal had ruled. Multiple musical genres – odes, cantatas, marches, symphonies, piano pieces – were composed with a nationalist purpose, even if they revealed clear influences of international models. This was rendered in the scope of the message, as in the will to constitute a Portuguese musical identity. Consequently, many works exhibited a connection with Camões, particularly with the author of *The Lusiads*, as they successively restaged the tripartite dramaturgy described above.

A Portuguesa (1890), the national anthem of the Portuguese Republic, is an example of the allusive effect and how the reference to Camões both continuously operates upon the imaginary of the nationalist romanticism and modulates the interpretation of the meaning of History. Composed by Alfredo Keil (Lisbon, 1850-Hamburg, 1907) on the lyrics by Henrique Lopes de Mendonça (1856-1931), it intends to relaunch the value of national identity against the humiliation inflicted by the British Ultimatum, and it finds in *La Marseillaise* its hypotext. (Castro, 2013, 760). But it is probably the intertextuality with Camões' epic that allows the anchorage of such a model on the Portuguese imaginary, granting at the same time an extreme efficacy to what appears to be a generic text.

The parallel between the first lines of *The Lusiads* ('Arms are my theme, and those matchless heroes / Who from Portugal's far western shores / By oceans where none had ventured / Voyaged to Taprobana and beyond', I. 1. 1-4) and those of the national anthem ('Heroes of the sea, noble people, / valiant, immortal nation') appears as unambiguous. The analogy also foresees the idea of a reformist scope based on the regeneration's metaphor, that always goes with the reception of Camões' poetry. The same Camões' effect overhanging on *A Portuguesa*, eventually explains why different regimes and ideologies have gazed in it.

But the work which reflects the best how the metonymical effect of Camões' reference contributes to strengthen the romantic vision of the nation is the Symphony in A minor, "To the Fatherland", composed by José Vianna da Motta (São Tomé, 1868-Lisbon, 1948), one of the main figures in the Portuguese musical scene. Written in 1895 and executed in 1897, it was also a response to the Ultimatum, constituting a 'work deeply symbolic of a certain mythology of a national "revival" (symptomatically inspired by Camões)' (Nery and Castro, 1991, 156). This inspiration is quite explicit in the full score. Following the classical model of the symphony in four *tempi* and a grandiloquent aesthetic, it is supported by a programmatic script. To this effect, three movements are headed by a quotation from *The Lusiads*, another by a sonnet. The form of the symphonic poem reinforces the correspondence of music and poetry.

In the first movement, *allegro eroico*, the passage comes from two excerpts of the fourth and fifth stanzas in Canto I. This is the moment when the poet asks 'the nymphs of the Tagus' for an inspiration adjusted to the epic heroism and a voice according to the greatness of the deeds described. Significantly, Vianna da Motta joins line five of the fourth stanza to the first four lines in the fifth stanza. This allows him to establish the sublime character guiding the symphony ('Return me now a loftier tone'), to associate his eloquence to that of the poet ('Fight me now with mighty cadences') and to underline an identical mobilizing function ('Stirring the heart, steeling the countenance').

For the second movement, *andante molto*, he turns to the quartets from the sonnet 'I will sing of love so sweetly.' The choice of the poem introduces an idyllic dimension towards love, reinforced by Wagnerian echoes. The poetic-musical language expresses love's sweetness and suggests the need of spreading it. Keeping aside the tercets, where Camões mentions a lady, the composer seems to acquit the spiritual dimension of the feelings in favour of the idea of love for the motherland.

The first two lines of the fifth stanza in Canto X of *The Lusiads*, when the poet describes the erotic practices rewarding the Portuguese sailors in the Isle of Love, entitle the third movement, *vivace*. Including themes from popular songs, stressing the nationalist character of the composition, this moment retrieves the utopia described by Camões to remind the joy of a life lived in harmony with the genuine patriotic ideal and to feed the trust in a future at least as glorious as the past of the Discoveries. Therefore, the expression of hope precedes the elegy of the present that constitutes the last movement.

This displays the full programme of the symphony (*Decadence – Fight – Resurgence*) in a complete accordance with the general scheme of appropriation described above. For this climax he chooses the last three lines of stanza 145 of Canto X, adapting them to one sentence: 'My country […] being given over […] and philistinism, heartlessness and degrading pessimism.' Through this allusion, the musical work integrates the analogy with Camões' phrase of sorrow for the state in which the country fell, unable to prosecute his heroic fate, to find in the pride of its history the strength to raise again and engender new values. At the same time, it assumes the idea defended by Camões, on those final stanzas, that the people keps the spirit intact, waiting for the creative impetus of the rulers. Finally, he makes his patriotic exhortation at the end of the poem to replace Portugal in the European leadership. The musical solutions completely accompany this incitement, reinforcing the piece's persuasive power and suggesting a circular movement to return to the initial civic enthusiasm (Delgado, 2002, 44).

These quotations disappear in a revision made in the subsequent century, leaving just a dedication to the fatherland. Was it the will to universalize the scope of the work or the influence of a new way to deal with Camões legacy? As a matter of fact, 20th century composers, though keeping active a context of reception in which aesthetic choices conjugate with other parameters, favour the relationship with Camões' more intimist poetry, recovering some lesser-known genres from his lyric and using the same ancestral matrix to think the history of Portuguese music in terms of continuity and modernity.

Luís de Freitas Branco (1890-1955), 'the pioneer of musical modernism to Portugal' (Nery and Castro, 1991, 157), adopted 'an outspoken and militant nationalism which brought him close to the ideologies of the Integralismo Lusitano' (Nery and Castro, 1991, 158), a movement similar to the *Action française*, lasting for a decade, in which he invested in a symbolist style. Approaching, since 1920, the leftist group of Seara Nova, he carries out a neoclassical turn, by which he combines a rationalist attitude with the 'recovery of certain cultural values of the Renaissance (polyphony, Gregorian modality, linearity, etc.), accompanied by a special valuation of the works of Camões.' (Nery and Castro, 1991, 160). If, in the previous period, he made the piano music for a few sonnets to be sung, in the decades of 30 and 40, he produced three series of *Ten Madrigals by Camões* to a feminine, mixed, and masculine *a cappella* choir, recurring to different genres of texts by the Renaissance author.

It appears that the composer did not abandon his nationalist ideas. He rather gave a new meaning to the continued appreciation of the Portuguese way of being, less fixed on identity features defined by a mythicized origin and more concerned with asserting a principle of rationality against the romantic propension of the coeval culture. In the same way, he turned his cyclic conception of history to the apology of the classicism in which he saw the only interesting way out for the national culture. (Pina, 2018, 379). Once again, it is a whole programme supporting this revivalism of Camões' poetic universe, having in the horizon the specific intention of settling the existence of an unbroken continuity of the history of Portuguese music (Pina, 2018, 376), as well as guaranteeing the opening to modernization processes tuned with other European countries.

The most significant aspect of this reception was probably determined by the representation of Camões as a man from a revolutionary context opposite to the ancient canon, quite different from the most usual understanding of the Renaissance, retrieved from the Antiquity (Pina, 2018, 375). Therefore, the idea that the encounter with Camões did not aim any longing for past times stands out. Instead, it shows that the main expectation relies on its propeller effect for the development of the national culture. This stimulating element, always connected with the maritime dimension, also contributed to secure the Portuguese Europeanist character, that henceforth defines one of the contemporary ways of reception of Camões' assets. Through it, the issue is no longer to choose between Classicism and Modernity, but to conciliate them.

The sixth symphony by Joly Braga Santos (Lisbon, 1924-Lisbon, 1988), written in 1972, confirms the presence of this working modality in the music field. The unique movement includes two different moments in an inverted chronological timeline. On the first one, fully tuned with the contemporary tendencies, the composer takes the atonality to the extreme. (Delgado, 2002, 126). On the second one, he goes back to the universe of tonal music, relaunching the dialectic between ancestry and novelty. (Delgado, 2002, 129). For this return to the classicism of forms, he introduces a madrigalian feature, echoing Freitas Branco's proposal, and he also recurs to the content of two poems by Camões, written in Galician-Portuguese. A choir sings the sonnet 'Waves walking all through the world,' followed by the poem 'I want to go, mother', sang by a soprano solo. By recurring to Camões' poems, Santos enhances the programmatic suggestion of an eternal return to the Classicism architectonic values, after going through Modernism. The choice of the texts in the medieval language probably suggests that this movement should not be strictly Portuguese, but also Iberian, if not universal.

Each poem introduces a specific determination, conferring an exacerbated emotivity from the poetic construction to the music rational serenity. The sonnet evokes a famous song of love, 'Waves of the sea of Vigo...', referring to a sort of *Urtext* from the origin of the nationality. The poetic-self entrusts the waves with the transmission to his beloved of his deep and complex feelings. The second poem, following the same line of the love song, expresses a girl's desire to her mother of becoming a sailor, so she could follow her seafarer sweetheart. They are both united by a maritime motive, which supposes the themes of desire, existential disquiet, longing, and the will to undertake an internal journey searching for a happiness in a symbolic overseas. They differ in the anguish expressed in the first one, stressed by the obsessive repetition of the verbal form 'Tell her,' to which opposes, in the second poem, the hopeful naivety of the hesitating and bold young lady.

Thus, are suggested the vicissitudes of a troubled artistic path that ends with the recovery of the creative-self authenticit. (Delgado, 2002, 129). As many others, he needed Camões' legitimation for that audacity to state the values in which he believed, rehearsing a commitment between the orientations of his own time and a kind of constant aesthetic value that would have been established in that idealized Golden Age.

The greatest *fado* singer that exists

The imaginary does not work with the expected coherence. Perspectives that should be harmonized, in the optic of conceptual reflexion, clearly show a conflict zone between opposed directions of the representation and the represented. It occurred with what would be, *a priori*, a most obvious marriage – the one between Camões' lyric and *fado*, namely during the period when both were incensed as references of the 'New State' ideology. (1933-1974). Indeed, the dictatorship turned them into instruments of a nationalist ideology, based upon the constant evocation of a Portuguese way of being that they would decisively display.

In *The Lusiads* could be found the supreme expression of this glorious exploit of a valiant Nation that was able to impose the Christian values and a civilizational order to peoples spatially and culturally distant regardless of the scarcity both of the population contingent and of material resources. The *Lyric* settled the contrasts of the sentimental universe of the national soul, between longing and hope, respectful moderation and adventurous spirit, endurance and passional enthusiasm, respect for perennial values and creative wit. A language cultivated in its absolute purity – a language that constituted the first link of national identity, wherever Portugal was in its vast colonial empire – sublimated these characteristics.

Fado, becoming the national song, would give voice to what was considered common in that Portuguese emotional scale. Without the cultural erudition or the stylistic resources of Camões' genius, but with the support of the pungent musical accompaniment, the *fado* would bring the people to itself. Longing, fatalism, exacerbated suffering, sadness, disillusionment, desire, compliant self-representation conferred a feeling of belonging to an organic identity. At the same time, the *fado* ensured the catharsis of a generalized unhappiness and allowed the reconciliation with a way of life that was intentionally kept miserable by the political power.

The institutional control and the censorship of themes, locals and people tended to normalize what rose in the previous century in street and bohemian environments. It benefited from the introduction, in the decade of 1920, of authorial poems, written intentionally, as lyrics for the *fado* (Pereira, 2008). It would have been expected, then, that Camões' poems constituted a significant heap of this union between authorized erudite poets and *fado*'s singers, being included in their music repertoire. The shared expression of the supposed *Volksgeist* and of the main *loci* of the national imaginary could have turned into a sort of symbiosis that would have been if not a creative one, at least a booster of ideological purposes. Yet, the reality was totally different, prevailing the respectful reverence towards the poet, the literary greatness of his production and the elevation of his message, with which the popular character of *fado* would not be able to deal with.

Amália Rodrigues (Lisbon, 1920-Lisbon, 1999), in partnership with Alain Oulman (Dafundo, 1928-Paris, 1990), was responsible to change this situation. In 1963, she sang 'Hard Memory', a title that recovers the last two terms of Camões' sonnet 'Memories of Happy Days Slain in their Primes'. The text shows how the memories of pleasant times combined with the present sorrows and the predicted future hardness torment the poetic-self, suggesting him the certainty for a lonely end. It conveys a fatalistic pessimism, decurrent from the sudden loss of happiness of the poetic-self in line with the spirit of the *Fado*. This attempt did not cause any reaction. Two years later, launches the disc 'Amália sings Camões'. Oulman set to music the sonnet 'My Errors, Evil Fortune, Ardent Love' and the villanelle 'Leonor. Barefoot to the Fountain Goes', which are linked to the previous poem.

The choice fell upon two of the most appreciated poems of the Renaissance author. The sonnet expresses the suffering of the poetic-self, who feels like having lived in a total nonsense because of his mistakes, of the excessive enthusiastic way he lived loves and of bad luck. In this reckoning, stands out the despair of those perceiving that the true cause of their misfortune is in themselves and their inability to avoid the effects of wrath and to stop the need of revenge. This reading, in which the poem's thematic axis is the personal feeling of guilt, is reinforced with the choice just of the two first words ('My Errors') to entitle the *fado*.

The villanelle depicts a girl going to a fountain to fetch water. The bucolic scenery, the detailed description of her clothes and her physical attributes with a strong sensual magnetism expressed by the game of words between scarlet and whiteness, and the suggestion of her swinging walking, contribute to idealize an absolute beauty, carnal and spiritual at the same time, statuary and alive. Those features superimpose themselves to the fragilities inherent to the humble condition of the girl. Entitling the *fado* 'Lianor', the name given by Camões to his character, Amália stresses these interpretative lines. The simplicity of the name reminds the humility of her social origins, while orientating the focus to the object of desire, the woman, in her femininity condition. The analogy between both universes – the one of the poet, and the one of the *fado* – does not offer any difficulty to a coeval listener: what Lianor had been to Camões corresponds now to the simple young woman, fishwife, maid, seamstress or laundress, who has nothing, but captivates everybody with the attributes given to her by a generous nature, as a compensation for what society denied her.

Yet this attempt to transform Camões into a *fados*' author, uniting two forms of culture around the presupposition of the fatherland's identity, was not welcome by everybody, raising the polemic. Another structure of the imaginary came in between, the one opposing scholarly culture to the popular one, as two impermeable and mutually exclusive fields, using either an elitist or an ethnic argument. To some detractors, connected with the literary field, it seemed appalling to see Camões suddenly chosen to embellish that popular music, muddled by the dominant ideology's dissemination. Others, namely *fado* singers, wondered about the authenticity of that encounter on behalf of *fado*'s popular legacy, which would suffer with the interference of the fineness of such an elevated writing, so alien to the People's truth. On the other hand, poets sung by Amália became allies to defend the boldness of the appropriation, insisting on the relevance of the effect of dissemination of a cultural patrimony only accessible to the educated elite.

After 55 years, in a democratic context already reconciled with a mythicised version of Amália Rodrigues, and after a double desacralization of the accessibility to Camões' universe and the corporationism about *Fado*, one of these poets, Manuel Alegre (Águeda, 1936-) resumes the issue. On the celebrations of Amália's 100th birthday, this personality who fought for freedom, finds it on her gesture. Away from any compliance with the regime and from any meaning that the dominant ideology could give to it, when she sang 'My Errors', for him Amália was giving expression to Portugal and its people. As it goes, the same legitimation factor remains uncontested as one of the main associations that keep on determining the reception of Camões – the one that sees in him the bard by excellence of national vocation. Amália and Camões meet in this miscegenation area where words and music sing the Portuguese identity that, in the past as nowadays, represents a yearning for liberation.

In short, if Alegre recovers the trope of Camões' updating by the *fado* singer, what seems to be relevant, besides the aesthetic result, is the relationship that both have with a collective psychology, described in terms of the common places of identity's mythologies. This decontextualization also solves the opposition between high and low culture, crossing Marxism and Nationalism. If, wherever people express themselves, something revolutionary happens, Amália, the child and the voice of the people, carries this source of revolution, even when she sings erudite poets.

This idea seems to echo what the *fado* singer enunciated as a response to her critics, reminding them that poets belong to the same people that she did. But for her, there is no political redemption in such statement, just the reminder of the right to use freely a common cultural patrimony to which the *fado* belongs. The true issue related to this Camões' freedom has to do with the voice, how it expresses itself and shares with others a significant content. This voice does not belong to anyone in particular, and so, it can be both Camões' and hers. In this cultural oecumenism, the *fado* appears as a central axis of secular national artistic expressions and Camões the greatest *fado* singer as he represents the incarnation of the Portuguese soul (Santos, 1987, 154). Significantly she resumes the beginning of the first line ('With what voice') of the sonnet 'With what Voice Will I Cry My Sad Fado' to entitle both her album and one *fado* included in it, produced in 1970.

Also in this context, an eventual marriage is thought in the dependence of identity presumptions, as well as of a vast fiction concerning culture, the poet's figure and *fado*'s meaning. As far as Camões remains a myth, the dialog between them requires the foreseeing of a utopic and uchronic dimension, where both go to a kind of uprooting enabling them to become equals in the partnership. Camões appears as the poet of spiritual states, which, though universal, are specific to the Portuguese soul. The *fado* loses all his historical and sociological features to immaterialize in the fiction of a languorous and nostalgic pathos. This effect makes for important changes in the traditional conception of the *fado*. As for Camões to enter this musical universe in a more expressive way depends on a loss of reverence for its mythical figure and its absorption by the consumer culture. But it becomes clear that the intellectualism of his poetry does not contribute to blurry the frontiers and make it a consistent source of lyrics.

Camões enters Democracy

Music had a significant role preparing the Carnation Revolution. Though the use of Camões's work, easily associated with a culture of the elites and considered as an expression of nationalist and colonialist values, is scarce, it still integrated the revolutionary song repertoire. In 1971, whilst exiled in France, José Mário Branco (Porto, 1942-Lisbon, 2019), exemplary adapts the sonnet 'The Times Change, the Desires Change' to a song inserted in an album of the same name. The song reflected the style *rive gauche* easily aligning with the leftist Sorbonne intellectualism (Corte-Real, 1996, 153). The choice falls into one of the most wellknown sonnets of the poet, making it easier to accept by the listeners the changes introduced on a series of classical tropes relating to the fugacity of time.

The poem nurtures some traces of neoplatonic ontology opposing the permanence of the being and the fluid evanescence of the appearing. The overwhelming change is amplified by the repeated use of change, changing, as well as connected words such as novelty. This effect induces a generalized pessimism, in which some readers see the whinings of an author fallen into disgrace due to the social and political changes of the reign. The suggestion of a disproportion between the scarce good moments to be remembered and the several evils kept in the memory is accentuated by the contrast between the vitality of the outside world, the arrival of spring, and the internal long-lasting grief of the poetic subject. Only the final hyperbole of an unstableness in the changing process, making it totally meaningless, seems to retrieve the *carpe diem* trope leaving room for hope.

Resuming the poem, Branco deeply changes the context of the enunciation. The idea of living in the present through the nostalgia becomes a diagnosis of the national ideology. It is no longer a sort of existential inevitability, becoming instead the background for the revolutionary impetus. The introspective and confessional dimension is replaced by the claiming expression of a generational collective such as that of May 68. The usage of a melody from a Jean Sommer (Paris, 1943-) song, titled *la nouvelle génération*, makes that intention clear. As a result, three words, all relating to the exterior become essential: world, will, change.

Such a meaning with the correspondent injunction become more explicit by the introduction of a chorus that is not part of the initial text, intended to establish a nexus of consequence: 'And if the whole world is made up of change / Let us twist it around as the day is still a child'. Henceforth, the sonnet is meant to express the idea of a present that anticipates and prepares the future. Since change is possible and nothing is established, change is the only way. The image of the rosy finger dawn reinforces the conviction that history is yet to be made, that, just as with childhood, nothing is decided. Therefore, the hope for the success of the revolutionary action is justified. The dithyrambic rhythm of the musical composition and its bright joy, that the vocal interpretation conveyed, give consistency to the conviction that, while the expected day approaches, the sun of equality will spread its light. In this way the imagery surrounding the rising sun, central to the communist ideology, comes to blend with Camões' sonnet to induce a feeling of trust in the Portuguese revolutionary movement.

Contrary to the usual version that stresses the value of an unchanged national identity suggested by the lines of Camões, this interpretation vindicates the alternative image of a popular revolutionary soul to whom the poet would, in his own way, been able to give voice to. Disconnected from the man and the context of his production, the work of Camões continues to benefit from a considerable amount of symbolic capital that operates as a kind of *cachet* of quality and high culture. However, the process of desecration is in progress, as it was essential to assert the programme of the Marxist philosophy of history. It turned also to be determinant for its accommodation in the democratic consumer imagery throughout several genres from *fado* to folk music or to rap.

Rapping Camões Poetry

Gisela Cañamero (Lisbon, 1960-), a multifaceted artist, begins in 2015 one of her performances titled 'Camões is a rap poet'. Combining vocals, drama and visual effects, this show resumes the two first stanzas of *The Lusíads* and sixteen of his sonnets in rap and hip-hop versions. It has the explicit purpose of conveying the actuality of the classical author, to reconcile the new generations with him. In this programme, Camões stands very traditionally as the 'Prince of Poets'. The epithet is anything but neutral, focusing on the excellence of a model of poetic expression that appears eternal. It is this same timelessness that sustains the bold assumption that Camões' prosody is easily transposed to the rhythms of rap. Therefore, the essence of the message corresponds to a new variant of the long-lasting process of receiving Camões' poetry through a supplementary cultural bias to its mere fruition. In this figuration, it is the 'personal tragedy' that works as a pledge of the human, cultural, literary, and linguistic value of the work. Presented as the protagonist of a drama of pain and suffering, in reply to the difficulties imposed by the mediocre society of his time, by a cruel nature and a ruthless fortune, Camões emerges akin to one of the multiple individuals that face the intensity of living a life of the marginalized and excluded in a contemporary metropolis. This hero of the quotidian is a resilient fighter who insists on proceeding with his art and being able to find in the suffering a way to creation. Camões is converted into an example of overcoming the encircling limits by imposing his own value and, thus, assuring a universal recognition. This rereading of the Camões' myth determines the set of selected poems. The inclusion of the two first stanzas of the epic poem, easily recognisable by those who frequent the Portuguese educational system, assures the *captatio benevolentiae*. The sonnets define the *inventio*, restoring the image of a figure profoundly lacerated between hope and disillusionment. Amidst these 'The Times Change, the Desires Change …' is included. This sonnet that we have mentioned in a revolutionary context is now placed to prove the fickleness of man's existence. It ends the show with the suggestion of a most needed sense of relativism that the townsman hero must deal with, just as Camões did. The perpetual mobile of the syncopated rhythms specific of rap and hip-hop induces the spectator to participate in the performance and simultaneously to resent the power of an identical creative impulse. At the end, each one of us should incorporate a part of Camões spirit.

Unique in the Portuguese literary scene, Camões became the symbol of the country and of the people. His poetry has been perceived as an accomplished example of 'art and invention' (*The Lusíads*. I. 2. 8), influencing different musical genres since the 19th century. As showed above, this relationship has not been based only on aesthetic values. Cultural conceptions, images and stereotypes constantly merge with more artistic intentions, therefore contributing to establish a sort of mythology around the poet and his works. That becomes determinant in his reception.

Bibliography

Aubertin, J. J. 1881. *Seventy Sonnets of Camoens. Portuguese Text and Translation*. London: C. Kegan Paul & Co.
Camões, Luís de. 1990. *Epic and Lyric*. Translations by Keith Bosley; illustrations by Lima de Freitas; edited by L. C. Taylor; with essays by Maurice Bowra, Helder Macedo and Luís de Sousa Rebelo. Manchester: Carcanet Press Limited.
Camões, Luís de. 1986-2002. *Lírica completa*. Lisboa: IN-CM (3 vols.).
Camões, Luís de. 1971. *Os Lusíadas*. Lisboa: Editora Arcádia, S.A.R.L.
Camões, Luís de. 1982. *Os Lusíadas*. Lisboa: IN-CM (facsimiled edition).
Camões, Luís Vaz de. 2008[3]. *The Lusíads*. Translated with an Introduction and Notes by Landeg White. Oxford: Oxford University Press.
Lisbon Poets. 2015. Translated by Austen Hyde and Martin D'Evelin; illustrations by André Carrilho. Lisboa: Lisbon Poets & Co.
Alegre, Manuel. 2020. *As Sílabas de Amália*. Lisboa: Dom Quixote.
Alegre, Manuel. 2020. Intervention at Academia das Ciências. Lisboa, 13/10/2020.
André, Carlos Ascenso. 2011. "*Eneida* e *Os Lusíadas*". In *Dicionário de Luís de Camões*, coordinated by Vítor Aguiar e Silva, 337-341. Alfragide: Editorial Caminho.
Baubeta, Patricia Odber de. 2014. "The Sonnets of Camões in English Transalation". *Revista de Estudos Anglo-Portugueses*. No. 23. 11-90. Casal de Cambra: Caleidoscópio – Edição e Artes Gráficas, S.A.
Beller, Manfred, and Leerssen, Joep. 2007. *Imagology: The Cultural Construction and Literary Representation of National Characters*. Amsterdam/New York: Rodopi.
Bernardo, Luís. 2017. "The New Golden Age: The Cultural Memory of the Discoveries in the Portuguese Enlightenment Imaginary". In *Literature and Cultural Memory*. Edited by Mihaela Irimia, Andreea Paris and Dragos Manea, 155-172. Amsterdam/New York: Rodopi.
Bomtempo, João. 2006. *Requiem, op. 23. Coleção Gulbenkian Música 01*. Lisboa: Público.
Bowra, C. M. 1972[9]. *From Virgil to Milton*. London: Macmillan.

Camões e a identidade nacional. 1983. Lisboa: IN-CM.
Cascudo, Teresa, and Trindade, Maria Helena, eds. 1998. *José Vianna da Motta: 50 anos depois da sua morte*. Lisboa: Instituto Português dos Museus.
Castro, Paulo. 2013. "A Portuguesa e a representação musical da República". In *Representações da República*. Edited by Luís Manuel A. V. Bernardo, Leonor Santa Bárbara and Luís Andrade, 751-764. Vila Nova de Famalicão: Edições Húmus.
Corte-Real, Maria. 1996. "Sons de Abril: estilos musicais e movimentos de intervenção político-cultural na Revolução de 1974". *Revista Portuguesa de Musicologia*. No. 6. 141-171. Lisboa.
Crowley. Roger. 2015. *Conquerors. How Portugal Forged the First Global Empire*. London: Faber & Faber.
Delgado, Alexandre. 2002. *A sinfonia em Portugal*. Lisboa: Caminho da Música.
Efetkari, Ladan. 2012. *Bomtempo (1775-1842), un compositeur au sein de la mouvance romantique*. Paris: Hachette.
Ferreira, Rui. 2006. "Amália Rodrigues: com que voz cho(ra)rei meu triste fado! A Poesia no Universo Fadista de Amália". MA diss., Lisboa: Universidade Aberta.
Kramer, Lawrence. 1990. *Music as Cultural Practice, 1800-1900*. Berkeley: University of California Press.
Langrouva, Helena. 2011. "Camões e a música". In *Dicionário de Luís de Camões*, coordinated by Vítor Aguiar e Silva, 153-158. Alfragide: Editorial Caminho.
Mattoso, José. 1998. *História de Portugal – O Liberalismo*. Lisboa: Estampa.
https://www.museudofado.pt/en
Monelle, Raymond. 2000. *The Sense of Music*. Princeton: Princeton University Press.
Murphy, Michael and White, Harry, 2000. *Musical Constructions of Nationalism. Essays on the History and Ideology of European Musical Culture 1800-1945*. Cork: Cork University Press.
Nery, Rui Vieira. 2012. *History of Portuguese Fado*. Lisboa: IN-CM.
Nery, Rui and Castro, Paulo. 1991. *History of Music*. Colecção Synthesis of Portuguese Culture. Lisboa: IN-CM.
Nillis, Ike. 2017. *Reception*. London: Routledge.
Picchio, Luciana Stegagno. 2012. "Para uma mitologia portuguesa". In *Actas da VI reunião internacional de Camonistas*, coordinated by Seabra Pereira and Manuel Ferro, 73-83. Coimbra: Imprensa da Universidade de Coimbra.
http://dx.doi.org/10.14195/978-989-26-0569-2_6.

Pina, Isabel. 2018. "O Integralismo Musical de Luís de Freitas Branco". *Revista Portuguesa de Musicologia*. V. 5, No. 2, 357-382. Lisboa.
Sadie, Stanley. Edited by. 2001. *The New Grove Dictionary of Music and Musicians*. London: Macmillan Publishers.
Santos, Vítor. 1987. *Amália, uma Biografia*. Lisboa: Editorial Presença.
Santos, Vítor. 2014. *O Fado da tua Voz – Amália e os Poetas*. Lisboa: Bertrand.
Saraiva, António José. 1966. *História da Literatura Portuguesa. Vol. 1: Das origens ao Romantismo*. Lisboa: Editorial Estúdios Cor, S.A.R.L.
Silva Dias, J. S. 1981. *Camões no Portugal de Quinhentos*. Lisboa: Instituto de Cultura e Língua Portuguesas, col. Biblioteca Breve.

Websites

CESEM – Centro de Estudos de Sociologia e Estética Musical da NVA FCHS: https://arquivojosemariobranco.fcsh.unl.pt/

Two Lodgers in Their Time: Dmitry Shostakovich and Sasha Cherny

Elena Lutsenko

Fig. 30: Galina Vishnevskaya, Dmitry Shostakovich and Mstislav Rostropovich after a concert.

Though many researchers argue that Dmitry Shostakovich was mainly a symphonist and opera theatre composer, more than any other Russian artist of the first half of the 20th century he was a song composer. In fact, chamber-vocal music is one of the most important genres for Dmitry Shostakovich. He began writing songs at the down of his creative life and proceeded throughout his career. Actually, he "turned the genre of the song cycle […] into a flexible and multi-layered means of expression for his autobiographical and philosophical musings," almost into a confession (Maes, 2008, 231).

His early vocal cycle *Two Fables of Krïlov* (1922) pays tribute to Modest Musorsky's song tradition and to its verbalization and conversational style. In *Six Romances on texts by Japanese Poets* (1928–1932) Shostakovich focuses on lyricism and poetic imagery. These romances are delicate and light in their manner of expression. In *Four Romances on Texts of Pushkin* (1936), the most famous Russian poet, "the sun of our poetry," the composer continues to explore the lyrical genre and also invites the listener to think of the fragility of a human life in the decay of Time.

In the 1940s, Shostakovich creates two vocal cycles, *Six Romances on Verses by Raleigh, Burns and Shakespeare* (1942–1943) that explore the idea of oppression and tyranny, and *From Jewish Folk Poetry* (1948). The latter should be regarded as a reflection on the harsh years of Stalin's regime and anti-Semitic repressions. The Jewish songs portray daily routine episodes of the epoch, the hardships and gritty realities of life like hunger and poverty, including such scenes as a father's warning to his young daughter, a cradle song, the death of a baby, etc. All the people depicted are true victims of the Soviet times.

After the Zhdanov affair and the accusations of formalism in 1948, Shostakovich focused on the Soviet Realist cantatas, film music, and songs on the texts by Yevgeny Dolmatovsky whom he met in 1949. One of the two cycles composed together with Dolmatovsky (*The Motherland hears*) was written for the first Russian cosmonaut Yury Gagarin and his space flight in April 1962. The songs glorify heroic deeds of the Soviet people and life under the communist regime.

At the beginning of the 1960s, Shostakovich turns to satirical genres. When scholars talk about the roots of Shostakovich's satirical intonations, they say that the composer owes much to the song tradition of the 19th century Russian vocal music, Alexandre Dargomïzhsky (1813–1869) and Modest Musorgsky (1839–1881) who explored the conversational opportunities of the melody.

In 1961, Shostakovich composes a new song cycle called *Satires (Sketches of the past)*, that is going to be the main focus of my attention in this essay. Many scholars argue that *Satires* should be mainly understood through the mirror of grotesque, a literary device that Shostakovich uses in many of his works[1]. This essay aims at analyzing the reception of this vocal cycle in the Soviet press. Such an approach is quite revealing as it helps to understand how the Soviet audience of the epoch treated Sasha Chorny's

---

[1] For further bibliography please see: [Dobrykin 1975], [Vasina-Grossman 1980], [Meyer 1998], [Vishnevskaya 1991], [Kremer 2005], [Maes 2008], [Rappaport 2012].

poetry that became known to the general reader in the early 1960s due to the vocal cycle by Dmitry Shostakovich.

Shostakovich's literary tastes

It's quite obvious that Shostakovich always showed deep interest in the current literary process. When action was taken against Joseph Brodsky, the composer sent a telegram to support the poet who was accused of social parasitism. Besides, Shostakovich was acquainted with Anna Akhmatova, one of the most prominent Russian poets of the 20th century. The circumstances of their first meeting are described in detail by Irina Shostakovich, his wife. Shostakovich and Akhmatova "met as two members of the Russian intelligentsia who understood each other because both of them had suffered a lot." (Shostakovich, 2008, 18)

In his younger years Shostakovich expressed his literary tastes quite directly stating in one of the application forms that he loved the poetry of Gavrila Derzhavin (1743–1816) and Vladimir Mayakovsky (1893–1930), appreciated Fyodor Dostoyevsky (1821–1881) and Nikolay Gogol (1809–1852). Concerning the European tradition, he adored Homer, Dante and Voltaire (Petrushanskaya, 2006, 109).

Not surprisingly, the list of authors did not yet include Sasha Chorny as by the early 1960s his poems had not been published in Russia for almost 50 years. Sasha Chorny (Aleksandr Glikberg, 1880–1932), a famous Russian poet, was forced to leave his motherland because his views on the Russian Revolution were openly hostile to the new regime. The rehabilitation of the poetic works by Sasha Chorny, Mikhail Zoshenko and Evgeny Shartz at the times of the Khrushchev Thaw captured a new *Zeitgeist*, the wakening interest to satirical genres.

The republication of Chorny's poetry in the Soviet Union belongs to 1960, when the volume in the prestigious series *The Poet's Library*, published by *Soviet writer*, came off the press with the introductory word of Korney Chkukovsky, a prominent children's poet and a literary critic of the epoch. Shostakovich received this book as a gift, perused it and almost immediately marked several poems in pencil for his new vocal cycle. This edition included over 600 works (1910–1923). It must be said that Sasha Chorny continues the tradition of Russian satirical genres (from Gogol, Leskov, Chekhov to Vladimir Mayakovsky, who Shostakovich collaborated with the music to *The Bedbug* reverberates in the *Satires*, in a certain sense).

The introductory word to Sasha Chorny's volume is full of compassion to Chorny's life (that was quite bold a step for the epoch) as Korney Chukovsky knew Sasha Chorny in person. No wonder that Shostakovich took this poetry to heart. Such perception of Chorny's life and poetry differed greatly from the point of view expressed in the Soviet press.

In the first decade of the 20th century, Chorny wrote a lot for the popular journal *Satirikon*. Chukovsky recollected that the poet was short, had a gaunt figure and never smiled. He would always wear a tight jacket and wrinkled trousers. The *Satires* were first published in Russia in 1910. Before the Russian Revolution the volume was reprinted four times and his poetry gained great popularity. Everybody from the student to the engineer knew his poems by heart. (Chukovsky, 1960, 5–6)

Fig. 31: *Satires*, Sasha Chorny. 1st ed.1910.

In 1918, Sasha Chorny left Russia for Europe, spent some years in Lithuania, moved to Berlin and then to Paris where he died. Isaak Glickman, a friend of Shostakovich, recalled that Shostakovich was attracted not only by Sasha Chorny's poetic world but also by his biography and death, in particular. The composer envied the way the poet abandoned this world. (Glickman, 1993). In fact, Sasha Chorny died in 1932 on helping to extinguish a fire in the little town of Lavandau in the South of France. As the legend goes, his dog Micky whom he depicted in *Micky the Fox Terrier's Diary* saw him dead, and died on his chest.

Chukovsky argues that the *Satires* should be perceived as a certain diary of its epoch that reflected the daily routine of Chorny's life in the slightest detail. (Chukovsky, 1960, 9). Sasha Chorny, "a blister on the skin of Russian literature" as he once called himself, rebelled against his epoch, full of platitude and cheap humour. When Petersburg was dying of hunger and filth, false patriotism flashed out the vulgarity of the "accursed questions," and the trivial love theme that Sasha Chorny derided in his poetry.

Shostakovich must have seen a certain likelihood between Sasha Chorny's and his own life. Of course, Shostakovich, who was born in Petersburg in 1906, remembered the prerevolutionary life quite vaguely, but the times of his adolescence were surely dark and penniless. He would work as a pianist at the cinema where (as he later confessed), he lost a lot of time and energy. (Yakovleva, 1980, 11).

The lodgers and the critics

Shostakovich completed his vocal cycle in June 1960. It was dedicated to the famous Russian opera singer Galina Vishnevskaya as well as *Seven poems of Alexandre Blok*, a vocal cycle composed seven years later. The vocal cycle comprises five poems by Sasha Chorny: *To a critic*, *Awakening of spring*, *Descendants*, *Misunderstanding*, and *Kreutzer Sonata*.

The poem *To a critic*, typed in italics, was separated from the others since it must have served as an epigraph to the first part of the book. In his cycle Shostakovich did the same thing. The first words of all five romances are quite colloquial, they repeat the title as if they were meant for a presenter that announces a new concert number. Galina Vishnevskaya, the first performer of the cycle, believed that the first words of each song must be performed impersonally without any anticipation of the future events (Shostakovich, 2000, 3).

Sure enough, Shostakovich knew what to tell the critic. It's worthwhile remembering the events of the campaign against the composer when his opera, *Lady Macbeth of the Mtsensk District*, was considered a mess and a muddle of sounds. That's why in this opening song of the cycle he laughed at the critic and scorned at his ignorance. In fact, this image descends from the hero of *The Donkey and the Nightingale* by a famous Russian fable writer Ivan Krïlov (1769–1844). The donkey that decided to judge the singing of the nightingale, is as dumb and clumsy in his assertions as any critic to whom the poet and the composer must explain the real meaning of the poetic "I":

If a poet, describing a lady, begins:
"I was walking down the street. My corset was pinching me in the side"
Don't, of course, take "I" here literally.
And if the lady is a poet

I will reveal a truth to you, my friend:
The poet is a man. He even has a beard[2].
(*To a critic*)

Needless to say, that in this song dedicated to the donkey critic (the attentive reader of the Russian literature certainly remembers Pushkin's use of this metaphor in the first lines of his novel in verse *Eugine Onegin*), Shostakovich warns the audience that the character of his poem bears no connection to him personally and this primitiveness is deliberate. Musicologists agree that the ignorance of the critic is also scorned in the piano postlude, composed as a trivial galop (Dobrykin, 1975, 27).

For Shostakovich the characters of the five poems are theatrical masks or puppets and he directs them as a deft puppeteer. Indeed, they are all victims of the epoch, whether it be a critic, a lodger with a fat laundry girl, or a vulgar poetess and her curly brunet admirer. The triviality of these images is underlined by the parody of the genre that serves the theme tune for this or that character.

In particular, when depicting a poetess from *Misunderstanding*, Shostakovich parodies the Russian social romance and cheap opera arias (Kremer, 2005). How does it happen? In this poem the vulgar poetess addresses her lover whom she asks to press his lips "to her foaming hips, beneath the scarlet garter" and claims that she's "as fresh as a flower's breath," thus provoking the young rake to join their "tired bodies." Implicitly, this text reminds the audience of the epigenous poetry of the epoch, pretentious poems of bad taste. That's why to describe the poetess, Shostakovich uses low register and chromatic intonations which taken together create an effect of a cheap opera aria.

Besides, the young rake (most probably, a poet himself?) is characterized by the frivolous sixths in the piano accompaniment that dramatically change the comfortable atmosphere of the sensual romance. The yelling of the poetess at one and the same musical interval when the rake embraces her "with the strength of a centaur" helps sour the atmosphere created by the "perfume wafted in the semi-darkness." The song finishes with one and the same vulgar phrase full of astonishment and offence that repeats three times: "He didn't understand the new poetry.".

As for *Descendants*, the third song in the cycle, the most transparent one from the ideological point of view, here the composer and the poet "took aim at the ageless injunction to sacrifice personal fulfillment so as to assure paradise for one's descendants; sentencing any descendants to fend for

---

[2] Hereinafter, the *Satires* are quoted in English after [Rappaport, 2012].

themselves, the poet [and the composer] peevishly demands a little reward from his own life on earth" (Fay, 2005, 221).

In the music to *Descendants* Shostakovich elaborates the theme of vulgarity with the help of a piano accompaniment that repeats one and the same waltz rhythm, so that it can be regarded as a beaten path of a vanilla plate, a caricature [Kremer, 2005]. Numerous repetitions in the music of *Descendants* symbolize the endless circle, the inability to get through the difficulties of the everyday routine:

> Our ancestors would crawl into cellars
> And whisper there to each other
> Times are tough, guys, But of course our kids
> Will live much better than us.
>
> The kids grew up. And they too
> Would crawl into cellars in parlous times.
> They too sighed: Our children
> Will see the sun after us…

In the romance that became a sticking point in the Soviet times, one hears the composer's reluctance to build a promising communistic future and to live under the regime. That is why all of a sudden, the monotonous intonation of the singer turns into a cry. As Maes put it, "the poem is a bitter critique of any rhetoric that justifies actual hardship with the promise of a better future for the next generations. The poem makes a powerful statement about the individual's right to happiness: let the descendants care for themselves…" (Maes, 2008, 245).

In comparison with *Descendants*, *The awakening of spring*, the second song of the cycle, is full of light humour. While the singer is telling a story of the March cats that are heralds of the spring and love, the resurrection of a cactus called Lasarus, in the piano part one hears the parody on the *Spring Waters* by Sergei Rachmaninov. The appearance of the genitor and a junk dealer is underlined by the quote from a traditional Russian folk song *Ah you, inner porch, my inner porch*. These two examples have already become very famous. The hymn to the spring might be regarded as an allusion to the Kchrushev Thaw (Rappaport, 2012), thus making a daily routine story quite political. Nevertheless, the end of the romance is still full of jokes and mild humour: "Who can I fall in love with, damn it?"

Galina Vishnevskaya thought that the character of this romance is an unlucky fellow dying from dullness of the winter and then overtaken by the spring feeling that made him rush towards adventures (Vishnevskaya, 2000, 3) On the contrary, Soviet critics accused Shostakovich of primitiveness and dull simplicity.

The same spring feeling changes the life of another citizen – a dull impoverished intellectual from *Kreutzer Sonata*. Though Shostakovich omitted the stanza about the blooming almond tree, the introduction is full of the spring feeling. With the introduction over, we see a lonely man sitting on his suitcase in a tiny room. His look is full of dull aversion. After the Revolution he has become a lodger in his own country, a penniless person deprived of civil rights. All his belongings include a quarter, a key, some sealing wax and a dime. Had he perhaps collected his things in order to leave the country as Sasha Chorny himself? It's quite obvious that Shostakovich felt pity to this man as he omitted a stanza where the lodger is compared to the donkey, thus refusing to fully deride his character.

The situations dramatically change when the intellectual notices a laundry girl who seduces him while washing the windows and bending amid the washing lines. Though Chorny and Shostakovich reflect on the one-size-fits-all approach, this thought is deliberately hidden by the love theme, that's why Shostakovich grotesquely accentuates the words, "*You* and *I*, at last we'll understand each other," at the end of *Kreutzer sonata*.

When the lodger finds himself on the sofa with Fekla it's not a bliss or a crowning moment as the text says. Shostakovich transforms the pathetic idea of *Kreutzer sonata* and reduces love to an odd coition after which both of the participants return to the daily routine as they are victims of the dead epoch with "no brother and no enemies." Having heard that the intellectual and the housemaid are sure to perfectly understand each other one feels but bitter irony as Chorny cynically denounces the idea of "going to the people," a mass movement of the democratic youth into Russia's rural areas.

Kreutzer sonata ends the cycle. Bit by bit, it becomes clear what lies behind the composer's grotesque. In fact, this music reveals the composer's attitude to the country where, being a public figure, Shostakovich felt himself lonely and could easily say with Sasha Chorny's words from "Descendants": "Times are tough [...] But of course our kids /Will live much better than us."

Two opening nights

Galina Vishnevskaya remembered that she had almost lost her voice when Shostakovich had offered her to sing "Satires." She first heard this vocal cycle at Shostakovich's. When the composer played his new work, she and Mstislav Rostropovich, a famous cellist and her husband, were amazed by its sarcasm and bitter humour. To perform "Satires," Shostakovich couldn't have chosen a better singer because Vishnevskaya started her career as a musical comedy singer and this vocal cycle was composed exactly for the variety performer (Wilson, 2006).

It was Vishnevskaya who suggested to Shostakovich to add a subtitle, *Pictures of the Past* to mask all contemporary references in the poems, and Shostakovich approved of it. Whenever the Soviet critics accused Sasha Chorny of thoughtlessness, they mentioned the subtitle as well. From their point of view, this poet aimed at showing characters of the past considered as prerevolutionary lower middle-class parasites. So, following Sasha Chorny, Shostakovich depicted the survivals of bourgeois views. In her memoirs Vishnevskaya later recollected that for this very reason Shostakovich was very anxious that the Satires wouldn't be authorized for performance (Vishnevskaya, 1984, 268–270).

In the commentaries to correspondence with Shostakovich, Isaak Glickman argues that in June 1960 the composer invited him to listen to his new vocal cycle, but this performance was suddenly postponed till 2 July. On 29 June, early in the morning, Shostakovich asked Glickman to visit him. He was desperate. Following Khrushchev's initiative, Shostakovich was to become the chairman of the Russian Music Union, and this position implied that he had to join the Communist Party, which he was reluctant to do (Glickman, 1993, 165).

Satires were first performed on 22 February 1961 by Galina Vishnevskaya and Mstislav Rostropovich. On 29 January, a famous Russian paper *Pravda* (*Truth*) published a small article about Galina Vishnevskaya in the section *People of our art* [Grosheva, 1961). The journalist described the vocal parts Vishnevskaya performed at the Bolshoi Theatre (Tatiana in the *Eugine Onegin*, Kathrine in the *Taming of the Shrew*, Natasha in *War and Peace*, etc.) and emphasized her ardent desire to work hard and the vocal skills, especially her pianissimo. The article ended with the announcement of the concert.

Fig. 32: The article about Galina Vishnevskaya in *Pravda* in January 1961.

Actually, many reviewers of the time were convinced that Vishneskaya had a real talent to perform contemporary music and that is why, Soviet composers eagerly dedicated their works to her. One more announcement of the concert appeared in the paper *The Moscow Evening*. It clearly said that the tickets to the Recital Hall of the Moscow Conservatory had been sold out very quickly. The author also mentioned that the piano part would be performed by Mstislav Rostropovich, a worldwide famous cellist who was to make his debut as a pianist on "A concert with a surprise," 1961.

Fig. 33: Galina Vishnevskaya and Mstislav Rostropovich.

The concert in the Moscow Conservatory consisted of two parts. In the first part, the singer performed the romances by Alexander Dargomyzhsky and *The songs and dances of the death* by Modest Musorgsky (1839–1881). After the interval, Vishneskaya sang some romances by Sergei Prokofiev, and *Satires*. The singer then recollected that on performing "Descendants," she saw fear at people's faces. Shostakovich was very pale. Everybody was moved because Lavrentiy Beria's and Joseph Stalin's ideas were still fresh in their minds. When she finished, the audience started crying and she sang the *Satires* once again from the very beginning to the end.

After the concert, one more review came out in the paper *Soviet Music*. On praising Vishnevskaya, the critic blamed Shostakovich for the choice of poems, stating that the selection was ill-founded (Lyakhotin, 1961), whereas the music was much more spectacular than Sasha Chorny's poetry.

From one of the letters addressed to Glickman we know that Shostakovich planned one more event in Leningrad as well (the letter from

26 February 1961), but due to different circumstances the concert in the Grand Hall of Leningrad's Conservatory was held much later, on 27 May. Afterwards, Shostakovich was severely blamed for ill-taste and frivolity. The song *Descendants* was censored, and Vishnevskaya was unable to record the vocal cycle on TV as she refused to sanction cuts in the *Satires* (Vishnevskaya, 1984, 268–270). It is only in May 1966 that the concert was recorded by Leningrad Television and then broadcasted for the general audience.

"He didn't understand the new poetry"

In 1962, the *Satires* were performed in Moscow, Leningrad, Gorky, and Edinburgh in Scotland. One of the reviews on the *Satires* called *The concert of the candidate to a party deputy* brought Shostakovich's name back to the political context (Golubovskaya, 1962). The journalist praised Shostakovich and named him but a comrade and a teacher.

In spring 1962, Shostakovich was elected deputy to the Council of Nationalities of the USSR Supreme Soviet (representing Leningrad). In fact, Shostakovich performed his duties quite industriously even at the expense of his creative work. This could also be considered one of the rituals of the Soviet past when a worldwide famous composer was obliged to perform as people's representative. In the archives of the Soviet documentaries, one can see Shostakovich in the Kremlin meeting room with dairywomen and cotton pickers.

In August 1962 the *Satires* were performed in Edinburgh at the International Music Festival, and the paper *Isvestiya* ("The Latest News") published an article called *The Englishmen cried: "Bravo, Shostakovich"* (25 August 1962. The music including the *Satires* was warmly welcome by the audience that burst in applause. Europe had known Shostakovich as a great symphonist, but in 1962 they saw him as a satirist, and one review was even titled *Dmitry is smiling*.

The article with almost the same title came off the press in the Soviet Union as well (Sokolsky, 1962). Its author was the first to mention the musical quotations in the vocal cycle by Shostakovich. But as predicted, Sokolsky turned a deaf ear to Sasha Chorny's poetry that he called bourgeois and lacking progressive ideas. In his perception, Sasha Chorny was not capable of "great social conclusions" as he was much alike his characters. In his perception, Soviet composer Shostakovich certainly goes further by unmasking philistine position of the poet and criticizing it from the point of view of the groundbreaking ideology. In the appraisal of Sasha Chorny, as a parasite, Sokolsky forestalls the ideas of the authorities concerning such "parasites" as Joseph Brodsky, also a curly young poet of the time, who lost his citizenship and never came back to Russia.

In the early 1970s, the *Satires* were mentioned in the Soviet press less and less. The journalists gave way to musicologists who were to reinterpret both the music and the poetry. Ironically, in the 1960s, Sasha Chorny's poetry was apprehended by politically biased journalists of the Soviet papers. These critics couldn't understand that the inner arrangement of the *Satires* reflects how deeply Shostakovich was moved by the *Satires*.

While working on the vocal cycle the irony couldn't have escaped Shostakovich, in his cycle he reflected on the modern Soviet society. The image of the donkey and the nightingale and the vulgar gallop can't but support this idea. Behind the clown's smile the attentive reader sees the weary face of the composer or the poet who, as it turns out, have so very much in common. Living in a Soviet country, being hugely involved in public activity, Shostakovich felt himself a lodger of his time who was unable to change anything. Only music gave him a chance to become a real puppet player. But the more efficiently he worked, the more the epoch manipulated him. The *Satires* and its reception in the Soviet press couldn't but serve the main proof to this idea.

Bibliography

Chukosky, K. 1960. Sasha Chorny. In *Chorny Sasha. Poems*. Ed. by L. Yevstegneeva. Leningrad: Soviet writer. (*In Russian*)

Golubovskaya N., 1962. Concert of the candidate to deputies. In *Music frames*. 15 March. (*In Russ.*)

Grosheva, Ye. 1961. Galina Vishnevskaya. In *Truth*. 29 January. P. 6. (*In Russ.*)

A concert with a surprise, 1961. In *The evening Moscow*. 22 February. P. 3. (*In Russ.*)

Dobrikin, E. 1975. Musical satire in the vocal works by Shostakovich. In *The problems of musicology*. №. 3. Moscow: Soviet composer. (*In Russ.*)

Fay, Laurel E. 2005. Shostakovich. A life. Oxford: Oxford U. P., 2005.

Kremer, A. 2005. *The vocal cycles by D. Shostakovich*. Moscow: The Russian Academy of Music named after Gnesin. (*In Russ.*)

Glickman Isaak Ed. 1993. *Letters to a friend. Shostakovich to Isaak Glickman*. Moscow: DSCH. (*In Russ.*)

Lyakhotin, B. 1961. Galina Vishnevskaya sings. Mstislav Rostropovich accompanies. In *Soviet Music*. № 4. (*In Russ.*)

Meyer K. 1998. *Shostakovich. Life. Creative work. The epoch.* Saint-Petersburg: Horison. (*In Russ.*)
Petrushanskaya, E. 2006. Shostakovich as a reader. In *Music Academy.* № 3. (*In Russ.*)
Rappaport, G. C. 2012. *Five Satires (Pictures of the Past) by Dmitrii Shostakovich* (op. 109*): The*
Mayes, Francis, 2008. Between reality and transcendence: Shostakovich's songs. In *The Cambridge companion to Shostakovich.* Ed. by. P. Fairclough, D. Fanning. Cambridge: Cambridge U. P. P. 231–258.
Musical Unity of a Vocal Cycle. In *Contemplating Shostakovich: Life, Music and Film.* Ed. by A. Ivashkin and A. Kirkman. Farnham: Ashgate.
Shostakovich, Irina. 2008. *Shostakovich and the book. An Interview with Irina Shostakovich.* In *Music life.* Vol. 4. (*In Russ.*)
Sokolsky, M. 'Shostakovich is laughing.' In *Izvestiya.* 1962. 4 September.
Yakovleva, M., ed. 1980. *Shostakovich on his epoch and himself* (1926–1975). Moscow: Soviet composer. (*In Russ.*)
Vasina-Grossman, V., 1980. Chamber-vocal music by Shostakovich. In *Soviet musical culture. History, tradition. Modernity.* Moscow: Music. (*In Russ.*)
Vishnevskaya, G., 1984. A Russian Story. San Diego, CA: Harcourt Brace Jovanovich.
Visnevskaya, G. 1991. *Galina.* Moscow: Horison. (*In Russ.*)
Visnevskaya, G. 2000. The Introduction. In *Shostakovich D. Satires., Britten B. The echo of a poet.* Saint-Petersburg: Composer. (*In Russ.*)
Wilson E. 2006. *Shostakovich's life told by his contemporaries.* Saint-Petersburg: Composer. (*In Russ.*)

POETRY AND WAR: MIGUEL HERNÁNDEZ SET TO MUSIC

PATRICIA PÉREZ BORRERO

Fig. 34: Miguel Hérnandez haranguing his fellow soldiers.

Music in Spanish Literature. Generation of 27.

The relationship between literature and music has been widely studied throughout the years. As Claudio Guillén (1924-2007) remarks in his study *Entre lo Uno y lo Diverso* (1985) the study of interdisciplinary arts must be carried out. Sometimes, there is no frontier between literature and other arts as is often with music. They are not different systems with individual characteristics, but rather, they are aesthetic ways to express interartistic convergences. Henry Remak (1914-2010) defines comparative literature as:

> "the study of literature beyond the confines of a particular country, and the study of the relationships between literature on the one hand and other areas of knowledge and beliefs, such as the arts (e.g., painting, sculpture, architecture, music)."
>
> (Stallknecht & Frenz, 1961, 3)

In the relationship between literature and other areas a lot of intersectionality arises. Multiple examples can be found in Spanish literature. From Medieval literature, whose religious chants and jugular poems were very closely linked to music, and to modern literature from the eighteenth to the twentieth century. Given that literature has always been related to music, in Spanish history this bond has been stressed during the twentieth century. During the Modernist era, movements such as "The Generation of 27" and war poetry have repeatedly been set to music. Spain was completely shocked by the Spanish Civil War (1936-1939) which led to new forms of expression through various artistic movements. There are many singers taking Spanish poets whose works were set to music. The "Generation of 27", formed by a group of poets that arose during 1923-1927, created avant-garde forms of poetry and connected such stylish literature to popular roots. Their poems place a lot of emphasis on music as shown by various studies about that. In 1986, on the 50th anniversary of Lorca´s death, the exhibition "Music in Generation of 27" was held in Granada, where several studies and publications were presented. That generation, unlike their predecessors, somehow reconciled Spanish literature with music, as it is remarked in the article 'Letters on music by Jorge Guillén' by Martín Moreno, Antonio:

> One of the main characteristics is their reunion with music, an attitude that had traditionallybeen a constant in our history of literature and that somehow had been lost in the "Generation of 98", suffering from, as Federico Sopeña points out, a strong musical deafness.
>
> (Moreno, 1995, 245-264).

They declared their utmost admiration for the *Cancionero of Barbieri*, a compilation of poetry and music from the 15th and 16th centuries, composed in 1830. Their first official meeting, dedicated to multiple musical references and studies, was held to commemorate the Spanish writer Luis de Góngora (1561-1627). Some of the poets of the group had a notable affinity to musical expression, especially Jorge Guillén (1893-1984), whose passion for music can be easily detected throughout his work. Many of his poems were addressed to music. According to him, as for many Spanish poets, there was a passion for the idea of composition, poetry, music, and rhythm. Besides Jorge Guillén, we can find numerous other examples, including Luis Cernuda (1902-1963), who dedicated a poem to Mozart, Garcia Lorca (1898-1936), who played the piano and recorded some songs, identifying himself with *cante jondo*, Gerardo Diego (1896-1987), who even wrote a book called *Offering to Chopin*, and Rafael Alberti (1902-1999), who spent the money he had won as a prize for Barbieri´s songbook. Then, from the 1960s onwards, followed a number of poems set to music by great poets such as Paco Ibáñez, Joan Manuel Serrat, Jarcha, and other Spanish singers. Miguel Hernández (1910-1942) is one of them and his poems were highly significant during the Civil War.

Miguel Hernández

Miguel Hernández was one of the poets of the 'Spanish Generation of 27', and his firm position during the War got him to become the voice of the Republican side during the Spanish Civil War. He was born in Orihuela, a village in the Alicante Province, in a low-income farming family. So, his childhood was strongly linked to peasantry, nature, and the working class in general. No wonder he grew up with deep proletarian ideas. Even though his father did not let him pursue a formal education, he was determined to become a poet. When he was young, he was in permanent conflict with his father because of that. Yet, that lack of diffused culture among the masses was so common in Spain at the time, clearly resulting from the Civil War and the subsequent dictatorship. Many intellectuals were exiled, some of them were killed or died in those years, and the war became a dark shadow in the history of Hernández's beloved country. Thus, his father refused to allow him to achieve his dreams as an artist. In spite of this paternal conflict, his relationship with his mother was totally different and she supported him. Finding allusions to this situation throughout his work is quite normal, just as it is frequent to see him confess his mother how he felt deep within himself.

In 1936, the Spanish Civil war broke out after a military coup led by Francisco Franco, and it drove Spain to three years of fighting between the Republican and Nationalist factions, leaving the country deeply devastated. Miguel was a member of the Fifth Regiment and he took part actively during the fight. He campaigned for the Republicans, writing poems for the troops, and even reading them aloud in the trenches. He referred to himself as "the wind of the nation," using the ideas expressed through his poetry as a weapon to lift people's spirits up in their darkest moments. He could not understand those artists who did not act to help. A poet had no other choice, he had to write about the horrors of the conflict: "Miguel points with his finger at those writers who close their eyes to the tremendous reality that surrounds them." (Cano Ballesta, 2017, *Intro.* 37)

For him, giving peasants the opportunity to get involved in cultural activities is part of his task as a poet. He participated in the "Pedagogical missions," developed in 1935-1936, which allowed him to present music, poetry, and theatre to the people in the villages. The peasants were deeply touched by this artistic expression when they could see it for themselves. His most famous biographer, Jesucristo Riquelme (1956-) recalls in his *Miguel Hernández, obra exenta que completa la obra completa* that "the social function of the artist is a concept strongly developed by Miguel Hernández." (Riquelme, 2012, 164). As it happens, he attacks other artists, such as Pablo Picasso, who from his point of view, "plays with new forms and runs away from the real art of painting." (Ibid.) For Miguel Hernández, reality is cruel enough to even be the only theme of an artist´s repertoire. His social function is almost an obligation. According to his own words: "the poet moves emotions like nobody else, the poet makes the revolution. I will never deny my destiny of poetry, that is the destiny of the nation, like another skin [...]" (Cano Ballesta, 2017, 13).

This explains his active participation and strong involvement in the Spanish war. Miguel could not escape as other Spanish artists did, and he was arrested when the war had just ended. He was accused of attacking Franco´s cause with his poetry. Even though he was initially condemned to death, in the end he was imprisoned for 30 years. However, he stayed in many different prisons and suffered from a lot of diseases. He eventually died of tuberculosis in 1942 in an Alicante prison, leaving a vast amount of poetry and writing to his beloved and broken Spain.

Miguel Hernández´s poetry deals with three main topics. For him, they are the crucial moments in one's lifetime: death, love, and life. The three of them are correlated in one: "without one of them the other two cannot exist." (Juan Cano Ballesta, 68). In his poem 'Three wounds,' he presents this interrelation that affects all his work, his world, and his sense of life. The war only amplified his perspective of death as a part of life and his longing for his wife's love, and he believed that the blend of soldier and man enhanced each other in himself. From his first book, "*Perito en lunas*" (1933), he portrays himself as an idealistic young man, "an expert in ethereal and romantic beliefs." And throughout the war years, his works ("The lightning that never stops," 1936; "The wind of the town", published in 1937; and "The man stalks", 1939) reveal himself as a strong figure in the cultural atmosphere of the Civil War. He matured through suffering for his country and friends, tried desperately to support the cause of the needy with his poems. His last and unfinished book "*Cancionero de romances y ausencias*," was published posthumously in 1958. It consists of poems written during his stay in various prisons throughout the country, pleading for the nonsense to stop the fight while yearning for help.

War poems set to music by Lan Adomian

Music and poetry have always had a strong bond. Although war is the main topic of most of Hernández´s poems during the years of the war, only three of them were set to music. His poems set to music became war songs that were sung in the trenches for and by the soldiers that were fighting. He used his words as weapons against the Nationalist side, sometimes attacking their barbaric actions, sometimes regretting the nightmare his beloved country was in, and other times trying to raise Republican soldiers' spirits for battle.

His first poems set to music are some of those written in "*Viento del pueblo*" ("The wind of the town"), a compilation of war poems written during 1936-1937, which transitions from the profound "I" to the socially committed "we." Miguel thus emerges as the voice of the Republican side. At the same time, he is named Delegate of Culture and he works actively during the first years of the struggle, writing texts for radio and to be read aloud in the trenches. He also fights in different battles (defence of Madrid, Teruel, etc.), so, he has both the experience of real struggle and the idealized values of the soldiers. Miguel didn't think of the war as an individual issue; rather, he reinforces the social and collective brotherhood that was necessary to defeat the opposing side.

In the prologue of this book, which is dedicated to his beloved friend and poet Vicente Aleixandre, Miguel writes the following words:

> "Vicente: for us, who have been raised poets among all men (…) We have been flowing from the spring of the guitars of the nation, and each poet that dies leaves in another´s hands, as a heritage, an instrument that has come since eternity (...)" (Hernández, *Viento del Pueblo*, 55)

For him, poetry and music are tied together and enhanced naturally, and he makes a metaphor with poetry and music as instruments that express themselves. Each poet must leave his legacy as an instrument to be played for the upcoming poets, so that they might create the music of their own nations by writing poems with a social purpose.

During the time he spent in Valencia, working as Delegate of Culture, he met Lan Adomian (1905-1979), a Russian Mexican composer and

International Brigadist who had come to Spain to meet intellectuals during the war. He met Adomian in 1938 and they collaborated together, being Adomian the one who first set Miguel Hernández's words to music. Two of his poems were musicalized by Adomian: "*Las puertas de Madrid*" ("The gates of Madrid") and "*La guerra, madre, la guerra*" ("War, mother"). Both of these poems were compiled in the Collection called *Songs of Fighting* (1938, by Carlos Palacio). When an article by Carlos Palacio titled "Songs for the defence of Madrid" appeared in the newspaper *Comisario* (number 3, published in 1938). On page 50, he made a reference to the historical defense and how it had inspired poets and musicians: "Poets and musicians have been inspired by the glorious defense of Madrid (...) Exaltation songs of the invincible spirit of *madrileños*" (Cano Ballesta, *Viento del pueblo,* 40).

'*Las puertas de Madrid*' refers to the heroic defense of this city during the war. It took over eight months of struggles, attacks from different zones, strategies, and historical battles until it was finally taken by Nationalists in March 1937. The poem was written in autumn 1937, one year after the siege of Franco's troops in Madrid had begun. Adomian set it to music in 1938 and got it published in a magazine. The poem emphasizes the power of the people of Madrid defending their beloved city from fascists: "The gates are of Heaven / the gates of Madrid. / Closed by the people / nobody can open them".

Madrid withstood various battles and Franco's troops had to struggle to take control of the city. Its inhabitants were proclaimed heroes for defending their city fiercely. Miguel Hernández's words delve into this feeling: "People are at the gates / as a wounding key."

People are the guardians of the place. For Miguel, the importance of the peasants and the laborers is vital to the nation's development. His words give them force to resist even more, idealizing their position during the fight. He also refers to the Manzanares river, which crosses Madrid, as an important part of the city: "Oh Manzanares river / without any other apple tree / that those people that make you / as big as the sea." Once again, people are holding up the city, supporting the attack and protecting the place. The Allegro music Adomian added to these proud words is completed with an heroic female voice who happily sings the importance of people defending their places. This piece of music was also interpreted by a group of soldiers within one of Hernández's plays ("Shepherd of death", 1938). As Riquelme points out in his exempt production of the poet:

> "The song is reproduced on page 639 (...) with little variations on punctuation and repeating the last two verses after each stanza" (Riquelme, 2012, 133)

Thus, not only was the song and poem known by soldiers, but it also appeared within his own works as a singing piece to emphasize people's power.

The second poem turned into music by Adomian is called "*La guerra, madre*" ("War, mother"). This poem was written by Miguel Hernández in 1937 too, and it has a different tone. With a devastated heart, the poet recounts to his mother all the horrors that he was witnessing: "War, mother: the war / my house lonely and empty." The tone is completely different, and Adomian reflects this; a slow piano intro is broken by the lament of the voice that sings languidly the terrible consequences of the war. The poem changes in the second part its topic and starts with "life, mother, life / life to be killed." Adomian introduces a female voice for this part, singing what life has become as a consequence of the war. The last part of the poem is sung by the two voices at the same time: "the deep steps can not be heard / in my soul and in the street / dying letters, dead ones / war, mother, the war." Both sing desperately the devastating effects of the struggle, the empty streets, the never-received letters, the disasters in people's souls. The poem was written in 1938 and Lan Adomian set it to music right at the same time. It signifies a contrast not only in reference to 'The gates of Madrid,' but also to the exaltation of war in some of his poems. In 'War, mother,' a profound reflection on the real meaning of the war can be seen. And Adomian's music reinforced its reflective and sad tone, even though it is an "andantino", but contrasting with the voices and words.

Both poems have had various versions over the years, from songwriters to punk bands. But Adomian was the first to set them to music. It was not the only collaboration with Adomian. In the same year, Miguel Hernández was in charge of writing the lyrics for the Sixth Division anthem. This Division was a unit of the Republican Army in Spain and they relied on Hernández to create a hymn for it. At the same time, the poet chose Adomian, as he revealed in his letters:

> "One day Miguel came to my house. I had a room there and I was composing music. He entered with some officials of the Sixth Division and told them I was the right person to compose the new anthem for the Division. He gave me the lyrics and just left. I stayed the whole night composing and I finished it completely for the following morning". (Riquelme, 2012, 135)

This time the music has a hymn tone, with praise and pride for the army. It is, again, addressed to his "mother," showing proudly how the Sixth Division would contribute to restoring peace in the country. The chorus repeats: "of Spain, mother, is Sixth Division / of Spain, mother, is Sitxh division / which will save Spain from the invaders / Homeland of my life / shore of my soul." The members of the Sixth Division were highly motivated by the hymn, which could be sung throughout the trenches and the marches toward the battle. This last piece of music was not included in Carlos Palacios' *Collection* of 1938, but it appeared with the other two in the compilation *Canciones de lucha 1936-1939. Selección* (Dahiz EGT 745 CD, 1998).

In 1957, some years after Hernández's death, the Republican exiled government asked Adomian to change the Republican anthem. Miguel Hernández's words from the Sixth Division lyrics and, with the help of the writer Margarita Nelken (1894-1968), an active Spanish politician, feminist, and writer created a new version of the Republican hymn. It was never published as the official new one, but Riquelme followed the trail of this piece until he discovered the links between both anthems in 2002. He makes a contrast between the poem of Hernández and the new proposed anthem with lyrics adapted by Margarita Nelken, and explains:

"Some of the belligerent allusions of Hernández's poem were blurred into more general and patriotic in Adomian's version (…)"
"We reproduced the score, with some instrumental arrangements for orchestra and choir" (Riquelme, *Miguel Hernández, obra exenta que completa la obra completa,* 139)

This hymn, never proclaimed as the new official one, was recovred by Miguel Hernández's scholars and it was set to music for the documentary on the poet released in 2004. Riquelme also exposes that Adomian used some other texts from the poet to produce in 1964, the 'Cantata de las ausencias' (p. 133). The strong bond between the poet and the musician can be seen in the extant productions as masterpieces of war poetry set to music.

Joan Manuel Serrat sets Hernández to music. 'Lullaby of the Onion'

Apart from the relationship and collaborations between Miguel Hernández and Lan Adomian, there can be no doubt that his poems were linked to music. He named some poems with musical references, as for example, 'The song of the poet-soldier,' 'Chant of independence,' 'Song of the antipilot,' and 'Song of the machine gun.' The devices he used throughout his poetry are highly connected to music: the tone, the chorus or central parts of the poem repeated with a constant cadence. In the 1960s, some musicians started to sing Hernández's poems. From then on, multiple versions have been produced by various Spanish singers and bands, such as the band "Jarcha," Paco Ibáñez, Manolo Sanlúcar, or even the flamenco singer Camarón de la Isla. But one of the most remarkable pieces of his poetry turned into contemporary music was led by Joan Manuel Serrat, influential Spanish songwriter and singer.

In 1972, Serrat published his work *Miguel Hernández*, a thorough homage to the writer, where he set to music ten of his most famous poems. Serrat released the album three years before the death of the dictator, Francisco Franco, and the historical facts that occurred after his death in 1975 were full of hope and a spirit of open-mindedness. Intellectuals were enthusiastic about the idea of having more freedom to express their ideas and the Transition years in Spain (from the dictatorship to modern democracy) were sometimes filled with those songs (e.g. 'Para la libertad' - 'For Freedom'). But the song that excites the audience most is the musicalized 'Lullaby of the Onion.'

This poem was written by Miguel Hernández in 1939, before the Civil war ended. The writer was imprisoned in Madrid and received a letter from his wife. She told him that they had only onion and bread to eat, as she was breastfeeding his little son, the milk would be as poor as onion. He had a strong impact and wrote the poem. It is addressed to his second son, and it reflects the extreme hunger, poverty, and desperation of so many families during those years. Luis Rodríguez Isern, who was sharing a cell with him, wrote for an interview in *El dominical* in 1992:

> "One morning, in the jail playground, Miguel read for us some "*coplillas*", as he called them, inspired by his wife's letter, which told she only had bread and onion to eat. (…) I made the transcription and put the title "Lullaby of the Onion", adding that note to all the editions explaining why Miguel had composed it" (Ferris, José Luis. *Miguel Hernández. Pasiones, cárcel y muerte de un poeta*, 486)

If we take a look at its content, two parts can be clearly distinguished. The first one is dark, sad, full of images that evoke starvation and pain: "The onion is frost / shut in and poor / Frost of your days / and of my nights. / Hunger and onion / black ice and frost / large and round." Miguel was having extremely hard times, alone in the dark and cold cell; and after that letter he sadly realises that his wife's reality was not very different from his. He moves his background to his wife's at home, so he can see his son trembling in cold and being fed by onion milk.

> "My little boy / was in hunger's cradle. / He was nursed / on onion blood / But your blood / is frosted with sugar, / onion and hunger /. A dark woman / dissolved in moonlight / pours herself thread by thread / into the cradle".

The cradle appears as a metaphor of the country they were living in "a hunger's cradle" also refers to Spain, where the baby was being raised. Blood and hunger are mixed at the very end of the war. And the figure of the mother, representing all the mothers of Spain, taking care of the poor people, and trying to sweeten the situation.

From that point, we can see the second part of the poem which turns into a more hopeful allegory. First of all, Miguel focuses on his son's laughter as a medicine to heal any disease. "Lark of my house / keep laughing / The laughter of your eyes / is the light of the world". Children's laughter is a promise of a better future, a peaceful world where Miguel wants his son to live. "Your laughter frees me, / gives me wings, / It sweeps away my loneliness / knocks down my cell." He imagines his son's laughing and all children in Spain laughing and he can feel free. As he uses his words to fight, children can use their laughter to stop this barbaric situation. "Your laughter is / the sharpest sword / conqueror of flowers / and larks. / Rival of the sun / Future of my bones / and of my love." Freedom, future, and flowers complete this part of the poem. Hope, faith, and trust in a better place.

Finally, Miguel reflects on childhood, and he pledges that his son will not wake up to this reality. "I woke up from childhood / don't you wake up. / I have to frown: / always laugh / Keep to your cradle / defending laughter / feather by feather." The poem ends by emphasizing that he'd better not know the horrors of the war: "Don't find out what's happening / or what goes on." (Poem translated by Robert Bly)

Music is present in the poem in different ways. First of all, the title suggests music itself. A lullaby, according to the Cambridge dictionary, is "a quiet song that is sung to children to help them go to sleep". We can also find another definition, that is "the music for such a song.". So, before we read the poem, we already know it is a song, a quiet one, with the intention of caring for a baby, letting him sleep peacefully. However, the title was not chosen by the poet, but rather it was named like that by Rodríguez Isern, his companion in the cell. He transcribed the poem and put the title as Miguel wrote it for his son, Rodríguez Isern named it as "lullaby", whereas the transcriptions of Hernández always name it as "The onion is frost". In a personal interview with Jesucristo Riquelme in 2004, Rodríguez Isern told him the story behind the title:

> "The Lullaby of the onion had no name, from the very first moment Miguel said they were some *"coplillas"* he had composed for his little son. (...) And I sent the verses to his friend Vicente Aleixandre and named it "Lullaby of the Onion" and so it has remained forever" (Riquelme, *Obra exenta*, 41)

Regarding its metric, the poem is enhanced directly to music. It is composed of twelve *"seguidillas"*, seven verses each. *Seguidillas* are a popular Spanish strophe structures, formed by seven/eleven syllables verses, that rhyme in the odd ones. It has a lot of variations, but the common trait is that the verses are short, and they have a musical cadence. It is because originally *seguidillas* were used as part of the folklore and were sung aloud. In the Collins dictionary, we find the following definitions for them:

1. a Spanish dance in a fast triple rhythm
2. a pience of music composed for or in the rhythm of this dance
3. *Prosody*. A stanzaic form consisting of four to seven lines and marked by a characteristic rhythm.

Seguidillas are the base of a wide variety of Spanish folklore, especially used in flamenco, such as *sevillanas* or *alegrías* from Cádiz. They have a popular origin and were used to sing aloud by people. In the eighteenth century, some poets started using them as a formal verse stanza, and Modernist writers recover it for their poetry. There are a lot of variations, and the one Miguel uses in his 'Lullaby of the onion" is the composed one (adding three verses to each four and rhyming assonant in a cadent way). *Seguidillas* were also used by some of his contemporaries, such as Lorca or Machado. They convey music in its form and can easily be sung while you read them.

Serrat, in his homage CD *Miguel Hernández*, made a version of the lullaby. But he moves away from the popular folklore and he emphasizes the childish tone of the music. It starts with little twinkles and a slow piano accompanies the song. Like a music box, notes appear repeatedly during the song. Violins and an in-crescendo music with more instruments appear step by step. Flutes appear in the hopeful part of the poem and towards the end of the song, Serrat has a stronger voice, a powerful way of marking words. Music accompanies the tone of triumph, hope, faith, and a better future for Spain. This version of Miguel Hernández's poem is widely known in Spain and Serrat was one of the musicians who set him to music and spread his poetry many years after this terrible episode of Spanish history.

***

It is said that Miguel's body was buried with his eyes open wide. According to Ferris's biography Nobody was able to shut them, and a lot of doctors tried to explain the cause of this unusual fact, attaching it to hypertoroids or even to Dalrymple's synpthom. (page 563). Undoubtedly, those eyes were never closed to the world they looked at. Vicente Aleixandre, his close friend, wrote an elegy for him right after his death and it starts:

> "I don´t know. / There was no music. / Your big blue eyes /
> were opened forever upon the ignorant emptiness"
> (Vicente, 2010, *Poesías Completas: Elegy on Miguel Hernández's death*)

This is how he recalls the analogy Hernández made years earlier between poetry and music. But once he died, there would be no music left. Aleixandre continued writing about the poet's death:

> "I saw your face, so shockingly Spanish. Lying, suffered, and harmed, (…)
> And in your big eyes, the absence of music, sunk. The music that had sounded so hard in your pupils".

He witnessed the horrors of the war and he was a sharp observer of his environment, putting voice to the disasters of the war. Miguel Hernández's eyes are still open since his words still exist in Spain's historical background. He still looks at us and tells us not to forget the most terrible event of our history: Civil War.

Bibliography

Aleixandre, Vicente. 2010. *Poesías completas*. Madrid: Visor Libros.
Bly Robert. *Selected Poems* by Miguel Hernandez, translated by Robert Bly. 1989 (edited by Timothy Baland) New York: White Pine Press.
Cano Ballesta. Juan. 1978. *La poesía de Miguel Hernández*. Madrid: Editorial Gredos.
Cano Ballesta, Juan. 2017. *Viento del pueblo*. Madrid: Catedra, Letras Hispanicas.

Fernández Palmeral, Ramón. 2015. *Miguel Hernández, el poeta de las tres heridas*. USA: Amazon Books.

Ferris, José Luis. 2020 (5ª edition). *Miguel Hernández. Pasiones, cárcel y muerte de un poeta*. Sevilla: Fundación José Manuel Lara.

Guillén, Claudio. 2005. *Entre lo uno y lo diverso. Introducción a la Literatura Comparada (Ayer y hoy)*. Barcelona: Marginales Tusquets Editores.

Hernández, Miguel. 2020 (15th edition). *Viento del pueblo*. Madrid: Cátedra, Letras Hispánicas.

Hernández, Miguel. 2017 (5th edition). *El rayo que no cesa*. Barcelona: Austral, Espasa Libros.

Martín Moreno, Antonio. 'Letters on music by Jorge Guillén'. In *Cuadernos de arte de la Universidad de Granada*, No 265. (1995): (https://doi.org/10.30827/caug.v26i0.10829)

Newton P. Stallkneicht and Horst Frenz. *Comparative Literature, its Definition and Function* 1961. Illinois: Southern Illinois University Press

Riquelme, Jesucristo. 2012. *Miguel Hernández, obra exenta que completa la obra completa*. Madrid: Editorial EDAF, S.L.

Riquelme, Jesucristo. 2019. *Epistolario general de Miguel Hernández*. 2019: Editorial EDAF, S. L.

Sánchez Vidal, Agustín. 1992. *Miguel Hernández, desamordazado y regresado*. Barcelona: Editorial Planeta.

Sopeña, Federico. 1974. *Música y literatura*. Madrid: Ediciones Rialp, S.A.

Website: www.flamencopolis.com
(http://ciposfred.blogspot.com/2015/12/estudio-literario-y-analisis-metrico-de.html)

Contributors

Gianfranca Balestra was Full Professor of American Literature at the University of Siena, Italy, until 2015. She has published extensively on nineteenth- and twentieth- century literature of the United States, with monographs on Edith Wharton, Edgar Allan Poe and F. Scott Fitzgerald. She edited and introduced the first Italian translations of Edith Wharton's *The Reef* and *The Touchstone,* and a new Italian version of Fitzgerald's *The Great Gatsby* (Marsilio, 2011). She is well known internationally for her scholarly work on Edith Wharton and is currently co-editing volume 29 ('Translations and Adaptations') of *The Complete Works of Edith Wharton* to be published by Oxford University Press. She has carried out research into the Wharton papers held at the Beinecke Library at Yale University, the Lilly Library at Indiana University, the Houghton Library at Harvard University. Her fields of research include: the literature of the fantastic, literary and intersemiotic translation, literature and music, women writers, and Canadian literature. She co-edited books on the literary canon, on portraits of women in literature, and on Alice Munro. Her essays have appeared in Italian and international journals and books. Her most recent book *Riflessi del Grande Gatsby. Traduzioni, cinema, teatro, musica* (2019) focuses on the Italian translations of Fitzgerald's novel as well as its many film, theatre, and music adaptations, from opera to musicals and ballets.

Luís Manuel A. V. Bernardo is a Professor at the Department of Philosophy of NOVA University of Lisbon Faculty of Social and Human Sciences (FCSH). He has held various academic management positions, more recently, as Assistant Vice-Dean for Curriculum Management and Teaching Assessment; Responsible for the NOVA FCSH Quality System; Head of the master's degree in Teaching Philosophy; Departmental Erasmus Coordinator. He is also a researcher at CHAM - Centre for the Humanities, of which he is also the Vice-Director for the publications and the Library. Main teaching, searching, and publishing fields: Philosophy of Knowledge and Language, Philosophy of Education, Philosophy of Culture. He is particularly interested in texts and discourses that contributed to define the direction of Modernity. Co-Director of *Cultura - Revista de História e Teoria das Ideias*, he has published several books, papers, and translations on different textualities.

Some recent publications: "The New Golden Age: The Cultural Memory of the Discoveries in the Portuguese Enlightenment Imaginary," Mihaela Irimia, Dragoş Manea, and Andreea Paris (eds.). In *Literature and Cultural Memory, Internationale Forschungen zur allgemeinen und vergleichenden Literaturwissenschaft*, vol. 194, Leiden, Brill/Rodopi, 2017, pp. 155-172; "Diderot, Mathematics and the Idea of a Scientific Revolution: Retake of a Recurrent Theme." In *META: Research in Hermeneutics, Phenomenology, and Practical Philosophy*, Vol. XI, N°. 1 / JUNE 2019, pp. 135-160; "A Science of the Probable: Epistemological Inventiveness according to Diderot," Mário Kong, Rosário Monteiro, and Maria João Neto. In *Intelligence Creativity and Fantasy, Leiden*, CRC Press/Balkema, 2019, pp. 363-368; "Rafael Bordalo Pinheiro, un 'Peintre de la modernité' au Portugal? Une lecture en dialogue avec Baudelaire." In *Hermeneia : Journal of Hermeneutics, Arts and Criticism*, n. 25, November 2020, pp. 5-28 ; "La fonction auteur entre éthique et épistémologie : sur les traces de Michel Foucault" *Études françaises*, 56(3), PUM, 2020, pp. 117-138. *Views on Eighteenth Century Culture – Design, Books and Ideas*, Leonor Ferrão and Luís Manuel A. V. Bernardo (eds.). In Newcastle upon Tyne: Cambridge Scholars Publishing, 2015, pp. 431; "Reasons of Violence, Violence of Reason: An Interpretation based on Eric Weil's Core Paradox", Diogo Pires Aurélio/João Tiago Proença (eds.). In *Terrorism: Politics, Religion, Literature*, Newcastle upon Tyne, Cambridge Scholars Publishing, pp. 35-67.

Izabel F. O. Brandão is Professor of literatures in English, and contemporary Brazilian women writers at Federal University of Alagoas, Brazil (now retired). She is also a CNPq grant holder for literature research. Her publications include a book on D. H. Lawrence (2009) and on feminist literary criticism both in Portuguese and English. She is one of the editors of a feminist anthology in translation (*Traduções da cultura:* perspectivas críticas feministas -1970-2010 ['Translations of Culture: Feminist Critical Perspectives 1970-2010'], Mulheres, Edufal & EdUFSC, 2017). Her latest book is *Literatura e ecologia: trilhando novos caminhos críticos* ("Literature and ecology: tracking new critical paths", Edufal, 2019, in collaboration). She is also a nationally established poet.

Nick Ceramella is Vice President of D. H. Lawrence Society of Great Britain.
 He taught, as contract professor, English Literature and Language, Italian American literature, Translation Studies, and History of English at the following universities: '*La Sapienza,*' '*Roma Tre,*' and *LUMSA* in Rome; Istituto Universitario *l'Orientale*, and Università *Federico Secondo*

in Naples; University for *Foreigners* in Perugia; Università dell'*Aquila;* and, lately, at the Università di *Trento*. He was visiting professor at the Universities of Moscow (Russia), Maceiò - Alagoas (Brazil), Nikšić (Montenegro). He lectured in many European Universities, at Stony Brook University (New York), Ottawa University (Canada), and Kyoto (Japan). Nick's eclectic teaching is reflected in his latest publications, in books and academic journals. He wrote extensively books and articles on D. H. Lawrence; W. Shakespeare; Renaissance theatre and poetry; Linguistics; Translation studies.

Particularly relevant to this book are these lectures, translations and presentations in concerts and talks:

- Nick is a passionate amateur guitar, mandolin and cavaquinho player. He used to be a clarinettist in a concert band.
- *A Rainbow Across the Atlantic.* William Neil (piano), Paula Velvet (singer), Eleonora Savini (violin), Nickn Ceramella presenter, reader and translator of poems put to music by W. Neil. Auditorium Convento SS XII Apostoli, Roma, 2017.
- *Verde, Bianco, Rosso.* William Neil (piano) & Nick Ceramella (presenter, translator of poems put to music by W. Neil). Event organiser Demetrio Ceramella. Accademia della Musica, S. Sofia d'Epiro (CS), 2015.
- *Literature and the Arts*, Keynote Speaker "Role of Music in Shakespeare's Theatre," Doctoral school: of Literary and Cultural Studies, University of Bucharest, 2014.
- *Where there is no autumn*; *The waters are shaking the moon* (Concert for Lawrence's Centenary at Gargnano auditorium). William Neil (piano & digital acoustics), Charlotte Stoppelenburg (mezzo soprano), Bethan Jones (clarinettist), John worthen (reader), Nick Ceramella (presenter and co-organiser), 2012.
- *Shakespeare and the Role of Music in his Theatre*, PhD Course, Russian State University for the Humanities, Moscow, 2007.
- *As multiplas faces de Vinicius de Morais : Canto e poesia.* Rita Namé (piano), Fatima de Brito (singer), Otávio Cabral (reading actor), N. Ceramella readings and translations. Teatro Casa de Cultura Latino-americana, Maceiò (Brazil), 2006.
- *Il ruolo della musica nel teatro elisabettiano*. In collaboration with Conservatorio di Musica "S. Giacomantonio" & Piccolo Teatro Rendano (CS), 2005.

Books: Nick Ceramella, 'Silence Symphony' Conducted by Pinter and Eduardo, Two World Theatre Maestri.' In *Harold Pinter on International Stages*, ed. Tomaž Onič. Frankfurt am Main: Peter Lang Edition, 2014.

Yuri Chung is a contract professor in English Literature at the University of Rome "La Sapienza," where he holds an M. A. course on "Literature and Opera." He has got a B. A. in "Modern Languages and Literatures," writing a thesis on the relationship between Sir Walter Scott's novel, *The bride of Lammermoor*, and Donizetti's eponymous opera. He also holds an M. A. in "Linguistics, Literary and Translation Studies," focusing on the collaboration between Stravinsky and Auden in *The Rake's Progress*. Ultimately, in 2020, he took his PhD, writing a dissertation on *Modernism and Melodrama: Effects on the Libretto*. Chung concentrated on the rise of librettos in English as valuable and independent literary texts, during the 20th century, after the librettists regained their poetic prominence. Chung's research interests include early and late modernist literature, the adaptations of novels to operatic librettos, comparative and ekphrastic literature. He has recently published the essay, "Napoleone e l'opera lirica" in *Letteratura e Storia* (Roma: Lithos, 2021).

Malcolm Gray: My joy as a teacher for over 40 years was that I felt I was forever learning, but that joy was enriched by the fact of being able to share what I learnt, to be passionate about learning and committed to sharing.

The enjoyment of shared ideas was significant in the creation of the Cantata "The Voice of Nethermere." Creating the cantata gave me the opportunity to share my love of D. H. Lawrence and literature with Alan Wilson as we explored together the novel *The White Peacock* using his passion for creative expression through music. To bring the two elements of literature and music together was a new step for us. An interest in the novels of D. H. Lawrence was the link that initially brought Alan Wilson and me together. I had been Chairman of the D. H. Lawrence Society for a number of years and when I retired Alan took on my role.

Christian Hänggi studied Communication Sciences at the Universities of Lugano and Toronto, received a PhD in Media and Communication from the European Graduate School, and a PhD in Anglophone Literary and Cultural Studies from the University of Basel, Switzerland. Over the past ten years, Christian has taught literature, English, history, and philosophy at various Swiss universities and at the Autonomous School in Zurich, as well as media and communication at Ramkhamhaeng University in Bangkok. He is currently the coordinator of the Doctoral Program in Literary Studies at the University of Basel and sits on the Advisory Board of the performance art space Fidget in Philadelphia.

His most recent monograph is *Pynchon's Sound of Music* (Diaphanes, 2020) and he is the producer of the album *"Now everybody—" Visit Interprets*

Songs by Thomas Pynchon (2020) by the NYC band Visit. He has also published monographs, articles, and encyclopedia entries on hospitality, outdoor advertising, South Park, Karlheinz Stockhausen and 9/11, Scientology, MOVE, the Kent State University Shootings, and the Haymarket Affair. As a lifelong amateur musician, he has played the baritone saxophone in numerous bands and orchestras, among which the Civica Filarmonica di Lugano, the Swiss Saxophone Orchestra, and the Lakeside Big Band.

Christa Jansohn is Professor of British Culture at the University of Bamberg, Germany. She received her PhD and Habilitation from Bonn University and is the author and editor of books and articles about D. H. Lawrence and Shakespeare (e. g. apocrypha, translation studies, stage history and reception of Shakespeare in Germany, sonnets, and narrative poems). For further information, see http://www.uni-bamberg.de/britcult/

Bethan Jones is a Senior Lecturer in Modern and Contemporary Literature at the University of Hull, UK. Her academic research has principally focused on the works of D. H. Lawrence but her extensive experience as a performing musician has led her to explore interrelations between text and music in a wide range of genres and contexts.

Her monograph *The Last Poems of D. H. Lawrence: Shaping a Late Style* was published by Ashgate in 2010 and was awarded a literary prize. Bethan co-edited *The Virgin and the Gipsy and Other Stories* for Cambridge University Press (2006) and was editor of the *Journal of D.H. Lawrence Studies* from 2001 to 2006. She contributes regularly to collections on Lawrence, modernism and music but is currently working on representations of visual impairment in literature.

Bethan is a clarinettist, jazz saxophonist, conductor, and librettist. She was principal clarinettist of the National Youth Orchestra of Great Britain (performing regularly at the London Proms and winning the Ivey Dickson Prize in 1991), and a founder member of the National Youth Chamber Orchestra of Great Britain. In recent years she has performed concerts by Mozart, Copland, Debussy, Weber, Nielsen and Finzi. She has played with Sinfonia Cymru (Cardiff), Meadows Chamber Orchestra and Scottish Sinfonia (Edinburgh), Hull Sinfonietta and Guildhall Orchestra (York). Through her involvement with D. H. Lawrence research, she collaborated with the American composer William Neil on a new work entitled *Where there is no Autumn*, performing in the world première at the First International D. H. Lawrence Symposium organised by Nick Ceramella in Gargnano in 2012. She coordinated a music and literature event in Bloomsbury as part of the 14th International D. H. Lawrence conference (2017).

Manuela Kustermann was very young when she made her debut as Ophelia in Carmelo Bene's version of Shakespeare's *Hamlet*. She was already very active since 1967, when she started to work with Giancarlo Nanni, interpreting the main plays of 'La Fede' Group. Thus, she became one of the icons of the experimental theatre which was flourishing in Rome in the mid-sixties. She impersonated a wide variety of female characters from the classic and modern repertoires directed by Nanni.

From the mid-sixties through the seventies, Manuela Kustermann was the 'prima donna' of the Italian theatrical avantgarde. She acted nude on the stage and triggered all sorts of provocations by taking part in all the pieces directed by Nanni with whom she debuted in *Il bando di Virulena* at the Margutta Theatre in Rome (1966).

From 1968 to 1972 the two of them - partners in real life as well as on the stage - founded the Compagnia Teatro La Fede and presented a play on Marcel Duchamp (1968) and revealed the Roman theatregoers some highly expressive texts such as Wedekind's *Risveglio di primavera* (*Frühlings Erwachen*, 1972) and rewrote classic works as *A come Alice e Carrol*. This is one of the crucial experiences of that period, characterised by spontaneity and vivid body language. In 1972, she played again the role of Bene's Ophelia. Following a quick experience in *Ondine* at the Stabile Theatre in Genoa, 1973, Kustermann established with Nanni, the Cooperativa 'La fabbrica dell'attore' and opened an experimental theatre in Trastevere (Rome).

Polyhedric and androgynous, Manuela often wore men's clothes (in *Faust* and *Franziska* she wears a tail coat). She returned to *Hamlet* with Nanni, but this time she played the role of the Prince of Denmark (1978).

Still engaged on the avantgarde front in 1979, when she and her partner took the roles of Jean Harlow & Billy the Kid. In 1982, Manuela Kustermann was the interpreter of a beautiful version of Ibsen's *A Doll's House* followed by many other performances. In 1986, the Coop. "La Fabbrica" (Factory) refurbished an old cinema in the Old Monteverde district, called 'Il Vascello', and in 1989 opened the season with Tadeusz Kantor staging "Qui non ci torno più" (*I'll never come back here again.*) Ever since Teatro Vascello has been one of the reference points for Italian and international theatrical research and dance. After the death of Giancarlo Nanni in 2010, Manuela Kustermann has been running the theatre on her own with her usual drive towards the innovation which has characterised all the seasons at The Vascello.

Elena Lutsenko is a senior research fellow of the Comparative Studies Centre (Russian State University for the Humanities, Moscow) and associate professor of The Russian Presidential Academy of national economy and public administration (the department of history and theory of literature). Her interests are in the fields of comparative studies, Elizabethan England, Russian Shakespeare and the history of music. She is the author of several books on Shakespeare, including *"Romeo and Juliet* by William Shakespeare: a guideline" (MSU, 2017), *"Romeo and Juliet"*: (a commented edition) (Ladomir, 2021). She also contributes comparative articles on music and literature, including "Shostakovich and Shakespeare" for Shakespeare encyclopedia (Moscow, 2015), "B. Britten's speech *On receiving the first Aspen Award*: Russian translation and commentary to the text" for the collection of essays *The composer's word* (Gnesin Academy, 2016) etc.

Elena is also a soprano, a graduate from Gnesin Russian Academy of Music (2014).

Cinzia Merlin: "Music has fascinated me since childhood. I had my first encounter with the piano at the age of nine and thenceforward I started a journey of academic studies as I went on to graduate from the Conservatory "F. E. Dall'Abaco" in Verona under the tutelage of Ida Tizzani. I immediately distinguished myself in numerous national and international piano competitions, achieving important milestones, among which winning first prize at the "Accademia Filarmonica" in Verona as the best graduate and then, another first prize at the 10th "Giulio Rospigliosi" Piano Competition in Pistoia. With a need to pursue my studies I took master classes with Peter Lang in Verona and with Mikhail Rudy in Nice. Continuously searching for new musical inspiration, I decided to move to Rome and to perfect my work with Lya De Barberiis. Starting off by refining my classical repertoire, an intense concert activity then began.

With a deep love of theater, art and literature, I graduated in History of Music at the Sapienza University of Rome, where I also collaborated in the project "Rediscovered Music" with the National Academy of Santa Cecilia in the premiere concert at the MUSA at the Auditorium-Parco della Musica.

Looking for new musical artistic forms, I discovered body music. This discovery opened up new perspectives in my artistic journey, which, in a natural way, has been enriched by contaminations and collaborations with various internationally renowned artists. After several performances in Italy, I debuted at the Teatro Vascello in Rome with 4Rhythm, an ensemble I had founded together with Jep Meléndez, Tupac Mantilla and Ruben Sanchez; this performance develops through the interaction between piano, movement, tap dance, body music, and percussion.

In the wake of these events, the meeting with Daniel Borak, one of the most extraordinary tap dancers on the international scene, gave rise to performing on the television program "Tu Si Que Vales" on Channel 5, enjoying great success and appreciation from the critics, and the synergic meeting with the actress Manuela Kustermann is finally bringing me through the experimentation with new connections in the theater and music worlds.

After a journey through intense artistic experiences, I've arrived here in "Metamorphosys" with a new interpretive idea of the repertoire that aims to break the "barriers" of cultured music and to bring it closer to a wider and more mixed audience. My artistic research remains in constant growth and continuous evolution."

Rita Luiza Percia Namé has a degree in Music Theraphy and has specialized in Musical Education, Ethnomusicology and Musicology by the Conservatório Brasileiro de Música – Centro Universitário of Rio de Janeiro. She holds an MA and a Doctorate from the Universidade Federal de Alagoas where she taught in the Music, Dance and Theatre Undergraduate course. Now she has retired. Founder and Director of the Technical School of Arts at the same university (2009-2016). Founder, presenter and head of the radio programme "Música de todos os tempos" (Music from all times) broadcast by Radio Educativa de Maceió-Alagoas, Brazil (107.7 MHz).

William (Grosvenor) Neil's compositions present the listener with an intense brilliant effect (FANFARE MAGAZINE) and represents contemporary writing at its most intellectual probing (CHICAGO TRIBUNE). His extremely characteristic harmonic world (CLASSICAL CD REVIEW) is fundamental to the unfolding of his music, and the range of sonic experiences (in his music) is astounding (SOUNDBOARD).

In the 1980s Neil was appointed as the first composer-in-residence with the Lyric Opera of Chicago, the first residency of its kind with a major American opera company. His opera, *The Guilt of Lillian Sloan* was premiered by Lyric in June of 1986. He then went on to produce award winning concerts and events at the New Music Chicago Spring Festival for several years. He has composed music for celebrated musicians including John Bruce Yeh and Chicago Pro Musica, guitarist Michael Lorimer and soprano Barbara Ann Martin. His *Rhapsody for Violin and Orchestra,* commissioned by the Abelson Foundation, was premiered in Prague by the Czech National Symphony conducted by Paul Freeman. It has been recorded and released on the New Albany label.

The Rome Prize and the Charles Ives Award are among his honors and his work has been recognized through grants from the National Endowment of the Arts, the Illinois Arts Council, fellowships from the Fulbright Commission and the American Symphony Orchestra League and awards from ASCAP and BMI. In 2008 he served as the McKnight Visiting Composer with the American Composers Forum for the city of Winona, MN.

Significant performances include the premiere of his piano trio, *Notte dei Cristalli*, at the Teatro alla Specola in Padova by Trio Malipiero, the premiere of his *Symphony No. 1* (*Sinfonia delle Gioie*) by The La Crosse Symphony Orchestra, directed by Alexander Platt and the premiere of *Out of Darkness Into Light* at the Cameron Art Museum in Wilmington, NC. Most recently, Italian pianist, Giacomo dalla Libera premiered *Nocturne No. 1*, *Prelude No. 3*, and *Tango No. 2* at Morely College in London and clarinetist, Fàtima Boix Canto' premiered *Concerto for Piccolo Clarinet* and Chamber Orchestra at the Music Academy of the West in Santa Barbara, CA, Duo Sureño premiered Love Poem with a Knife and pianist Martin Jones premiered Six Preludes for piano at Radford University.

Recent CD releases have featured his music including *Out of Darkness into Light* on Ravello Records, *Spiritual Adaptation to Higher Altitude*s on Mark Masters Recordings and *Six Preludes for Piano* on PnOVA Recordings. His music will be featured on several live broadcasts on WFMT radio in Chicago in 2019 including his Six Preludes for piano solo by pianist Martin Jones. In the fall of 2020, Neil served as an Artist in Residence at Badlands National Park in South Dakota. His latest composition, the premiere of Concerto for Clarinet and Orchestra, was performed at Texas Christian University, on 12th October 2021.

Adrian Paterson is a Lecturer in English at the National University of Ireland, Galway, Director of Graduate Research for the Discipline of English, and Chair of the Humanities Research Committee. A graduate of Worcester College, Oxford, and Trinity College, Dublin, he is the curator of NUI Galway's Yeats & the West exhibition for Yeats 2015, the author of Words for Music: W. B. Yeats and Musical Sense (forthcoming) and completed an Irish Research Council fellowship at the Moore Institute at NUI Galway entitled Perfect Pitch: Music in Irish Poetry from Moore to Muldoon.

Patricia Pérez Borrero is an English teacher and Head of Studies at the secondary school, "Rafaela Ybarra," Madrid. She graduated in English Philology at Complutense University (DEA), with a double specialization in English literature and Italian language and literature in 2007. She has presented various papers on literature at various international conferences (University of Edinburgh, Scotland, 2003; Nottingham, D. H. Lawrence Conference, 2009; Paris X University of Nanterre, 2010; the First International D. H. Lawrence Symposium, organised by Nick Ceramella in Gargnano, Italy, 2012. Her essay "The triumph of the body" was compiled in the volume "Lake Garda: Gateway to D. H. Lawrence's Voyage to the sun", ed. Nick Ceramella in 2013.

Currently working on different areas of English teaching, she has never left literature aside. Great lover of Spanish literature and writers, she has been working through Spanish history of literature during these last years.

Alessandro Portelli has taught American Literature at the Universities of Rome "La Sapienza" and Siena. He has served as Advisor of Historical Memory to the Mayor of the city of Rome and is the founder of the Rome-Based Circolo Gianni Bosio "for the critical study and historical presence of people's cultures." His works published in English include *The Death of Luigi Trastulli and other Stories. Form and Meaning in Oral History* (1991); *The Text and the Voice. Orality, Writing and Democracy in America Literature* (1995); *The Battle of Valle Giulia. Oral History and the Art of Dialogue* (1997); *The Order Had Been Carried Out. History, Memory and Meaning of a Nazi Massacre in Rome* (2003); *They Say in Harlan County: An Oral History* (2011); *Biography of an Industrial Town: Terni, Italy 1831-2014* (2014); *Bruce Springsteen's American: A Dream Deferred* (2017); *Hard Rain. Bob Dylan, oral tradition and the meaning of history* (due in 2022). A collection of his field recordings of American folk and topical song has been released as a book and 4-CD set as *We Shall Not Be Moved. Voci e musiche dagli Stati Uniti 1919-2018* (Rome, 2019).

Doc Rossi's Education goes from literature to music. After teaching English literature and language at the John Cabot University in Rome, Doc concentrated on music. His professional life in music has been evenly split between performing and teaching. He held university degrees in Music and Literature (Ph.v D. University College London, 1992 (Awarded Overseas Research Scholarship); BA English Language and Literature, Oakland University (USA), 1988 Magna cum laude; Diploma in Music, The Open University (UK), 1998; Certificate in Sampling and Audio Production, Berklee College of Music (USA), 2004. So, his experience of more than thirty years in performance and teaching has been built on solid foundations that he has continued to enrich through the many encounters he had been fortunate to have had along his musical journey.

His work has involved blending the ancient sounds of early music, the intricacies of traditional dance music, and the mystery of "The Old Weird America." He discovered an affinity with Irish traditional music by first falling in love with the dance music of medieval, renaissance and baroque Europe. His passion for the cittern led him to Fado and the deep Portuguese *guitarra* tradition. He plays historical as well as modern citterns, and has, so far, recorded two albums of music for the 18th-century cittern, often called the English "guittar."

His latest solo recordings are
Parlors Porches & Islands (Xacutti 2020); These Are My Rivers (Cetra 2020).

His recordings with other artists include:
Mighela Cesari & Ensemble Phémios. *A Brama Ghjirandulona, Cetera Andarina.* (Cetra 2019). Ange Lanzalavi Trio. *Passiunata.* (Casa Editions 2014).

His latest books comprise:
Parlors Porches & Islands. (Anaheim Hills, CA: Centerstream Publishing, 2021).
Etern' Amore - The Mandolin of Ange Lanzalavi. (Pigna, France: Casa Editions, 2019).
The Irish Mandolin ASAP. (Anaheim Hills, CA: Centerstream Publishing, 2014).
The Irish Guitar ASAP. (Anaheim Hills, CA: Centerstream Publishing, 2012).
The Celtic Guitar. (Anaheim Hills, CA: Centerstream Publishing, 2011).
The Celtic Cittern. (Anaheim Hills, CA: Centerstream Publishing, 2010).

Selected Articles and Reviews
'Lute Connections with the English Guitar' *Lute Society of America Quarterly v. XLV, n.1* (Spring 2010): 46-52. 'Citterns and Guitars in Colonial America.' *Gitarre und Zister: Bauweise, Spieltechnik un Geschichte bis 800.22.* Musikinstrumentenbau-Symposium Michaelstein, 16 bis 18. November 2001. Ed. Monika Lustig. (Dossel, Germany: Stiftung Kloster Michaelstein and Verlag Janos Stekovics, 2004) 155-168.

Tabrizi Alizadeh Sanaz was born in Iran in 1978. She received her second BA (2010) and her MA (2015) in English Language and Literature. In July 2020, she completed her PhD with a dissertation entitled: *Reading Music in Henry James' Fiction.* She started her teaching career in 1999 and is currently an assistant professor at the Department of English Language and Literature at Istanbul Aydin University, Turkey. Her main interests lie in

Victorian and early Modernist literature, intermediality, multimodality, interdisciplinary studies in literature and music, and narrative theory. She is a member of several associations for intermedial studies, including ISIS and WMA. She is working on her monograph, which will be published by Cambridge Scholars Publishing soon.

Leonor Santa Bárbara is an Assistant Professor at the Department of Portuguese Studies at NOVA FCSH, teaching undergraduate courses related with Ancient Greek Language, Literature and Culture, as well as an MA seminar on the reception of Classical Antiquity in the Portuguese Culture. She is also a researcher of CHAM - Centre for the Humanities (NOVA FCSH/UAç). Her research interests cover Ancient Greek culture and literature, particularly the Hellenistic age, with both national and international publications. She has recently participated in an international conference at the University of Coimbra (Conference in Classics & Ancient History) where she proposed, with two colleagues, a panel on the reception of ancient myths (The Reception of Ancient Myths in Iberian and Latin-American Contemporary Literature), and also presented a paper at another panel (Displacing Greek Drama in the Modern World) on the reception of Greek tragedy in a Portuguese play of the 21st century.

She is the Portuguese translator of numerous works in both French and English: E. R. Dodds, E. Havelock, Jacqueline de Romilly and Félix Guirand. She translated both Greek and Latin texts, including epigrams from the *Greek Anthology*. In the last few years, she worked on the reception of ancient authors and/or themes, as it can be seen in two of her most recent publications: "Two Giants in Love: Epic and Bucolic Poetry", *in Literature and Cultural Memory* (eds. Irimia, Mihaela, Dragoş Manea and Andreea Paris), Leiden/Boston, Brill/Rodopi, 2017, pp. 136-144; "Sappho's Poems – Portraits of a Poetess", in Proceedings from the International Conference Sources to Study Antiquity: Between Texts and Material Culture (coord. Trindade Lopes, Maria Helena, Maria de Fátima Rosa and Susana Mota). *Res Antiquitatis. Journal of Ancient History*, 2nd Series, Volume 1, CHAM-NOVA FCSH, May 2019, pp. 208-213.

Jemana Stellato Pledger holds a PhD. She is a multidisciplinary arts practitioner and Human Rights Artist/Advocate who has worked extensively in Australia, as well as Samoa and Europe. She has been awarded numerous grants to write and produce her work. These include *Blood in the Garden*: The Malthouse Theatre, Melbourne; Explores the relationship between Italians and Indigenous Australians in Gippsland Victoria. *Calabrian Eyes-Installation* - Piers Festival. *Limbo 24/7*: Installation of photography; digital media and live performance. Melbourne. *Singing in Siena*: Documentary of choirs in Tuscany: *Bondi Films Sydney*. *Waves of Love and Emotion*: Group Art exhibition: Storytelling-second generation migrants. Emerald Hill Heritage Centre. *Walking with my Ancestors in Recalling the Journey*. 2nd Edition, E- Book: Multicultural Arts Victoria. "Operation Mare Nostrum: It's Affect in Creating a Mediterranean Identity." In *The Mythical Mediterranean Sea: Crossroads of Cultures, People, and Civilizations* (Eds) Ceramella, N. & Gori U. *On the Eve of All saints*. In Tapestry Series: Jessie Street National Women's Library. *The Temporary Incarceration of Elisabeth San Paola's Soul* –Melbourne University Zine: *Physical Theatre, Circus and Storytelling*: Raising the Curtain Performance in Cultural Institutions; National Museum of Australia, Canberra. *Disturbing the Storm*: Narratives from the liminal space: Investigating the Commonalities between older Hazara Afghan women and Calabrian exiles: Interdisciplinary PhD by creative project and exhibition.

Charlotte Stoppelenburg is a mezzo-soprano, who studied at the Conservatories of Utrecht (The Netherlands) and Cologne (Germany). In addition to her work as a professional musician, she completed her German Studies at the Universities of Utrecht and Amsterdam, where she specialized in the interaction of literature and music.

She has contributed to lectures, symposia, and concerts in which literature and music take a central place, such as a lecture on translating *Winterreise* (2015, Utrecht University), and *Caribbean Letterendag* about Louis Lichtveld (Amsterdam 2016, OBA Theatre). She has specialized in music inspired by great poets as Heinrich Heine, Rainer Maria Rilke, and Paul Celan. Some of her other writings have focused on the collaboration between the composer Hans Werner Henze and the poet Ingeborg Bachmann.

Charlotte has premiered contemporary works such as *Le Bel Indifférent* (1943) a one-act play-opera by Willem Stoppelenburg), based on a play by Jean Cocteau, as well as songs on poetry of Pablo Neruda, Johann Wolfgang von Goethe, Christian Morgenstern, and Dylan Thomas. Through her growing interest in D. H. Lawrence, she collaborated with the American composer William Neil on his work, inspired by a selection of poems by Lawrence, entitled *The Waters are Shaking the Moon*, performing in the European première at the "First International D. H. Lawrence Symposium," organised by Nick Ceramella in Gargnano in 2012. Charlotte performed in the Netherlands, Germany, Italy, the United States, and German, and appeared in concert with orchestras such as Gürzenich Orchester, WDR Rundfunkorchester, Noord Nederlands Orkest and Amsterdams Promenade Orkest.

Alan Wilson has been Director of Music at Queen Mary College, University of London and performing organist and choral director at both the London University Church of Christ the King, followed by the famous 'Bow Bells' Church of St. Mary-le-Bow in Cheapside, London. He has also made many broadcasts on the BBC, as performer, choir director and composer. As performer he has played in many of the leading Early Music ensembles, and as a published composer has been very active throughout his life.

Now, in his retirement, he is Director of Music and Organist at the iconic church of Holy Trinity, Eltham, with its fine Gallipoli Chapel (near where he lives), and during the last two years has played a major part in Eastwood (Nottinghamshire) where he was born. Several concerts based on local themes have been devised; absorbing his fascination for heritage based sociological and historical research. He loves meeting up with people, both young and old - gathering up information, as well as delving through archives at the libraries. He has also discovered some neglected names from the past, especially the musical entrepreneur Arthur Linwood, and is combining his own composing and performing skills with the output of such newly discovered gems.

Alan regards it very humbling to be the new chairman of the D. H. Lawrence Society of Great Britain, following the position held by Malcolm Grey.

INDEX

Addison, Joseph, 3-4
Adomian, Lan, 319-322
Alighieri, Dante, xix-xx, xxiii, xxxv, li, lxv, lxvi, lxxix, 33, 303
  Divine Comedy, The
  Convito
Aristotle, xvii
Armstrong, Louis, 80, 82, 87, 133
Asquith, Cynthia, 55
Austen, Jane, xli, lxxx
Avalos, Bolaño, Roberto, lxviii, lxxxi-ii
Azzinnari, Giovanni, xii, 14-15
  Through all the employments of life, transcription of Air, Act One, *The Beggar's Opera*

Bach, Johann Sebastian xiv, lxxi, lxxviii, 53, 172, 174, 200, 206, 236-7, 240, 242-3
  Art of the Fugue,
  The St. Matthew Passion,
  Well-Tempered Clavier
Baez, Joan, xxii
Bakhtin, Michail Michilovič, lvi, 19
Balestra, Gianfranca, 146-157, 328
Ballesta, Cano, 318, 320, 326
Barthes, Roland, 20
Baudelaire, Charles, 1, lxxii, 30, 329
Beatles, The, xxxi, lxiv, lxxi, lxxv, lxxvii, 132, 152, 160, 163, 266
Beethoven, Ludwig van, i, lviii, lx-i, lxv, lxvii-iii, lxxi, lxxv, lxxviii, 19, 21-22, 30, 40, 78, 105, 117-8, 138, 174, 206

Bellini, Vincenzo, xxxi, 29, 178
  I Capuleti e i Montecchi
  Sonnambula, La
Benda, Georg, Anton, xxxi, 172-195
  Romeo und Julie (Singspiel)
Berlioz, Hector, 176
  Roméo et Juliette (dramatic symphony)
  Symphonie Fantastique
Bernardo, Luís A. V., 281-299, 329
Bizet, George, 52
  Carmen
Blake, William, xliii-xlvii, lv, lxxvii, lxxix, lxxxii,
  Songs of Experience, Marriage of Heaven and Hell, The,
Boccaccio, Giovanni, xxiii
  Decameron, The
  Elegy of Madonna Fiammetta
Boito, Arrigo, xxxii, lxxix
Brahms, Johannes, l, 53, 285
Brandão, Izabel, xvi, 248-266, 329
Brecht, Bertolt, xiii, 2,11,14,16
Brett, Francis, 53
Brontë, Charlotte, lii
  Jane Eyre
Burgess, Anthony, lxvii-lxix, lxxxii, 55, 78
  Clockwork Orange
Burns, Robert, xliii, xlvi, 302
Byron, Lord George, xxi, xlvii, lxxix, 204
  Hebrew Melodies

Calvino, Italo, xiv, lxxviii, 220-235
  Invisible Cities

Camões, Luis de, 281-300
  Lusiads, The
Capelli, 54
Camus, Marcel, 261
Ceramella, Nick, x, xii-xvi, xlvi, lxvii, lxix, 51-68, 77, 200, 248-279, 329-330, 332, 337,340
Chaucer, Geoffrey, xxiii-xxvi, lxxix
  Canterbury Tales, The
  Book of the Duchess
  House of Fame, The
Chopin, Fryderyk, xxxi, xlix, li, 240, 243, 317
Chorny, Sasha, xi, 302-305, 303-313
Chung, Yuri, 2-15, 321
Clerc, Charles, 164, 169
Cocteau, Jean, **261**
Cohen, Leonard, lxviii, lxxii, lxxiv, lxxxii, 130, 135
Cortàzar, Julio, lxviii, lxxxi-ii
Cowper, William, 102, 107, 124

D'Arezzo, Guido, xvii
De Andrade, Mario, 249, 259, 265, 267
De André, Fabrizio, lxviii, lxxii-iv
De Bonis, Rosalba, xiii
De Bonis, Vincenzo, xiii
De Machaut, Guillaume, xix
De Morais, Vinicius, 248-269
Debussy, Claude, i, lxxi, lxxix, 40, 48, 237, 240, 244, 332
Defoe, Daniel, 11, 16
Delillo, Don, 132
Dickens, Charles, liii
  American Notes
  Christmas Carol, A
  David Copperfield
  'Fiddler of the Reels,' The
  Sketches by Boz
Donne, John, xxix
Dostoyevsky, Fyodor, 303
Dryden, John, xxxvi
  A Song for Saint Cecilia's Day

Dylan, Bob, xiv, xxii, xxxi, xlv, lxviii, lxxi, lxxii, 10, 128-137

Eliot, George, xiv, 18, 21-33
  Mill on the Floss, The
Eliot, T. Sterne, lvii-lviii, lx, 55, 79-80, 265, 268.
  String Quartet
  The Waste Land

Faulkner, William, 79, 92
Fitzgerald, Ella, 134
Fitzgerald, Francis, Scott, xiv, 79-80, 82-83, 98, 146-157, 328
  Great Gatsby
  Tales of the Jazz age

Garborg, Arne, 56
Gautier, Théophile, lxxii
Gay, John, xii, xxxviii, xli, 2-14, 29
  Beggar's Opera, The
Gesualdo, da Venosa, xxviii
Getz, Stan, 256, 266
Gilberto, João, 256, 259
Gluck, Christoph, Williband, 262
  Orpheus (opera)
Gogol, Nikolay, 303
Goldsmith, Meredith, 156, 158,
Goldsmith, Oliver, xxii, 179-180
  'Deserted Village'
Goodman, Benny, 81, 87
Gotter, Friederich Wilhelm, 172-195
  Romeo und Julie (libretto)
Gray, Cecil, 54
Gray, Malcolm, xiv, 34-50, 331
Grieg, Edvard, 52, 56, 78
Guthrie, Woody, xxii, 129, 133

Händel, G. Frederic., xxxvi, 3-6, 8, 10, 14, 16, 22-3, 26-7,
Hänggi, Christian, lxxviii, 159-169, 331
Hardy, Thomas, liii-liv, lv, lxxix, 50
  Tess of the D'Urbervilles

Index

Hernandez, Miguel, 315-326
Heseltine, Philip, 54
Hesiod, 253
Hindermith, Paul, 58
Hogarth, William, 3
Homer, xvi, lxxiii
  Iliad, The
  Odissey, The
Hopkins, Gerald Manley, 59
Hugo, Victor, xx, xxxi, lxv, lxxix
Hughes, Langston, 79, 81, 83-4, 95, 98, 157
Huxley, Aldous, xlvii, lxiv, lxv, lxxvii-lxxix, 54, 160

Ishiguro, Kazuo, lxxviii, lxxxi-ii

Jansohn, Christa, 172-199, 332
Jobim, Antonio, 250, 255-9, 261
Jones, Bethan, 56, 77, 79-97, 330, 336
Johnson, Samuel, 7,10,16
Joyce, James, xiv, xl, lvii, lxi-lxiv, lxviii, lxx, lxxvi-lxxviii, lxxx, lxxxii, lxxxiii

Keats, John, xxxvi, xlviii, 147
  'Ode on a Grecian Urn'
Kennedy, Fitzgerald, John, 130-4
Kerouac, Jack, lxx,i, lxxx
Kinkead-Weekes, Mark, 53-4, 78
Knezević, Tanja, xii
Kundera, Milan, lxviii, lxxxi-ii
Kustermann, Manuela, 236-244, 334
Kutcha, Edwards, 221-23, 232-34

Lawrence, D. H., x, xiv, lvii, lxviii, 34-50, 51-79, 80, 329-332, 337, 340-341
  Aaron's Rod,
  Apocalypse
  David
  'Piano', The
  'Piano'
  Rainbow, The

  Trespasser, The
  Twilight in Italy
  White Peacock, The
  Women in Love
Leibniz, Gitfried, Wilhelm, xxxviii, xlix,
Listz, Franz, xx
London, Jack, xiv, 137-145,
  Call in the Wild, The
Lorca, Garcia, 317
Lutsenko, Elena, 301-313, 334

Macartney, H. B., 53
Machiavelli, Niccoló, xviii, xxvii
Mansfield, Elizabeth, 53
Mansfield, Katherine,
  Garden Party, The
Marlowe, Christopher, xxviii, xxix, xxx
  'Come live with me / be my love'
Mellown, Elgin W., 54
Merlin, Cinzia, 236-244, 334
Milton, John, xxxv-vi, xlviii, lxxx, 46
  Comus
  Paradise Lost
Mitchell, Anäis, 263
Monteverdi, Claudio, 262
  L'Orfeo (opera)
Morrison, Toni, xiv, lxix-lxx, lxxvii, lxxvii, lxxxii 79, 89-98, 157
Mozart, Wolfang, Amadeus, xxxvii, lix, lxv, lxxv, lxxvii, 174-5, 179, 189, 202, 205, 317, 322.
  Entführung aus dem Serail, Die
  Zauberflöte, Die
Müller, Wilhelm, x, 200-217
  Winterreise (Winter Journey)
Mussorsky, Modest, 55

Namé, Rita, xvi, 248-268, 329, 335
Neil, William, xii, xiv, 58, 67, 137-144, 256, 330, 332, 335-6, 340,

Newton, Isaac, 35
Newton, John, 52
Nietzsche, Friederich, li, liii, lxxx-xxxi, 18-19, 33, 52, 167
Birth of Tragedy, The

Oates, Joyce, Carol, lxxi,
Offenbach, Jacques, 262
Orpheus in the Underworld (opera)
Ovid, xiv, 23, 236-245, 253
Metamorphoses, The
Epistles, The
Pater, Walter, lv, lxxx, 124
Paterson, Adrian, lxxxiii, 99-125, 336
Pepush, Johann Cristoph, xxxviii, 10, 13, 15, 29,
Pérez, Borrero, Patricia, ix, 315-327, 336-7
Petrarca, Francesco (Petrarch), xx, xxi
Piazzolla, Astor, xiv, lxv, lxvi, lxvii, lxxi, 55, 78-9, 117,
'Milonga de l'Angel'
Pope, Alexander, 4-5, 7, 10
Porteli, Sandro, 128-136, 337
Porter, Cole, 93-95, 98
Pound, Ezra, xix, lxv-lxii, lxxxiii, 55, 78,79, 117
Proust, Marcel, lxxiv-v, lxxxii, 33
Pushkin, Aleksandr, Sergeevič, 302, 306
Pynchon, Thomas, xiv, lxxviii, 159-170, 331-2
Pythagoras, xvi, xxxv

Rhys, Jean, xiv, 79, 83-89, 96, 98
Richardson, Samuel, xli, lxxx
Riquelme, Jesucristo, 318, 320-322, 325, 327
Rimsky-Korsakov, 55
Roach, Archie, 221-28, 232-35
Rodrigues, Amalia, 293-4, 298-300
Rossi, Doc, xii, xiv, xxii, 337

Rossini, Gioachino, xxxi, xxxvii, lxxvii, 21, 122, 164
Rostropovich, Mislav, 300-313
Rushdie, Salman, lxix, lxxxii
Rimsky-Korsakov, Nikolaj, 55

Santa, Barbara, Leonor, 281-298, 339
Scher, Paul steven, lvii, lxxx, 19-20, 33
Schubert, Franz, xxxi, li, lxxvii, 53, 200-217, 240, 244
Schumann, Robert, xxxi, 1
Self, Will, v, lxiv, lxxxii
Serrat, Juan Miguel, 317, 322-3, 325-6
Seth, Vikram, lxviii, lxxxi-ii
Shakespeare, William, xiii, xxix-xxxiii, xlvii, lxv, lxx, lxxix-lxxx, 30, 37-8, 50, 102, 131, 164, 175-6, 178-182, 185-187, 194-199, 302, 330, 332-4
All's Well That Ends Well
As You Like It
Hamlet
Henry IV
Macbeth
Merry wives of Windsor
Midsummer Night's Dream, A
Romeo and Juliet
Othello
Tempest, The
Shaw, George, Bernard, xxxii-iii, lxx, 158, 162
Shopenhauer, Arthur, xlviii, xlix, li, lxxx
Shostakovich, Dmitry, xiv, 302-314, 334
Sidney, Philip, xxviii-ix, lviii, lxxx
Smith, Zadie, xiv, 79-80, 93-97
Spencer, Joseph, xlviii
Spenser, Edmund, 4, 16
Springsteen, Bruce, xxii, 129, 132, 136, 337
Stellato, **Pledge**r, Jema, 220-235, 339

Sterne, Laurence, xxxix
  Sentimental Journey
  Tristram Shandy
Stoker, Bram, 140, 145
Stoppelenburg, Charlotte, xii, li, 200-17, 330, 340
Strauss, Richard, 52
Stravinsky, Igor,
  Orpheus (ballet)
Swift, Jonathan, 5, 7

Tabrizi, Sana Alizabeth, 18-32, 338-9
Tisano, Massimiliano, 243
  Prelude After Bach

Ulhôa, Marta, 259-60, 269

Verdi, Giuseppe, xxxi-ii, lxi, lxxix, lxxxi, 21, 55, 164, 262, 285
  Falstaff
  Macbeth
  Othello
  Rigoletto
Vesterman, William, 164, 170
Vishnevsaya, Galina 301, 302, 305, 308-314
Vivaldi, Antonio, 40
  Le quattro stagioni ('The Four Seasons')
Virgil, Publius, Marone, 253, 284, 298

Voltaire, François-Marie Arouet, xxxvii, 303

Wagner, Richard, xxxi, xxxiii, xlix, li, lxv, lxvii, lxxv, 13, 18-19, 21-22, 30-31, 48, 52-3, 162, 167, 185, 190, 199, 216, 289
  Lohengrin
  Tannhäuser
  Tristan und Isolde
  Valkyrie, Die
Whiteman, Paul, 80, 149-151, 154
Whitman, Walt, lvi-lvii, 131-2
  Leaves of Grass
Williams, Tennessee, 262
Wilson, Alan, xiv, 34-50, 331, 341
Wittgenstein, Ludwig, xv, lxxxi
Woolf, Virginia, lvii-lxiv, lxxxi, 55, 79, 80
  Diary II,
  To the Lighthouse,
  Waves, The,
  'String Quartet,' The
Wolf, Werner, xxxix, lxxxi, 20, 33, 78,
Wordsworth, William, xlvi-xlviii, 35, 38-9, 44, 162,
Worthen, John, 52, 77-, 330

Yeats, William, xiv, lxxiii, 117-123-125